Yale Broadway Masters

KANDER
and EBB

JAMES LEVE

With a Foreword by Geoffrey Block, General Editor

YALE UNIVERSITY PRESS NEW HAVEN & LONDON

Set in Electra Roman by Tseng Information Systems, Inc.
Printed in the United States of America by Sheridan Books, Ann Arbor, Michigan.

Library of Congress Cataloging-in-Publication Data
Leve, James.
Kander and Ebb / James Leve; with a foreword by Geoffrey Block, general editor.
p. cm. (Yale Broadway masters)
Includes bibliographical references and index.
ISBN 978-0-300-11487-4 (hardcover: alk. paper)
1. Kander, John—Criticism and interpretation. 2. Ebb, Fred—Criticism and interpretation. 3. Musicals—United States—20th century—History and criticism.
ML2054.L47 2009
782.1′4092—dc22
2008040304

A catalogue record for this book is available from the British Library.
This paper meets the requirements of ANSI/NISO Z39.48-1992 (Permanence of Paper).
It contains 30 percent postconsumer waste (PCW) and is certified by the Forest Stewardship Council (FSC).

10 9 8 7 6 5 4 3 2 1

To James Quincy Leve

Contents

Foreword

J AMES LEVE'S *JOHN KANDER AND FRED EBB* FOLLOWS JOHN SNELSON'S *Andrew Lloyd Webber* (2004) and precedes Kim Kowalke's forthcoming *Stephen Sondheim* to round out a trio of Yale Broadway Masters volumes devoted to Broadway creators active since the 1960s. Since composer Kander (b. 1927) and lyricist Ebb (1932–2004) worked seamlessly and almost exclusively together for over forty years (usually in the same room), longer than any composer-lyricist team in Broadway history, it is fitting that this volume display shared billing on the marquee. Their twelve Broadway musicals begin in 1965 with *Flora, the Red Menace*—directed and co-written by the legendary George Abbott, then a spry seventy-eight-year-old—and was the first of several collaborations with Liza Minnelli, who at the age of nineteen received a Tony Award. Their final bow, the fittingly titled *Curtains* (2007), by necessity presented lyrics completed by Kander and Rupert Holmes after the death of Kander's long-time creative partner. The other ten Kander and Ebb shows that appeared during their forty-two years on the Broadway stage are *Cabaret* (1966), *The Happy Time* (1968), *Zorbá* (1968), *70, Girls, 70* (1971), *Chicago* (1975), *The Act* (1977), *Woman of the Year* (1981), *The Rink* (1984), *Kiss of the Spider Woman* (1993), and *Steel Pier* (1997). As I write this in early June 2008, *Curtains* rests on the verge of closing its first Broadway run at 511 performances at the end of the month.

Despite their consistently excellent scores, most Kander and Ebb shows were at best modest hits—only three shows initially ran more than nine hundred performances, six shows ran under three hundred performances, and three of these closed under one hundred performances—and most remain less well known than the mega-hits of Lloyd Webber and the acclaimed musicals of Sondheim. In addition to their uniformly fine music and lyrics, the backbone of the present study, Kander and Ebb shows feature often outstanding and memorable work by major librettists, directors, choreographers, stage designers, orchestrators, and stars, especially larger-than-life divas. Many of these players will figure prominently in the chapters to follow:

Librettists: Terrence McNally (*The Rink, Kiss of the Spider Woman*); Joe Masteroff (*Cabaret, Zorbá*); N. Richard Nash (*The Happy Time*); Joseph Stein (*Zorbá*); Peter Stone (*Woman of the Year, Curtains*)

Directors: George Abbott (*Flora, the Red Menace*); Walter Bobbie (*Chicago* [revival]); Gower Champion (*The Happy Time*); Bob Fosse (*Cabaret* [film], *Chicago*); Rob Marshall (*Chicago* [film]); Sam Mendes (*Cabaret* [revival]); Hal Prince (*Cabaret, Zorbá, Kiss of the Spider Woman*); Martin Scorsese (*New York, New York* [film], *The Act*)

Choreographers: Gower Champion (*The Happy Time*); Graciela Daniele (*The Rink*); Ron Field (*Cabaret, Zorbá*); Bob Fosse (*Chicago*); Rob Marshall (*Chicago* [film]); Ann Reinking (*Chicago* [revival]; Susan Stroman (*Steel Pier*); Onna White (*70, Girls, 70*)

Stage Designers: Boris Aronson (*Cabaret, Zorbá*); Tony Walton (*Chicago, Woman of the Year*)

Orchestrators: Ralph Burns (*Chicago*); Don Walker (*Flora, the Red Menace, Cabaret*)

Stars: Lauren Bacall (*Woman of the Year*); Alan Cumming (*Cabaret* [revival]); Jack Gilford (*Cabaret*); Robert Goulet (*The Happy Time*); Joel Grey (*Cabaret*); Lotte Lenya (*Cabaret*); Liza Minnelli (*Flora, the Red Menace, Cabaret* [film], *New York, New York* [film], *The Act, The Rink*); Debra Monk (*Steel Pier, Curtains*); Mildred Natwick (*70, Girls, 70*); Jerry Orbach (*Chicago*); David Hyde Pierce (*Curtains*); Natasha Richardson (*Cabaret* [revival]); Chita Rivera (*Chicago, The Rink, Kiss of the Spider Woman*); Barbra Streisand (*Funny Lady* [film]); Gwen Verdon (*Chicago*); Karen Ziemba (*Steel Pier, Curtains*)

Two Kander and Ebb shows, *Cabaret* (1966) and *Chicago* (1975), are widely regarded as among the most artistically imaginative and historically influential of their time. Moreover, in their staged revivals and film incarnations this illustrious pair now ranks among the most popular shows of our time as well. *Cabaret* innovatively combined book scenes outside its cabaret habitat and what would soon be known as "concept" scenes within, the latter, according to Hal Prince's vision, standing as a metaphor for Germany's moral disintegration on the eve of the Third Reich. Bob Fosse's *Chicago* ingeniously adapted the venerable genre of vaudeville and created an idiosyncratic angular choreographic style to convey a cynical view of crime, celebrity, and legal manipulation and corruption in decadent 1920s America. In both shows, the acerbic and unsentimental lyrics of Ebb and the atmospheric musical styles of Kander—an original hybrid of German jazz and Kurt Weill theater songs in *Cabaret* and American jazz and popular song in *Chicago*—gave the Broadway musical a fresh new voice and sound.

Although the revival has consistently offered some of the most exciting and competitive Broadway fare in recently decades (evolving from a Tony Award shared with plays in 1977 to its own category in 1994), only two of the longest-running musicals in Broadway history are revivals: *Cabaret* and *Chicago*. The 1998 revival of *Cabaret*, directed by Sam Mendes, closed in 2003 after 2,377 performances—more than double the show's successful but unspectacular initial run of 1,165 performances—and currently ranks as the eighteenth-longest-running Broadway musical. Meanwhile, the still-running 1996 revival of *Chicago*, a relatively inconspicuously popular musical from 1975 directed by Fosse, was overwhelmed by the critical and popular juggernaut of *A Chorus Line* (6,137 performances), which had opened a few weeks earlier. This revival now ranks as the eighth-longest-running musical in Broadway history and likely will surpass the soon-to-close *Rent*, also from 1996. With enough irony, the *Chicago* revival might even catch up with the astronomical first-run totals of *Chorus Line*, the work that cast *Chicago*'s debut run in the shadows. Adding to this newfound glory, six years into *Chicago*'s revival a film version directed and choreographed by Rob Marshall in 2002 became the first film musical to be nominated for an Academy Award for best picture since Fosse's *Cabaret* (1972), and the first film musical to win this coveted award in thirty-four years. Perhaps nothing in Broadway history comes as close as these two shows to validating the generally erroneous perception that some works are ahead of their time.

Cabaret and *Chicago*, as well as *Kiss of the Spider Woman*, will receive extensive treatment in this volume. The underrated or at least controversial *Spider Woman*, in my view a powerful, convincing, and beautiful show (even if less gritty than its source novel by Manuel Puig), is centered on the evolving relationship between a homophobic political prisoner and his gay cellmate, and was directed by Prince. In this volume we will learn more about its arduous odyssey and numerous revisions before its eventual popular but mixed critical success in 1993.

Leve, a National Institute for Music Theater Fellow who studied composition privately and enjoyed numerous sessions of coffee and gooey *schnecken* with Kander in the 1980s, obtained the composer's cooperation as well as unlimited access to invaluable personal manuscripts and papers and to a complete collection of Kander and Ebb's impressive recorded demos of songs from each of their shows (only a few of which are commercially available). His thorough study of Kander's papers, his conversations and correspondence with the composer, and his interviews with others who worked with both Kander and Ebb gave Leve an unprecedented glimpse into one of the most intimate creative collaborations in Broadway history. For the first time readers will be able to gain a reliable and comprehensive compositional history of the famous shows and their major revivals and films as well as a comprehensive overview of the often fine but little-known output (including the unpublished early works, abandoned works, and promising works in progress) of this outstanding team.

GEOFFREY BLOCK
General Editor

Acknowledgments

R ESEARCH FOR THIS BOOK WAS CONDUCTED WITH THE SUPPORT OF a 2004 National Endowment for the Humanities Summer Stipend and two Intramural Grants from Northern Arizona University. Many of the people who know/knew John Kander and Fred Ebb personally and professionally are part of this book, and I thank them for their contribution: Larry Alpert, Hank Beebe, Ruth Schoeni Bent, Ellen Gibson, Norman Leyden, Marty Richards, Mary Rodgers, David Rogers, and Mary Stone. I am grateful to Ron Cowen, Michael Gibson, Rupert Holmes, Daniel Lipman, Terrence McNally, Hal Prince, Chita Rivera, David Thompson, Tony Walton, and Karen Ziemba, all of whom were enormously generous with their time, knowledge, and materials. Albert Stephenson needs to be thanked separately for his patience and help throughout the project.

I thank Theodore S. Chapin, the president of the Rodgers and Hammerstein Organization, for providing Fred Ebb's additional lyrics for the 1997 version of *Cinderella*; the Kurt Weill Foundation for providing a copy of the original script and score for *Love Life*; and Fuerstner Musikverlag GmbH, Mainz, Germany, for permission to quote from Frederick Hollander's "Die Pijetät." Paul McKibbins, musical administrator for Kander and Ebb, was instrumental in procuring the permissions to reproduce Kander and Ebb's music and lyrics. Brad Lohrenz of Samuel French Inc. provided statistical data on Kander and Ebb's musicals. Any book of this nature involves the efforts of numerous anonymous faces making up the staffs at public and private libraries and archives, in this case the New York Public Library of the Performing Arts at Lincoln Center, Charles E. Young Humanities Research

Library Rare Books Division at UCLA, and the Tamiment Library at New York University. George Boziwick, while still Curator of the Music Division's American Music Collection at the New York Public Library, helped get me access to materials that had not yet been catalogued.

Without David "Bone" McKeon, John Kander's personal assistant, this book would simply not have been possible. I will forever be grateful for his generosity of time and spirit. Special thanks also go to Jeffrey Scott Neuman, who generously shared the research that he did on Kander and Ebb for his master's thesis at the University of Colorado–Boulder. Thanks also go to Janet Ruwe for her assistance when it was most needed.

Although it is a bit unusual to thank the subjects of the book one is writing, in this case I must acknowledge Fred Ebb and John Kander. They gave me the type of access to their materials that no researcher should ever expect. They were inordinately generous with their time and forthright with information, sitting for hours upon hours of interviews. They have spoiled me beyond measure for any future book projects that I might undertake.

A very special thanks to Geoffrey Block, who had the insight to include a book on Kander and Ebb in the Yale Broadway Masters series and who was opened to the possibility of my writing it. I am deeply grateful for his unwavering support and assistance throughout the process. I thank Keith Condon, the acquisitions editor at Yale University Press, and the editorial staff, especially Jeffrey Schier, for their assistance, care, and dedication to this project. Lastly, without the expertise and support of Donelle Ruwe, this book would be a far inferior work. A mere sentence cannot adequately express my gratitude and indebtedness to her.

Yale Broadway Masters Advisory Board

Kander and Ebb

Introduction

They were so willing to go to a place that they knew was theatrically so dangerous. They couldn't get there fast enough.
—DAVID THOMPSON

F RED EBB'S DEATH IN 2004 ENDED THE LONGEST COMPOSER-lyricist collaboration in the history of musical theater. For nearly forty-two years, Fred Ebb and John Kander literally worked together in the same small room with an old, banged-up spinet piano, writing over twenty musicals, twelve of which opened on Broadway; music for several Hollywood films; and a wide range of specialty material. They won numerous awards and honors, including the Kennedy Center Award for Lifetime Achievement in the Performing Arts.[1] They were among the most resilient Broadway writers of their generation (Kander still is) and continued to write provocative new musicals steadily into the twenty-first century (Table I.1).

Ebb preferred to write at home, so Kander, the sprightlier of the two, usually walked the six blocks to his partner's apartment to work. It was a pattern established in 1962 with their very first meeting, which was arranged by Tommy Valando, their mutual music publisher, who sensed that they might make a good team. This first meeting went well, but their collaboration got off to a slow start. Their first musical, *Golden Gate*, was never produced, and their second, *Flora, the Red Menace* (1965), was a flop. Their groundbreaking third musical, *Cabaret* (1966), earned them their first of three Tony Awards

Table I.1. Kander and Ebb's twelve Broadway musicals

Title of Musical	Year Opened	Theater Venue
Flora, the Red Menace	1965	Alvin Theatre (today Neil Simon Theatre)
Cabaret	1966	Broadhurst Theatre
The Happy Time	1968	Broadway Theatre
Zorbá	1968	Imperial Theatre
70, Girls, 70	1971	Broadhurst Theatre
Chicago	1975	46th Street Theatre
The Act	1977	Majestic Theatre
Woman of the Year	1981	Palace Theatre
The Rink	1984	Martin Beck Theatre
Kiss of the Spider Woman	1993	Broadhurst Theatre
Steel Pier	1997	Richard Rodgers Theatre
Curtains	2007	Al Hirshfeld Theatre

for best score; the others were for *Woman of the Year* (1981) and *Kiss of the Spider Woman* (1993).

Since 1996, not one day has passed without at least one Kander and Ebb musical occupying a Broadway theater. As of this writing, the Broadway revival of *Chicago*, which opened in 1996, is the longest-running revival in Broadway history and is still going strong, and *Curtains* just closed after playing for well over a year. *Cabaret*, *Chicago*, and *Kiss of the Spider Woman* are among the most innovative and provocative musicals of the post–Rodgers and Hammerstein era. The film versions of *Cabaret* and *Chicago* both won the Academy Award for best film and are the biggest Hollywood musical hits since *The Sound of Music*. Despite these and other accomplishments, Kander and Ebb are seldom acknowledged for their pivotal role in shaping the course of musical theater for the last forty-five years. Because their musicals do not generate the same level of controversy as Stephen Sondheim's and Andrew Lloyd Webber's musicals, Kander and Ebb are usually left out of the debate that Sondheim and Webber engender regarding art and commerce. The only published work on Kander and Ebb is a relatively recent book of conversations with them about their musicals.[2]

The present book, the first full-length study of Kander and Ebb's work, establishes a historical and stylistic framework for analyzing their musicals and appreciating their remarkable collaboration. I survey Kander and Ebb's collaboration in its entirety and, as in all of the volumes in the Yale Broadway Masters series, provide in-depth studies of their most important works.

Kander and Ebb is one of only two volumes in the series dedicated to a composer and lyricist team, the other being on Lerner and Loewe. It is fitting that Geoffrey Block, the general editor of the series, decided to include Kander and Ebb in a single volume, given the fact that their names are inseparable. That Block privileged them (along with Sondheim and Lloyd Webber) over the other writers of their generation is itself recognition of Kander and Ebb's importance in the history of the musical.

This book is based on Kander's and Ebb's private papers (which contain song sketches, early drafts of scripts, correspondence, and demo recordings and live recordings of the musicals), interviews with the authors and a number of their collaborators, the Tamiment Papers at New York University, and manuscript collections at the New York Public Library for the Performing Arts and the Special Collections Library at UCLA.[3] Kander and Ebb made studio demo recordings of nearly everything they wrote, thereby documenting in sound their entire career. These recordings are a treasure trove of information, and they allowed me to reconstruct the evolution of each show. The writers were known as great performers of their own material, and these recordings convey musical and dramatic nuances that are sometimes missing from the Broadway recordings.[4] Ebb sings the majority of the comic songs and showstoppers, whereas Kander, a less gregarious performer than his partner, sings most of the ballads.[5] Kander also provides lush piano accompaniments intended to simulate an orchestra. The recently reissued original Broadway cast recording of *Cabaret* and the tenth-anniversary edition of the Broadway revival of *Chicago* include bonus tracks of heretofore unknown songs from these demos. Unfortunately, the other demo recordings are inaccessible to the general public.

Kander and Ebb grew up during the Rodgers and Hammerstein era, when musicals dominated American popular music and captured post–World War II optimism, but the Broadway musical was in a precipitous decline when the two men met in the early sixties. The Rodgers and Hammerstein model, established in 1943, was incapable of responding to the uncertainty created by the Cold War and Vietnam, and rock was replacing Broadway music as the primary popular idiom. The Broadway musical was starting to move in an increasingly serious direction just as Kander and Ebb found their distinctive voice. They welcomed this development and started to experiment with new forms. Their success was due to an ability to assimilate the past into something new. While moving away from linear narratives toward more fragmented structures, they also reached back to old song styles and theatrical venues. This approach helped to transform the musical into a more commentative, self-reflexive, and ironic genre, and one that resonated with modern audiences.

Kander and Ebb's breakthrough musical, *Cabaret*, defined a new type of musical theater for the postmodern era. Most critics call this type the "concept musical," although some have opted for more idiosyncratic labels such as "metaphorical musical" and "fragmented musical."[6] Whatever the preferred term, such musicals reject the storytelling mode of shows like *Oklahoma!* in favor of a less linear and more self-referential mode of presentation. The music, lyrics, book, set, and costumes are conceived not individually but as a whole in order to articulate the theme or metaphor of a musical.[7] Rodgers and Hammerstein's *Allegro* (1947) and Kurt Weill and Alan Jay Lerner's *Love Life* (1948) are early experiments in the concept musical, but neither fully created the marriage of form and content that the concept musical demands and that *Cabaret* achieved. Nor have they found a stable place in the Broadway repertoire.

Concept musicals not only experimented with structure, they also shifted the focus from the celebration of community, as in *Oklahoma!*, to the Self, as in *Cabaret*, *Company*, and *A Chorus Line*. In Kander and Ebb's musicals, the individual, usually a disenfranchised member of society, confronts existential challenges within a hostile, cynical, and nihilistic world. The typical protagonist of a Kander and Ebb musical, such as Flora (*Flora, the Red Menace*), Jacques (*The Happy Time*), Angel (*The Rink*), and Rita (*Steel Pier*), struggles to discover or assert his or her true identity, sometimes with tragic consequences, as is the case for Sally (*Cabaret*) and Molina (*Kiss of the Spider Woman*).

Kander and Ebb are provocateurs and arguably the most subversive practitioners of the concept musical. They owe something in this respect to Bertold Brecht, who emphasized the intrinsic disconnect between narrative and musical performance.[8] Brecht, like Kander and Ebb, responded to the Wagnerian ideal of integrating all elements of music theater by cultivating an aesthetic of disjunction between song and narrative. But Kander and Ebb developed their own unique sense of irony by exploring serious topics within various forms of popular entertainment: for example, a decadent cabaret embodies German society during Hitler's rise to power; the Hollywood musical provides a wrongly imprisoned homosexual an escape from an oppressive society; vaudeville is a metaphor for a legal system that rewards the most dazzling courtroom performances; a dance marathon represents possibilities for a better life; and a minstrel show reveals the ingrained racism of the American criminal justice system. By exploring serious issues through the lens of American popular culture, Kander and Ebb virtually invented the self-referential musical and exploited the inherent contradiction of breaking into song in the middle of a realistic scene.[9] Their musicals draw attention to the artifice of theater. Although *Curtains* is their only musical about a musical, most of their works adopt some variation of the show-within-a-show framework. The theatrical settings of their musicals make the use of presentation songs (songs sung directly to the audience) seem natural. Such songs lure the spectator into a self-reflexive mode (such as "If You Could See Her Through My Eyes"). In this regard, too, Brecht might have been the model, as his epic theater emphasizes the separation and palpable disjunction between song and speech in order to distance the audience from the emotional tug of the story.

In the first chapter of this book, I set out to define what we mean when we talk about Kander and Ebb. To answer the question "What is a Kander and Ebb song?" is no easy matter, and neither Ebb's response—"the songs that have become what people think of as Kander and Ebb songs are purely accidental"—nor Kander's rejoinder—"I wouldn't recognize a Kander and Ebb song if it walked in the room and slapped me in the face"—is much help. Kander and Ebb are a study of opposites, as different from each other as two collaborators could possibly be. I explore how each writer individually influenced the single entity that Kander himself calls "KandernEbb."[10] The composer has an unabashed lyrical and romantic side, and the lyricist a strong sense of irony, a pairing not unlike Rodgers and Hart. The marriage of these two extreme aesthetic positions produced whatever it is that people have identified as a Kander and Ebb song.

Chapters 2 and 3 explore *Cabaret* and *Chicago*, respectively. These shows epitomize Kander and Ebb's unique approach to musical theater and continue to be their most popular works. In *Cabaret*, Ebb's cynical and wickedly funny lyrics find a home in Kander's blend of pastiche and lyrical music *Cabaret* began as a traditional book musical, but when Hal Prince and his creative team came up with the idea of featuring an emcee and using a cabaret named the Kit Kat Klub as a metaphor, they changed the face of musical theater forever. At one point, Clifford Bradshaw, the romantic male lead, had several numbers to sing, but by opening night, he was left with a single song. In Sam Mendes's 1998 Broadway revival of *Cabaret*, even this song was gone. Clifford's ever-diminishing musical role is significant when considered in the context of his sexuality—in the original Broadway version he is heterosexual (or a closeted homosexual), but in later versions he is bisexual or gay (Christopher Isherwood, the novelist on whom the character was based, was one of the first major openly gay writers). The sexual ambiguity of this role made it difficult for the writers of *Cabaret* to find a musical voice for Clifford.

Chicago has long been heralded as a "Fosse musical," but it bears all the hallmarks of a Kander and Ebb musical. The concept for *Chicago*, which is the perfect marriage of content and form, relies on Kander and Ebb's ability to adapt vaudeville tropes and Tin Pan Alley styles to a modern musical theater sensibility. *Chicago* is cynical and subversive, exploiting American cultural mythologies in order to attack American celebrity culture. Ironically, as celebrity culture has become an increasingly corrosive force in America, *Chicago* has become more relevant. After *Cabaret*, it is Kander and Ebb's most often produced musical.

Individually, Kander and Ebb each have several major achievements. These works and the writers' artistic activities before they met, including student projects, are the subject of Chapter 4. Kander and Ebb both received similar top-notch academic training; each one attended a private undergraduate program and earned a master's degree at Columbia University. Unfortunately, not a page of Ebb's student writing remains. However, Kander has held on to his student compositions, thus providing us a window into his early growth as a composer. Like his contemporary Stephen Sondheim, Kander received conservatory music training. Whereas Sondheim's exposure to modernist trends can be heard in the percussive and fragmented musical textures that often take precedent over his melodies, Kander's academic background reinforced the operatic tendencies of his melodic writing. He has always aimed for directness and breadth of melody supported by unencumbered musical accompaniments. Unlike Sondheim, who admittedly never "got" opera, Kander has made three pilgrimages to Bayreuth and is a regular subscriber to the Metropolitan Opera. In college, Kander experimented with both opera and musical theater composition. When he decided that he was going to write musical theater, he initially suppressed his operatic instincts, but he soon dropped any distinction between the two forms that he might have seen and started to allow himself a greater degree of lyrical expression. He has acknowledged that there is a continuum between musical comedy and opera and that "I'm free to write in any form I want to." In fact, as Kander's late serious compositions reveal, he is just as likely to draw from musical theater for his serious arias as the other way around. It should be noted that

Kander's taste in music has always been far-reaching. He is just as passionate about Mahler and Brahms, whom he calls the "human Beethoven," as he is about Wagner and Puccini, although Debussy and Ravel "just drive me crazy."

After graduating from Columbia University, Kander and Ebb both worked with several different writers in the hope of finding the ideal partner. After achieving a certain degree of success as collaborators, Kander and Ebb continued to work on independent projects, often with people they had met earlier in their careers. Ebb wrote and produced a number of acclaimed television specials, and Kander composed art songs and music for dramatic films. Ebb also devoted considerable energy to playing Pygmalion to Liza Minnelli's Galatea. Although Kander did compose music for Ebb's specials and concerts for Liza, his own independent projects rarely intersected with his collaboration with Ebb.

Chapter 5 examines the transformation of the musical *Kiss of the Spider Woman* from a flop to a hit. The last major diva musical of the twentieth century, *Spider Woman* first appeared on stage in 1990 at Purchase College in upstate New York. The critics disparaged the overblown movie-musical sequences. Ironically, they had no difficulty with the scenes depicting defecation, homosexual sex, a male-male kiss, or torture. When a revised version of *Spider Woman* opened on Broadway in 1993, these same critics declared the musical a triumph, and it won the Tony Award for best musical. After Purchase, the writers replaced the glitzy Hollywood musical sequences with a series of exotic scenes filled with Latin dances and south-of-the-border rhythms. These scenes, featuring Chita Rivera, provided enough entertainment for the audience to accept the main story, which, even though it was a mere shadow of Manuel Puig's rich novel, was still more provocative than that of most Broadway musicals.

Half of Kander and Ebb's Broadway musicals were flops in the financial sense. Nevertheless, over the years many of these works have developed a following and are perennial favorites in regional and community theater. Chapter 6 discusses these musicals, each of which boasts a solid Kander and Ebb score. Kander and Ebb continued to make improvements to these works after they closed on Broadway. In its revised form, *Flora, the Red Menace*, is more serious than its original incarnation. *The Happy Time* was revised by Kander, Ebb, and the playwright N. Richard Nash for a production at the Goodspeed Opera House. The new version restores some of the initial charm and dramatic conflict of the original material that was lost under the guidance of

Gower Champion, the director of the Broadway production. *Zorbá* closed on Broadway before turning a profit, but it did well on the road and several years later returned to Broadway in a successful revival starring Anthony Quinn. This revival adopted many of the changes that Kander and Ebb made for the first national touring company in 1970. *70, Girls, 70* (1970) has developed a cult following and is one of Kander and Ebb's most frequently produced works today. There are dramaturgical problems that Ebb was never able to solve, but the score is a delight from start to finish. Neither *The Rink* (1984) nor *Steel Pier* (1997) was a commercial success, but Kander regards them with great fondness. They might even be his personal favorites; he most enjoys composing music for stories about human interaction, as was the case for both. Kander and Ebb maintained close personal relationships with the people involved in these projects, especially Scott Ellis, David Thompson, Susan Stroman, and Karen Ziemba.

Chapter 7 focuses on two of Kander and Ebb's diva musicals, *The Act* and *Woman of the Year*. Although both were financially successful, neither rates very high in Kander and Ebb's own assessment of their work. In *Woman of the Year*, the more successful of the two, the leading female character chooses to compromise her professional ambitions in order to save her marriage. The female protagonist of *The Act* saves her personal relationships by achieving a degree of professional independence. Broadway's diva musicals—*Gypsy*, *Mame*, *Chicago*, and *Evita*, for example—usually provide figures of identification for gay audiences. The leading ladies of *Woman of the Year* and *The Act* are not the sort of nonconformist divas that have become part of the currency of gay subculture.

The penultimate chapter is an overview of Kander and Ebb's incomplete and abandoned projects. These works, which exist in various states of completion, share features characteristic of Kander and Ebb's twelve Broadway musicals, in particular, the use of theater as a metaphor for real life. The last chapter of this book examines Kander and Ebb's final four musicals. *Curtains*, which opened on Broadway after Ebb's death, took half of Kander and Ebb's career to reach fruition. The other three are still bound for Broadway: *All About Us*, *The Visit*, and *Minstrel Show*. These are daring and innovative works, as challenging and interesting as anything else Kander and Ebb wrote. Finally, Kander and Ebb's television and film work and minor stage projects, although relegated to the appendix for reasons of organization, were a vital part of their collaboration.

I initially resisted the temptation to discuss Kander and Ebb in relationship to Sondheim, but the more I immersed myself in their work, the more difficult it became to ignore how often their career paths crossed. Hal Prince produced and directed many of Kander and Ebb's and Sondheim's most important musicals. Kander arranged the dance music for *Gypsy*, for which Sondheim wrote the lyrics. In 1962 Sondheim urged Prince to consider producing Kander's musical A *Family Affair*, which he co-wrote with James and William Goldman. James Goldman wrote the book for Sondheim's *Evening Primrose* and *Follies*, and Sondheim wrote songs for two of William Goldman's screenplays, *The Thing of It Is* and *Singing Out Loud*, neither of which was ever made.[11] Like Sondheim, Ebb also collaborated briefly with Mary Rodgers Guettel. N. Richard Nash, whose play *The Girls of Summer* featured a song by Sondheim, wrote the book for *The Happy Time*. By acknowledging the intersections in Kander and Ebb's and Sondheim's careers, we begin to see that their musicals lie not on different planes but on different ends of the same spectrum.[12]

I have had the great fortune of knowing Kander, Sondheim, and, to a far lesser extent, Ebb. In the mid eighties, I received a grant from the now defunct National Institute of Music Theater to study composition with Kander. I was working with a lyricist named Dennis Stranz at the time, and we wrote a musical called *Ball of Fat*, based on De Maupassant's *Boule de suif*, under Kander's tutelage. A few years earlier, I had had several opportunities to play my music for Sondheim and receive his feedback. As teachers, neither Sondheim nor Kander is ever prescriptive. Kander encouraged me to build on the work that I brought him, and Sondheim barraged me with questions about the choices I had made. Occasionally, each would spontaneously disappear into his vast record collection and reemerge a few minutes later with something to illustrate a point, Kander with the comic finale from Ermanno Wolf-Ferrari's *Quattro rustechi*, Sondheim with the rhythmically complex Brazilian folk song "Bambalele." Years later, when the opportunity to write this volume presented itself, I asked John Kander, with whom I had not had direct contact for several years, if I could have access to his manuscript materials. To my surprise and delight, he literally gave me a key to his house in New York. He also convinced Ebb, who was somewhat reluctant at first, to talk with me and to share his personal manuscripts. And so, during the summer of 2004, and with the support of a National Endowment for the Humanities summer stipend, I immersed myself in a study of a collaboration that was even more fascinating than I had first realized.

When I was studying with John Kander, we would always begin a session

with coffee and schnecken. That was over twenty years ago. By the time I re-
connected with him I had gained a far better understanding of musical theater and opera. In the interviews I held with him for this book—which only
occasionally involved schnecken, as the years had made us both more aware
of our waistlines—we discussed music and theater from a broader perspective. I will always cherish the hours that we spent discussing the differences
between musical theater and opera, the trajectory of Renée Fleming's career,
and the qualities that make a good Broadway dance arranger. I still question
the wisdom of pointing out to him that scholars no longer consider the closing
duet of *L'incoronazione di Poppea* to be composed by Monteverdi, a fact that
Kander would prefer not to accept. My contact with Fred Ebb amounted to a
few compact hours during the summer of 2004, just months before he died.
He was acerbic, sharp-witted, and solipsistic. Several of the stories he told me
I subsequently heard or read elsewhere, as though they were a fixed part of
his repartee. That was Fred Ebb, a man of the theater. I was so grateful for his
time that I invited him out for dinner, assuming that he would turn me down.
To my surprise, he responded, "I accept." So I searched for a convenient restaurant near his apartment, for it was difficult for him to get around in those
days. However, whenever I tried to confirm our date, his assistant informed
me that he was out of town visiting his nephew. Eventually, I gave up, accepting the fact that the dinner was never going to happen. It was only then that
I realized that he had simply taken the path of least resistance and graciously
accepted my invitation. He had made a similar dodge years earlier, when he
avoided a social engagement by claiming that he was going to Greece to do
research for *Zorbá*. He had to hide out in his apartment in New York for three
weeks for fear of being found out.

   In the years since that summer in New York I have interviewed many
of the people who worked closely with Kander and Ebb, including Chita
Rivera, Michael Gibson, Rupert Holmes, David Thompson, Tony Walton,
and Karen Ziemba. From these conversations emerged a portrait of Kander
and Ebb as generous, unpretentious, and dedicated "Broadway babies," as
Hal Prince has called them. They built a family out of their friends and associates, many of whom are considered to be the most talented people working on Broadway today. In interview after interview, I heard about Kander
and Ebb's collaborative process, their eagerness to revise, their dedication
to a single artistic vision. They were model collaborators, nondictatorial and
receptive to any and all suggestions. As Terrence McNally once said, "For
every Kander and Ebb, there is an Attila the Hun." These words come from

the librettist who worked with Kander and Ebb on three musicals and thus ought to know.[13]

Like many writers of their generation, Kander and Ebb have had their share of revivals and tributes, but they never allowed these events to get in the way of progress on a new musical. Kander remains active today and is open to working with other lyricists. Fred Ebb, were he still around, would be pressuring Kander to come over to his house so that they could get some work done on their latest project. And Kander would go, sometime reluctantly, sometimes eagerly, but he would go. Ebb once complained that Sondheim received all the major awards before they did. Eventually, Ebb and Kander were rewarded. And now it is time that they be duly recognized.

CHAPTER 1

Forty-Two Years of Musicals

We walk into the studio as John Kander and Fred Ebb, but what comes out is authentic Kander and Ebb.

—JOHN KANDER

JOHN KANDER AND FRED EBB WERE AS DIFFERENT FROM EACH OTHER as two collaborators could possibly be. Kander grew up in Kansas City, raised by nurturing parents and surrounded by the comforts of a middle-class household.[1] Fred Ebb grew up in New York City. He was the only male child in a dysfunctional and undemonstrative family of modest means. Since the late seventies Kander has lived with his partner, Albert Stephenson, in a modest brownstone on the Upper West Side. For years Ebb bounced between his Manhattan apartment in the San Remo, one of the most desirable residential buildings on Central Park West, and his Bel Air home in Los Angeles.[2] Ebb, who had a roommate for decades, was living alone with a small dachshund when he died. He had amassed an impressive art collection dominated by German and Austrian paintings and sketches from the first half of the century, all of which he bequeathed to the Morgan Library and Museum in New York. By contrast, Kander spends as much time as possible at his country house in upstate New York. Being more aurally than visually oriented, he never cared much for art collecting, but he has long been an assiduous collector of sound recordings. At eighty-one years of age, Kander still subscribes to the Metropolitan Opera.[3] Ebb had little affinity for opera, and he preferred Gian Carlo Menotti to the masters of grand opera.

John Kander was born on March 18, 1927. His father, who worked in his father-in-law's egg and poultry business, instilled in John and his brother Edward a love of life and a healthy interest in the arts. Kander's fondest recollection of his childhood was of the time his "Aunt Rheta [put] her hands over my hands on the keys. That made a chord, and as a boy, it was about the most thrilling thing that ever happened to me."[4] To this day, Kander associates music with happy feelings and positive memories. Kander's parents regularly brought their two sons to local theater and orchestra concerts, and every year treated them to a trip to New York City to see theater. As a nine-year-old, Kander attended his first opera performances when the San Carlo Opera came to Kansas City with productions of *Aida* and *Madama Butterfly*: "My mother took me and we sat in the first row. There were these giants on the stage, and my feet were dangling over my seat. It was overwhelming for me, even though I could see the strings that held the beards on the Egyptian soldiers. . . . My interest in telling a story through music in many ways derived from early experiences like those." Opera soon became an important part of Kander's world.

In the mid 1940s, Kander joined the United States Merchant Marine Cadet Corps. He completed basic training in California, after which he sailed between San Francisco, the Philippines, Shanghai, and Hong Kong.[5] He left the Corps on May 3, 1946, but rule changes governing national service forced him to enlist in the Army Reserves in September of the same year, after having already completed one semester at the Oberlin Conservatory of Music. He served for a year at Fort Bragg in North Carolina. By organizing a seven-piece dance band, which performed at the Officers' Club, Kander was able to remain musically active as well as in good standing with his superiors. As if trapped in a proverbial Catch-22, during the Korean War Kander was again ordered back into active duty. In preparation, he gave up his apartment in New York, but after a medical physical revealed scars on his lungs he was forced to remain in the city for six months of observation and was officially discharged on July 3, 1957.

Taking advantage of the G.I. Bill, Kander returned to Oberlin and earned a degree in music composition in 1951. He then entered the master's program in composition at Columbia University and received his degree in 1954. Columbia, which had one of the most conservative composition programs in the country, suited Kander's artistic temperament. He was not inclined to write in an atonal idiom, the trend at many music programs at the time, but he did feel compelled to compose serious works. Jack Beeson and Otto Luening, his primary composition teachers at Columbia, were open to any music he wanted to write. Beeson improved Kander's understanding of musical form from a composer's perspective, and Luening taught him to stay out of his own way, to avoid self-imposed roadblocks. Luening's enthusiasm for new music bordered on the uncritical, a trait that perhaps rubbed off on Kander. Even at his most critical, Kander uses humor to couch his comments, as in the time he called a writer of a new work produced at the Metropolitan Opera "the composer of no fun." Kander participated in the highly regarded Columbia Opera Workshop during its heyday and was either musical assistant or assistant conductor for the premieres of Arthur Kreutz's *Acres of Sky* (1951) and Jack Beeson's *Hello Out There* (1954), as well as for a production of John Gay's *The Beggar's Opera* (1954).[6] Other workshop participants at the time included Marvin David Levy (*Mourning Becomes Electra*), Ezra Laderman, Ulysses Kay, and John Crosby (founding director of the Santa Fe Opera). The workshop was extremely important to Kander's development as a theater composer, even though at the time he was undecided between art music or popular music, and opera and musicals held his interest equally. Douglas Moore, the head of the music department, admitted to the still impressionable Kander that, if he himself could start over, he would write musicals. Moore's confession meant a lot to Kander, for it freed him to become a theater composer.

Ebb was secretive about the year of his birth, and sources for that date range from (April 8) 1928 to 1936.[7] Ebb likened Kander's childhood to a Norman Rockwell painting and was aware of how much it differed from his own: "Looking back, I can honestly say I don't believe my mother and father ever touched each other in my presence. I never saw them kiss or embrace. . . . They stayed together with their children as their only common interest, me and my two sisters, Norma and Estelle."[8] Ebb told a humorous story about the Broadway premiere of *Cabaret*. His mother attended the opening night party at Sardi's East. When the reviews came out, Ebb went over to her and said, "they were all raves, . . . it's a huge hit." She responded with a single monosyllabic "Good." He offered to buy her a mink stole. This time her response was more expansive: "It's about time." When Ebb asked her opinion about the show, she said, "The show? Well, it didn't have to be so dirty, big shot." Whether true or revisionary, this story is telling about the way Ebb wanted to depict his family. His parents never took him to the theater or a concert. His first exposure to musical theater came in the form of cast recordings. When he was old enough he started attending theater on his own, and it became his escape. Later Ebb turned to his friends and the theater for the approbation he felt that he never received at home. "And that's been my story with my family. Nobody ever says it's magnificent, you're marvelous, you're very talented, congratulations, none of that. Right up until the Oscar for *Chicago*. They don't do that . . . I can't say it never did [bother me]. . . . Of course I always had resources, which is my friends and my contemporaries. And I got a lot of respect in the business and from people I loved and friends I loved and admired and respected, who were close to me and good to me and warm and affectionate and smart."

People who knew Ebb admired his wit and unassuming erudition. By all accounts he was precocious and perspicacious. He graduated early and as valedictorian from DeWitt Clinton High School, earned a bachelor's degree from New York University in record time, and earned a master's degree in English literature from Columbia University in 1957. In contrast to Kander, who found his life's work early in life, Fred Ebb did not decide to pursue writing until college. He first became interested in writing when he took a seminar on the short story at New York University, but even after Columbia he accepted a variety of unrelated jobs, such as bronze shoes salesman and credit authorizer at Ludwing, Mauman & Spear. Meanwhile, he dabbled in limericks and other light verse, impressing his friends so much that they encouraged him to try writing professionally. Soon Ebb was peddling song lyrics to record companies, which assigned them to various staff composers with whom he had little or no contact. Around this time, Patsy Bamos, who was dating Ebb, introduced him to a composer named Phil Springer, whom she was also dating.[9] Springer taught Ebb the mechanics of songwriting, tutoring him on structure and rhyme scheme. Their first song, "I Never Loved Him Anyhow," was recorded by Carmen McRae, but their promising collaboration ended abruptly when Springer took a permanent job with a music publishing firm.

In 1951, Ebb met a composer named Paul Klein, with whom he later wrote his earliest theater music, including three full-length musicals: *It Gives Me Great Pleasure, Simon Says,* and *Morning Sun. It Gives Me Great Pleasure,* an adaptation of Emily Kimbrough's 1948 book of the same name, and *Simon Says,* an original musical comedy set in a New York advertising firm, were never produced. *Morning Sun,* based on a 1953 short story by Mary

Deasy, was produced Off Broadway in 1963. Ebb and Klein also contributed songs and sketches to the Broadway revue *From A to Z*. They had a couple of popular hit songs, including "Little Blue Man" and "That Do Make It Nice." Had Klein not quit the business to pursue a more secure livelihood, Ebb and Kander might never have gotten together.

While Ebb was working with Springer and Klein, Kander was earning a living by coaching singers, playing auditions, and conducting summer stock productions. A serendipitous encounter at the Variety Club in Philadelphia led Kander into the epicenter of Broadway musical theater. While waiting in line to order a drink, he met a man named Joe Lewis, who was the piano player for *West Side Story*. When Lewis went on vacation, he asked Kander to substitute for him. The young composer thereby met Jerome Robbins, who hired him to accompany the auditions for *Gypsy* and later to write the dance music. The production stage manager for *Gypsy* was Ruth Mitchell, the long-term associate of Hal Prince. David Merrick, the producer of *Gypsy*, later hired Kander to write the dance music for *Irma la Douce* and produced Kander and Ebb's *The Happy Time*.

In 1962, the music publisher Tommy Valando, who had successfully brought Bock and Harnick together, arranged a meeting between Kander and Ebb. They met at Ebb's apartment and discussed songwriting and musical theater. Based on this first conversation, they agreed to test their compatibility by writing a mock title song for the comedy *Take Her, She's Mine*, which was running on Broadway in a Hal Prince production. *Take Her, She's Mine* is about a father's struggle to accept his daughter as a woman.[10] Kander and Ebb's song, a nonfussy affair, imparts the bittersweet resignation that one might expect at the end of a hypothetical musical version of this play. The lyric twice contains the line "take her, she's mine," but for the final line of the song Ebb inserts "from me" to create "take her from me, she's mine." Kander reinforces the father's feeling of loss with a pause on a secondary dominant. The melody on this line recalls the melodic segment first heard in measure 3 on "take her, she's mine" (example 1.1a) but at a higher pitch level (example 1.1b). The melodic apex of the song coincides with the final "her" of the lyric. Not to overstate the case but these simple devices inject just the right degree of musical tension at just the right time. "It was a case of instant communication and instant song," Ebb recalled. "Our neuroses complemented each other, and because we worked in the same room at the same time, I didn't have to finish a lyric, then hand it over to [Kander] to compose it."[11] This first experience paved the way for the atmosphere of fun that both writers have

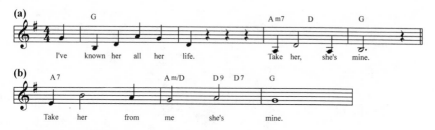

Example 1.1. Kander and Ebb's First Song, "Take Her, She's Mine" (chorus)
(a) first 4 measures (b) last 3 measures

referred to on several occasions: "When we first began to work together we
fell into a way of working that allowed us to enjoy what we were doing. . . . We
just fell into a way of writing that was pleasurable." Soon Freddie and Johnny,
as they liked to call each other, were writing novelty numbers for club acts
and industrials, anything that would keep them working and earning enough
money to pay the rent.

The turning point in Kander and Ebb's collaboration occurred when Kander suggested that they try a ballad. The result, "My Coloring Book," became
an instant hit. They wrote the song for Kaye Ballard, who planned to sing it
on the *Perry Como Television Show*, but the producer of the show, Nick Van-
noff, felt that Ballard was too much of a comedienne for the sentiment of the
song and gave it to Sandy Stewart to perform.[12] The song brought attention to
Kander and Ebb, and Stewart's recording of "My Coloring Book" was nominated for a 1962 Grammy Award.[13]

In Kander and Ebb's case, the perennial question "What comes first, the
lyrics or the music?" is not germane. They usually worked together in the
nonthreatening atmosphere of a small studio in Ebb's apartment, which had
a window air conditioner and an old spinet piano. They relied on spontaneity
rather than on any systematic method of writing. They felt free to try out any
idea that popped into their heads, and if one or the other did not like what
they came up with, they simply discarded it and moved on to something else.
In an interview Kander reluctantly described the moment-to-moment process of a typical writing session:

We used to sit around the kitchen table first and have some coffee or tea
or something and talk. We'd gossip. Then lead into whatever it was we were
going to attack that day. And sometimes Fred would have a line or an attitude

Emmy Award nomination for "My Coloring Book." From left to right: Fred
Ebb, Sandy Stewart, Tommy Valando (?), and John Kander (1962)

. . . or we would have a conversation in which we would be the people, trying
to find what they're talking about. And then we'd gradually get into the little
room. And we'd go to the piano. [I'd] find a rhythmic feeling, or sometimes
just a whole melodic idea, whatever my fingers happened to [be doing] that
day. . . . And maybe it won't feel right. And we'll both know it. And then we'll
take another tack. . . . Or first I have this quatrain. I'll mess around with it
for a little bit. I'll say, well what if we give this a different rhythmic life, if we
altered the pattern just a little bit—he's always accommodating. . . . And here

he will start to think and to write. And then if I have a musical setting, even if it's not the piece that I'm going to end up with, if I have a kind of structure, then I'll go sit in the other chair and we'll play with it lyrically. And Fred will go to the typewriter. . . . When I say we write together, we literally do.

Can we claim that there is such a thing as a Kander and Ebb song (or a Kander and Ebb musical, for that matter) when the writers themselves deny having any awareness of what this might be or that it exists at all? Kander and Ebb's portfolio of songs includes recurring harmonic progressions and exhibits preferences for certain stanzaic structures, but what best defines their voice is the contradictory nature of their collaboration: the composer and lyricist have strikingly different artistic temperaments, the former demonstrably sentimental and lyrical, the latter campy and cynical. Their collaboration is a perfect balancing act. Some critics have suggested that Kander was tolerant of Ebb's "soured idealism" and that Ebb reciprocated by tolerating Kander's "unquenchable optimism."[14] Ebb liked to joke about his partner's irrepressible sanguinity: "Johnny doesn't know how not to be sympathetic. Johnny is the Christ child. Reborn. He really is." The palpable tension between the opposing qualities that each embodies produces the dramatic energy underlying their scores. In "Maybe This Time," for instance, the melody striving to go higher and higher and the forward momentum of the harmonic progression force the singer to deny the possibility of failure even though the lyric and physical exertion required to perform this song create a sense of desperation.

One song in particular exemplifies Kander and Ebb's approach to musical theater: "How Lucky Can You Get," the opening song in the film *Funny Lady*, starring Barbra Streisand. It starts out as a suave vaudeville number but ends up revealing the interior emotional life of the singer. One can see a connection between this song and the searing "Rose's Turn" from *Gypsy*. In performance, these numbers reveal some psychological truth about the characters. As *Funny Lady* begins, Fanny/Streisand is onstage performing the song accompanied by a chorus of boys, but as the number turns inward and reveals her state of mind, it becomes a book song. This shift is accomplished both visually and musically. The melody winds chromatically and in syncopation around the sixth scale degree. Harsh parallel fourths in the accompaniment suggest an emotional fragility, which Fanny conceals beneath her flashy showbiz veneer. (Kander often uses parallel fourths to impart a sense of tension.) In Kander's original version of the song an abrupt modulation to the dominant and a change in the accompaniment announce the change in focus from the public Fanny to the private Fanny (the version used in the film modulates upward by half steps). The pounding bass on every beat creates a sense of urgency as the vocal part starts to fragment. Here, Fanny sings only the first half of each phrase, the second half taken over by the orchestra as she turns inward. When the music modulates up a half step, Fanny leaves the tune behind altogether, soaring on a countermelody over the original tune in the orchestra, a technique right out of Puccini ("O soave fanciulla," at the end of the first scene of *La Bohème*).

> Hey there, gorgeous!
> Big success!
> What's your secret?
> Just lucky I guess.

The music oozes with irony. An abrupt return to the tonic key effects a merging of Fanny's onstage and offstage psyches (the film version does not return to tonic but instead continues modulating upward). Streisand's stunning vocalization realized the dramatic potential of this number, and Kander and Ebb received an Oscar nomination for best song.

Kander and Ebb's most famous songs, including "Theme from New York, New York," "Cabaret," and "Maybe This Time," are "hyperbolic anthems of survival."[15] Ebb loved to write them and perform them; Kander calls them "screamers." Comprising a major portion of the Broadway diva repertory, such Kander and Ebb songs push the female chest voice increasingly upward, thereby forcing the singer into a heightened vocal physicality. The singing required to execute these songs, which has been called "positive singing," is itself an act of self-determination.[16] By literally overcoming the strenuous physical challenge of these numbers, the performer also expresses her (or his) will to survive. It is no coincidence that Liza Minnelli—who is closely identified with the songs listed above—has built a career based on this type of performance. Kander and Ebb's "screamers" are balanced by a body of introspective ballads, a natural expression of Kander's lyrical impulses. For these songs, Ebb, who best expressed himself in sarcastic commentaries on life, rose to the occasion with unexpected moments of poignancy. "It's a Quiet Thing," from *Flora, the Red Menace*, their first hit theater ballad, is one of the most self-reflective numbers in the Broadway repertory. With a deceptively simple melody and unfussy lyric, the song has the austere quality of a late nineteenth-century French chanson.

Ebb identified musical theater with his own life: "I find that the musical theater is metaphorically very close to my own life. When I succeed, the
happiness it brings me, when I fail, the despair it brings me . . . I find are just
about the same." For Ebb, musical theater, like showbiz, was "the business of
putting out love and getting it back . . . Life, like show business, is a series of
exchanges . . . some real, some phony, but they all spring from very human
needs. I guess Johnny and I use show business as a . . . symbol for life because
we believe that musical theatre can reflect human nature."[17] Putting theory
into practice, Ebb always looked for the intrinsic musical theater element in
a project: "When it [musical theater] is already there, already built into the
framework, it is so much easier for me to identify the musical source."[18]

Kander and Ebb viewed the world through the lens of theater, but no
form captured their interest more than vaudeville. Ebb once commented,
"By writing in the vaudevillian vein, you have a wealth of conventions that
are available to you . . . Johnny and I . . . love those conventions, and we
wanted to use them to entertain an audience and to tell a story."[19] This approach produced the unsettling mixture of nostalgia and sardonicism that
is characteristic of Kander and Ebb's brand of musical theater. Ebb could
superimpose a vaudeville motif onto practically any subject. For example,
in a projected television special on ecology, Ebb envisioned the star-studded
cast—Fred Astaire, Mama Cass Elliot, Bill Cosby, Tatum O'Neal—traveling
"the 'ecology circuit' offering through song and dance and comedy construc-
tive suggestions that will enable the average American to do a small part in
helping the current environmental crisis." Their means of travel is a vessel—
"a combination travel home and mini vaudeville theatre." For his part, Kander loves to write rags and songs in popular styles from the late nineteenth
century through the 1930s.

Kander and Ebb's veneration of popular entertainments of the past
(vaudeville, cabaret, minstrel shows, Hollywood musical) and incorporation
of camp are expressions of their gay sensibilities and a desire to assert their
identity. As part of gay subculture, camp has traditionally been a strategy to
undermine repressive hegemonic constructions of sexuality, racial prejudice,
and even class distinctions. By camping outdated forms of American popular
entertainment, Kander and Ebb draw attention to life as theater, one of the
main tenets of camp. Jack Babuscio's explanation of camp attribution seems
tailor-made for Kander and Ebb's musicals: "To appreciate camp in things or
persons is to perceive the notion of life-as-theatre, being versus role-playing,
reality and appearance. If 'role' is defined as the appropriate behaviour asso-

ciated with a given position in society, then gays do not conform to socially expected ways of behaving as men and women. Camp, by focusing on the outward appearance of role, implies that roles, and, in particular, sex roles, are superficial—a matter of style. Indeed, life itself is role and theatre, appearance and impersonation."[20] The camp aesthetic of Kander and Ebb's musicals is part of their diversionary, edgy quality. Their musicals always entertain, but they are never superficial. Their reliance on camp, in addition to being an expression of who they are, is part of their strategy for exploring themes that are of great importance to them.

Kander and Ebb's music is highly referential because they conceive their musicals in relation to popular culture. Pastiche and nostalgia in musical theater date back at least to *Show Boat* (1927). For decades, composers incorporated melodic and harmonic features associated with the historical and geographical settings of their musicals. Rather than striving for authenticity, however, they incorporated stereotypical surface details, those perceived "gross features" that suggest ethnicity or nationality, into a standard musical theater idiom—such as the use of the pentatonic scale for the "exotic" songs in *The King and I* ("My Lord and Master," for example).[21] In Kander and Ebb's musicals, form and content dictate musical style just as much as time and place do. The suggestive musical patina of *Cabaret* originates in the cabaret metaphor as well as in the historical backdrop. It does not have as its goal nostalgia or authenticity. Although the referentiality of Kander and Ebb's music can evoke an earlier era and a specific geographical location, it is more likely to draw attention to the theatrical milieu in which the story is presented: *Cabaret*'s music evokes the decadence and four-square jazz playing of Berlin nightclubs in the thirties; *Steel Pier*'s music incorporates Depression-era dance styles; and *The Act* features Las Vegas brassiness and brashness with a healthy dose of disco. In all of these works, the musical style is evocative and decidedly theatrical.

The Lyrics and Music

Kander's classical training in counterpoint, orchestration, and form prepared him for a career in concert music and opera. Ebb had a strong literary pedigree and the erudition to be a novelist. Notwithstanding their academic background, Kander and Ebb's music conveys an almost deliberate lack of pretension. They could be vulgar in one instance, as in "Two Ladies" from *Cabaret*, and disarmingly sentimental in another, as in "It Couldn't Please

Me More" from the same musical. Counterpoint in the title song from *The Rink* joyously captures in sound the whirling motion of the choreography without drawing attention to the lyricist's cleverness or the composer's solid technique. It was important to Kander and Ebb that their music be accessible. Ebb in particular deliberately avoided any hint of artistic pretension: "I think there are a lot of guys writing for the theatre who write in an elitist way. They write to please a small group who come the first three months or the first three weeks. They're content to write that way, and I think everybody has to do his own thing. As for me, I always want to be popular, and I always want to be well liked."[22] Ebb may have been taking aim at Sondheim, but he meant what he said about himself. For his part, Kander has made it his goal to move the emotions, not to intellectually engage the connoisseur. He hopes to "be remembered as an emotional stirrer . . . emotions that have impact, feelings that don't just wash over you and do nothing."[23]

Ebb's effort to write accessible songs is manifest in the smooth cadence of his lyrics. They are unencumbered by gratuitous wordplay, but when appropriate they are as clever as any lyrics written for the theater. Although Ebb could engage in the sort of wordplay ascribed to Lorenz Hart, Cole Porter, and Sondheim, his lyrics never seem labored. He could be acerbic, desperate, ironic, and at times sentimental, and his self-deprecation was second only to Lorenz Hart's. He loved to be risqué but reserved off-color humor for moments governed by the characters or the situations, such as Shelby's "Everybody's Girl" in *Steel Pier* and "Two Ladies" in *Cabaret*. Ebb has his share of poignant moments, but he found humor in unexpected places and in unlikely situations. He found a way to use the word "Dubrovnik" on three separate occasions. Ebb avoided linguistic pomposity in favor of natural language, and he had a nonchalant way with occasional vulgarity and the vernacular, writing lines like, "No one says oops while they're passing their gas / What ever happened to class?" Finally, Ebb always worked from a dramatic premise, even when writing novelty songs, such as "Sara Lee" and "Liza with a Z."

Ebb was fond of telling stories through song, adopting the long verse-short refrain format popular in early American popular ballads. He concocted discursive episodic narratives that progressed toward a surprise conclusion or moral. In these songs, long expository verses alternate with a pithy or sententious refrain, which provides a moment of repose for the listener and an opportunity for the performer to indulge in a catchy tune. "Ring Them Bells," one of his earliest examples of this type of song, is a fable about a single woman who travels the globe in search of her soul mate, who, as it ultimately so happens, lives in the apartment next door. Liza Minnelli made a splash with this song in her 1972 television special *Liza with a Z!*[24] Ebb also wrote a number of anecdotal songs for musicals, such as "Meeskite" (*Cabaret*), "Each Time Is the First Time" (*Zorbá*), "Where Does an Elephant Go" (*70, Girls, 70*), and "You Better Make Friends with the Truth" (*Minstrel Show*). The verse-refrain structure is ideal for the anecdotal nature of "Meeskite," which Herr Schultz sings to the guests at his and Fraulein Schneider's engagement party.[25] "Meeskite" is supposedly a "real" song that Schultz learned as a child. Schultz's ingratiating performance of "Meeskite" has an uncomfortable ring of irony because it reinforces his outsider status, the opposite of his drunken intentions.[26]

Some of Ebb's story songs reflect directly on a character or dramatic situation. A good example is found in *The Act*, which is about a one-time movie star, Michelle Mayer, who attempts to make a comeback as a nightclub singer. She performs "Bobo's," a song of survival but with a veil of desperation, as part of her club act immediately after a flashback in which the man she loves proposes to her. "Bobo's" is autobiographical, describing Michelle's mother's piano bar in Omaha, a place "where the losers ruled." Michelle, we are led to believe, escaped this environment and became a Hollywood star. The song's hard-edged imagery, coupled with a honky-tonk accompaniment, belies the heroine's happiness and portends the divorce that she will have in a future flashback scene.[27] It is quintessential Kander and Ebb.

Kander places melody above all other musical elements of a song. As he himself once noted in an article he wrote about one of his musical heroes, Jerome Kern, "It's hard to explain why one is attracted by a particular composer's style, but with Kern it's simple. Melody. Incredible, elegant melody that seemed to pour out of him endlessly and effortlessly. And how profligate he was with those melodies, and how abundantly they populate his scores. . . . He's my favorite. And when I grow up I want to be just like him."[28] Kern's naturalness and ability to lay out the melodic direction of a song in the first line left an indelible impression on Kander.

Ragtime has also been a steady influence on Kander's music. He still recalls that as a boy he responded to the "sweetness and cleanliness" of the music by Scott Joplin and other ragtime composers. Kander's love of vaudeville partially explains the ragtime tendencies in his own music. Another reason is Kander's piano skills, which he developed at an early age. When he started to compose music, Kander instinctively relied on his piano playing ability and ever since has trusted his fingers to do a lot of his creative work.

Kander's piano instructor at Oberlin, Joseph Hungate, encouraged him to connect what he was hearing with what he was playing: "the whole point was to . . . have your technique so that you went directly from what you wanted to hear, to what your ear heard, to what you heard coming out of the piano with no thought, no conscious thought of what your fingers are doing." An experience that Kander had during *Steel Pier* vividly illustrates this last point:

> There's a melodic idea in *Steel Pier* which I find quite lovely. It's a little piano piece. . . . It comes in the end. . . . Nobody ever sings it, but it's the emotional climax of the whole piece, when they [Rita Racine and Bill Kelly] say goodbye. And we're in a meeting, [Susan] Stroman, Tommy Thomson, Scott Ellis, and me. There was a piano right to my left. . . . And they said, "there should be something which is connected with that girl." It was almost like they were teasing me. And I said, "oh, you mean something like this." I swear to God. I had no idea. I put my left hand on the piano, and I said, "something like this." I had no idea what I was going to do. And the thing came out whole, just exactly like it is in the show. . . . It was like you put your hook in the water, and a fish grabbed it right away, and you don't know how it happened. I've thought of that moment often. It's a musical idea that I still find touching. Maybe because it's connected with all those people whom I love so much. . . . It still touches me. I still get teary when I think of those two people who are never going to see each other again.

Composers of Kander's generation elevated the dramatic importance of the vamp, a repeated musical figure introduced at the beginning of a song—often marked "vamp till ready"—and establishing the mood. The vamp is sometimes carried over into the accompaniment and often recurs between verses and at the end of a song. Some of Kander's vamps, such as the opening of "Theme to New York, New York," are among the most recognizable vamps in the musical theater repertory. For Chita Rivera, they are part of what defines a Kander and Ebb song.[29] They capture the entire essence of a dramatic moment in a few brief measures, and often define the rhythmic and melodic profile of the song, as is the case for "Life Is" from *Zorbá*. Many of Kander's vamps are pianist in nature and incorporate features from ragtime (example 1.2). These typically employ a stepwise melodic figure, often syncopated, moving obliquely against a repeated pitch in either the top or bottom voice. This devise is the basis for the vamp of "Theme from New York, New York." The vamp of "Life Is" is constructed along similar lines. The ostinato in the upper voice is imitative of the drone of the Greek bouzouki, a strummed folk instrument, which Don Walker's orchestration makes explicit.

Example 1.2. Two of John Kander's Vamps, (a) "Theme from New York, New York" (b) "Life Is"

Scott Joplin's 1909 composition "Solace" incorporates a similar texture in the right hand in the B section. It occurs over a Latin-inflected ostinato in the left hand based on the rhythm of Bizet's famous "L'amour est un oiseau rebelle" from *Carmen*. Rhythms like this, which Jelly Roll Morton dubbed the "Spanish tinge," were popular in jazz music during the twenties. The A section of "Solace" features a sinuous, chromatic melody consisting of sixteenth notes. The B section has a different melodic profile: the lower voice of the right hand carries the main melody, which turns about E. A pedal point in the higher voice forms oblique counterpoint against the stepwise melody in the lower voice. Five measures later, the two voices come together in parallel thirds. Many of Kander's vamps incorporate the syncopated right hand and stride left hand observed here. Kander also embeds ostinatos set against stepwise melodies within the accompaniment of songs, such as "Bobo's," "Chief Cook and Bottle Washer" (*The Rink*), and "We Both Reached for the Gun" (*Chicago*).

In a more lyrical mood, Kander is likely to express himself in three-quarter time, so much so that he could be called the Waltz King of his generation, although some would bestow the title onto Sondheim. During the first decades of the twentieth century, the waltz, with its European pedigree, was associated with a bygone era. Richard Rodgers found effective ways to incorporate the waltz into his scores. "Out of My Dreams" from *Oklahoma!* and "This Nearly Was Mine" from *South Pacific* are just two of many excellent

Example 1.3. "Maybe This Time" (chorus, first 4 measures)

examples. Likewise, Kander has breathed new life into the waltz, and some of his biggest hits are waltzes: "My Coloring Book," "I Don't Care Much," "Married," "The Happy Time," and "Kiss of the Spider Woman."

Counterpoint plays a limited but effective role in Kander's music. One of his favorite contrapuntal devices, especially for his signature ballads, is an ascending chromatic line embedded into the accompaniment moving in whole notes over a static bass and against a short repeated theme in the vocal part. Usually rising from $\hat{5}$ to flat $\hat{7}$, this counter line builds tension throughout the phrase and pushes the harmony in a subdominant direction. In the opening phrase of "Maybe This Time," the inner ascending line forms the harmonic progression I–I+–I^{+6}–I^{b7} [V7/IV], which is followed by a shift to IV (a harmonic structure intended to evoke the blues) (example 1.3). In measure 4, a whole note on "stay" coinciding with the secondary dominant builds the momentum toward the subdominant. "Nowadays" from *Chicago*, "We Can Make It" from *The Rink*, and "But the World Goes 'Round" from *New York, New York* all incorporate this device.

The scores for Kander and Ebb's first two musicals, the unproduced

Golden Gate and *Flora, the Red Menace,* are the stuff of fifties musical comedy. *Cabaret* marks a distinct change in Kander and Ebb's style, no doubt inspired by the dark subject matter and unconventional dramatic structure of the musical. The music exhibits an expanded harmonic palette, an increase in chromaticism, and a more inventive use of the minor mode. With *Cabaret,* Kander incorporated nondiatonic pitches, borrowed harmonies, and shifts between the major and minor key with increased dramatic effectiveness. Key changes, as Kander has noted, occur "where it seems appropriate . . . where you don't want the listener to get too comfortable. . . . It has to do with the feeling." The lyrics for *Cabaret* exude a more pronounced sense of irony than anything Ebb had written before. For example, "If You Could See Her Through My Eyes" has the bounce and playful lyric of a novelty vaudeville number, but it also serves a didactic purpose. The emcee performs the song for the cabaret patrons, but it is intended to shock the theater audience.

Kander and Ebb's Musical Theater

Shaped by the Depression and World War II, Kander and Ebb, along with other writers of their generation, were uniquely positioned to make the musical more socially aware, more political, and more international. They opened up the genre to a range of topics unheard of in previous eras—pogroms, Communism, Jesus Christ, Eva Peron, Nazism, presidential assassination, cannibalism, homosexuality, prostitution, and AIDS—and thereby transformed the musical theater genre into something more than just entertainment. This transformation has an evolutionary aspect. Musical theater writers emerging during the late fifties and early sixties were products of vaudeville, Tin Pan Alley, the book musical, and the mainstreaming of jazz, and yet professionally speaking they came of age at the precise moment that these cultural forces were fading into the background. Along with the loss of popularity of the Broadway musical in the sixties came the aggrandizement of the musical theater genre, which bestowed upon it a canonical, nearly high-art status. As a result, young writers (as well as directors) felt an "anxiety of influence," to borrow Harold Bloom's term, and a fear of "belatedness," and musical theater started to become a more self-referential genre.[30] Pastiche became a stylistic imperative, and Kander and Ebb were generationally predisposed to capitalize on this change.

It is no coincidence that between the passing of the Civil Rights Act of

From left to right: Fred Ebb, Charles Strouse, Cy Coleman, John Kander, and Jerry Herman. This photograph was taken at a benefit for the hospital where Chita Rivera was being treated following an automobile accident (November 1986). Cliff Lipson/cliff lipson photography (copyright 1986) (TIFF C10)

1964 and the Stonewall riots in 1969, the concept musical emerged as a viable means of responding to changes in the status of the musical and of addressing a wider range of social concerns. These and other events drove the musical in a more serious direction, as it became increasingly difficult to ignore the issues affecting many Americans. Kander and Ebb continued to honor musical theater's traditional purpose of entertaining, but they exploited this purpose in order to tell serious, mature stories. They negotiated difficult subjects by viewing the world itself as a stage. The playwright David Thompson,[31] one of their frequent collaborators, puts it best: "John and Fred looked for work that has much more at stake, much more danger, much more sense of an important story that they're taking you to under the guise of entertaining you. And that to me is their hallmark, is how you think you're being entertained but at the same time you're being given a story that's incredibly dark, or complicated, or desperate, or extremely theatrical. That's their hallmark."

Kander and Ebb continued to write integrated book musicals and musical comedies even as they experimented with new forms and serious themes. The

Table 1.1. Kander and Ebb's Broadway and Broadway-bound musicals*

Title	Theme or Topic	Dramatic Genre	Form
Flora, the Red Menace	Communism	comic	book musical
Cabaret	rise of Nazism	serious	concept musical
The Happy Time	family and self-deception	comedy	book musical
Zorbá	celebration of life	serious	concept musical
70, Girls, 70	old age and survival	comedy	concept musical
Chicago	collusion of the media and the criminal justice system	comedy	concept musical
The Act	self-renewal	serious	concept musical
Woman of the Year	gender roles	comedy	book musical
The Rink	forgiveness and reconciliation	serious	concept musical
Kiss of the Spider Woman	intersection of sexuality and politics	serious	concept musical
Steel Pier	love and self-renewal	serious	hybrid**
Curtains	endurance of theater	comedy	book musical
All About Us	the human condition	comedy	concept musical
The Visit	revenge, responsibility, and guilt	serious	book musical
Minstrel Show	racism and the American criminal justice system	serious	concept musical

*For a discussion of Kander and Ebb's incomplete and unproduced musicals see Chapter 8.
**Steel Pier, according to David Thompson, has elements of both the book musical and the concept musical.

topics of their musicals range from the collusion of the press and the American criminal justice system (Chicago) to the battle of the sexes (Woman of the Year), to issues of gender (Kiss of the Spider Woman), to the Scottsboro Boys trial (Minstrel Show); and sunny and dark themes occur with nearly equal frequency. Table 1.1 denotes the theme, dramatic genre, and form of their twelve Broadway and three Broadway-bound musicals.[32] In some cases, the category is not definitive, a reflection of the ever growing ambiguity between comedy and drama in musical theater after 1960. For instance, Flora, the Red Menace deals with a serious topic, but it is framed as a romantic musical comedy, and All About Us, a musical version of Thornton Wilder's The Skin of Our Teeth, is a very serious comedy. Kander and Ebb's comedies tend to be book musicals, the serious dramas concept musicals, but there are exceptions. For instance, *70, Girls, 70*, a light comedy, is also a concept musical; and *Steel Pier*, a serious romance, is essentially a book musical.

The pronounced eclecticism of this list would seem to preclude an answer to the question, What makes a Kander and Ebb musical a Kander and Ebb musical? And yet, one can indeed talk about a unified body of work. First, issues of identity and self-actualization are ubiquitous in their work. Flora loses her man but gains a sense of self. In *The Happy Time*, Jacques returns home and discovers who he really is. The protagonist of *The Act* changes herself from an overly dependent wife into a self-sufficient woman. The mother and daughter in *The Rink* confront the truth about their past in order to share a brighter future. *Kiss of the Spider Woman* features an openly gay window dresser. Ethnic identity figures in *Flora, Cabaret, Zorbá, The Minstrel Show*, and, to a lesser extent, *Chicago*. *Woman of the Year* asks, albeit in nonconfrontational terms, questions about gender. Another distinguishing feature of Kander and Ebb's musicals is their limited historical scope. They all take place within the time frame of the writers' own lives. Like the best book musicals of the forties and fifties, Kander and Ebb's musicals also have colorful and exotic locales, but they replace the vivid backdrops of places like the Oklahoma Territory, nineteenth-century Siam, and the mystical Brigadoon with the darker American milieus of Jazz Age prisons, Las Vegas, and Depression-era dance marathons. Moreover, death or the implication of death occurs in nearly every one of their musicals, comic and serious alike.

Like so many Broadway composers and lyricists, Ebb was, and Kander is, Jewish as well as gay. They thus bring a particular outsider's perspective to musical theater. Scholars have begun to take a keen interest in how ethnicity and sexuality shaped the Broadway musical. Andrea Most views the history of Jewish acculturation in America and the development of the musical as intertwined and inextricable from each other. Jewish writers, Most claims, negotiated their concerns about race and ethnicity through the musical theater genre.[33] By the early sixties, writers felt freer to write directly about their ethnic heritage. However, the success of *Milk and Honey* (1961) and *Fiddler on the Roof* (1964) might have also made it unnecessary to do so, and writers continued to worry about appearing too narrow, lest their work lack universal appeal.[34] Inexplicably, Most left Kander and Ebb off her list of Jewish-American musical theater writers, even though Kander's first Broadway musical, *A Family Affair*, written with James and William Goldman, is a comedy about a Jewish wedding.[35]

Kander's secular Midwest upbringing contrasted with that of his Jewish New York collaborator: "[My family and I] were much less tied to the traditional Jewish neuroses, those famous neuroses that supposedly exist."[36] Ebb also grew up in a secular household, but he suffered all of the demands and pressures of trying to be a good Jewish boy without any of the approbation. Religion played no significant role in either Kander's or Ebb's adult life, and the Jewish characters in their musicals reflect the writers' ambivalence about their ethnic heritage. Of all of their musicals, there are only two Jewish characters whose religious background is relevant to the story, Herr Schultz from *Cabaret* and Samuel Liebowitz from *Minstrel Show*. Herr Schultz is an epitomized victim of Nazi anti-Semitism, and his song "Meeskite" marks the only time that Ebb expressed an overt sense of Jewishness. Samuel Liebowitz, an important figure in their last musical, is an opportunist, serving a worthy cause for personal gain. His nemesis in the musical, a southern lawyer, sings a song called "Jew Money," which Kander wrote immediately after Ebb's death. Uncharacteristically, Ebb had difficulty coming to terms with the potentially controversial topic of this song. In between these two extremes one finds no strongly marked Jewish character—*Chicago* did include an avaricious, implicitly Jewish, theatrical agent, but his role was cut.

Kander and Ebb recognized the Jewish hegemony of Broadway, and Ebb made fun of it in a contrafactum to the music of Jule Styne's "People":

> Jewish
> People who are Jewish
> Are the luckiest people in the world
> Commercial
> Oy, are we commercial
> Take "Funny Girl" for the proof
> Plus "Fidd-a-ler on the Roof"

Once Sondheim boldly, and perhaps jokingly, suggested that Jews have a monopoly on passion, and they are "smarter."[37] Kander prefers to believe that what Jews "have, as opposed to gentiles, is a tradition of expressing passion just like Italians. . . . the Irish also . . . What you don't find is Presbyterians." Hal Prince feels that American Jewish exceptionalism as it regards the Broadway musical stems from the historical deprivation of the Jewish people, and he has noted that "there are other races and religions out there and they don't always turn adversity into creativity."[38] Ebb tacitly shared Prince's attitude and expressed it in the songs he wrote and the characters he helped to create.

The history of homosexuality in musical theater is even more problematic than ethnicity. Sexual identity has played nearly as important a role as
ethnic identity in the development of musical theater, but explicit portrayals
of homosexuals are practically nonexistent before the 1970s. As Stacy Wolf
suggests, "Gay male culture is produced in part through engagement with
musicals . . . [they have] offered personal, emotional, and cultural validation
for gay men."[39] John Clum calls the golden age of the book musical the "era of
the closet."[40] One only need consider the work of Cole Porter and Noël Coward to understand how gay writers devised strategies to express the sexually
inexpressible.[41] Their favorite device, the double entendre, "was a product of
an era repressive of homosexuals, which was characterized by anti-gay legis-
lation and regulations."[42] The double entendre (such as Porter's "Tom, Dick,
or Harry") is at the center of musical theater's "highly charged 'camp' atmosphere," which, as Raymond Knapp has noted, reveals a gay sensibility.[43]

Even during the sixties, musical theater writers were more reticent than
writers of spoken drama to openly portray gay characters. Their initial appre-
hension might explain the rash of popular diva musicals, "the pinnacle of gay
musical theater,"[44] in the sixties. This was the decade that saw the ascension
of Barbra Streisand, Liza Minnelli, Bernadette Peters, and Bette Midler. Gay
men identify with the diva musical because it gives voice to concerns that
they themselves cannot express in a homophobic society, and they project
their own outsiderness onto the diva. Kander and Ebb kept the diva musical alive into the twenty-first century, but it was not until *Kiss of the Spider
Woman* that they dealt openly with the homosexual subject. Like the Reagan-
era hit musical *La Cage aux Folles*, *Spider Woman* incorporates camp, but
unlike *La Cage aux Folles* it does so not for the benefit of the heterosexual
segment of the audience, although, as Clum has indicated, the musical over-
whelms Puig's politics with a "stereotypical representation of queerness."[45]
Ebb thought that *La Cage aux Folles* and *Falsettos* "were phony as hell. Not
an ounce of validity or sincerity in each of them." He took enormous pride
in the fact that *Spider Woman* succeeded in making a positive statement in a
"gutsy way."

It should be noted that the book writers and directors with whom Kander
and Ebb worked also influenced the thematic focus and treatment of the
source material of their musicals. That *Flora, the Red Menace* deals almost
flippantly with a hot-button political issue (Communist organizing) is not
particularly surprising given that George Abbott, the director of the musical, had little affinity for the subject matter. Terrance McNally, the librettist

for *Kiss of the Spider Woman* and an openly gay writer, is sympathetic to the issues of Puig's novel. McNally's script for *The Rink* reflects his love for opera, albeit obliquely. Joseph Stein, the librettist for *Zorbá*, is Kander and Ebb's only non-American-born collaborator, and he brought a certain European sensitivity to the material. David Thompson, the youngest of Kander and Ebb's book writers, comes from a generation that is more inclusive and sensitive about issues of gender, race, and identity.

The trajectory of Kander and Ebb's career, which began the same year that President Kennedy was assassinated, was partly determined by a confluence of events and changes in musical theater. Their career also coincided with the post–Rodgers and Hammerstein era, the rise and fall of the so-called rock musical, the British invasion, the age of the mega musical, and the incursion of Disney on Broadway. It intersected with the passage of the Civil Rights Act, the Vietnam War, the Stonewall riots, the Chicago riots, the creation of NOW, the Nixon/Watergate scandal, the collapse of the Soviet Union, the 9–11 terrorist attacks, and the so-called war on terrorism. Their musicals reflect these events and other social concerns and thus belong with those cultural texts that accommodate, to quote Raymond Knapp, "changes in American culture and society and, in turn, [help] to shape their development in profound ways."[46] These musicals have mattered to people and will likely continue to do so.

CHAPTER 2

The Divinely Decadent Lives of *Cabaret*

We're looking for a new form of musical theater, one that'll break away from what's become stale and static, and self-imitative. We're looking back in time only to look forward in form.

—FRED EBB

ABARET, THE GROUND-BREAKING MUSICAL BASED ON CHRISTO-pher Isherwood's *The Berlin Stories*, takes place in Germany during the rise of Nazism and tells the story of the relationship between a struggling American novelist, Clifford Bradshaw, and an expatriate British nightclub singer, Sally Bowles, who performs in a seedy Berlin cabaret and hopes to be discovered by a film director. In hindsight, *Cabaret* seems an ideal vehicle for Kander and Ebb's brittle and self-referential brand of musical theater. It was their first project to fully capitalize on their opposite artistic temperaments. The combination of Ebb's acerbic wit and Kander's broad stylistic range produced powerful results. However, when they began work on the show in 1965, Kander and Ebb had not yet discovered their unique voice, and a serious musical about Nazism was daring for writers who had not yet had a major hit.

Cabaret opened on Broadway in 1966 and ran for 1,165 performances; there have been two Broadway revivals, one in 1987 and the other in 1998. There is talk of a third Broadway revival in the near future. The original production won Tony Awards in seven categories, including best composer and lyricist, best director, and best musical. Like *Show Boat, Candide,* and a handful of other musicals, *Cabaret* exists in several versions, most notably Prince's original, Bob Fosse's 1972 film, and the 1998 Broadway revival directed by Sam Mendes. *Cabaret* also produced a number of hit songs, which were covered by a wide range of popular artists, including Louis Armstrong.

Source Material

Isherwood's *The Berlin Stories,* which was published in 1945, is presented as two separate novellas, *The Last of Mr. Norris,* first published by itself in 1935, and *Goodbye to Berlin,* first published in 1939. Both parts explore the insinuation of Nazi attitudes into the daily affairs of people living in Germany during the decline of the Weimar Republic. *The Berlin Stories* warns that, to borrow a phrase from the architecture critic Paul Goldberger, "To romanticize aesthetics divorced from political reality is a dangerous mistake."[1] *Goodbye to Berlin* contains six stories, including "Sally Bowles," the basis for *Cabaret.*[2] The stories explore Isherwood's impressions of Berlin, where he lived from 1929 to 1933. These stories, which Isherwood described as "an absurd jumble of subplots and coincidences," are about inconsequential characters from the dark niches of Berlin society: "crooks, gold-diggers, spent artistes, prostitutes, nervy bourgeoisie, and would-be revolutionaries."[3] These characters collectively symbolize the growing fatalism of the period. Unifying the seemingly disparate stories of *Goodbye to Berlin* is a single point-of-view character, a homosexual English writer living in Berlin whom Isherwood named after himself. This narrator observes society through the eyes of the other characters, the people to whom he is closest. He claims to provide the objectivity of a camera lens and merely to record what he sees: "I am a camera with its shutter open, quite passive, recording, not thinking. Recording the man shaving at the window opposite and the woman in the kimono washing her hair. Some day, all this will have to be developed, carefully printed, fixed." However, his professed disinterest forces the reader to make his or her own moral judgment about the events he describes.

Isherwood manages to depict the horrors of a society whose moral fabric is unraveling by focusing on the banality of everyday life. In this way, the novel reveals as much about the daily downward spiral of German society at the time as would a political tome on the Third Reich. The narrator illuminates various facets of economic, sexual, cultural, and political life in Berlin. The opening segment, titled "A Berlin Diary," introduces Christopher Isherwood, his landlady (Fräulein Schroeder), and the people who come and go at her boardinghouse. The next section is about the narrator's relationship with Sally Bowles. In "On Ruegen Island," Isherwood, writing during a seaside sojourn, observes a homosexual relationship between Peter Wilkson and Otto Nowak. "The Nowaks" also involves Otto; Isherwood, being hard up for cash, rents a room from Otto's family, who live in a squalid section of the city. "The Landauers" is about a wealthy Jewish family, the daughter of whom takes English lessons from Isherwood. Her cousin, Bernhard, befriends him but is eventually killed. The narrator is unable to achieve any real intimacy with any of these characters. As the Isherwood scholar Claude J. Summers has noted, "his inability to connect meaningfully even with the characters with whom he is in most intimate contact mirrors the state of Berlin itself. His personal failure is symptomatic of the social disease that blights the whole city and that culminates in the spiritual death represented by Hitler's eventual triumph."

In 1951, John Van Druten adapted *The Berlin Stories* for the stage, titling his play *I Am a Camera*, a line taken from the novel.[4] *Cabaret* has long overshadowed *I Am a Camera*, but Van Druten deserves credit for bringing the character of Sally Bowles to theatrical life and for devising a workable plot structure out of Isherwood's sprawling narrative. The playwright overcame the episodic nature of Isherwood's novel by limiting the action to four months and to the boardinghouse of Fräulein Schroeder, whom he renamed Schneider. The plot centers on Sally's relationship with Christopher Isherwood, the homosexual writer based on the narrator of *The Berlin Stories*: they meet, develop an intimate but not a sexual relationship, and grow apart. Sally casually mentions having a lover, her accompanist Klaus, who has abandoned her for England. When Sally learns that she is pregnant, probably by Klaus, Christopher and Fräulein Schneider arrange for her to have an abortion. At the end of the play, Sally and Christopher part company as he decides to return to England. In effect, Van Druten turned the "Sally Bowles" episode into a drawing room comedy and dissipated the ominous cloud looming over *The Berlin Stories*. The parting of Sally and Christopher at the end of the play is maudlin and bittersweet, and it lacks the pathos of the parallel account in Isherwood's *Goodbye to Berlin*.

Van Druten invented a subplot involving two other characters in *The Berlin Stories*, Fritz Wendel and Natalia Landauer. Fritz is an amiable gigolo who introduces Christopher and Sally to each other. In the play, Fritz is Jewish, but he conceals his religious identity until late in the play, when an anti-Semitic incident involving Natalia impels him to reveal the truth and to

confess his love for her. Van Druten also concocted a new character, Sally's
overbearing mother, Mrs. Watson-Courtneidge. She is a broadly drawn
comic character whose unannounced appearance in Berlin pushes the limits
of believability and runs the risk of turning the story into a British farce. The
dreary film version of *I Am a Camera*, directed by Henry Cornelius, wisely
does away with Mrs. Watson-Courtneidge, but this change did little to save
the bland film.[5]

Plot and Theatrical Conception of *Cabaret*

Hal Prince was not the only person who thought about the possibility of a
musical version of *I Am a Camera*. Interest was generated by several actresses,
including Gwen Verdon, who wanted to play the role of Sally Bowles. Sandy
Wilson worked on an adaptation for Julie Andrews, but he did not get very
far. When Prince decided to take on the project in 1965, he hired Joe Masteroff, who had written the book for *She Loves Me* the year before. Masteroff,
Kander, and Ebb's natural inclination was to think of the story in terms of a
traditional book musical. Masteroff initially adopted the three-act structure
of *I Am a Camera* while also restoring the political undercurrents of *The
Berlin Stories*. Musical theater convention dictated a primary love story and
subplot, so Masteroff altered the very nature of Sally and Christopher's relationship by making them lovers, and substituted the Natalia-Fritz subplot of
I Am a Camera with a politically naïve romance between Fräulein Schneider
and a newly invented character, Rudy Schultz, an elderly Jewish proprietor
of a fruit shop (table 2.1). In both the original novel and play, the landlady is
an anti-Semite. That Lotte Lenya, Kurt Weill's wife, agreed to play the role
might explain why Masteroff turned her into a sympathetic character. Both
romantic relationships fail, affected by the mounting tensions and nihilism
of the world around them. The parallel unhappy endings were rather bleak
for a Broadway musical in 1966, but they were the perfect expression of what
the writers wanted to say.

Masteroff changed the Christopher character to an American writer
named Clifford Bradshaw (borrowing the surname of the narrator in *The
Last of Mr. Norris*) and made no attempt to explore his homosexuality. In
Contradictions, Hal Prince openly regrets the decision to turn Cliff into a
heterosexual.[6] Van Druten's play had been successful and had hardly disguised the homosexual orientation of Isherwood's novelist-narrator. Neither
he nor Sally seems interested in a sexual relationship, and Christopher de-

Table 2.1. Characters in *The Berlin Stories*, *I Am a Camera*, and *Cabaret*

The Berlin Stories	I Am a Camera (1951)	Cabaret (1966, '87, '98)	Cabaret (film)*
Sally Bowles (English)	Sally Bowles (English)	Sally Bowles (English)	Sally Bowles (American)
Christopher Isherwood (English)	Christopher Isherwood (English)	Clifford Bradshaw (American)	Brian Roberts (English)
—	—	Ernst Ludwig	Ernst Ludwig
Fraülein Schroeder	Fraülein Schneider	Fraülein Schneider	Fraülein Schneider
Fraülein Kost	Fraülein Kost	Fraülein Kost	Fraülein Kost
Clive (American)	Clive (American)	—	Maximilian von Heune
—	—	Max (club owner)†	Max (club owner)
Bobby (bar mixer at the Troika)	—	Bobby†	Bobby
Fritz Wendel (not Jewish)	Fritz Wendel (Jewish)	—	Fritz (Jewish)
—	—	Herr Schultz	—
—	Mrs. Watson-Courtneidge	—	—
Klaus Linke (Sally's accompanist and lover)‡	—	—	Klaus (stage manager)
Natalie Landauer	Natalie Landauer	—	Natalie Landauer
—	—	Emcee	Emcee

*Sally Bowles's father was going to appear in the film, but his scenes were cut.
†The roles of Max and Bobby are expanded in the 1998 version.
‡There is a passing reference to a person named Klaus in *I Am a Camera*.

flects Natalia's flirtations. One of Masteroff's riskiest calculations was to include Sally's out-of-wedlock pregnancy and abortion. Sally's resolve to have an abortion is tantamount to leaving Cliff, and the bleakness surrounding her actions reflects the atmosphere of Berlin. Masteroff also invented a character named Ernst Ludwig, a Nazi who befriends Cliff as his train is about to arrive in Berlin.

Cabaret begins as Cliff arrives in Berlin, where he hopes to write his second novel. He rents a squalid room from Fräulein Schneider. During his first evening out on the town, Cliff meets Sally. Their flirtatious encounter precipitates Sally's being fired by her one-time boyfriend, the proprietor of the

Kit Kat. With nowhere else to go, she shows up at Cliff's apartment and convinces him to take her in as a roommate. Their relationship becomes intimate,
and Sally gets pregnant. Faced with the responsibility of supporting a family,
Cliff accepts an offer from his German friend Ernst to smuggle contraband
from Paris. Cliff is unaware, however, that Ernst is a member of the Nazi
party and that the work he has been asked to do will benefit the Nazis. In a
parallel subplot, Fräulein Schneider and her tenant Herr Schultz decide to
marry, but the escalation of anti-Semitism in Berlin causes her to break off
the engagement. Her unilateral decision parallels Sally's unilateral decision
to get an abortion. Hoping against hope that Sally will join him in Paris, Cliff
leaves Germany as the Nazis are poised to take over the government.

The musical and theatrical viability of *Cabaret* became a reality when
Hal Prince and the "boys," as he liked to call his writers, decided to use the
cabaret as a metaphor for German society. Prince came up with the notion
of interspersing the narrative book scenes with scenes set in a cabaret that
comment on the events affecting the main characters. Masteroff, who gave
the musical its title, began to interweave the book scenes with Expressionistic nightclub sequences. By adopting this unusual approach and perfectly
matching form and content, the writers turned what might have been a traditional book musical into the first fully realized concept musical.

The narrator in *Goodbye to Berlin*, Christopher Isherwood, describes
several of the cabarets he frequents: Troika, Salomé, Alexander Casino, and
Sally's place of employment, the Lady Windermere. For *I Am a Camera*, Van
Druten replaced the panoramic scope of *The Berlin Stories* with a single location, the boardinghouse, thus precluding any scene set in a cabaret, although
there is a passing reference to one. In the film version of *I Am a Camera*,
Christopher and Sally meet at the Lady Windermere. Prince and Masteroff
might have had this scene, which is reminiscent of the nightclub in Joseph
von Sternburg's 1930 film *The Blue Angel*, in mind when they conjured up
the Kit Kat Klub. In subsequent productions of *Cabaret*, the cabaret atmosphere became increasingly more decadent, from the "divine decadence"
of Bob Fosse's film to a "raunchy kind of decadence" in Sam Mendes's version.[7] Fosse shot the film on location in Germany and featured a particularly
seedy cabaret in the name of authenticity. His camera, with its odd angles
and disturbing vantage points, becomes the film's point of view. Mendes's
production transformed the entire theater — the original Studio 54 — into the
cabaret, and then the cabaret into a Nazi gas chamber, the final shocker of an
already provocative production.

The dramatic strength of *Cabaret* rests on the effectiveness of the cabaret metaphor. As Scott McMillin observes, "The rise of Nazism seems to take place in a seedy Berlin nightclub."[8] The libidinous cabaret entertainment offers the Kit Kat Klub customers temporary respite from the restraints of daily life. The permissive atmosphere is innocuous until Nazi propaganda begins to creep into the Kit Kat stage show. As it has often been noted, the cabaret songs comment on the book scenes. However, the songs are more than commentary; they are the mood of the piece, and any direct connection between them and the book scenes is secondary to their ability to establish a point of view. Collectively, the cabaret songs reflect the moral decline in Germany: they start out as risqué diversions but gradually become racist political propaganda.

When Kander and Ebb started writing, they created essentially two parallel scores, one consisting of traditional book songs and one of novelty numbers. The score that audiences heard on opening night contained a nearly equal number of cabaret numbers (eight, plus a kick-line dance) and book songs (seven). The writers began by creating a group of songs that collectively captured the decadent milieu of Berlin in the late 1920s. They intended these numbers, which they called the "Berlin Songs," to be sung throughout the show by various characters—a fat man, an aging operatic tenor, a streetwalker, two Chinese girls on the radio, a group of college boys. Written to expose the underbelly of Berlin society in the late 1920s, the "Berlin Songs" explore a wide variety of topics, including economic hardship, prostitution, and sexual adventurism:

Berlin Songs[9]
 "Angel of Love" (never incorporated into a script)
 "I Don't Care Much" (in early draft of Masteroff's script)
 "I Never Loved a Man as Much as Herman" (early draft)
 "If You Could See Her Through My Eyes" (final script)
 "A Mark in Your Pocket" (early draft)
 "The Money Song" ("Sitting Pretty") (final script)
 "Tomorrow Belongs to Me" (early draft and final script)
 "Two Ladies" (early draft and final script)[10]
 "Willkommen" (early draft and final script)

Prince and Masteroff's idea of mixing realistic book scenes with cabaret scenes was strikingly innovative. How this concept took shape is a remarkable part of musical theater history. Prince's vision of using realistic scenes and a metaphorical cabaret coalesced when he saw a production in Moscow of

Taganka Theatre's *Ten Days That Shook the World*, which incorporated an array of experimental theatrical techniques. These "alien theatrical devices," as Prince calls them, were the catalyst for moving beyond *I Am a Camera*.[11] They freed him to exert more directorial vision and convinced him that the musical could go beyond a linear plot. At this stage in the process, Prince experimented with incorporating a purely psychological or mental space, which he called "Limbo," to represent the German mind. During the middle of the song "Cabaret," Sally leaves the cabaret stage and enters this metaphorical space.

Initially, the cabaret scenes themselves had no unifying element. But this changed when Prince recalled the haunting image of a grotesque performer whom he had seen in 1951 at a nightclub near Stuttgart called Maxim's: "There was a dwarf MC, hair parted in the middle and lacquered down with brilliantine, his mouth made into a bright-red cupid's bow, who wore heavy false eyelashes and sang, danced, goosed, tickled, and pawed four lumpen Valkyres waving diaphanous butterfly wings."[12] Kander saw a similar character while attending the Tivoli in Copenhagen, where Marlene Dietrich was performing. There was a diminutive emcee who announced each act in three languages. The collective memory of Prince and Kander gave birth to the androgynous Mephistophelian emcee who has become an epigrammatic image for *Cabaret*. The emcee's material, located entirely in the cabaret, helps to bridge the real space and the abstract space. As originally conceived, the emcee was going to sing a set of songs, including some of Kander and Ebb's "Berlin Songs," in a single scene.

The success of this concept for *Cabaret* (a hybrid between a traditional book musical and concept musical) depended on a single vision shared by all the contributors, which, in addition to Masteroff, Kander, and Ebb, included the set designer Boris Aronson, who had designed the sets for *I Am a Camera*, lighting designer Jean Rosenthal, costume designer Patricia Zipprodt, choreographer Ron Field, and orchestrator Don Walker. The designers brilliantly incorporated Prince's concept into their designs, distinguishing between the book scenes and cabaret episodes by giving the former a representational style and the latter an expressionistic atmosphere.

Prince was closely involved in all facets of the production, including the dramatic structure and the decision to make Cliff heterosexual. He sent his writers suggestions for scenes and songs, some of which never materialized, and some of which were tried and rejected—for example, a singing competition that recalls one of the memorable nightclub scenes in the film

Casablanca: "Fritz [changed to Ernst] enters with Sally and Cliff. They join a group of Fritz's friends—young men who look like college students. The men sing. Another group enters—looking more like workingmen. The singing gets louder—as the two groups compete. Fritz's friends start putting on their swastika armbands. Cliff is surprised to find that Fritz is a Nazi—But Cliff is far more interested in making love to Sally."[13] Another one of Prince's suggestions involves Sally and Cliff's declaration of love, which the director thought could occur in counterpoint to the music of a German street band. "Act II—To musicalize the street scene two ways, with a love statement by Cliff and Sally against an umpahpah German round for the street people."[14]

An early outline by Prince reveals his directorial instincts and an already well-formed sense of dramatic timing for the musical. For instance, he wanted the third act to build rapidly toward the moment in which Cliff ceases to be a camera, which Prince saw as the dramatic turning point in the story. He intended to open the act with "I Don't Care Much," staging it as a production number in which the emcee is backed up by "girls in men's suits." Prince eventually cut this number, but he reinstated it for the 1987 Broadway revival. In Mendes's 1998 version, the emcee sings the song while tripping on heroin (see below). "Act III—Open with 'I Don't Care Much'—MC and girls in men's suits. Then to Cliff's room. Sally is finishing dressing to go to the Kit Kat Klub. . . . She tells him she's been offered a job and that they need the money and she's going. He refuses to let her. . . . Schneider arrives—'What would you do?' When she leaves, they pick up where they left off, only now Cliff has ceased to be the camera. She has shamed him into waking up and doing something." When Prince decided against the three-act structure, Masteroff conflated act 1, which ended as Sally moved in with Cliff, and act 2, which ended with Schneider and Schultz's engagement party. This change created two balanced acts with a single intermission occurring at the dramatic high point of the story.

Camp Strategies in *Cabaret*

Most commentaries on *Cabaret* note the importance of camp in the portrayal of decadent and deviant sexuality. The creators of *Cabaret* saw a parallel "between the spiritual bankruptcy of Germany in the 1920s and our country in the 1960s" and wanted to send a warning signal about the moral decline in America. They used camp in order to emphasize similarities between the grotesqueness of German culture regarding gender and sexuality and certain elements of American culture. Camp, according to Raymond Knapp, is "an important lens for understanding [*Cabaret*] through the figures of the Emcee . . . and Sally Bowles," who are the primary representatives of "divergent sexuality" in the cabaret scenes and book scenes, respectively.[15] The emcee's numbers rely on camp humor to achieve their dramatic function within the musical as a whole.

Camp, whether a performance or an interpretative strategy, is notoriously difficult to define. Jack Babuscio, a leading scholar of camp, describes it as "those elements in a person, situation, or activity that express, or are created by, a gay sensibility."[16] Scholars agree that camp discourses emerge from a gay sensibility, which Babuscio defines as the "creative energy reflecting a consciousness that is different from the mainstream; a heightened awareness of certain human complications of feeling that spring from the fact of social oppression." Jonathan Dollimore describes camp as "an invasion and subversion of other sensibilities, and words via parody, pastiche, and exaggeration."[17] Al Lavalley calls camp "a gay version of irony and critical distance."[18] As a "transgressive mode of cultural engagement," as Brett Farmer has described it, camp "disrupts and refigures dominant cultural forms, especially sexual forms," mostly in the form of parody.[19] Sally Bowles is the most self-consciously campy figure in *Goodbye to Berlin*. Everything Sally does is a camp performance designed to help her escape from her banal middle-class English existence. She performs the part of a bad girl. She mocks respectability and everything that is serious, one of the hallmarks of camp. In Sally's first appearance in *Cabaret*, she performs "Don't Tell Mama," adopting the attitude of a girl who mockingly expresses guilt for her life of sin, as though to thumb her nose at her judgmental mum. Minnelli's portrayal of Sally in the film version of *Cabaret*—a melding of Marlene Dietrich, Mae West, and Judy Garland—embodies the heart and soul of camp performance.[20]

Camp resists precise definition because there is confusion over its conceptual status. As Andrew Britton has asked, "is camp an attribute of something or is it attributed to something?"[21] Camp recognition requires a cultivated taste for and sensitivity to those aspects that signify an expression of camp. Whether camp is the result of the text or the reading of the text, there is a general consensus among scholars that it sees life as theater and uses the medium of performance to expose societal incongruities, such as the dichotomy or lack thereof between maleness and femaleness or high art and low art. In this respect, the emcee in *Cabaret* is camp personified. Dressed in a tux and wearing lipstick, his/her every leer, wink, grin, and innuendo evoke camp's primary elements: irony, aestheticism, theatricality, and humor. His songs celebrate sexual deviance, cross-dressing, and bestiality. *Cabaret's* camp strategies "neutralize moral indignation," to use Susan Sontag's phrase, by subversively luring the viewer into the cabaret atmosphere and its dehumanizing entertainment. "If You Could See Her Through My Eyes," the campiest and most unsettling number in *Cabaret,* produces this effect. The song has a camp flippancy, not unlike the quality of some of Isherwood's campiest discourses, such as his comical descriptions of the drag queens frequenting the Berlin nightclubs, but the emcee's gleeful detachment from the song's sinister intent coupled with the knee-jerk reaction of the cabaret audience is intended to solicit sympathy from the theater audience. This point is made clear by the heart-wrenching scene that follows the song. In Isherwood's own words, "you can't camp about something you don't take seriously. You're not making fun of it; you're making fun out of it."²²

The Kit Kat Klub scenes in *Cabaret* fulfill the traditional function of camp by undermining expectations of respectability through parodic humor. The emcee performs sexual deviance. Hidden behind a painted face, he pushes the limits of perversion in order to titillate the middle-class Kit Kat Klub patrons, who, at least momentarily, are escaping the dreariness of their mean existence. As *Cabaret* begins, the emcee lures the audience into the decadent world of the cabaret, telling them, "Leave your troubles outside.... In here life is beautiful," at which point a spotlight reveals a quartet of homely female musicians (which in some productions includes at least one male musician in drag) who perform a horribly out-of-tune, jazzed-up rendition of "Willkommen." The cabaret patrons take pleasure in this sort of mockery. The theater audience, on the other hand, sees the cabaret entertainment within a bigger framework, one that encompasses Berlin, its inhabitants, and its politics. The theater audience can enjoy, if only as voyeurs, the lewd performances of the emcee and Sally, but it is never allowed to lose sight of the metaphorical function of the cabaret. (As we shall see, Mendes attempted to obliterate the physical and psychological line separating the theater audience from the cabaret audience.)

The cabaret songs share a lewd sense of campiness. Three numbers in particular exemplify this feature: "Two Ladies," the untitled kick-line dance at the top of act 2, and "If You Could See Her Through My Eyes." "Two Ladies" boldly and bawdily celebrates a ménage à trois. The music incorporates a suggestive triplet figure ending with an upward leap on the nonsense syllables "beedle dee dee dee dee." This playful figure depicts three-way sex by occurring three times in immediate succession, with the leap at the end growing larger with each repetition. The kick-line music begins with an instrumental martial variation of "If You Could See Her Through My Eyes." The kick line itself features the cabaret girls and, unknown to the audience until late in the number, the emcee in drag and high-heel shoes. When the emcee reveals himself, the kick line turns into "a row of goose-stepping" troops giving the "Heil Hitler" salute, accompanied by "Tomorrow Belongs to Me" arranged as a march. Two scenes later, the emcee returns to perform "If You Could See Her Through My Eyes." The "her" of this song is a female gorilla in an apron. The emcee swoons and dances with the gorilla, and then kisses it on the lips. The full impact of the number is achieved during the final line, which starts, "If you could see her through my eyes." The emcee sings the main theme over a schmaltzy secondary dominant and then jumps up to the highest note of the song on "eyes," which he sustains in a sugarcoated falsetto as the orchestra drops out. After a provocatively long fermata, he lets loose with the wickedest line in musical theater: "she wouldn't look Jewish at all."[23] The cabaret audience bursts into uncontrollable laughter; the theater audience sometimes does not know whether to laugh or sit silently (sometimes the former is the case).

In the original production, to further magnify the effect of this song, when the emcee delivered the punch line, the distortion mirror that Boris Aronson incorporated into his set design stopped distorting the audience. As Bruce Kirle recalls, "The audience was able to witness its individual reactions to this racist joke. Some laughed, some were shocked, while others were simply hypnotized into watching their own reactions and those of their fellow spectators."[24] Humor in "If You Could See Her," as in many camp events, is ironic and transgressive. The dancing gorilla and the emcee's unctuous sentimentality seem funny because they are incongruous, but the humor is racist hatemongering. The emcee's dancing and crooning give the appearance of a vaudeville turn, but the number is revealed at the end to be Nazi agitprop theater. The song follows on the heels of Schneider and Schultz's engagement party and anticipates the collective response that ultimately destroys their union. It is a powerful example of Kander and Ebb's pointed use of irony in musicals like *Cabaret* and *Chicago*, both of which rely on diegetic music to entertain as well as to make a statement and elucidate a theme. The cabaret numbers are strategically staggered to imply an evolving hatred in

German society toward Jews, homosexuals, and any other perceived threat to the Fatherland.

Christopher Isherwood has been regarded as one of the first important gay writers of the first half of the twentieth century and one of the first writers "to define camp as a strategy of self-identification."[25] He experienced Germany as an outsider, as a foreigner and a homosexual, and this experience informs every page of *The Berlin Stories*. *The Last of Mr. Norris* has been called "a camp comedic romp through contemporary Berlin starring a dandy-aesthete with . . . a penchant for S&M." The narrator in *The Last of Mr. Norris* takes in the "sexually perverse culture" and patronizes the "sexual dives" of Berlin. In his early writings, including *The Berlin Stories*, Isherwood artfully "silenc[es] his gayness" for personal reasons, but it is clear to all except the most imperceptive reader that the writer presents a gay point of view.[26] It is never openly stated whether the narrator of *Goodbye to Berlin* is homosexual (the same is the case for the narrator of *The Last of Mr. Norris*). Sally flirts with him, and so do several of the men he encounters but, unlike his counterpart in *Cabaret*, he does not have a sexual encounter.

In the original version of *Cabaret*, Cliff is heterosexual, which might have made him a suitable male lead for audiences in 1966, but it rendered him a rather bland character. Starting with Fosse's film version of *Cabaret*, the role of Cliff was brought more in line with his literary counterpart (see below). Directors staging *Cabaret* today have the option of reading Masteroff's heterosexual Cliff as a closeted homosexual or as bisexual. After all, Cliff's first encounter in Berlin is with Ernst Ludwig. Ernst promises to show Cliff the fun spots in Berlin, starting with Kit Kat Klub, "the hottest spot in the city." He even helps him to find a flat. Their homosocial relationship ends only when Cliff takes a stand against Ernst's politics.

Goodbye to Berlin observes the role that aestheticism (the nineteenth-century movement, especially popular in British culture, that gave birth to camp) played in Berlin during the decline of the Weimar Republic, if only by mentioning the names of the cabarets that the narrator visits, Lady Windermere's Fan and Salomé, both of them titles of works by Oscar Wilde, the dandy and aesthete to whom twentieth-century camp is indebted. Isherwood describes the theatrical spectacles fashioned by Nazi propagandists and fraught with homoerotic potential. As Antony Shuttleworth notes, "Nazism gains its power by spreading mass delusion: the delusion arrived at by the imposition of aesthetic structures on experience, and by the individual experience of a fake authenticity."[27] Crowds fell under the spell of Hitler's carefully

Drama Critics Circle Award for *Cabaret*: (from left) Fred Ebb, Hal Prince, Ruth Mitchell, Joe Masteroff, and John Kander. From the personal collection of John Kander

staged Nuremberg Rallies. By conveying the mixed theatricality and hysteria of such orchestrated events, Isherwood draws attention to the role of artifice, fantasy, and spectacle during the creeping totalitarian policies of the Nazis.

Since Clifford Bradshaw is not detached, not passive, and not gay, he experiences Germany differently than does the narrator of *Goodbye to Berlin*. Whereas the narrator of *Goodbye to Berlin* sees Germany through the lens of camp, the book scenes of *Cabaret* suppress this feature of the novel, lest the story lose its dramatic immediacy. The true genius behind *Cabaret* is that the cabaret scenes make up for the loss of camp in the book scenes. That said, it is important to recognize that the presence of camp in *Cabaret* is not limited to the Kit Kat scenes. "Tomorrow Belongs to Me," the only diegetic song in *Cabaret* that occurs outside of the Kit Kat Klub, invokes the mob mentality of the Nazi rallies and the youth marches, as well as the potential homoeroticism of Nazi propaganda. This song is reprised by the prostitute

Fräulein Kost at Fräulein Schneider and Herr Schultz's engagement party. In an earlier scene, Kost embarrasses Schneider when she catches Schultz sneaking out of her apartment. At first, Kost feigns moral outrage, not because Schultz is a Jew but because she wants to turn the tables on Schneider, who disapproves of her line of business. Later at the engagement party, Kost leads the guests in a rousing rendition of "Tomorrow Belongs to Me," in part to provoke Schneider; but now she is a Nazi sympathizer, and her earlier performed moral outrage has turned into a defense of Nazi opposition to marriage between a German and a Jew. The other guests at the party—except Schneider, Schultz, Sally, and Cliff—join in, losing themselves in the nationalistic fervor of the moment. The use of "Tomorrow Belongs to Me" to accompany the kick-line goose stepping of the cabaret girls in the next scene makes it clear that Nazism has begun to seep into German culture. The song has been camped, subsumed into the cabaret.[28]

The Score of Cabaret

With its angular rhythms, sudden bursts of lyricism, razor-sharp observations, blistering humor, and show-stopping belting numbers for the leading female role, the score of *Cabaret* resonates with all of the traits that would come to distinguish Kander and Ebb's style. Arriving at the final score, however, took considerable trial and error (table 2.2). To acclimate themselves to the musical style of the locale and era, Kander and Ebb listened to every period recording of Berlin jazz that they could get their hands on. Kander discovered the "sound" of Berlin in the stylized piano playing of Pater Kreuger and the incongruous harmonies and rhythms of Friderick Hollaender's cabaret songs.

Hollaender was the composer for *The Blue Angel*, which was released in 1930, the second year of Isherwood's stay in Berlin and the year in which *Cabaret* takes place. His cabaret songs have a cosmopolitan sweep that reflects Berlin before the wave of xenophobia that washed over Germany in the thirties. These songs range in style from two-step rags to chromatically inflected lyrical ballads. "Die Pijetät" from 1919 is representative.[29]

Die Welt war rosig wie ein holder Maien graum,	The world was rosy as a dream when my parents lived under the linden
Als noch die Eltern lebten unterm Lindenbaum!	tree. Four children were we in the house. They all died. My parent's
Vier Kinder waren wir im Haus, die starben aus;	house became cold and empty. Sweet little mother, who was

da ward es kalt und leer im Eltern-
 haus!
Das liebe Mütterlein, kaum dreiund-
 neunzig Jahr,
ging ab mit Tod, der Vater kriegte
 graue Haar!
Dann starb auch er, und ich war ganz
 allein,
und schluchzend sang ich auf dem
 Leichenstein.
Die Pijetät ans Eltern grab,
das ist die einz'ge, die ich hab!
Sitz ich allein im Lampenschein,
dann juckt der Tod durchs Fenster
 rein!

gespr[echen]. "Du—Kellner! Gibt es
 ein Leben nach dem Tode?"

almost 39, died. My father got
gray hair, and then he died, too.
I was left totally alone. I sang at
the gravestone while sobbing.
Respect for my parents' grave is all
that I have. When I sit alone in the
lamplight, death peeks through
the window.

spoken. You—waiter! Is there life after
death?

Hollaender marked the music polylingually, "Schmalzig, trivial, lamentabile," perhaps intentionally to create ambiguity regarding the way that the piece was to be performed. Hollaender creates a dialectical contrast between the introduction and interludes, which are highly chromatic and unpredictable, and the vocal sections, which are almost entirely diatonic and regular. The verse melody contains the type of simple symmetrical phrases found in some German Lieder, especially those with a folk influence (such as Franz Schubert's *An Sylvia*) (example 2.1a). The chorus has a darker, more ironic mood (example 2.1b), as more dissonance appears in the accompaniment. An ascending linear line (A–B–C-sharp) is embedded into the refrain melody (the downbeat of each measure in example 2.1b), supported by I, ii6 (+ lowered 3rd), and V. Cross relationships, such as E-flat and E-natural sounding simultaneously in measure 21, produce a pang of melancholy. The entire refrain melody reoccurs in the piano but reharmonized with three consecutive unstable diminished seventh chords (C^{o7th}-$B^{ø7th}$-$E^{ø7th}$) over a D pedal point. At a pause toward the end of the song, the singer asks, "Du—Kellner! Gibt es ein Leben nach dem Tode." The last four measures of the accompaniment mock the singer with a lilting eighth note–sixteenth note rhythm. In the cabaret songs for *Cabaret*, Kander tried to capture the ironic mixture of sentimentality and sarcasm that characterizes Hollaender's cabaret songs.

Critics have linked the score of *Cabaret* to Kurt Weill's music, but the

Table 2.2. Preliminary and final score of *Cabaret*

Preliminary Score	Final Score
Act 1	**Act 1**
Scene 1	Scene 1
"Willkommen"	"Willkommen"
Scene 3	
"Two Ladies"	
Scene 4	Scene 3
"So What"	"So What"
Scene 5	Scene 4
"Telephone Song"*	"Telephone Song"
"Don't Tell Mama"	"Don't Tell Mama"
	Scene 5
	Telephone cross-over
Scene 6	
"Tomorrow Belongs to Me"	
Scene 7	Scene 6
"My Room-mate"	"I Met This Perfectly Marvelous Girl"
	Scene 7
	"Two Ladies"
Act 2	
Scene 1	
"A Mark in Your Pocket"	
Scene 3	
"You're Such a Good-Time Charlie"	
Scene 4	Scene 8
"Guten Abend"	"It Couldn't Please Me More"
Scene 6	
"I Never Loved a Man as Much as Herman"	
	Scene 9
	"Tomorrow Belongs to Me"†
	Scene 10
	"Why Should I Wake Up?"
	Scene 11
	"I'm Sitting Pretty"
Scene 7	Scene 12
"Married"	"Married"
"Tomorrow Belongs to Me" reprise	Scene 13
"Meeskite"	"Meeskite"
"It'll All Blow Over"	"Tomorrow Belongs to Me" reprise

Table 2.2. (*Continued*)

Preliminary Score	Final Score
Act 3	**Act 2**
	Scene 1
	Dance of high kicks
Scene 1	
"I Don't Care Much" (Sally)	
Scene 2	Scene 2
"Married" refrain	"Married" refrain
	Scene 3
	"If You Could See Her Through My Eyes"
	Scene 4
	"What Would You Do?"
Scene 3	
"Room-mates" refrain	
Scene 4	
Cabaret Interlude (song not specified)	
	Scene 5
	"Cabaret"
Scene 9	Scene 7
"Willkommen" reprise	"Willkommen" reprise

*The version of this song on Kander and Ebb's demo recording is much more musically complex than the final version.
†This song was originally going to be sung by a group of German college students.

similarities are limited to a few details shared by "Willkommen" and "Ballad of Mack the Knife," such as the centrality of the 6th scale degree and offbeat eighth notes. What connects these two songs most, however, is their shared cynicism. Kander claims, "I very consciously didn't listen to Kurt Weill. . . . Kurt Weill was doing very early on what I was doing many years later. . . . He was really using the vernacular of that period." Kander was afraid of being accused of imitating Weill, but Lotte Lenya put his mind at ease in a conversation that he has often recounted: "I said to Lenya before we opened, 'When the reviews come out, I know that they're going to say that I was cribbing from Kurt Weill, but I just want you to know that was never my intention.'

. . . I remember she took my head in her hands and said, 'No, no, it's not Kurt. When I'm on the stage, it's Berlin that I hear when I sing your songs.' I thought, if she feels that way, then fuck everybody else."[30]

Cabaret dispenses with the traditional Broadway medley overture. In the famous opening scene, the emcee welcomes the cabaret crowd, as well as the theater audience, to the cabaret. The first sound heard is a disembodied drumroll crescendo followed by an anemic cymbal crash. A pregnant pause then gives rise to the plodding vamp of "Willkommen," arguably the most familiar two measures in musical theater (example 2.2). This vamp evokes a smoky cabaret atmosphere, and perhaps Berlin itself, and it contains the seeds of the rest of the score. The opening chord, a tonic chord with an added sixth, and repeated eighth notes on the offbeats encapsulate the naughty burlesque milieu. The vamp recurs throughout the opening scene, underscoring the emcee's salacious remarks to the audience. Coupled with the emcee's lurid punch lines, it captures the menacing artifice of German culture during this period. The vamp foreshadows Sally's, as well as Germany's, downward spiral, as Kander sneaked it into the end of "Don't Tell Mama," just before Ebb's final wordplay, "If you see my mummy, mum's the word!," and also employed a tightly wound version of it in the minor key at the opening of "Cabaret" as an allusion to the ultimately sad outcome of Sally's decision to have an abortion.

The opening melody of "Willkommen" hinges on an appoggiatura gesture consisting of three elements (approach by downward leap, strong-beat dissonance, and pointed resolution to the 6th scale degree over a tonic chord) on the first English word in the musical, "welcome," the English translation of the German "willkommen" and the French "bienvenue." The dissonant downbeat and syncopated resolution upward to G beckon the audience like the salacious grin and come-hither finger wag of the emcee.[31] Don Walker, the orchestrator of *Cabaret*, instructed the accordion (an instrument commonly used by Broadway orchestrators to suggest a European milieu) in measure 5 to echo the F-sharp–G resolution. The appoggiatura motive reoccurs twice in succession on "Glucklick zu sehen" and "happy." Kander had this terse ascending semitone motive in mind when he stated, "Cabaret is about a minor second."

Schneider's cheery "So What?" and dreary "What Would You Do?" are opposite sides of the same coin, reflecting the acceptance of a pragmatist who has experienced many setbacks in her life and has done her best to overcome

Example 2.1. Friedrich Hollaender: "Die Pijetät," (a) introduction and verse
(b) chorus

(b)

them. In the narrative middle section of the song, Schneider twice brushes aside any regrets she might harbor about the trajectory of her life with the rhetorical question "So what?" G-natural, a pitch borrowed from the parallel minor key, is prominent during this section, first serving as a chromatic upper-neighbor prefix on "So what?," and then sustained through the phrase "now I scrub up the floors . . ." before resolving down to G-flat, and finally appearing as a lower-neighbor to A-flat at the beginning of the conclusion of Schneider's stoic defense (example 2.3).

"What Would You Do?," an implicit indictment of Nazi collaborators, is one of Broadway's bleakest ballads and a virtual study in nonchord tones. Embedded into the vamp is an unprepared dissonant A-sharp, which occurs three times in succession, evoking a funeral march, and then resolves to B (example 2.4). The melody on "What would you do?" also recalls the downward leap and appoggiatura of "Willkommen," the first dissonant pitch in the score. The arduous chromatic vocal line avoids a cadence until measure 18, but only after an unexpected and direct modulation to F major on the key word of the phrase "free."

The more convivial "Married," a duet for Schneider and Schultz, also

Example 2.2. "Willkommen"

incorporates the ascending half-step motive first heard in "Willkommen" on "welcome," and Schultz's pickup notes to the main strain of "It Couldn't Please Me More" wind chromatically around a B-flat. The melody of Schultz's "Meeskite" also relies on chromatic inflections, in this case an allusion to Jewish music. In contrast, "Tomorrow Belongs to Me" is blatantly diatonic. Its folklike melody gains force through several repetitions, each of which involves more Germans, as though the song were taking place at a Hitler youth rally.[32]

Kander and Ebb's score for *Cabaret* brilliantly articulates Prince's dual structural framework as well as portrays the book characters. It took them some time to come up with the right mix of book and cabaret songs, and they ended up discarding an unusually large amount of musical material. They started writing the so-called Berlin songs even before Masteroff had completed the first draft of his script. The Berlin songs appropriate popular musical traditions, the male choir and folk song ("Tomorrow Belongs to Me"), lascivious cabaret music ("Willkommen" and "Two Ladies"), and the drinking song. Ultimately, the emcee sang two of the original Berlin songs, "Willkommen" and "Two Ladies." "Tomorrow Belongs to Me," also one of

Example 2.3. "So What" (mm. 36–51)

end - ed that way, and I   shrug and I say: So   what?

Example 2.3. (*Continued*)

the original songs, was transformed into a book song; as a Berlin song it was intended to be sung by a group of college boys. To the emcee's solo spots were later added "The Money Song" ("I'm Sitting Pretty") and "If You Could See Her Through My Eyes." Many of the "Berlin Songs" lost their viability after the emcee was born. One of these songs, "Angel of Love," is a spoof of the overly ingratiating sentimental ballads that Richard Tauber sang during the decline of his career.[33] "Herman the German" is sung over the radio by two Chinese girls.[34] Kander and Ebb composed "I Don't Care Much" on a party bet, completing it in the time it took the other guests to eat dessert. As a Berlin song, it was originally assigned to a streetwalker.

The evolution of the "The Money Song" ("Sitting Pretty") reflects the ever-mounting irony that the score acquired over time. "A Mark in Your Pocket," an early attempt at a song about money, is a rather mild commentary about economic deprivation during the Depression. Money, the lyric claims, buys love and impunity from the law as well as provides for daily sustenance.

> The cupboard is terribly bare
> But you get a frown from the grocer
> Well, you'll get a smile from the grocer
> But first put a mark in your pocket.
>
> You're spending the evening alone
> You'd rather be out with a boyfriend
> Well, you can have many a boyfriend
> But first put a mark in your pocket
> A mark in your pocket.
>   . . .

Example 2.4. "What Would You Do?"

> They take you in front of the judge
> You wish that he weren't so honest
> You'll find that he isn't so honest
> But first put a mark in your pocket.

Finding this sentiment too tame, Kander and Ebb wrote "Sitting Pretty," which gradually grew into a vitriolic attack on capitalism. Ebb's original lyric parodies the love-will-see-us-through sentiment of Depression-era Tin Pan Alley songs. His final version of the lyric portrays the beneficiaries of the capitalist system as being the most impervious to the abject poverty of their friends and family:

Early version
    The grocer wants money
    The baker wants money
    They tell me my rent's overdue

Final version
    My father needs money,
    My uncle needs money,
    My mother is thin as a reed.

But me, I'm sitting pretty
Life is pretty sitting with you.

. . .

If I could make it, which I
    couldn't
Or could win it, which I wouldn't
Or could steal it, which I
    shouldn't even possibly
    consider
Could I ever be more dreamy
Or contented than you see me
    now?

But me, I'm sitting pretty-
I've got all the money I need.

. . .

I know my little cousin Eric

Has his creditors hysterical,
And also Cousin Herman
Had to pawn his mother's ermine,

And my sister and my brother
Took to hocking one another, too.

Fosse went even further and replaced "Sitting Pretty" with a new, implicitly anti-Semitic "Money Song," which both Prince and Mendes later used in their respective Broadway revivals of *Cabaret*.

Two of the unused Berlin songs are light commentaries on prostitution. In pure Ebbian fashion, "Liebchen, Liebchen" considers the topic from the client's point of view. A "deedle deedle dum" refrain, which Kander assigns to a chorus, suggests the same type of musical treatment as found in "Two Ladies":

Liebchen liebchen
Look out the window, look out the window
Liebchen, liebchen
Look out and see me there.

Liebchen, liebchen
Throw me the key down, throw me the key down
Liebchen, liebchen
So I can climb the stair.

Once knew a liebchen in Berlin
Yahwohl, yahwohl
Threw down the key and asked me in
Yahwohl deedle dum yahwohl
I ran up the staircase, feeling fine
Yahwohl, yahwohl
And I was the twenty third in line
Yahwohl deedle dum yahwohl.

(Liebchen) etc.

Once knew a liebchen in Bombay
Yahwohl, yahwohl
She ran a well-known cabaret
Yahwohl deedle dum yahwohl
The waitresses ran around in slips
Yahwohl, yahwohl
You've never seen girls get [written above: "with"] bigger tips
Yahwohl deedle dum yahwolh.[35]

"This Life," performed by six cabaret girls dressed as angels, treats prostitution more seriously. Its tone is similar to the nihilistic streetwalker's "I Don't Care Much."

There must be a better life
Far away from here
There has to be a better life
For one thing's more than clear
. . .
Once I fell in love, well, in love, but it did me no credit
First he said forget me not then forgot that he said it
So if I had a slug or a plug nickel why would I bet it?
On the cheating kind of a man women find in this mean ole life . . .
. . .
This life, this mean ole life
Will be the death of me!

Sally is the only character in the musical who inhabits both the realistic book scenes and the surreal world of the cabaret (as well as the actual physical space of the cabaret where Sally and Cliff first meet). On a couple of key occasions involving Sally, the cabaret song and book song categories bleed into each other. For example, "Don't Tell Mama," Sally's first cabaret song, is virtually autobiographical and thus functions as a character-defining song as well as a Kit Kat Klub number. The song "Cabaret" functions on two levels: on the surface, it is an upbeat cabaret star turn, but during the middle section ("I used to have a girlfriend known as Elsie"), Sally drifts mentally (and in some productions physically) into the abstract "Limbo" space as she struggles with the decision of whether or not to have an abortion (changing locations is not important, as the shift is written into the music). An early script includes the following stage directions after the line "I remember how she'd turn to me and say": "Sally has walked off the Kit Kat Klub stage. She heads directly downstage as the light-curtain comes on behind her. The Kit Kat Klub disappears. Sally stands alone on the fore-stage." Prince experimented with the placement of "Cabaret," even trying it out as the opening number of the musical, an option he quickly rejected.

The book songs also underwent an extensive period of trial and error. Kander and Ebb wrote nearly fifty songs that ended up in the proverbial trunk. Finding effective music for Cliff was unusually difficult and, in the end, elusive. Kander and Ebb wrote at least eighteen songs for Cliff (some of them duets with Sally), only four of which were incorporated into the early version of the script.

"Anywhere You Are" (Cliff and Sally)[36]
"Come the End of November" (Cliff and Sally)
"Down, Down, Down" (Cliff and Sally)[37]
"The End of the Party" (Sally, Cliff, Schultz)
"Goodtime Charlie" (Sally, Cliff, and Schneider) (incorporated into early draft)
"I Wish I Never Met Her/Him" (Cliff and Sally)
"I'll Be There" (Sally and Cliff)
"It'll All Blow Over" (Sally, Cliff, Schultz) (incorporated into early draft)
"Mama Loves Papa" (Cliff and Sally)
"Man in the Mirror" (version 1) (Cliff and Sally)
"Man in the Mirror" (version 2) (Cliff and Sally) (incorporated into early draft)[38]
"Maybe Down That Street" (Cliff)
"My Room-mate" (Sally and Cliff) (incorporated into early draft)
"Never in Paris" (Cliff)
"Perfectly Marvelous" (Sally and Cliff) (different from the version used)
"Practical People" (Cliff and Sally)
"Soliloquies" (Cliff and Sally)
"We Can't Stand Still" (Cliff and Sally)

By the time *Cabaret* premiered on Broadway, Cliff was left with a single ballad, "Why Should I Wake Up?," which happens to be the most generic number in the score. Perhaps Cliff's character resists song because his romantic involvement with Sally contradicts the nature of his counterpart in Isherwood's novel, who is homosexual and, as mentioned earlier, remains emotionally detached from the people in his life. Masteroff's script mandates a heterosexual romantic relationship for Cliff, and musical theater convention requires him to sing romantic ballads. These two aspects cut against the grain of Cliff and might explain why he ended up a flat, middle-class charac-ter, from Pennsylvania of all places (a closeted homosexual cast as a straight leading man), and unable to express himself in song.

Many of the songs written for Cliff are responses to Sally's unwelcome pregnancy. For example, in a scene that was eventually cut, Sally and Cliff, facing parenthood, make a pact to reform their reckless behavior. They re-nounce smoking and drinking, and Cliff, caught up in the emotion of the moment, proposes marriage. The idea for this scene comes directly from an episode in *I Am a Camera* in which Chris and Sally promise to turn over a new leaf, and Prince urged them to write it and provided several ideas for the lyrics: "In scene three, Sally and Cliff duets . . . 'What do you think? I don't want a baby yet. I'm not ready, but it's something that would happen anyway eventually . . . so . . .' And for her, 'If it were Max's, I wouldn't be here telling him. I wouldn't have to be having it. But I'm here, and anyway, maybe it will be wonderful." Kander and Ebb wrote two numbers to be sung as a pair— "Soliloquies" and "Man in the Mirror." In the first, Cliff and Sally react am-bivalently to the unexpected news. Like *South Pacific*'s "Twin Soliloquies," the song alternates between the male and female protagonists, who sing their private thoughts. Spoken dialogue with musical underscoring connects the sung portions and creates an extended musical scene:

CLIFF
Ask me how I feel.
What am I to say?
I don't know myself, that's right.
I don't know myself, not yet!

Everything's mixed up,
Anger, fear, surprise.
What am I to say that's right.
I don't know myself, not yet!

I do know some things,
One of which is
I haven't got a job.
If I played poppa,
I'd pick a better place,
I'd pick a better time,
I never would have planned it now.
. . .

(speaking) I feel all right.

SALLY
You do?

CLIFF
I feel all right.

SALLY
You really do?

CLIFF
I really do. How do you feel?

SALLY
Me? I feel . . . I don't know.

(singing)
I do know one thing
If it were Max's
I'd have never told
I'd ask around and
Find a place somewhere
. . . Have it taken care of . . .
But he says it's all right
So maybe it's all right.

CLIFF
Maybe we can make it work

SALLY
Maybe we can make it work

CLIFF
All we have to do is change.

SALLY
All we have to do is change.

. . .

(Spoken)
I feel all right, too.

CLIFF
Hey, we're going to be somebody's parents. Will you marry me?

CLIFF
See that man in the mirror.

Well, that bum's on his way out.
See that man in the mirror.
He's through with knocking about.
He's going to be a father in November.
So that image you see,
As a favor to me,
Please forget to remember.

SALLY
See that girl in the mirror.
Well, that girl's on her way out.
See that girl in the mirror.
She's through with mucking about.

She's having an original creation.
So that dissolute lass
That you see in the glass
Wants some modification.

She'll be wildly adorable
As she's pushing the pram.
Though her past was deplorable
Now, she's meek as a lamb.

The music for "Soliloquies" is in recitative style, marked "freely" in Kander's sketch. Mixed meter and dissonance in the accompaniment help to impart the characters' agitated frame of mind. The dissonance, an appoggiatura on the downbeat of the first two measures resolving upward, reflects Kander's earlier comment about the importance of the half step in *Cabaret* (example 2.5).

"Soliloquies" segues directly into "Man in the Mirror," in which Cliff and Sally resolve to turn their lives around. A vamp consisting of propulsive eighth notes in the upper voice and a reference in the bass voice to the appoggiatura figure at the beginning of "Soliloquies" suggests a degree of desperation, as though Cliff and Sally have to work hard in order to convince themselves of what they are saying. After Cliff's verse, Sally repeats the music with her own set of lyrics. When she cries out, "Maybe we can make it," the recitative music from the beginning of the scene abruptly returns, as though to underscore the futility of Cliff and Sally's efforts.

Scott McMillin has discussed the "mirroring effect" of many musical theater songs. Songs that provide a literal or metaphorical mirror "[enlarge] the book characters into new versions of the themselves, song-and-dance ver-

Example 2.5. "Soliloquies"

sions. . . . [They] are invasions of interiority, subtext disguised as song and dance."[39] For the characters who sing these songs, the mirror reveals something psychologically repressed, something that may be contradictory to the characters' normal sense of themselves. "Man in the Mirror" seems out of place in *Cabaret* because it implies a sense of reality and action for two characters who live an illusion and are emotionally disconnected. The song also suggests a maternal instinct that does not seem even hypothetically possible for Sally. The downfall of Cliff and Sally's relationship is predicated on their inability to see themselves honestly. Cliff and Sally's other duets also have a forced musical comedy optimism. "Practical People" is a song of utter domesticity that seems out of place in *Cabaret*, and "We Can't Stand Still" has an upbeat, dreamy quality that is not right for the musical.

Cliff's other cut songs allude either to his writer's block or to the growing political storm in Berlin. In "Never in Paris," Cliff explains to Sally why he came to Berlin to write his novel rather than stay in Paris. On the word "Paris" he sings the same appoggiatura figure that the emcee sings on the word "wel-

Example 2.6. "Never in Paris"

come" in the opening song "Willkommen," as though the city has the same
sort of seductive pull as the cabaret (example 2.6). (The main theme of this
song is similar to that of Vernon Duke and E. Y. Harburg's "April in Paris,"
which was published just shortly after the year in which *Cabaret* takes place.)
The song is haunting and romantic, and a fine expression of Cliff's worldli-
ness. Ironically, it is arguably the best number that Kander and Ebb wrote for
Cliff, but the scene for which they wrote it was eventually cut.

Clifford Bradshaw and the Act of Singing

That Kander and Ebb made so many attempts to find a musical voice for Cliff,
that he ended up with a single song, that this song was replaced for the 1987
revival with little notice, and that this new song was expunged from the 1998
revival might clearly signal the inherent contradiction between his character
and his status as a male romantic lead in a musical. Though Masteroff's plot
places Cliff into a heterosexual role, it does not entirely erase his homosexual
orientation. Cliff goes through the motions of making love to Sally, but he
is unable to fully engage his voice or body, which runs counter to the modus
operandi of the traditional romantic lead in musical theater. To fully understand this interpretation, it is necessary to place Cliff in the context of gender
construction and Isherwood's novel.

As Judith Butler has shown, performance is a locus for the working out
of constructions of gender and sexuality.[40] Cliff's acting the part of a heterosexual is just one of many instances of gender performance in *Cabaret*. Singing is a special performative mode in that the act itself has the potential to
connote gender and sexuality.[41] At least since the Victorian era, singing has
been closely aligned with the female gender. This bias toward the feminine

stems from the association of singing with emotionality, which was, from the mid-nineteenth century onward, the domain of women. By contrast, men were expected to be rational and stoic. Because this ideology of gender ("ideology of separate spheres") affected attitudes about singing well into the twentieth century, musical theater singing, which enshrines open emotiveness, has been associated with gayness.[42] However, in the strict context of a musical, male characters escape the emasculation or feminization that men in the real world might experience through the act of singing. In fact, singing in musical theater often reinforces gender through the exaggeration of the natural vocal timbres of the female and male voice. Singing can even emphasize maleness because it has the agency to move a character to resolve and action, and most leading men in musicals are fully in touch with their sexuality and launch lustily into song. Cliff's abnegation of song is thus conspicuous. It might be explained as an extension of his preferred emotional distance as a writer (or camera).[43] In fact, when Cliff does become emotionally involved, he neglects his writing and loses all sense of objectivity. Cliff can perform the outward duties of traditional masculinity (for example, he wants to protect Sally and provide for their child). What he cannot do, however, is express himself musically as either a heterosexual or homosexual. His musical silence is wrapped up with his ambiguous sexual identity.[44]

Cabaret at the End of the Millennium

When the studio heads of Allied Artists decided to make a movie version of Cabaret, Bob Fosse was the last person they had in mind for the director. His 1969 film adaptation of Sweet Charity had been a colossal failure, and he had a reputation of going over budget. The studio wanted someone with a much bigger name, such as Joe Mankiewicz, Gene Kelly, or Billy Wilder. Fosse got the job only because the producer of the film, Cy Feuer, agreed to back him.[45] Fosse recognized the unhealthy state of the film musical at the time, and he knew that his adaptation would have to respond to the shift in cinema toward greater realism. By "resurrecting elements of the classical film musical into contemporary concerns," as Stephen Bowles has observed, he made the musical work at a time when Hollywood was no longer interested in the genre.[46] Fosse essentially reinvented Cabaret according to own vision, and his film was recently chosen by the Smithsonian Institute as one of ten representative films from the twentieth century to be preserved for posterity.

Ernest Martin, Cy Feuer's longtime business partner, suggested that he hire the screenwriter Jay Presson Allen, who had been nominated for an Academy Award for her adaptation of *The Prime of Miss Jean Brodie*.[47] Hoping to present *Cabaret* in a more realistic light than the Broadway version did, Allen made drastic changes to the story, rethinking the characters, plot, and music. She renamed the male lead Brian Roberts, changed him to an Englishman, and made him more sexually ambiguous or, as Morris Mitchell puts it, "at least situationally bisexual."[48] After Sally and Brian fail miserably at making love, Sally suggests to Brian, "Maybe you just don't sleep with girls." This line made it into the final cut of the film, although Brian's response in a draft of the screenplay, "Actually, I don't," does not appear in the film. Nor does Sally's rejoinder: "Bri, I just didn't get it, you know. I mean it's so hard for Americans to *tell* with Englishmen. Whether they're queer or just well-bred." Brian's campy response lessens the tension that Sally has introduced into their conversation: "The conditions do occasionally overlap."

From the beginning, Feuer felt that "the entire secondary story—that soupy, sentimental, idiotic business with the little Jewish man courting Sally's landlady by bringing her a pineapple every day—had to be thrown out."[49] Allen reverted to Natalia and Fritz's relationship from *I Am a Camera*. Compared to Masteroff's Schneider-Schultz engagement, Natalia and Fritz's marriage has a greater ring of truth and elicits a greater amount of sympathy from the audience, who can predict the imminent fate of these doomed Jewish lovers. The screenwriter created a German aristocrat, Maximilian von Heune, who fills the same role as the American character of Clive in Isherwood's *The Berlin Stories* ("Sally Bowles") and *I Am a Camera*. When Sally and Brian visit Max at his country villa, it is implied that the three of them have a ménage à trois (and it is later revealed that both Sally and Brian are sleeping with Max independently).[50] This scene gives a whole new meaning to the song "Two Ladies," which immediately follows this encounter.

The most radical change made for the movie involves Kander and Ebb's score. The decision was made to eliminate all of the book songs except "Tomorrow Belongs to Me," which was assigned to a Nazi youth to sing in a beer garden. Snippets of some of the Broadway book songs are heard, including "Married" sung in German, but only as diegetic music coming from a gramophone or radio. According to Stephen Bowles, the newly configured score utilizes "music as an essential ingredient in a dramatic social comment on . . . Germany in the post-war reconstruction."[51] This approach to the music also played into Fosse's desire for realism. It solved the problem of verisimilitude and also magnified the commentative nature of the cabaret songs.[52] Left with only five of the original numbers, Fosse asked Kander and Ebb to write two new ones, a Marlene Dietrich-like ballad, "Mein Herr," and a new "Money Song" to replace "Sitting Pretty." Fosse also interpolated "Maybe This Time," which has the feeling of a Dietrichesque torch song. His filming of the number, which cuts from Sally singing in the street to Sally singing on the stage of the Kit Kat, connects the two worlds of *Cabaret*.[53] Kander and Ebb were not involved with the shooting of the film, and they did not see it until it opened in New York.[54]

Allen wanted to portray more vitriolic and virulent forms of German anti-Semitism than were ultimately permitted for the film. For example, in an early draft of her screenplay, Kost and Schneider go on an anti-Semitic diatribe when they hear that the national banks are shut down. In one of the more violent scenes taken from *The Berlin Stories*, the Landauers' department store is vandalized by three Nazis, who paint "Juden" in bright yellow paint on the show windows. Natalia confronts them and hits one of them with her purse. Following the confrontation between Natalia and the Nazi youths, Fritz accompanies her home and confesses to her that he is Jewish. "If You Could See Her Through My Eyes" follows immediately. In this draft of her screenplay, Allen only implied Natalia and Fritz's marriage, but in the final cut of the film their wedding follows "If You Could See Her Through My Eyes."

Allen's Sally is insensitive to the targeting of Jews. For instance, when Sally meets Natalia, she blurts out, "I'm an actress. I spent all afternoon making love to an old Jew producer who's promised to give me a contract." Of course, Sally deliberately tries to shock Natalia, whom she sees as her competition, but her rudeness is later met with a stern scolding from Brian: "And incidentally, Natalia Landauer is *Jewish*." Suggested by Isherwood and Van Druten, Sally inherited her lack of tact from her father, a mid-ranking member of England's diplomatic corps, who shows up in Berlin on official business. Allen originally included an awkward encounter between Brian, Sally, and her father. Lightly admonishing Sally's admiration of Sarah Bernhardt, he quips with cool condescension, "Bernhardt had very little choice but to be 'fascinating.' She was an illegitimate Jewess." Sally is no more sensitive to homosexuals. Later, when Maximilian abandons Sally and Brian, Sally calls him a "lousy faggot!"

In the original stage version of *Cabaret*, the parallel love stories, one conventional and romantic, the other nonconformist and decadent, played to the expectations of the audience steeped in the Broadway tradition as well as audiences concerned with the new social agenda of the 1960s. Mitchell Morris has observed that the "traditional" courtship of Fritz and Natalia (heterosexual and leading to marriage) is morally superior and thus taken more seriously than Brian and Sally's impetuous and libertine affair. Sally and Brian are sexually outside the mainstream, and they experience an unfulfilled sort of love. On the other hand, Natalia and Fritz's love leads to the reward of marriage. Their love contrasts with "the queerly desiring characters in Cabaret [who] participate in an endless play of mask and mirrors."[55] Fritz's decision to expose himself as a Jew is a sacrifice done out of pure love for Natalia. His confession is a sort of Liebestod. For the original Broadway version of Cabaret, it was enough that Sally's destructive actions destroy Cliff's plans for the future; in the film, Brian's sexual ambiguity contributes to the destructive nature of his relationship with Sally, although Sally's actions push their relationship to its tragic conclusion. Sally and Cliff's affair cannot bear the weight of their narcissism and passivity, whereas Fritz and Natalia's love will endure, which makes their likely extermination all the more poignant.

Like the original Broadway musical, Fosse's film links the decadence of German culture to the downfall of the Weimar Republic, but it emphasizes sexual deviance (embodied in the cabaret scenes and Sally and Brian's relationship). In the aftermath of the war, many critics of the Nazis propagated the theory that sexual deviance was one of the causes of the Holocaust. Fosse implicitly accepted this fallacious argument and made sexual deviance — with homosexuality its most blatant form — a conspicuous aspect of German society. He justified this aspect of the film by purporting to be "authentic," but, as Morris has argued, he ended up triangulating contemporary myths about homosexuality with myths about the Weimar Republic, mapping the "exotic perversions and plain sluttishness, opium / tobacco / booze, and popular music" onto sex, drugs, and rock 'n' roll, and propagating his own "myths of divine decadence."[56] Ironically, this aspect of the film helps to explain why it resonated so strongly with American audiences, but it also inculpated the very thing it seemed to be celebrating. Responding simultaneously to 1930s Germany and contemporary America, Fosse's film, despite its many artistic merits, seems to be both an endorsement and condemnation of sexual deviance.[57]

In 1987, a year after a revival of Cabaret in London, Harold Prince decided that the time was right to bring the musical back to Broadway. By this time, the concept musical had more or less run its course. Prince returned to the original script and score, but he could not ignore the notoriety of Fosse's film. He knew that he had to let Cliff out of the closet, which made him "a person worth playing." The change, however, was not a simple matter, as the musical calls for a sexual relationship between Cliff and Sally.[58] Masteroff ended up splitting the difference between his original Cliff and Isherwood's character, making him bisexual, which further complicates his status as a musical theater romantic lead. Kander and Ebb replaced Cliff's song "Why Should I Wake Up" with a new one, "Don't Go," hoping that it would better personalize Cliff and Sally's relationship. The song, however, is weak from a dramatic standpoint. Cliff's plea in the song for Sally to stay has a hollow (or perhaps desperate) ring to it. Midway through the song, Cliff seems to be saying that only Sally can make a real man—a straight man—out of him: "You're more than just a girl. You are the only girl. And maybe my last chance." Other musical additions include "I Don't Care Much," which had been cut from the 1966 version, and the combining of "Sitting Pretty" with the new "Money Song."

These changes notwithstanding, the revival lacked the shock of the original production. It also placed too much weight on Joel Grey, whose fifth-spot billing for the original production was elevated to the top spot. As Frank Rich quipped in his review, "To have a '*Cabaret*' reliant on its emcee is almost like reviving 'Oklahoma!' as a star vehicle for the actor playing Jud."[59] The production was visually drab, the costumes were cheesy, and Alyson Reed's Sally and Gregg Edelman's Cliff had a passionless onstage romance. Rich went out of his way to note that "Mr. Edelman's writer, though also of pleasant voice, is so mild that one is constantly taken aback to discover he is the toast of two sexes in at least that many nations." More sympathetic was the courtship of Regina Resnick's Fräulein Schneider and Werner Klemperer's (of *Hogan's Heroes* fame) Herr Schultz.

In 1993, the Donmar Warehouse, an experimental theater space in London, presented a radically new version of *Cabaret* conceived and directed by Sam Mendes.[60] In this production camp and sexual deviance are aesthetic imperatives. For example, "Two Ladies" is performed not by the emcee and two cabaret girls, but by the emcee, a cabaret girl, and a cabaret boy in drag. There is nothing gratuitous about these features, however, for Mendes fully integrated them into his thematic reading of *Cabaret*. He set the entire musical—cabaret scenes and book scenes—in the cabaret, which also took in the seating of the theater. The audience sat at tables placed close to the stage. Life *is* a cabaret, after all. Bombarded at close quarters by the production's conspicuous sexuality, the audience could not escape from the entertainment at hand, and they were practically made complicit participants in the action. Mendes used every means available to him to enhance this effect, even waiting until after the performance to pass out programs. The shocker of the evening occurred at the very end, when the emcee took off his coat to reveal striped prison clothes with a yellow star and a pink triangle, Nazi labels for Jew and homosexual. As the emcee turned upstage, the cabaret metamorphosed into a death camp.

Michael Gibson reworked Don Walker's 1966 orchestrations, transforming the 1960s Broadway pit orchestra into a 1930s cabaret band, which was made up mostly of actors, all of whom could play one or more instruments.[61] The actor-musicians performed from everywhere, the band platform, the stage, the spiral staircase stage-left.[62] This band is the final coup de grâce, the last element working to break down the traditional fourth wall. Kander considers "Michael's orchestrations a work of absolute genius," for which he never got the credit he deserved.

In 1998, the Roundabout Theatre Company brought Mendes's production to New York, opening it at the Henry Miller Theatre and then transferring it to the old Studio 54, which was refurbished explicitly for the production, for an open-ended run. Rob Marshall was hired to redo the choreography. Natasha Richardson starred as Sally Bowles, Alan Cumming as the emcee (repeating his role from the Donmar production), John Benjamin Hickey as Cliff, Ron Rifkin as Schultz, and Mary Louise Wilson as Schneider. Tony Awards went to Richardson, Cumming, and Rifkin, as well as to the producers for best revival of a musical. Among the actresses who appeared in the role of Sally during the run were Gina Gershon, Molly Ringwald, and Brooke Shields. With 2,377 performances, the revival far exceeded the original Broadway production.

Whereas Prince's original production of *Cabaret* used metaphor and analogy to show parallels between Germany during the onslaught of Nazism and America during the Civil Rights movement, and to warn that it could happen here, Mendes was more concerned with explaining how Nazism and the Holocaust could have happened at all.[63] The production, however, was no mere history lesson. According to Roger Copeland, the earlier versions of *Cabaret* relied on the fallacy that decadence led to the rise of Hitler. Mendes's Kit Kat Klub "is the first to do justice to the complex historical relationship between German Expressionist Weimar decadence and the rise of the Third Reich."[64] Mendes's emcee is decadence incarnate, an "all-seeing theatrical dominance defining the production."[65] Cumming achieved the impossible by making his own a role that for nearly three decades had belonged to Joel Grey. His is an emcee without the Expressionist color of the earlier stage productions and film; he is covered with tattoos and the physical scars of drug use and brutality:[66] "Unlike the more subliminal character played by Joel Grey [on the stage and in the film], Cumming's shape shifts before our very eyes. He's a man, he's a woman, he's Hitler. He speaks all languages. He struts, he leers, he mocks, and he observes everything. At one point, he cajoles an audience member onstage for a dance, forever erasing any barrier between him and us."[67]

In this version of *Cabaret*, the character of Clifford is the closest theatrical reincarnation of Christopher Isherwood. Although the character is still bound by Masteroff's romantic story line, Mendes was able to bring Cliff's homosexuality out into the open. Early in act 1, immediately after Cliff and Sally meet, Cliff and Bobby, whom he met in England, engage in a long, passionate kiss. But there is no getting around the fact that Cliff is Sally's lover. When Mendes first experimented with *Cabaret* at the Donmar Warehouse, he included the 1987 song "Don't Go," but when he restaged the production for Broadway, he cut the song, leaving Cliff with a mere few measures to sing with Sally in "Perfectly Marvelous." A Cliff who does not sing is perhaps the ultimate expression of what Kander, Ebb, Masteroff, and Prince were aiming for all along. This production argues that there is no musical voice for Cliff (certainly not after Stonewall). Amidst the ubiquitous camp of this production, Cliff finally became the objective camera lens observing those around him, not unlike what the original writer in Isherwood's novel professed to be.

The role of Sally has also undergone some changes. She is more raw and dangerous, a contrast to the middle-class, style-over-content American Sally of the film whose "acquaintance with the darker side of bohemia was pretty much confined to green nail polish, soigné cigarette holders and casual sex."[68] Richardson's rendition of "Cabaret" caught the attention of critics:

> When Minnelli belted out those lyrics, the word was happiest. . . . Not so for Mendes's revisionist conception of Sally. As she prepares to sing the line "But when I saw her laid out like a queen," Richardson (later Leigh) closes her eyes and begins what looks like a ritual of self-hypnosis. We see this Sally working hard—very hard!—to convince herself that her story (somehow, against all odds) is going to end happily. But what follows is one of the most omi-

nous pauses in the history of the musical theatre—and the ultimate effect of her halting delivery is to place the emotional emphasis squarely on the word *corpse*. In that split second of silence, Sally's glazed-over eyes open wide and she seems to be staring into Elsie's coffin. But the body she sees there is undoubtedly her own.[69]

At the end of the song, Sally violently tips over the microphone stand and stomps off stage, physicalizing both her fatalism and self-loathing. The only power she can exercise is to reject Cliff and with him her only chance for true happiness.

Musically speaking, this production is a hybrid of the original and the film. Since every scene occurs in the physical cabaret space, on the stage, as it were, Mendes had to rethink the presentation of each book song. For Fräulein Schneider's songs, the playing area of the stage is set to suggest her apartments. Mendes cut "The Telephone Song," which Prince had himself shortened for the 1987 revival, in order to allow time for the interpolation of the salacious "Mein Herr." "It Couldn't Please Me More" remains intact, but giant pineapples descend from the ceiling, thus turning the song into one of Hollywood's tropic or exotic fantasy production numbers, as though to mock Herr Schultz's awkward attempts at courtship. Mendes uses "Married" simultaneously as a book song and cabaret song. A chanteuse performs it in German at the cabaret alongside Schultz's English version. In a radical departure from the original production, "Tomorrow Belongs to Me" is first heard as the emcee squats over a portable wind-up gramophone and listens to a recording of a boy soprano. He hisses the final words, "to me," while imitating Hitler. "Maybe This Time" and the "Money Song" are incorporated from the film version of *Cabaret*. The former, a cabaret number for Sally, reflects on the action and, as in the movie, suggests that she dreams of a better life. (Prince also used the new "Money Song ["Money Makes the World Go Around"] in the 1987 revival, but in combination with "Sitting Pretty.") Mendes retained only the newer, more vitriolic song. Michael Gibson's orchestration for this number invokes the whining timbre of a Klezmer band, orchestrally suggesting the stereotypical image of a greedy Jew. This brilliant stroke on Gibson's part echoes the exaggerated gyrations of the chorus and emcee. Mendes also found a powerful way to include "I Don't Care Much." The emcee, having become a ubiquitous physical presence, sings it in a heroin-induced state as a foreboding of Sally's decision to have an abortion. The song effectively sets up the next scene, during which Cliff is beaten up by Nazis and Sally sings "Cabaret."

Mendes's production "entertains us to *death.*"[70] It forces us to experience the musical viscerally by setting the whole thing in a cabaret that turns into a death camp. Mendes uses a figurative mirror—just as Prince and Fosse used an actual mirror—to confront the audience with its own complicity. In America at the end of the millennium, homosexuality was not viewed in the main as deviant behavior, and Mendes's *Cabaret* does not treat the gay subject as derogatorily as the film did. It reminds the audience that "hate crimes and human rights violations still persist worldwide, including but not limited to recent outbreaks of homophobia, gay-bashing, and gay murders in the United States."[71]

Cabaret is arguably one of the most influential musicals after *Oklahoma!*, and it placed Kander and Ebb at the forefront of musical theater during the post–Rodgers and Hammerstein era. With its interweaving of plot and commentary, book scenes and cabaret revue, political history and cultural critique, *Cabaret* showed an entire generation of writers a new brand of musical theater, one flexible enough to respond to the concerns of a nation in transition. *Cabaret* is no mere history lesson; its dramatis personae of inconsequential and disenfranchised members of society express what mere historical facts cannot. In this way, the musical captures in theatrical form the same thing that Isherwood's novel does in literary form. *Cabaret* remains Kander and Ebb's most produced musical. The latest professional production is a revival of Mendes's version at a remodeled Folies Bergère in Paris. It opened in October 2006 to rave reviews, with *Le Monde* calling it "vif et impeccable."[72]

CHAPTER 3

Chicago

Broadway to Hollywood

Twenty years from now, they'll die to see it [*Chicago*] —but . . . *Chicago* will be a wild
card already played. It won't even be in the discard pile. It's over.

—ETHAN MORDDEN

W HEN ETHAN MORDDEN MADE HIS DOUR PREDICTION FOR CHI-
cago, it was 1983 and the Broadway musical as he had known it
seemed a thing of the past. He could not have imagined that,
twenty-five years later, *Chicago* would be playing to sold-out houses on
Broadway. Maurine Dallas Watkins's 1926 play *Chicago*, the source material
for the musical, is a prescient satire depicting how the press, in collusion with
the American criminal justice, turns criminals into celebrities. Although set
in the twenties, her story is as relevant today as it was seventy-five years ago.
As of this writing, the 1996 Broadway revival of the musical *Chicago* is still
going strong and has become the longest running revival in Broadway history. This production inspired the 2003 Miramax film version of the musical,
which garnered three Golden Globes and six Academy Awards, including
best film. The soundtrack of the film went platinum in 2004 and triple platinum in 2005.

Gwen Verdon provided the impetus for the musical *Chicago*. She had
wanted to play Roxie Hart, one of two main parts in the play, ever since seeing the 1942 Warner Brothers film *Roxie Hart*, which starred Ginger Rogers

and which is loosely based on Watkins's comedy. In this film, Rogers performs the Black Bottom for the press and gets them to join in. It is no wonder that Verdon and Bob Fosse, her husband since 1960, saw musical potential in this story. Verdon's tough-dame exterior and inner vulnerability seemed ideal for the role of Roxie. In the late 1960s, she and Fosse tried to obtain the musical rights, but Watkins refused to grant them because she felt uneasy about her journalistic connection to the subject. When her play opened in New York, she even concealed the fact that she had been a reporter for the *Chicago Tribune* in order to defend herself against accusations of having been involved in the very process that the play mocks. After Watkins died in 1969, her estate agreed to sell the rights to Fosse, Verdon, and the producer Robert Fryer. By then, Fosse and Verdon had separated, but they both remained committed to the project. News of the musical appeared in the *New York Times* as early as 1972, but it was another three years before *Chicago* opened on Broadway.[1]

Ironically, what has now become one of Kander and Ebb's biggest successes was one of their most unpleasant experiences and a project that almost collapsed. A major setback occurred when Fosse suffered a heart attack, which precipitated a suspension of rehearsals. In the hope of keeping the cast intact while Fosse recovered from his now infamous bypass surgery, the producers scrambled to find temporary jobs for the out-of-work actors and dancers. With Fosse out of commission, they also made inquiries into the availability of other directors, including Hal Prince and Jerome Robbins. Rehearsals resumed as soon as Fosse emerged from the hospital.

Watkins based her play on two real murder cases that she covered while working as a reporter for the *Chicago Tribune*. Belva Gaertner, a cabaret singer, shot and killed her lover, Walter Law. Although the murder weapon was shown to be hers, she claimed to have been drunk at the time of the murder and therefore unable to recall anything about the incident. Shortly after Gaertner's arrest, Beulah Annan allegedly murdered her lover, Harry Kalstedt, and then swore to her husband that he had tried to sexually assault her. Two days after Annan's arrival at the Cook County jail, Watkins wrote an article that forever linked the two purported murderesses, noting their shared interests: "A man, a woman, liquor and a gun." Watkins titillated her readership with her juicy reportage of these cases and her dry sense of humor. She knew a good quote when she heard one, such as Gaertner's "Gin and guns—either one is bad enough, but together they get you in a dickens of a mess."[2] Nor did it escape Watkins's attention that Annan's cover story underwent several alterations during the lead-up to her trial, and that during the proceedings she claimed to be pregnant. In the end, the women were acquitted within ten days of each other.

Shortly after Gaertner and Annan were released from prison, Watkins abandoned her job at the *Tribune* for an editorial assignment in New York and to attend the playwriting program at Yale Drama School. She wrote *Chicago* in 1926, two years after the conclusion of the Gaertner and Beulah cases, and the play ran on Broadway for 172 performances.

In the prologue of Watkins's play, Roxie Hart shoots Fred Casely, an auto salesman and her latest lover. After the gunshot and a brief blackout signifying the passage of three and a half hours, her husband, Amos, confesses to the crime, claiming that he was protecting his wife. The assistant state attorney, Harrison, punches holes in Amos's story and informs him of Roxie's infidelity. Jake Callahan, a news reporter, is on hand to shape events into spectacular news copy. Jake predicts that Roxie's crime will turn her into an overnight sensation: "lay off men and booze till when you come to trial yuh look like Miss America . . . Why, you'll be famous!" He also convinces the opportunistic lawyer Billy Flynn to represent her.

When act 1 begins, Roxie is already enjoying her public notoriety. She and Mrs. Morton, the matron of Cook County Jail, collect paper clippings recounting the murder. Velma Kelly is also in jail, awaiting trial for killing her philandering husband. Billy Flynn, who has accepted both cases, concocts a self-defense strategy for Roxie: "you both grabbed for the gun." As the curtain rises on act 2, Roxie, who is being upstaged by the arrival of "Go-to-Hell Kitty"(Kitty Baxter), who is also accused of killing her husband, gets the reporters' attention by announcing that she is pregnant. Roxie's trial occupies most of the third act. Her testimony, from the tilt of her head to the tone of her speeches, is literally staged by Billy Flynn. Toward the climax of the trial, Flynn dramatically confronts his client: "Roxie Hart, the State charges you with the murder of Fred Casely . . . guilty or not guilty." Roxie cries out that she killed him, yes, but only to defend her "husband's innocent unborn child." The jury returns a not-guilty verdict. When gunshots are heard from outside the court building, Jake and the rest of the press dash off, leaving Roxie alone with Billy. "You're all washed up," he tells her, but Roxie insists that she is going to become a famous vaudeville star. The press reemerges with the new female killer. "Gee, ain't God good to the papers!" cries Jake. "Come on, sister, you gotta play ball: this is Chicago!" he adds as flashes go off and the curtain falls.

Watkins enlists sarcasm as her main weapon in the battle against the collusion between the press and the criminal justice system. The play teaches that in America being a bad celebrity is just as advantageous as being a good one. Once Roxie learns this lesson and how to "play ball," the original title of the play, her acquittal and stardom are practically guaranteed.[3] Of course, she receives plenty of assistance in her rise to fame both from Billy Flynn, who takes her case on only to secure his own fame, and from Jake Callahan, who exploits Roxie's crime in order to catapult his own newspaper career, usurping true justice in the name of readership. Watkins's character descriptions are as wry as her dialogue, and they telegraph her cynical viewpoint about the subject matter. Roxie is "the prettiest woman ever charged with murder in Chicago"; in profile, "there's a hint of a Raphael angel—with a touch of Medusa." Her description of the publicity-savvy Billy Flynn is a parody of the Romantic hero mixed with commentary on the ethnicity suggested by his features: "a rich voice . . . with a minor undertone that's Gaelic . . . a little man, like Napoleon, and he carries himself with the Corporal's air. A magnificent iron-gray mane, with a forelock he tugs at to convey the impression of thought, or tosses back now and then to reveal the Caesarian brow. The eyes are deep-set and keen; the nose starts out to be Semitic, but ends with an Irish tilt; the mouth is broad without being generous, and the jaw is pugilistic."[4]

When Fosse started work on Chicago, he enlisted Fred Ebb to coauthor the script. Perhaps taking his cue from Roxie's final lines in Watkins's play— "I am not washed up! I'm goin' in vaudeville—I'm famous"—Ebb decided to tell the story as a vaudeville show, even though when he had tried to do the same thing with 70, Girls, 70, the audience had difficulty following the plot (see Chapter 6).[5] 70, Girls, 70 proved to be a valuable training ground for Chicago and illuminated some of the pitfalls of telling a story as a vaudeville. In 70, Girls, 70 the vaudeville structure was a fun gimmick, but it had no metaphorical purpose. In Chicago the vaudeville is a metaphor for the American justice system in which the best performance wins over the press and the jury. This time Ebb structured the entire musical as a vaudeville bill, presenting the story through a series of vaudeville songs and vignettes, each of which evokes a well-known vaudeville act, such as ventriloquism or the "dumb show," or a particular performer, such as Sophie Tucker ("When You're Good to Mama"). The result was a much more organic and seamless work than anything Kander and Ebb had written before or have written since.

The vaudeville concept was perfectly wedded to the theme of Chicago.

After all, vaudeville producers willfully featured notorious, even criminal, figures and freak acts, such as Lillina Graham and Ethel Conrad, who were nicknamed the "Shooting Stars" for killing W. E. D. Stokes.[6] By superimposing a vaudeville framework onto Watkins's comedy, Ebb implicitly linked showbiz to the tawdry, parasitic practices of the press and the corruption of the American justice system. The musical literally conflates courtroom performance and stage performance. Further, the vaudeville format suited Fosse's background and aesthetic leanings. He had grown up in Chicago during the twenties and was a product of vaudeville and burlesque.

Ebb played up the vaudeville concept as much as possible. For example, he wanted to project vaudeville legends (captions) before each scene to summarize the action. One of Ebb's outlines gives the legends for act 1. Eventually, the legends were replaced with spoken announcements made by the conductor, Stanley Lebowsky, who can be heard on the original cast recording.

Vaudeville Legends for Act 1

> Scene 1 "VELMA O'ROURKE SINGS THE OPENING NUMBER WITH A BRIEF APPEARANCE BY MISS ROXIE HART"
>
> Scene 2 "MR. AND MRS. AMOS HART PERFORM A LOVE DUET"
>
> Scene 3 "THE COOK COUNTY SEXTETTE, CELL BLOCK FOUR SING A LAMENT"
>
> Scene 4 "A PIECE OF THE ACTION"
>
> Scene 5 "VELMA O'ROURKE SINGS OF THE IMPROBABILITIES OF LOVE"
>
> Scene 6 "ALL I REALLY NEED"
>
> Scene 7 "MISS ROXIE HART SINGS OF A GLORIOUS FUTURE"
>
> Scene 8 "THE AMAZING BALLANTINE AND HIS [C]OERCE BALLOON BUSTING"
>
> Scene 9 "MISS VELMA O'ROURKE DOES A SELLING JOB"
>
> Scene 10 "MISS ROXIE HART, SONGS, DANCES AND SAD SAYINGS"

Ebb started work on the script in 1973. He elevated the character of Velma to leading-role status. Like Belva Gaertner, the person on whom she is based, Velma is a nightclub entertainer. As soon as Roxie arrives at the jailhouse, she and Velma become rivals and vie for the attention of the press and their mutual lawyer. Jealous but not self-defeating, Velma invites Roxie to form a duo act with her. Roxie tauntingly rejects Velma's proposition because she thinks that she can make it on her own, but, after her trial, Roxie comes to the realization that she has a better crack at vaudeville with Velma than alone. Ebb replaced the role of Jake with a theatrical agent of his own invention,

Henry Glassman, who is known aptly as "the worm." Glassman represents Velma, but because he is having a hard time booking her act, he urges her to team up with Roxie.

The name Bob Fosse remains closely associated with the musical *Chicago*, and the Broadway revival bears his signature finger snaps and hallmark cynicism. But *Chicago* is also quintessential Kander and Ebb in that it uses performance to draw attention to the relationship between theater and everyday life. Lionel Abel calls this type of theater (theater about theater) "metatheater."[7] Richard Hornby has identified five major types of metatheater that writers such as Kander and Ebb employ to draw attention to the artifice and overt theatricality of their work: 1) the play within the play, 2) performed ceremony, 3) role-playing within the role, 4) literary and real-life references, and 5) self-reference.[8] *Chicago* employs all five: Roxie and Velma's stage act at the end of the musical (play within the play); Hunyak's hanging and Roxie's trial (performed ceremony); Roxie's imitation of a ventriloquist dummy during "We Both Reached for the Gun" (role-playing within a role); references to entertainers such as Sophie Tucker (literary and real-life references); musical calling attention to itself as a musical entertainment (self-reference). The references to past performers have been called "performative reiterations."[9] Performative reiterations force "the spectator to reevaluate his or her relationship with the dramatic fiction and to theatre as a whole."[10] *Chicago*'s self-referentiality occurs in the form of asides and direct addresses to the audience in songs such as "Roxie," "I Know a Girl," and "Mister Cellophane"; the conductor's announcements; and Roxie and Velma's ingratiating speech to the audience at the end of their stage act. The orchestra for *Chicago* sits not in a pit but on the stage, in the original production high atop a cylindrical platform that also served as part of the scenery. This idea, brilliantly realized by the scenic designer Tony Walton, helped to draw the audience's attention to the fact that they were in a theater. (Mendes borrowed this idea for his version of *Cabaret*.)

Nearly all of the songs and scenes in *Chicago* are allusions to real vaudeville entertainment and performers (table 3.1). For example, "When You're Good to Momma" is the type of number that Sophie Tucker sang, and "We Both Reached for the Gun" is a parody of the vaudeville ventriloquist routine. Velma's appearance at the beginning of both acts recalls Texas Guinan, a woman and owner of a speakeasy who famously greeted her clientele with the epithet "suckers."[11] At the beginning of act 2, Velma looks at the audience just back from intermission and says "Hello suckers, welcome back."

Table 3.1. Vaudeville musical references in *Chicago*

Songs	Vaudeville Associations
"All That Jazz"	Texas Guinan (1884–1933) (during prohibition owned the famous speakeasy called the 300 Club)
"Funny Honey"	Helen Morgan (1900–1941) ("Can't Help Lovin' Dat Man," "Bill," and "Don't Ever Leave Me")
"When You're Good to Mama"	Sophie Tucker (1884–1966) ("You've Got to See Mama Every Night")
"All I Care About Is Love"	Ted Lewis ("I'm Crazy 'Bout My Baby, And My Baby's Crazy 'Bout Me")
"A Little Bit of Good"	Julian Eltinge (1883–1941) and Bert Savoy (female impersonators)
"We Both Reached for the Gun"	Ventriloquist acts
"Me and My Baby"	Eddie Cantor (1892–1964) ("Yes Sir, That's My Baby" and "My Baby Just Cares for Me")
"Mister Cellophane"	Bert Williams (1876–1922) ("Nobody")

The black performer Bert Williams, the most revered comic of the vaudeville era, has been described as "a pathetic stage figure, hesitant in its delivery of lines, executing a song like 'Nobody' to the 'plaintive sound' of a slide trombone, which he made 'apparently desperate efforts to catch up with.'"[12] Williams's rendition of "Nobody" is the model for Amos's self-deprecating performance of "Mister Cellophane." A number of scenes in *Chicago* feature a traditional vaudeville routine or sketch: tap dance (act 1, scene 6), ventriloquist act (act 1, scene 8), card game trick (act 2, scene 3), rope trick (act 2, scene 4), and courtroom scene (act 2, scene 6).[13] These references help to reinforce the staginess of the proceedings, even for those members of the audience who know little or nothing about vaudeville. One need not be familiar with vaudeville to appreciate *Chicago*, as the current revival, which mutes the 1920s aura, proves.[14]

These referential songs draw attention to the artifice of the vaudeville structure.[15] For example, "Funny Honey" evokes the melancholy figure of Helen Morgan, whose tragic stage persona spilled over into her real life. Morgan, the famed chanteuse known for singing on top of an upright piano, was an alcoholic and died of liver disease. In Fosse's staging of "Funny Honey," Roxie, perched atop a piano with a drink in her hand, sings about Amos as he is being questioned by the district attorney. With each passing verse, Roxie knocks back another drink. The tone of the song takes a sour turn when Amos rats on Roxie, who, now completely inebriated, loses her composure and lashes out at him. Roxie's Helen Morgan stylization lulls the audience into the sentiments of the song (that she feels affection for "that funny, sunny, honey hubby of mine"), but she negates this effect with her outburst ("that scummy, crummy, dummy hubby of mine").

By the end of 1973, Kander and Ebb had completed a draft of the score, which included a song for Henry Glassman called "Ten Percent," a country-swing version of "We Both Reached for the Gun," "It," and "Looping the Loop" (table 3.2).[16] When *Chicago* went into rehearsals in the fall of 1974, the score contained only a few changes, such as a new version of "We Both Reached for the Gun." One of the changes to the score was the result of the audition of the actor Michael O'Haughey, who sang the "Bell Song" from *Lakme.* Fosse was so impressed with O'Haughey's abilities as a falsettist and female impersonator that he cast him in the role of Mary Sunshine. Kander and Ebb replaced Sunshine's earlier song, the cloying "Rose Colored Glasses," with the even more ingratiating and operatic "A Little Bit of Good." Billy Flynn de-wigs Mary Sunshine at the climax of his closing arguments at Roxie's trial, thus demonstrating that everything that happens in court is a performance.[17] The Playbill listed the actor as M. O'Haughey in order to conceal his true sexual identity.

The tryout period in Philadelphia was tense for Kander and Ebb. Fosse was still recovering from his heart attack and the prolonged hospital stay. His mood had darkened, and he suspected that the producers and writers were scheming behind his back. He took out his paranoia on the cast and on Ebb. When Ebb would go off to work on a lyric, he would return to rehearsals only to find entirely new scenes improvised without his approval.[18] Kander remembers going back to his hotel room, flopping on the bed, and thinking, "I could die right here." He once physically had to drag Ebb out of the rehearsal hall, lest his partner and the enfant terrible director come to blows. Fosse's 1979 movie *All That Jazz* is a fictional account of his own experience working on *Chicago.* The single composer-lyricist character in the movie is allegedly a composite of Kander and Ebb, although on the surface he is much more Ebb than Kander. In any case, the depiction offended Ebb.[19] Many people, including Kander and Ebb, found Fosse's postoperative frame of mind to be darker than it had been before, and it started to adversely affect the tone of the musical. Jerry Orbach observed that "There was no room in Bobby's concept of the show for real sentiment. He wanted something with an undertone of corruption." Fosse's original staging of "Razzle Dazzle" was "orgiastic": he

Table 3.2. Preliminary and final score of *Chicago*

Original Score		Final Version of Score	
Song	Character(s)	Song	Character(s)
Act One		**Act One**	
"All That Jazz"*	Velma and boys	"All That Jazz"	Velma and boys
"Funny Honey"	Roxie	"Funny Honey"	Roxie
		"When You're Good to Momma"	Matron Morton
"Cell Block Tango"*	The girls	"Cell Block Tango"	The girls
"Ten Percent"*	Henry and Velma		
"No"*	Male quartet		
"All I Really Need"	Billy and chorus	"All I Really Need"	Billy and girls
"Rose Colored Glasses"*	Mary Sunshine	"A Little Bit of Good"	Mary Sunshine
"We Both Reached for the Gun"* (first versions)	Roxie, Billy, Mary, and chorus	"We Both Reached for the Gun" (third version)	Roxie, Billy, Mary and chorus
"Roxie"*	Roxie and boys	"Roxie"	Roxie and boys
"Pansy Eyes"*	Male quartet		
"I Can't Do It Alone"*	Velma	"I Can't Do It Alone"	Velma
"My Own Best Friend"*	Roxie and chorus	"My Own Best Friend"	Roxie and Velma (with chorus)
Act Two		**Act Two**	
"I Know a Girl"*	Velma	"I Know a Girl"	Velma
"Me and My Baby"	Roxie and boys	"Me and My Baby"	Roxie and boys
"Mister Cellophane"*	Amos	"Mister Cellophane"	Amos
"When Velma Takes the Stand"	Orchestra and quartet	"When Velma Takes the Stand"	Orchestra and quartet
"Razzle Dazzle"*	Billy, Roxie, Mary Sunshine, judge, jurors, and chorus	"Razzle Dazzle"	Billy and company
"Class"	Velma and Matron	"Class"	Velma and Matron
"It"*	Roxie and Velma	"Nowadays"	Roxie and Velma
"Loopin' the Loop"*	Roxie and Velma	"Hot Honey Rag"	Roxie and Velma

*Included on Kander and Ebb's demo recording.

had the chorus members copulating on the spiral staircases leading up to the orchestra platform above the cylindrical set.[20] The producers hated it, but Fosse agreed to restage the scene only when Orbach convinced him that he was missing the Brechtian subtlety intrinsic in the number.

The reviews in Philadelphia were devastating, sending the creative team back to the drawing board. They made many changes, but the hardest choice they had to make was to cut the character of Harry Glassman and his song "Ten Percent," which had been well received during performances. Since Glassman and Mama Morton were both parasitic characters, Fosse and the writers realized that one of them should be cut. After much deliberation, they decided to keep Matron Morton because she was a more integral part of the story.[21] It was at this point that Kander and Ebb composed the song "When You're Good to Mama," which offset the loss of "Ten Percent." Before *Chicago* reached Broadway, several other good numbers were cut in the service of the overall flow of the musical. In Philadelphia, *Chicago* featured a barbershop quartet, which sang "No, No, No"—a waltz in close harmony— while Roxie pleaded with Amos to put up $5,000 for her legal defense. The quartet returned later and sang "Pansy Eyes" as Roxie posed for a series of photographs arranged by Billy: one while embracing a group of nuns, another while accepting a bouquet from a boy on crutches, and another while accepting a puppy from a lonely lady.[22]

In Philadelphia, Roxie and Velma's double act, which constitutes the finale of *Chicago*, was not coming off as Fosse had hoped. They sang a well-matched pair of songs, "Loopin' the Loop"—which featured Gwen Verdon on saxophone and Chita Rivera on drums—and "It."[23] Despite the excellent music and lyrics of these numbers, the scene seemed too much like an amateur act, so Fosse asked for something more "glamorous in pretty gowns and kinda like the toast of the town." Kander and Ebb went back to their hotel and wrote "Nowadays." Ebb proudly recalled, "He loved us and loved the song, and everyone loved the song. . . . That's when we became heroes." A short dance section occurs in the middle of "Nowadays," sometimes called "R.S.V.P." The band conductor whistles a debonair melody, and Roxie and Velma sing "wa-wa" vocals, a holdover from "It." "Nowadays" segues into an upbeat dance routine entitled "Hot Honey Rag." Peter Howard, the rehearsal pianist and dance arranger for *Chicago*, composed "Hot Honey Rag" over the harmonic foundation of "Funny Honey."[24] Kander, Ebb, and Fosse salvaged "Loopin' the Loop" by using it for the overture to *Chicago*.[25]

Chicago opened at the 46th Street Theater on June 1, 1975, with Gwen

Verdon as Roxie, Chita Rivera as Velma Kelly, and Jerry Orbach as Billy Flynn. Barney Martin, best known as Morty Seinfeld, Jerry's father on *Seinfeld*, gave a strong performance as Amos, Roxie's hum-drum husband. The reviews were generally favorable, although many critics had trouble with the show's bleakness and cynicism. The most insightful statement about the musical appeared in a review by Stephen Farber: "Bob Fosse's love-hate letter to Broadway razzle dazzle—a valentine engraved in acid." Farber interprets Fosse's invective against the American tendency to treat criminals like celebrities as tantamount to accusing entertainers of being like killers: "The show blasts the ruthlessness, egomania and duplicity of performers, the coldbloodedness and opportunism of the promoters who merchandize and exploit them, as well as the fickleness and brutality of the vampire-like fans who feed on celebrities. . . . the intensity of the musical seemed to enjoy the form over content."[26] Walter Kerr failed to appreciate the vaudeville concept and felt that, unlike *Cabaret*, *Chicago* lacked the evil force to justify its gloomy point of view: "Al Capone wasn't Hitler and Cicero wasn't Munich." Clive Barnes dismissed the premise out of hand: "A comedy melodrama of a girl who shoots her lover and is then acquitted through the chicaneries of the Chicago criminal system—you can only wonder who ever thought it was suitable for a musical."[27] However, Barnes had a change of heart when Liza Minnelli later substituted for Verdon, describing this version as "Bob Fosse's Brechtian outpost of glamour, squalor and sublime discontent."[28] *Chicago* could not compete with *A Chorus Line*, which was playing two blocks away. It is ironic that the 1996 Broadway revival of *Chicago* is still running. In the fall of 2006, *Chorus Line* returned to Broadway for the first time. It will have to stay nearly as long as the original production to overtake *Chicago*'s record.

Kander and Ebb's Score

Kander and Ebb's score for *Chicago* has a singular sense of purpose, and the songs seem to be cut from the same cloth. The jazzy style of the score provides a metaphor for the corruption on display as well as creates a sense of time and place. A few musical features in particular suggest the 1920s: "blue" notes, minor mode inflections, melodies centering on the 6th scale degree, and syncopated rhythms. The bluesiest song in the score, "Funny Honey," reserves the evocative lowered 3rd of the blues scale for the cadence on "that funny honey of mine" right before the bridge. The first phrase, a rising chromatic line embedded into a repeated melodic fragment, drives toward the

Example 3.1. The 6th scale degree as melodic focal point in songs from *Chicago*: (a) "All I Care About Is Love"; (b) "We Both Reached for the Gun" (chorus); (c) "I Can't Do It Alone" (vamp); (d) "I Know a Girl" (verse); (e) "Me and My Baby"; (f) "Class"

(e) ROXIE:

Me and my ba - - - - by, my ba - by and me.

(f) VELMA:

What - e - ver hap-pened to fair deal-ing and pure eth-ic and nice man-ners?

lowered 7th scale degree, which pushes the music in a subdominant direction. A minor subdominant in the next measure sets up the "blues" cadence. The bridge, which starts, "He ain't no sheik," is in the relative minor.[29] The 6th scale degree is the melodic focal point of no fewer than six songs in *Chicago* (see example 3.1a–f) plus three new songs that Kander and Ebb composed for the film. Most of the excerpts in example 3.1 also incorporate syncopated rhythm. For instance, "We Both Reached for the Gun (example 3.1b) is a variation of a common figure in rags around 1925.[30] The secondary rag, as it is called, superimposes a group of three notes of equal duration over a steady beat in duple meter, the result being a constantly shifting accent pattern:

```
>       >       >       >       >
1   2   3   1   2   3   1   2   3   1   2   3   1   2   3
1       2       3       4       1       2       3       4
```

An example of secondary rag is found in the B section of Scott Joplin's *Pine Apple Rag*.[31] In "We Both Reached for the Gun," the pattern is displaced and truncated, starting on the third reiteration of "oh yes." The first beat of each triple eighth-note grouping is subdivided into sixteenth notes, the second of which is tied over the beat. The melody simply alternates between two pitches, which, coupled with the syncopated rhythmic, gives the impression that the ventriloquist dummy (Roxie) is mouthing to a broken record.

Over half of the seventeen songs in *Chicago*—as well as most of the cut-out songs and the numbers written for the film—either are in a minor key or incorporate pitches from the blues scale or minor scale.

Broadway Score	
Overture ("Loopin' the Loop")	shift from major to minor in the A phrase (mm. 5–8); bridge starts in relative minor
"All That Jazz"	lowered 3rd on final cadence of refrain

"Funny Honey"	lowered 3rd on final cadence of refrain; bridge in relative minor
"Cell Block Tango"	introduction in minor key; oscillation between major and minor harmonies
"When You're Good to Mama"	refrain begins in major but cadences in the parallel minor
"All I Care About"	bridge begins in minor subdominant
"Roxie"	lowered 3rd (blue note) on final cadence of the refrain
"I Can't Do It Alone"	minor inflection during the bridge
"Mister Cellophane"	shift to minor key mediant in verse; lowered 3rd on "never know I'm there"; final cadence on minor tonic
"Class"	shift to parallel minor in refrain; lowered 6th scale degree and minor iv on "ass"
"R.S.V.P." (dance break in "Nowadays")	lowered 3rd and 7th scale degrees (blue notes)
"Honey Rag"	minor inflected chord (based on harmonic progression of "Funny Honey")

Cutout Songs

"Ten Percent"	verse in minor key
"No, No, No"	bridge in minor key; minor inflection on "live"
Verse to "Roxie"	verse in minor key

Songs Written for the Film

"It's a Criminal Thing"	in minor key
"In Other Words . . . Chicago"	minor bridge

"When You're Good to Mama" and "Cell Block Tango" are full-fledged minor songs. Both have the tendency, however, to slip into the major mode. Occurring back to back early in act 1, they introduce the audience and Roxie to the prison world in which most of the story takes place. "Cell Block Tango" begins with a sultry introduction in the minor key, but the song starts in the parallel major key (example 3.2). The opening line moves along an axis stretching from the "blue" A-flat down to A-natural. The cross-relationship between

Example 3.2. "Cell Block Tango"

A-flat and A-natural creates a high degree of tonal ambiguity, but the chorus cadences definitely in F minor. The refrain starts out like a real blues number—four measures on the tonic chord followed by two measures in the subdominant—although it does not fully complete the twelve-bar-blues pattern. Kander and Ebb might have had W. C. Handy's "St. Louis Blues" (1914) in mind, which Bessie Smith recorded in 1925. Like Handy's song, the refrain of "Cell Block Tango" incorporates the habanera rhythm ("Spanish Tinge") discussed in reference to Scott Joplin's "Solace" in Chapter 1.

The introduction to "When You're Good to Mama," an orchestral fanfare in A major, accompanies Mama Morton's first entrance. The verse starts in the parallel minor and ends on a half cadence. A burlesque bump-and-grind vamp follows, but the first phrase of the song—a two-measure theme occurring three times in a descending sequence—starts out in the parallel major key (example 3.3). The melody quickly shifts back to the minor key, and, on the aphoristic ending of the line "Mama's good to you," the voice traces the bottom six notes of the F-sharp minor scale, skipping over B.

The unusual emphasis on the minor mode in *Chicago* is not just connected to the influence of the blues. It also carries implicit ethnic associations (Latino, African-American, and Jewish), which lie just beneath the surface of the story. Even before the twenties, Tin Pan Alley composers regularly wrote songs in the minor key. Jack Gottlieb has shown that this tendency derived from Jewish and Yiddish musical traditions. The identification of minor melodies with Jewish music was so strong that Cole Porter, the only non-Jewish Golden Era composer to conquer Broadway, confessed to Richard Rodgers that he consciously tried to write "Jewish music," by which Rodgers and Porter understood to mean languid minor melodies. Porter must have meant it, for he composed some of the greatest minor ballads in the musical theater repertory—for example, "So in Love" from *Kiss Me, Kate,* and "I Love Paris" from *Can-Can.* Broadway composers occasionally used minor keys to denote ethnicity, race, and otherness (for example, "Can't Help Lovin' That Man" from *Show Boat* and "Wintergreen for President" from *Of Thee I Sing*). In *Cabaret* (especially the film version) and *Chicago,* Kander and Ebb adopted the old practice.

It should be noted that Ebb's early drafts portray racial tension among the inmates, especially between Roxie and Velma. Roxie's lines are laced with racial epitaphs, a trait also found in Watkins's play, albeit to a lesser degree. Because Ebb had Chita Rivera in mind for Velma, he used her Latin-American ethnicity as the main target for Roxie's bigoted slurs (even though Velma's last name is Irish). For example, while feasting on the dinner sent to her by a secret admirer, Roxie goes out of her way to provoke Velma: "I'd offer ya some, but it ain't one of it [*sic*] enchiladas. . . . Don't you know anybody could send you dinner from the Palmer House? Some nice . . . bull fighter or somethin'?" Later, in the presence of Mary Sunshine, Roxie continues to antagonize Velma: "I find people of . . . Spanish origin very . . . jealous, don't you? It must be that hot climate. And all them bananas." These lines were

Example 3.3. "When You're Good to Mama"

eliminated during tryouts in Philadelphia, perhaps because they would have squelched any sympathy that the audience might have for Roxie.

The song "Ten Percent," although cut from the show after Philadelphia, provides a good case study of how Kander and Ebb subtly slipped traces of ethnic stereotypes into the score, as Watkins did with her character descriptions. It also sheds additional light on the composition of "When You're Good to Mama." Harry Glassman, the character who sings "Ten Percent," can be read as Jewish, if only because of his name and theatrical profession. In addi-

Example 3.4. "Ten Percent"

tion, musical details of "Ten Percent" mark him as a Jew. As Glassman first
enters the stage, the orchestra plays an ethnically tinged vamp in the minor
mode, with strong offbeat accents (example 3.4). Kander probably modeled
the vamp for "When You're Good to Mama" on this vamp. It is closely related to the opening measures of the "Money Song" from the film version of
Cabaret, sounding like a cross between Eastern European Klezmer music
and burlesque. Henry's opening melody outlines an inverted G minor triad,
with an emphasis on the minor sixth interval between D and B-flat. A figure
reminiscent of a cantorial trope on "The worm is here" centers on the interval
of a diminished third formed between the upper neighbor E-flat and C-sharp.

Such a melodic gesture has its roots in popular Yiddish song. The C-sharp in this example is borrowed from one of two prominent melodic types of Jewish folk music that contain an augmented second. This version contains a raised 4th scale degree, which forms the augmented second with the lowered 3rd of the minor scale.[32] An abrupt modulation to the major key and a broadening of the tempo occur during a grandiose melody on "I'm a theatrical agent," at which point Glassman performs an Italianate recitative. The refrain that follows is in the relative major and is evocative of the Charleston.

There is a historical precedent for the minor verse–major refrain structure of "Ten Percent." This harmonic relationship between verse and refrain was common in early popular Jewish-American music and reflects the process of acculturation of Jewish musicians: as Jack Gottlieb notes, "For while this [minor] verse portrayed the Jew in traditional garb, the chorus in major showed him off in American Cloth."[33] The syncopated rhythms (a symbol of the American vernacular and modernity, and the cause, as Watkins's Mary Sunshine suggests, of Roxie's crime) simultaneously reflect Glassman's theatrical vocation and his self-consciousness about his Jewish roots. The end of the chorus (on "ten percent") features a pre-cadential cantorial melisma crowned by a flat third, here intended as a "blue" note, as opposed to a borrowed pitch from Eastern European music.

With its verse in the minor key and jazzy refrain in the major, "Ten Percent" also epitomizes the cross-pollination of Jewish and African-American music in vernacular song in the twenties. Jewish Tin Pan Alley composers, none more important than George Gershwin, incorporated jazz elements into their music. There is, of course, an exploitative aspect to this sort of ethnic borrowing. As Samson Raphaelson claimed in his preface to the stage version of The Jazz Singer, "Jews are determining the nature and scope of jazz more than any other race—more than the Negroes, from whom they have stolen jazz and given it a new color and meaning."[34] When the role of Harry Glassman was excised from Chicago, the writers transferred the exploitative aspect of his character onto the role of Mama Morton. It is important to bear in mind that Sophie Tucker, the model for Matron Morton, was Jewish and performed in blackface. Thus, "When You're Good to Mama," which mixes jazz and features associated with Jewish music, reflects the exploitive practices of blackface singers like Tucker, Al Jolson, and Eddie Cantor—as well as Jewish composers. By association, Mama Morton is a thinly veiled stereotype of the avaricious Jewish businessman. Glassman's music acknowledges his ethnic roots, but Mama Morton sings what is intended as a jazz number disassociated from its African-American roots. Such a relationship is less pronounced when a black actress plays the role of Mama Morton, which is often the case in the current Broadway revival and which is the case in the film, which stars Queen Latifa as Morton. What remains strongly in place in these versions is the vaudeville associations with the part.

The Broadway Revival and Film

The City Center "Encores!" series has been one of the darlings of the New York theater establishment since its inception in 1991. It has presented semi-staged versions of musicals from the past with their original orchestrations, including *Fiorello!, The Boys from Syracuse, On a Clear Day You Can See Forever, Carnival, Damn Yankees,* and *The Apple Tree.* None of these shows generated the excitement surrounding the production of *Chicago,* which took place in May 1996. As Kander and Ebb entered the theater, "the atmosphere was all of a sudden electric. You could sense it almost before the show started." Ebb joked, "It was like we had invited everyone in the audience." Ann Reinking appeared as Roxie, a role she had played during the original Broadway run, Bebe Neuwirth as Velma, James Naughton as Billy Flynn, and Joel Grey as Amos.

The Encores's production spawned the Broadway revival, now in its tenth year, which in turn inspired the Academy-Award-winning film version in 2002. Reinking, Neuwirth, Naughton, and Grey all signed on to repeat their respective parts on Broadway, Walter Bobbie directed, and Reinking re-created Fosse's original choreography, thereby introducing his style to a new generation. Ironically, Kander and Ebb were happy but not surprised that their 1975 musical still had some relevance. Not lost on Ebb were the headlines that made their "jaundiced worldview" seem almost fashionable, like the O. J. Simpson trial and the Monica Lewinsky scandal.[35] Kander humorously noted that the revival proved that "corruption never goes out of fashion," and saw a historical connection to the successful revival of *Pal Joey,* which was first considered "just too mean."

Marty Richards, one of the original Broadway producers of *Chicago,* was the driving force behind the film. He had purchased the movie rights for about $500,000 during the final months of the original Broadway run. What followed was an arduous, twenty-seven-year period of ups and downs leading to the 2003 Academy Award for best motion picture.[36] So many directors, actors, and writers were considered for the film that its success is nothing short of a miracle. Richards knew that turning *Chicago* into an effective film was not just a simple matter of reconfiguring the songs in cinematic terms and opening up the physical space of the Broadway version. To successfully transfer *Chicago* to film, the writer and director would have to find a filmic equivalent for Fosse and Ebb's concept. They would have to find, to quote Scott McMillin, "its own version of the theatre's fixed space." The Broadway version of *Chicago* draws attention to itself as a theatrical experience framed inside the proscenium of a vaudeville theater. Film can go anywhere, and the audience is willing to go along.[37]

Richards's first choice for director was Fosse, who agreed only after much arm-twisting. When Fosse died of a heart attack in 1987, Richards lost all hope of getting the film made, but, a few years later, he got a call from Harvey Weinstein, the co-chairman of Miramax Films, who was interested in reviving the project. They signed an agreement in 1994.[38] Finding a new director who was agreeable to all parties was a long and arduous process. Richards wanted Baz Luhrmann, the director of *Strictly Ballroom,* but Luhrmann turned him down for fear of being compared to Fosse. Herbert Ross agreed to direct the film and stuck with the project for over a year, until he saw the Broadway revival. During this period, Larry Gelbart agreed to write the screenplay. In 1998 Richards turned to the director Nicholaus Hytner and sent him Gelbart's screenplay. Hytner in turn asked Wendy Wasserstein to write a new screenplay. Miramax did not like either one. Word spread at the time that Goldie Hawn would play Roxie and Madonna Velma,[39] but Hytner felt that Hawn was too old for the part. He wanted Nicole Kidman for Roxie, but he soon left the project. Richards considered several other directors, including Milos Forman, Martin Scorsese, Alan Parker, David Fincher, and Robert Iscove, but eventually the studio hired Rob Marshall to direct and choreograph the film.

Ironically, Miramax courted Marshall for *Rent,* but he had his hopes pinned on *Chicago* and won over the studio with his concept for the film. Marshall brought a contemporary vision to the musical. More importantly, he came up with a filmic analogy for the vaudeville concept: all the songs occur in Roxie's imagination. The film medium allowed him to shift back and forth fluidly between the reality of the prison and a world of fantasy. Richards, who admired the use of this technique in the television series *Ally McBeal,* was confident that it would work for the film.[40] With Marshall signed, the studio and Richards still had to find a screenwriter, and Miramax suggested Bill Condon, the writer of *Gods and Monsters* and *The Usual Suspects.*

Marshall and Condon understood that the postmodern Hollywood musical needed to incorporate music more realistically than did its Broadway counterpart, and that one does not hear, or listen to, songs in film in the same way as one does in a Broadway musical. The different medium reorients the listener's relationship to music.[41] As Fosse had done for *Cabaret*, Marshall and Condon established "a diegetic world in which the audience can recognize that song and dance are valid modes of expression."[42] The film rests on the premise that Roxie imagines all of the musical numbers as a showbiz fantasy in which she is the star. This format maintained the performative framework of vaudeville but also provided the verisimilitude demanded by the film medium. Although a brilliant application of the film medium, this idea, as McMillin claims, "is a far cry from the metaphorical use of the stage in the musical as a space that stands for the places of the Chicago justice system."[43] What is lost in the new interpretation is the Brechtian disorienting effect of the stage version, which constantly draws attention to the artifice of theater. But the film succeeded in dealing with the reluctance of average filmgoers to accept the innate staginess of Broadway musicals and to overlook the fact that people do not break into song in real life. Marshall and Condon deconstructed Fosse and Ebb's material and humanized Roxie in a way that the stage musical never attempted. In effect, they focused on Roxie as the point-of-view character, whereas Fosse himself provided the point of view for the Broadway version.

An overview of Larry Gelbart's and Wendy Wasserstein's screenplays for the film illustrates why Marshall and Condon's works so well. Gelbart purposely avoided a film equivalent for the vaudeville framework and in general was not comfortable devising fantasy sequences. He sought cinematic realism, an aesthetic stance that kept him from fully embracing the proper frame of mind for the project. For instance, the female inmates in his version are scantily clad not to create a steamy sexuality with metaphorical potential, as Fosse did, but rather to reflect the insufferably hot conditions of the prison. Gelbart felt that the style should have a hard, cynical edge—not the sort for which Fosse was famous but more like that found in the films *Public Enemy* and *Little Caesar*. Whereas Marshall and Condon's version imparts a modern attitude about the topic without making any contemporary references, Gelbart wanted explicitly to link the theme of the story to modern times by starting with "Nowadays," the last song in the Broadway version, heard as underscoring during an opening montage made up of news clippings from the trials of O. J. Simpson, Lorena Bobbit, Michael Jackson, Mike Tyson, and the Menendez brothers. Segments from television tabloid news shows, such as "A Current Affair" and "Entertainment Tonight," are interspersed throughout. The bandleader counts out the beats "5, 6, 7, 8," taking us back to Chicago of the 1920s.[44] Another change that he made to the story involves the Hungarian convict Hunyak, the only unequivocally innocent prisoner in the story. She dies not by hanging as in the Broadway version but in the electric chair. This change epitomizes the flatness of Gelbart's version. On Broadway (and ultimately in the film), Hunyak's hanging, witnessed by her sister inmates, is a powerful visual image, and it marks a turning point for Roxie, who finally takes seriously the possibility of her own execution.

Gelbart's approach to the music was too literal, and it limited the ways in which he incorporated the songs, which have surprisingly little dramatic effect. For instance, in his second treatment, Billy Flynn, for whom he envisioned John Travolta, sings "All I Care About Is Love" after we already know all that there is to know about his character.[45] "Roxie" is reduced to a conventional wanting song, which Roxie sings between signing her confession and going to prison. "Cell Block Tango" occurs after Roxie and Velma meet, thus providing no suspense about the prison world into which Roxie is about to enter. Matron Mama sings "When You're Good to Mama" directly to Roxie while squeezing her for money, thus robbing the song of its metaphorical value. In "We Both Reached for the Gun" Roxie, now nobody's dummy, simply answers the barrage of questions from the reporters herself. By way of contrast, Marshall and Condon found an effective way to incorporate the majority of the songs from the Broadway score.[46]

Wendy Wasserstein's version is no more effective than Gelbart's. It is a movie-within-a-movie told by Velma in an interview with Frankie Callahan, a female reporter who covered the trial and built her reputation thereupon. Throughout the film, we hear Velma introducing the scenes, starting with "The night it all started, I was playing a joint called Butch O'Malley's." Only at the end of the film is it revealed that Velma is giving an interview. Wasserstein tried unnecessarily to strengthen the connection between the action and the characters' motivation. She invented a district attorney named Felix Fingerman, a son of Russian immigrants who wants to rid the city of corruption. Fingerman goes after Roxie's conviction in order to set an example to other potential murderesses, and he believes he has an open-and-shut case. However, the mayor, who plays golf with Billy Flynn, pressures him to lay off the case. Once he realizes that pursuing Roxie is not in his best interest, he goes after Hunyak because he anticipates another easy conviction.

Mama Morton, an ex-theatrical agent, helps Roxie because she sees her as her ticket back into show business. During the end credits Wasserstein revives the old film convention of providing summaries about the ultimate fate of each character. Frankie ("Francine") Callahan wins the Pulitzer Prize for her book, Chicago, which is the story told to her by Velma. The movie version of her book, the one we are watching, is a big hit. Roxie attends the premiere of the film with Cary Grant, Velma with Clark Gable. Mama Morton purchases the William Morris Talent Agency. Flynn wins in his bid to become mayor of Chicago. Felix Fingerman is arrested and exposed as a communist infiltrator.

Casting of the film was as difficult as signing a director and coming up with a workable screenplay. Back when Hytner was working on the project, both Bette Midler and Pam Grier were considered for Morton. At one point, the trio of Rosie O'Donnell, John Travolta, and Nathan Lane were envisioned in the roles of Mama Morton, Billy Flynn, and Amos Hart, respectively. Toni Collette was a contender for Roxie, and Kathy Bates for Morton. Miramax tried to get Brittany Spears to play a small part, but Marshall and Richards vehemently objected. When casting began in earnest, Richards wanted Kevin Kline to play the role of Billy Flynn, but the actor was unwilling to take on any negative roles. Richards's second choice, Kevin Spacey, also turned down the role. Richard Gere agreed to play the role but would not audition, as was also the case for Catherine Zeta-Jones and Renée Zellweger.[47]

In the buildup to the release of the film, the press made much of the fact that Catherine Zeta-Jones, Renée Zellweger, and Richard Gere were appearing in a musical. However, only Zellweger lacked significant stage musical experience. Raymond Knapp has argued that her lack of any musical theater experience was one of the film's strengths. "The strategic casting shakes the characters loose from the glib dance-based personae of the stage versions, allowing then—particularly Roxie—to achieve a kind of reality that the highly stylized Broadway mounting categorically denies them, for the 'real world' of more naturalistic film is where they most seem to belong for audiences familiar with their other work."[48] Not only was Zellweger's inexperience effective in the role of Roxie, but it also allowed for the film to find itself in cinematic terms. The brilliant editing of the film makes Zellweger's dancing appear seamless and polished, as no single shot takes in enough movement to reveal her lack of dancing experience.

Kander and Ebb were generally pleased with the film. However, Ebb had one major complaint regarding the opening setup.

There's a terrific mistake in the movie. I kept quiet about it . . . it makes me crazy, but it's there. It doesn't make any sense. She [Velma] gets out of her car. She walks into a nightclub. She washes her hands. She tears a sheet. I mean, obviously you're supposed to think that she just committed the crime. He says, "where's your sister?" "Oh, I'm gonna do it alone tonight." Another spotlight comes on. She comes out and sings "All That Jazz." Where did that act come from? This is Velma. And all the boys appear. Where the hell are you? Who is that girl? Later, you hear in "Cell Block Tango," "I was in Cicero with my sister. I went out . . . I came back and shot em." So what's that beginning ["All that Jazz"]? Where was she then? It makes *no sense*. . . . And then John writes *reams* about what a wonderful opening that is. It's not. I mean, it is. It's a wonderful number, but it's not dramatically sound. It's not logical. It's not true. It's not right. And it drove me nuts.

Despite this objection, Ebb, like Kander, was happy that the film was such a big hit. Kander and Ebb did not participate in the development or shooting of the film, but they did retain control of the musical material. Late in the process, Miramax Studio hired Janet Jackson to write and record a song to play during the credits, hoping to snag an Academy-Award nomination for best song. Harvey Weinstein was so determined to use Jackson that he even asked Kander and Ebb to collaborate with her, an indignity reminiscent of what the writers suffered during the filming of *Funny Lady* (see Appendix). They flatly refused and wrote "I Move On," which, in the final cut of the film, the two divas sing during the credits. (Sony did include Jackson's song, "Love Is a Crime," recorded by Anastacia, on the soundtrack, and Kander and Ebb were powerless to do anything about it.)[49] "I Move On" received an Academy-Award nomination, although it lost to "Lose Yourself" from the film 8 *Mile*.[50]

Chicago is one of the most unsympathetic musicals ever written, second only to *The Threepenny Opera* in its cynical view of humanity. It takes great pleasure in attacking the mythology of fame in America. It has no love story, and every attempt to include one, such as a request by Miramax Studio, was ultimately rejected. The darkness of *Chicago* may account for why ticket sales for the original production paled in comparison with those for *A Chorus Line*. It is ironic that *A Chorus Line*, which recently returned to Broadway, comes off today like a period piece, whereas *Chicago* seems timely. *A Chorus Line* is about feeling, and we sympathize with each of the young dancers. *Chicago* lacks the warmth of *A Chorus Line*. Only Amos and Hunyak are honest human beings, and they alone deserve our sympathy, but the system destroys them.[51] The film, as Knapp claims, "performs a major act of rescue, making the reality of Roxie's limited perspective and resultant pain sufficiently vivid, through montage, that we can take her seriously as someone who suffers and may not be discounted as *merely* cynical." Ebb probably never looked at the film in these terms, and if he did he probably would not have approved of the change. Of course, the film offers a healthy dose of cynicism mainly through the realistic scenes when Roxie is not imagining herself a star.

The success of the film spurred the making of other movie musicals, such as *Dream Girls*, *Hairspray*, and *Sweeney Todd*. *Chicago* had a relatively small budget of $45 million, but it grossed over $450 million. Kander and Ebb received little actual revenue from the film, though, and Richards claims that Miramax owes him money, for which he has initiated legal proceedings.[52] Despite this unpleasantness, Richards has few regrets. He has confessed, "This picture has been like a present, a joy, but it's always come with a little bit of heartache."

CHAPTER 4

Fred Without John and John Without Fred

Can you imagine how lucky [our] generation was. That we, all of us, got a chance. . . . Jerry Herman did an Off Broadway show. You could do that. You didn't have to mortgage your mother to do it.

—JOHN KANDER

BEFORE KANDER AND EBB FIRST MET EACH OTHER IN 1962, THEY each worked with many different writers in the hope of discovering the right partner for a long-term collaboration. When they started working together, they did not yet realize that they had found in each other what they were looking for. There was never a definitive moment in which they consciously agreed to a permanent collaboration. They were simply having too good a time to bother trying to work with anyone else. Ebb even turned down an opportunity to be Richard Rodgers's lyricist for *Rex*, and Kander refused to work with one of his closest friends when it was suggested that they write a musical together without Ebb.[1] When it came to writing musicals, Kander and Ebb were monogamous. However, throughout their career they each took on several extracollaborative projects.[2] Kander wrote music for television and film and occasional vocal compositions. Ebb wrote and produced concerts and television specials. These projects kept them active in between musicals and perhaps provided a buffer during trying times.

Ebb's independent projects are an extension of the work he did with Kander in that they express a fascination with the entertainment world (theater, television, movies, nightclubs) and usually incorporate a play-within-a-play format. For instance, most of his television specials were backstage musicals of sorts. In these independent projects, he was most comfortable when speaking as a showbiz insider, and through the voice of a Broadway or Hollywood diva. Kander has always been more catholic in his artistic interests and aesthetic tastes. He enjoyed composing music for dramatic films, dance companies, spoken plays, and classically trained singers, and he experimented with eclectic styles and techniques. Kander believed that art should rise above the mundane and aspire to reach the audience on an emotional level. Throughout his career, Kander has gravitated toward projects that reflect this philosophy and move him personally.

Fred Ebb

Ebb loved to entertain his friends with light verse, limericks, and other short poetic forms on topics ranging from Herman Wouk to King Lear to Mahatma Gandhi to the Lunts.[3] He aimed for economy and searched for the most direct way to land a joke, as in this homage to the composer of *Guys and Dolls:* "No one is greater than Loesser." Encouraged by his friends, in the late 1940s Ebb started to experiment with popular song lyrics. He submitted some of these lyrics to record companies in the Brill Building, then the epicenter of the pop music industry. Several staff composers set Ebb's lyrics, including Larry Coleman, Norman Leyden, Red Evans, Les Paul, Michel Emer, Paul Giasson, Ben Allen, Dick Charles, and Bernie Weston, although Ebb had little if any contact with any of them. Ebb also coauthored a few pop lyrics with Joan Javits, the niece of the late Senator Jacob Javits of New York, and wrote a few songs with the as yet undiscovered Charles Strouse: "Drummer Boy," "Calypso Rock," and "One Small Voice."[4]

Before Kander, Ebb's chief collaborators were Phil Springer and Paul Klein. Springer taught Ebb the craft of songwriting, and Klein was the first composer with whom Ebb wrote musical theater material. Ebb first met Klein in 1951. They wrote nearly one hundred pop songs, ranging from ballads to special material for nightclub performers.[5] One of the ballads, "Are You a Dreamer?" demonstrates Ebb's ability to develop a simple idea over the course of the song and end with a surprise finish.

Are you a dreamer?
With dreams to spare?
Do you build castles
High in the air?

Do you believe someday a love will come to you?
Chasing the clouds away,
Changing skies to blue?

Do you imagine,
When you're alone
Somewhere there's someone
To call your own?

And do you even think you'll know the way he'll sigh?
Are you a dreamer?
Well,
So am I!

"Are You a Dreamer" contains several pop-song clichés from as early as the twenties—"build castles high in the air" and "chasing the clouds away"—but the shift to the first person in the last line gives the song an unexpected poignancy. As simple as this lyric might seem, it anticipates some of Ebb's later songs, such as "Meeskite," that tell a long story in several verses building to an unexpected conclusion. Several artists recorded Ebb and Klein's songs, including the Mills Brothers, who made a single of their first published song, "Every Second Of." "That Do Make It Nice," which Eddie Arnold recorded, won the publishers' Country and Western Award.[6] They also wrote the second act of a musical revue called *Isn't America Fun* (1960), which starred Shelly Berman.[7] Ebb spoke only anecdotally and selectively about this period of his career. The one fact that he liked to share was that Judy Garland recorded his song "Heartbroken" (1953).

Ebb's specialty material reflects an era in which coffeehouses, cabarets, and nightclubs were in vogue and provided young songwriters an opportunity to hear their material in front of a live audience. Ebb tested a broad range of offbeat ideas, anything for a laugh. For example, in "Here Comes the Bride," a song he wrote with Paul Klein, a bride blurts out, "If I'd gone for that damn operation / This might never have come to pass." Ebb experimented with political satire in "I'm So Happy," a song about life behind the Iron Curtain in which three Russian cosmonauts sing, "Not so young, spot on lung, / Only yesterday, my wife was hung." Ebb also enjoyed dabbling in the sort of double entendres and inner rhymes that Noël Coward and Cole Porter did so well. "Civilized" is one of many examples.

> I enjoy the South of France
> and a fly by night romance
> Almost anything in pants has me hypnotized,
> I'm so
> Civilized!

Better still is the lyric for "Oh John," which Ebb created by systematically reducing a six-word sentence to a single word.

> Oh John, please don't kiss me.
> Oh John, please don't kiss.
> Oh John, please don't
> Oh John, please
> Oh John,
> Oh!

In 1959 Ebb spent the summer working at the playhouse at Camp Tamiment. This experience was seminal to Ebb's development as a musical theater writer. Also in attendance that summer were Paul Klein, Mary Rodgers [Guettel], Woody Allen, Dorothy Loudon, Christopher Hewett, Bob Dishy, Virginia Vestoff, Jonathan Tunick, and Gary Geld. As was the custom, the playhouse presented one new show each week during the first half of the summer and repeated some of them, often in a revised form, during the second half. Ebb contributed material each week and also appeared in a number of sketches. Unfortunately, little of the material that Ebb wrote has survived, but according to programs for 1959 he worked on about six sketches and wrote lyrics for about twenty songs. The Tamiment Library, housed at New York University, contains only a few of Ebb's lyrics: "I Said to Love," sketches for "Waltz with Me" (marked "Three Echoes" on the manuscript) and "The Philosophers," and a musical manuscript of "Mr. Klein." "Waltz with Me," conceived by Christopher Hewett, is a macabre story about a child who hears music in the room where his grandfather died. Death in the form of a woman appears and waltzes with the boy's father. When the dance is done, the father is discovered dead. "The Philosophers," a much lighter skit, features four beatniks in a San Francisco coffeehouse who espouse the philosophy that "Negative Thinking" is superior to Zen Buddhism, Dianetics, and Yoga.

Tamiment introduced Ebb to many of the actors and writers who figured later on in his career, such as Bob Dishy, the original Harry in *Flora, the Red Menace*, and Norman Martin, the coauthor of the book for *70, Girls, 70*. At Tamiment, Martin wrote a skit called "Watch Out for Mr. Klein," which gives new meaning to the term "sexual harassment."[8] The Tamiment program does not credit Ebb with this skit, but a lyric credited to Ebb exists in his papers, as does a recording of him performing it. The scene takes place in a department store, where a new model of the sportswear line receives the advice to beware of her male bosses:

> So you're the new model they picked for the junior line
> I can tell right away you're gonna do just fine
> You'll like the place, I'm sure of it
> You'll like the bosses, too
> You'll meet all twenty-six of them
> Before the week is through
> But because I know you're new here
> And I don't suppose you've checked
> Let me give you some idea of what you can expect
>
> Mr. Bernstein gets a yen
> For a quick kiss now and then
> Just watch out for Mr. Klein, he pinches
> Mr. Schwartz'll make you groan
> Cause he thinks he's Myron Cohen
> Just watch out for Mr. Klein, he pinches
> Mr. Segal likes to practice the Pachanga
> So you'll dance amidst the wrapping and the twine
> Though his dancing's far from great
> You'll at least be losing weight
> Just watch out for Mister Klein.[9]

Several years later, Ebb again worked with Martin when they contributed material to the Off-Broadway revue *Put It in Writing* (1963), which opened at the Lucille Lortel Theatre. The *New York Times* critic Howard Taubman, who found the revue's topicality tasteless and ineffective, singled out Ebb and Norman Martin's contribution, a song called "Emmy Lou," for special praise. The song "pays its respects to the storms in the South. Jane Connell as Emmy Lou is a sweet little thing with blond braids who's out on a backyard swing with three young admirers. They sing a ballad whose refrain is, "Who's gonna take you to the lynchin' Saturday night, Emmy Lou? Miss Connell, a versatile comic performer, gives Emmy Lou, the Mississippi belle whose boy-friends cannot find toys lethal enough to amuse her sadistic tastes, the keen edge of slashing satire."[10]

While at Tamiment Ebb also collaborated with Mary Rodgers Guettel and Jay Thompson.[11] In previous summers, Guettel collaborated exclusively with Marshall Barer, but in 1959 Ebb filled in for Barer when he was having problems working. Ebb and Thompson wrote a skit called "The Happy Medium" (variously titled "Tiger, Tiger" and "Tina and the Tiger"), a backstage look at a television production of "The Lady and the Tiger." Rodgers and Barer wrote the songs.[12] Dorothy Loudon, Virginia Vestoff, and Bob Dishy starred in the skit, and Ebb appeared in the role of Smithers. "The Happy Medium" may be Ebb's first piece with a show-within-a-show format.[13] It is structured like *Kiss Me, Kate*, with segments from "The Lady and the Tiger" alternating with scenes about the triangular romantic relationships among the actors and unsolicited advice from the sponsors.[14] When Rodgers and Ebb returned to New York after the close of the season, they worked on a musical called *Carte Blanche*, which was based on a true story about a boy who charged thousands of dollars to his parents' credit card without their knowledge. They wrote a few numbers, but when Rodgers showed them to Hal Prince, he urged her to find a more talented lyricist. It was clearly one of Prince's few misjudgments in a long and distinguished Broadway career.

Musicals with Paul Klein

Ebb and Klein chose for their first musical a story about a mother whose son is sentenced to hang. It probably never occurred to them that something a bit more uplifting might be easier for two unknown writers to get produced. The musical, *Morning Sun*, is based on a 1952 short story by the Cincinnati-born Irish-American author Mary Deasy (1914–1980).[15] Ebb was drawn to the story because he saw in it a parallel to modern life: "The mother fears that her oldest son will desert her the way her husband did. They can't communicate with each other. It's the same problem many people have today."[16] Ebb and Klein started working on the musical shortly after the story first appeared, but any chance of a production was delayed because CBS had tied up the rights.

Either too busy with other projects or too distracted by the unknown fate of *Morning Sun*, Ebb and Klein did not write another musical until 1959, perhaps inspired by their summer at Tamiment.[17] They chose a source as different from *Morning Sun* as possible, Emily Kimbrough's *It Gives Me Great Pleasure*. Ebb co-wrote the book with Keith McClelland, about whom nothing is known. They wrote three different versions, two of which exist in script form, one dated July and one November, and a detailed plot outline. The plots differ, but a synopsis of any one of these versions is enough to give an idea of what the writers had in mind.

An author named Louise McKinley is on a book tour to promote her latest opus, *Permanent Values in Marriage*. At a stop in Idaho, she meets Harry Weightman, the owner of a chain of exercise gyms, who has organized a contest to find the scrawniest man for the purpose of a television promotional campaign. The winner will appear on Harry's program in New York and have his meager physique transformed into an Atlas. Al, the man who wins, is the editor of a local newspaper. Louise is impressed with his writing talent and urges him to turn down the prize and pursue a literary career. When Harry gets wind of Louise's meddling, he threatens to sue Al for breach of contract. Back in New York, Louise and Harry continue their feud, but they eventually give in to their mutual attraction. The script for this version contains lyrics for fourteen songs, although no music has been found.

Act 1:
    "It Gives Me Great Pleasure"
    "About the Author"
    "Welcome"
    "That's Out, Forget It"
    "I Must Have Done Something Wonderful" (reused for *Simon Says*)
    "The Honorable Thing"
    "Whatever Happened to Me?"
    "Him"
    "The Sweetest Potato in Idaho"
Act 2:
    "Travelogue"
    "Gain It or Lose It, But Use It"
    "That's Out, Forget It" (reprise)
    "I Wrote the Book"
    "I Must Have Done Something Wonderful" (reprise)
    "May I Have the Next One?"
    "When You Grow Up"
    "It Gives Me Great Pleasure" (reprise)

Ebb, Klein, and McClelland attempted to interest a producer in *It Gives Me Great Pleasure* (although it is not clear which version they peddled), but no one came forth with the funding. The score, at least, made a positive impression on Martin Tahse.

> Dear Fred:
> It was a difficult decision to make, my decision not to do IT GIVES ME GREAT PLEASURE, and I made it with quite a heavy heart. All of my reservations are with the book, because I was greatly impressed with the contributions you and Paul made in the musical department. In fact I was so impressed that I told Dick [Seff] I would be the first producer to knock on his door for your talents when I find a book possibility. Let us hope it will be soon.
> Kindest regards and all best wishes.
> Cordially, Martin
> Martin Tahse[18]

Tahse eventually made good on his promise. In the meantime, Ebb and Klein joined other Tamiment alumni, including Mary Rodgers, Woody Allen, Jerry Herman, Jay Thompson, and Norman Martin, in contributing original material to the revue *From A to Z*, which Tahse produced. It opened on Broadway on April 20, 1960. Buoyed by their first Broadway credit, Ebb and Klein decided to write a second musical, *Simon Says*.

Dick Seff, the talent scout with MCA mentioned in Tahse's letter quoted above, introduced Ebb and Klein to a writer named Lionel Wilson. Wilson and Ebb co-wrote the script in 1962, and Wilson wrote a new version in 1964 because Tahse was planning to produce it. *Simon Says* is one of several musicals from the era that satirize the corporate business world (for example, *"How to Succeed in Business Without Really Trying"*). The 1962 version of *Simon Says* is a modern takeoff on *Alice's Adventures in Wonderland*, set in the world of advertising.[19] Alice Hammersmith, a commercial artist, has left her provincial home of Sequoia Falls, Idaho, to come to New York. She finds employment with an advertising company after the elevator she is riding in plummets several floors into the zany world of Keen Kartoon. She and her boss, Doug Kibby, fall in love, but their relationship suffers many setbacks. The title character, Simon, is a cartoon figure that Alice had created before coming to New York and that she now uses to snag an account. In the 1962 version of *Simon Says*, Alice hoodwinks Doug in order to advance her career; in the 1964 version Doug tricks Alice into allowing Keen Kartoon to use the Simon cartoon. An extant demo recording, which corresponds to the later version, contains fourteen numbers.[20]

"I Wonder What It's Like"
"Sequoia Falls"
"Very Important Person"
Dance
"Out of a Clear Blue Sky"
"It's a Living"
"I Must Have Done Something Wonderful"
"Little One"
"Simon Says"
"My Kind of People"
"Just Forget About Love"
"Think"
"Let Me Say It Over and Over Again"
"Gotta Be Busy"

It should be noted that both *It Gives Me Great Pleasure* and *Simon Says* anticipate Kander and Ebb's 1980 musical *Woman of the Year* (discussed in Chapter 7) in several ways. They are both are about a successful woman who inadvertently emasculates the man she loves. The plot of *Simon Says* foreshadows the rocky relationship between Sam and Tess in *Woman of the Year* and features a cartoon character who, like Sam's Tessie Cat, sings and dances with one of the leads. The musical contains a song called "The Two of Us," which is remarkably similar to the song of the same title in *Woman of the Year*. Another song from *Simon Says*, "It's a Living," has a built-in encore, a vaudeville device that Ebb reused for "The Grass Is Always Greener." In *It Gives Me Great Pleasure*, Louise McKinley arrives in Idaho to receive the Woman of the Year Award, and two of the songs share titles with songs in *Woman of the Year*, "Woman of the Year" and "I Wrote the Book."

At some point in the fifties, Ebb and Klein played *Morning Sun* for Frank Loesser, whose manager, Mike Sukin, was so impressed that he decided to promote the work for them. A few years later, when Tahse accidentally overheard the score for *Morning Sun*, he contacted T. Edward Hambleton, one of the owners of the Phoenix Theatre, and together they produced the musical. Nearly a chamber opera, *Morning Sun* is one of a series of "offbeat little show[s]" that flourished during the sixties and that provided an alternative to the "'bourgeois' Broadway style," to use Ethan Mordden's phrase.[21] Set in post–Civil War America, *Morning Sun* centers on the hanging of a young man, Rome, who, like his father before him, left home in search of excitement. He allegedly kills a man in a barroom brawl. His mother, a dogmatic,

Bible-thumping woman whose husband had abandoned the family to fight in the war, brings Rome's siblings to witness their older brother hang for his crime, hoping to use the experience as an object lesson on righteousness. Deasy tells the story through the eyes of the mother's only daughter, who describes the walk from the train station to the town square, where the scaffolding has been constructed for the execution of her brother, and then back to the station.

Ebb had to come up with a story line and flesh out the characters, including Rome. He invented a love interest for Rome, a seventeen-year-old woman named Melissa, who waits patiently for him to be released from prison. Deasy never states whether Rome is guilty, but Ebb leaves little doubt that it was Rome who delivered the fatal blow, although he entered the fight in the first place only to defend his friend, a character named John Atzel. Both boys are initially charged with the murder, but Atzel's influential father gets him released from jail. Rome, at one time the favorite of everyone in town, is sacrificed by the townspeople for the killing. The mother still harbors anger toward her dead husband and is unable to divorce these feelings from her literal interpretation of the Bible. While visiting Rome in jail, she confronts him in what might be one of the most unrelenting scenes in musical theater. Ebb based this scene on a brief passage in Deasy's novel in which Rome's sister mentions the mother's visit to the jail and notes that thereafter things changed.

MOTHER: Did you strike the man who died?
ROME: Ma . . .
MOTHER: Answer me.
ROME: I can't. It'll come out wrong.
MOTHER: Did you?
ROME: Set down, Ma. I'll tell you everythin.'
MOTHER: Did you?
ROME: Yes.
(The Mother closes her eyes. She raises her head as if in silent prayer)
Ma, let me talk to you, please. Let me.
(She stands, eyes shut)
I just stepped in the fight to . . . stop it, like. I never meant to hurt that man. I didn't even know him.
MOTHER: (even)
The discretion of a man deferreth his anger, and it is his glory to pass over a transgression.
ROME: It was an accident.

MOTHER: The Lord taketh pleasure in them that fear him, in those that hope in his mercy. He lifteth up the meek, he casteth the wicked down to the ground.

ROME: I never meant to hurt anybody.

MOTHER: (Opening her eyes. To Rome, quiet)
You're lyin.'

ROME: I ain't.

MOTHER: When you lifted your hand to stop that man, was there wrath in you, Rome? Was there anger in you?

ROME: You're twistin' it.

MOTHER: I'm seein' it.

ROME: It was an accident.

MOTHER: Was there murderin' rage in you, Rome? Answer me.

ROME: Don't be the avengin' angel, Ma. Help me.

MOTHER: I will. I will. If you answer 'no' to me now. Did you lift a hand in anger? Was there murderin' rage in you?

ROME: Don't.

MOTHER: Answer.

ROME: Yes. That's what I have to say. Yes, yes, yes.

MOTHER: Thou shalt not lift a hand in anger. A man of great wrath suffers punishment. That's the word of the Lord. All your life that's what I've tried to make you know. But you wouldn't learn, Rome. You wouldn't learn.

The mother's moral argument crumbles when she confuses her husband's actions with her son's.

ROME: Please Ma, for once, don't be what you are.

MOTHER: (Turning, screaming)
I am what your father made me!

ROME: (Rome turns away. He walks to the bars and clutches them.)
Leave my father out of it. I loved him. Leave me that.

MOTHER: I loved him more.
. . .
You are guilty. And you'll be punished. Punished as he should have been.

This confrontation leads directly to the mother's decision to bring Thad and Rome's other siblings to witness the hanging, believing that the sight of their brother's execution will prevent the same thing from happening to them.

Act 2 focuses on the growing conflict between the mother and Thad, who defies his mother by running away from home in order to save Rome. However, he is too young and physically weak to make it beyond the outskirts of town. After the hanging in the final scene, Thad assails his mother—"Damn your evil heart! Witch!"—and accuses her of turning her back on Rome not for God but for herself: "If God's your only friend, Ma, then damn Him too! Damn God for lovin' you!" When she strikes him, Thad shouts, "Is there mur-derin' rage in you, Ma!" This is a scene of Ebb's own invention. In the short story, Thad vomits on the street while walking back to the train station. He cries out "If I was a man!" as he smashes his fist into a brick wall. *Morning Sun* is brutal musical theater and it portends Ebb's growing interest in racy, dark topics. However, the musical is unforgivingly dark. There is no relief from the bleakness of the story, rarely any humor, and not enough nuance of character. It was a good lesson for Ebb, who later with Kander devised more effective and entertaining ways to present such serious topics.

No written score for *Morning Sun* has been found, and the musical was never commercially recorded, but an extant demo recording attests to the inventiveness of the score. The songs are sophisticated, vocally demanding, and dramatically wrenching.

Act 1:[22]
 "Morning Sun" (Rome)
 "This Heat" (Mother)
 "Tell Me Goodbye" (Rome and Mother)
 ["Rome's Journey" (Rome and Company)]
 "New Boy in Town" (Townspeople)
 "Good as Anybody" (Rome and John)
 "Mr. Chigger" (Mother, Mary, Thad, and Halleck)
 "The Pebble Waltz" (dance)
 "Follow Him" (Mother)
 "Missouri Mule" (Caller and Townspeople)
 ["Rome's Dance" (Rome and Woman)]
 "Square Dance" (Townspeople)
 "Seventeen Summers" (Melissa and Mary)
 "It's a Lie" (Mother)
 ["Rome's Dance" (Rome and Woman)]
Act 2:
 "My Sister In Law" (Thad, Melissa, Mary, and Halleck)
 "Why" (Mother)
 "That's Right!" (Townspeople)
 "Morning Sun" and "Tell Me Goodbye" reprise (Rome)
 "For Once in My Life" (Thad and Melissa)
 "Thad's Journey"
 "All the Pretty Little Horses" (Mother)

["Dialogues" (Townspeople)]
"I Seen It with My Very Own Eyes" (Townspeople)
"I Will Take Good Care of You" reprise (Thad)

The title song establishes the poetic tone for the rest of the score while capturing Rome's restless nature.[23] Ebb took the first line directly from Deasy's story:

> Mornin' sun like a fiddle playin'
> Sets my head to spinnin'
> Mornin' sun like a fiddle playin'
> Beckons me away!
>
> Mornin' sun like a piper pipin'
> Sets my face to grinnin'
> Mornin' sun like a bugle crowin'
> Says, "Today's the day!"
>
> . . .
>
> Come away!
> Come away!

Klein's music is folksy and lyrical, suggesting a Copland influence or perhaps the Loesser of *Greenwillow,* which had opened just two years earlier. The "Morning Sun" theme reappears in various melodies and accompaniments later in the score. For instance, "This Heat" uses the "Morning Sun" theme as the foundation for a recitative passage. "That's Right!" effectively conveys Deasy's chilling description of the mob at the hanging through chanted unison accompanied by the pulsating beat of a drum.[24] The most complex and contrapuntal number in the score is "I've Seen It with My Very Own Eyes," in which the townspeople present different versions of the murder. This number is about recapturing the truth about the past—a theme that Sondheim later explored in "Someone in a Tree" from *Pacific Overtures* and "Something Just Broke" from *Assassins*—and it attests to Ebb's growing sophistication as a lyricist and dramatist.

Morning Sun "led a charmed life," according to Ebb. Patricia Neway, fresh from her triumph in Menotti's *The Consul,* accepted the role of the mother, which, for Ebb, "validated the whole piece," and Bert Convy signed on as Rome. Agnus DeMille was the first choice as director, but when she declined Dick Seff got Bob Fosse interested in the project. Ebb claimed that a disagreement between Fosse and the producers led to his departure from the

project, but the composer's son, Jonathan Klein, suggests that Fosse left the
project because Ebb and Klein objected to many of the changes he wanted to
make, such as opening the show with the hanging in order to ease the shock
of the story for the audience. Daniel Petri was hired to replace Fosse before
the show went into production. Donald Saddler did the choreography and
Patricia Zippordt the costumes.

Morning Sun opened on October 6, 1963. To everyone's surprise, the
critical reception was not positive. Several critics praised Klein's music but
went out of their way to criticize Ebb's libretto. Howard Taubman called the
book "pretentious and empty" and overly "psychologizing."[25] He took issue
with the mother, who, were it not for some good music, "would be in danger
of setting back motherhood farther than it has been pushed by the devour-
ing mothers who have infested our stage in recent years." Gene Palatsky of
the New York Evening News wrote, "The drama resembles a series of Scan-
dinavian Biblical wall paintings in which stock, bloodless characters work
out a simple morality play." He complimented Klein's music but took issue
with Ebb's work: "Packed with clichés, the book and lyrics by Fred Ebb seem
awfully close to parody."[26] Worse, Norman Nadel called the musical "a lugu-
brious leaden, musical play [that] . . . denies us the psychological catharsis
of tragedy, thought it is almost obsessively steeped in misery." Like Palatsky,
Nadel praised the music but hammered the lyrics and book.[27] The only enthusiastic praise came from the theater critic of radio station WNYC.[28] It was
not enough to help, for Morning Sun closed after just nine performances.

In later years, Ebb played down any disappointment that he might have
felt about the demise of Morning Sun. Perhaps to make light of the subject,
he called his script "lachrymose" and claimed, "I didn't have a clue how
to write it." Nevertheless, he must have felt some residual affection for the
show, for he later tried to adapt it as a television musical. Against his better
judgment, he drastically changed the story, probably feeling pressure to alter
the tragic ending for a television audience. He omitted the character of John
Atzel and made Rome the sole agent in the killing. When Rome is taunted by
a stranger, he fights back and kills the man. He is found innocent of murder
but goes to jail for two years for manslaughter. In the context of the lighter
sentence, the mother's harsh reaction seems incongruous, almost as though
she were insane: "They may have found you innocent Rome, but I still find
you guilty . . . Ain't nothing been said to correct that Rome. I brought the
children here to show them, as a lesson to them. Well, they let you off Rome,
but in my mind, you're still guilty." Thad calls her crazy and repudiates her,

but when Thad's sister makes him realize that the ability to forgive is part of being a man, he takes his mother in his arms. Ebb turned the story into a tale of forgiveness. It was not a winning formula, and the program was never made.

Had *Morning Sun* been a hit, Ebb and Klein's collaboration might have taken off. Ebb believed that his collaboration with Klein, who was a few years his senior, came to an end because the composer's "insecurities played right into my insecurities so that I almost couldn't write. He had an overriding philosophy that nothing good could ever happen to us." Klein struggled with the decision over what to do with his career. Unknown to him at the time, his wife, concerned with the mixed praise from the critics about her husband's score, sought the advice of Richard Rodgers, who offered some guarded words of encouragement:

> I listened to your husband's score for "Morning Sun" with careful attention and I am now trying to write to you with equal care. The fact that the critics, who are not particularly sensitive to music, were able to recognize the value of the lighter pieces in the score and were confused by the ones with greater depth should have no influence on anybody at all. My own impression was not that one type of music was any better than the other. My feeling was that all of it had great value . . . I'm sure that, as your husband continues to write, he will find out where his musical life lies and, with his particular talent, he'll be able to live with it. What I heard the other night is not only talent but musicianship. Obviously there is also the will to succeed. I don't know how to tell you or him to be patient because this is a quality I have never been able to develop myself. . . . This will bring you my wishes for success and the uncalled-for remark that you must be a nice wife.[29]

Klein's self-doubt and the responsibility he felt to provide for his family soon caused him to quit the theater business in favor of a more stable career.

Liza Minnelli and the Television Specials

Fred Ebb and Liza Minnelli were each other's greatest fan, fueling each other's self-delusions and fulfilling each other's insatiable need for approbation. A videotape from 1974 located at the New York Public Library for the Performing Arts contains what was supposed to be an informal conversation about musical theater between Liza Minnelli, Kander, and Ebb.[30] It is telling of the nature of their three-way relationship. Shortly into the conversation

Ebb and Minnelli get caught up in a mutually sycophantic dialogue of their own. Before long, Kander gives up trying to get a word in edgewise.

Minnelli has proudly acknowledged that she was a figment of Fred Ebb's imagination. There is more than a grain of truth to this statement, as Ebb helped Minnelli to invent her "glam" persona, the occasional mid- or post-song giggle, the confessional tone when talking to her audience. Reciprocally, Minnelli served as the vessel through which Ebb lived out his own fantasies of stardom. The concerts, televisions specials, and musicals that Ebb created for Minnelli were an extension of their personal relationship and a reflection of his own personality.

In 1970, two years before Minnelli's meteoric rise to stardom, Ebb wrote his first television special, *Liza*, which aired on NBC on June 29. The special helped to boost Minnelli's national profile. The reviews were generally positive, although one of the critics bemoaned, "rarely have more energy, enthusiasm and production skill gone into a TV special with such meager results."[31] Through this and subsequent television specials and concerts, Ebb shaped the legend of Liza Minnelli, "a unique confluence of talent and biography, persistence and collapse," as one critic has describes it.[32] *Liza* was an entertainment about musical theater traditions, such as the eleven o'clock number, vaudeville, and movie songs. Minnelli opened with "Tradition" as a way of introducing the musical theater theme of the evening, followed by "Get Happy," her mother's signature song. She then explained to the home viewers what the special is about: show business, "the tradition I was born into."[33] In these opening moments, Ebb constructed a show business identity for Minnelli, that of a legend in the making. It was an image of a star's daughter wrapping herself up in her mother's reputation while at the same time trying to escape from it.

A defining moment in Minnelli's career was the 1972 television special *Liza with a Z!*, which Bob Fosse and Fred Ebb co-created immediately after the release of the film version of *Cabaret*. Filmed live with eight cameras, the special featured an eclectic range of music, from specialty numbers by Kander and Ebb such as "Liza with a 'Z'!" and "Ring Them Bells," to rhythm-and-blues numbers such as "I Gotcha" and "Son of a Preacher Man." The special had no overriding theme. It was simply about Liza being Liza, dancing Bob Fosse's signature choreography and wearing Halston dresses. *Liza with a Z!* was a show on which showbiz legends are made, and it garnered Emmy Awards for Minnelli, Fosse, and Ebb. It gave national exposure to Minnelli's stage persona, which by this time was already a fixed and self-referential cliché. In a recent review of the newly issued DVD of the concert, Alessandra Stanley, with the hindsight of more than three decades, sees the Minnelli of 1972 already as "an anachronism," at once "riveting and ghastly."[34]

In 1974 Minnelli played the Winter Garden Theatre for three weeks. The concert, called *Liza*, used a lot of the music from *Liza with a Z!* and involved many of the same artistic staff. Fosse and Ron Lewis choreographed, Ebb wrote the dialogue, and Marvin Hamlisch directed the orchestra. For this concert Ebb created a narrative and used songs to illustrate Liza's life (or his version of it) as she was growing up, with an affectionate tribute to her "daddy," Vincent Minnelli. By this time, Liza had a solid fan base, and she had mastered her mother's ability to feign spontaneous surprise at the audience's adulation. Clive Barnes recognized that much of her "act" was contrived, but, in a strange sort of star adulation, he felt that this very contrivance "adds to the total reality." There are times when Minnelli actually seeks Ebb's approbation from on stage, crying out "Freddie."[35]

Shortly after the Winter Garden concert Ebb started to pair Minnelli with other stars in self-referential television specials about themselves. Structured as a show-within-a-show, these specials deconstruct the backstage musical genre by having the stars play themselves and by taking the viewer backstage. In *Goldie and Liza*, Minnelli and Goldie Hawn rehearse for the very same television special that we are watching. Minnelli is a song-and-dance veteran who teaches Hawn about the Broadway musical. Ebb exploited Hawn's ditzy-blond persona from *Laugh In*. In the opening scene, Hawn rushes out of her house carrying a garment bag in one hand and a trash bag in the other. She tosses her costumes in the trash and gets into her Volkswagen with the garbage. In a parallel vignette, Minnelli emerges from the Beverly-Wilshire Hotel. She starts to drive off before the doorman has finished loading her luggage into the trunk, leaving him holding her garment bag. As they each drive to the television studio, Hawn sings "I'm doing' a special with my friend, Liza / Something I've always been / anxious to do." Minnelli responds obsequiously, "Goldie, blond and adorable / Lit by some interior spark." They pull into their respectively reserved parking spaces at exactly the same time and just seconds before the first commercial break. In the next segment, Hawn and Minnelli, now in their third day of rehearsals, are working on "It's What You Can." The scene, which depicts a grueling workout, dissolves into a sneak peek at what the number will ultimately look like when they are through. The remaining segments show the backstage machinations of a television special. There is a scene in a recording studio with a thirty-piece orchestra where Minnelli teaches Hawn how to do an overdub. Finally, the day of the telecast has arrived, and, as in the first montage, Minnelli and Hawn pack up their cars and drive to the studio, this time singing "Insecure." This special is a testament to Ebb's dedication to the revue format and the show-within-a-show.

In *Baryshnikov on Broadway*, which aired in 1980, Minnelli appeared as the guest star, along with Nell Carter and the cast of *A Chorus Line*, which performed "One." Like the previous special, this one too is about rehearsing the special that we are watching. In *Goldie and Liza*, Minnelli played the seasoned Broadway star patiently acclimating her inexperienced and fawning Hollywood counterpart to the world of musical theater. Here, too, she mentors the classically trained superstar in the more plebeian art of the two-step and kick line. Speaking directly into the camera, Minnelli sets the tone with Ebb's words: "Broadway. It's more than a word. It's a world. Some magic world no one's ever been able to describe. I used to dream about it. And when I got there, it was everything I thought it would be. Well, maybe the dressing rooms were a little small and the halls were a little drafty, and maybe it was a little less glamorous than Ruby Keeler had led me to believe. But the excitement of it was exactly what I had imagined. I'll tell you one thing. Broadway is unique." Liza and Mikhail use a looking glass to travel back in time to some of Broadway's greatest hits of the past. At the end of this magical Broadway tour, they return to the rehearsal studio, where Mikhail is still rehearsing the chorus line kicks for "One."

In 1973, Carroll O'Connor, at the height of his popularity as patriarch Archie Bunker on *All in the Family*, appeared in his own television musical special, *Three For the Girls*. O'Conner played a husband, father, and son in three respective skits. Ebb wrote the second segment, "Clothes Make the Girl," in which O'Connor, in the role of the father, attends an Off-Broadway play in which his daughter appears in the nude. Ebb's scenario was little more than an excuse to feature O'Connor in a vaudeville entertainment consisting of four numbers. At one point, O'Connor imagines himself performing a bubbly trio called "In the Same Boat," which Kander and Ebb wrote several years earlier (see Appendix, section on the Ford show) and later interpolated into *Curtains* (see Chapter 9). O'Connor is joined by four mermaids and the wardrobe mistress, played by Nancy Walker. At the end of segment, the father reconsiders his reaction to his daughter's decision to appear nude, and they leave the theater together, arm-in-arm.

In the same year Ebb also wrote *Ol' Blue Eyes Is Back* for Frank Sinatra. Gene Kelly appeared as a special guest star, and Ed McMahon was the announcer. The special was touted as a "return" for Sinatra following a brief retirement. Ebb organized a number of Sinatra hits into thematically unified segments—old songs, saloon songs, and new songs—and provided the singer with conversational interludes to string the segments together.[36] Ebb incorporated "I Can't Do That Anymore," a song probably originally written for *Wait for Me, World* (see Chapter 8), as the centerpiece for a segment about the movies.

In 1976, Ebb and Cy Coleman co-produced *Gypsy in My Soul* for Shirley MacLaine. Like Ebb's other specials, this one also used a self-referential, show business plot in which the star rehearses for her television special about a dancer's life. MacLaine explains: "You see those dancers? They're chorus dancers. The ones that do the hard stuff while the star takes the bows. In show business, they're called 'gypsies.'... Wherever the work is—the gypsy is.... I was a 'gypsy.' And I never forgot it. No matter what happens to me, or where I go, or what I do, some part of me will always be back there in the chorus. With the gypsies. I guess you could say, I've got a gypsy in my soul." The nostalgic tone of this insider monologue echoes similar sentiments in Minnelli's opening speech for *Baryshnikov on Broadway*. In these speeches, the stars channel Ebb's voice and express his love of the theater. MacLaine performed a wide range of songs, including "Lucy's Back in Town," during which Lucille Ball made a "surprise" appearance.

Throughout his career, Ebb took on various small projects, including writing additional material for the 1967 Off-Broadway revival of *By Jupiter* at Theater Four directed by Christopher Hewett, one of Ebb's associates from Tamiment, and for the third television incarnation of *Cinderella* (1997), which starred Brandy Norwood in the title role. His assignment for *By Jupiter*, which he accepted without any financial remuneration, was to rework some of the song lead-ins and remove the topical references. Ebb was particularly proud of getting Richard Rodgers's permission to reinstate the song "Wait 'til You See Her," which had been cut before the show opened on Broadway in 1942. For *Cinderella*, Ebb provided a new verse for "Your Majesties."

> Surely you'll need a side of ham,
> And lots of beef filets.
> Some marbleized steaks, a rack of lamb,
> And veal you raise to braise!

Limburger cheese and gourmandize,
Gouda, Gruyère and blue.
Chunks of Swiss in barrels,
Please make sure it's holey, too.

Pudding and pies and rum soufflé,
Succulent chocolate rounds.
Cream puffs we can eat all day
To gain some royal pounds.

Regrettably, these lyrics are not included in the version of *Cinderella* currently leased for performances by the Rodgers and Hammerstein Organization.

John Kander

A program for *Stay at Home and Like It*, a show presented in Kansas City at the Oakwood Country Club on December 29, 1943, includes a bio for John Kander: "Who wrote most of the music, shows great promise in 'show' business. He has had songs published and entrenous [*sic*] he is Irving Berlin's right-hand man. Really a swell guy and the girls are all 'mad' on him." By this time the fifteen-year-old composer had already been writing music for several years. Kander's oldest surviving composition is a song from 1937 called "In a Manger" (example 4.1). The song's nativity theme caused his elementary school teacher enough concern to inform her Jewish student's parents. They were not worried about their son's choice of topic. "In a Manger," despite a few mis-stressed words, exhibits an intuitive sense of melody and sensitivity to text.

Early Musical Training

When Kander first took up music, Schoenberg and Stravinsky had already accomplished their greatest achievements; George Gershwin was a household name; and Aaron Copland was about to abandon his modernist inclination and move in a more populist direction. When it was time for Kander to go to college, he chose Oberlin, which gave him a solid academic and musical background. He studied composition with Herbert Elwell. Throughout college, Kander preferred the neotonal vocabulary of composers like Hindemith, Barber, and Menotti to atonal techniques. His compositions are saturated with quartal harmonies, free dissonances, extended chords, chromatic

Example 4.1. John Kander's first song, "In a Manger" (1937)

counterpoint, and asymmetrical and mixed meters (table 4.1). The raised 4th scale degree is ubiquitous. He wrote primarily art songs and small instrumental works, which he calls "the worst chamber music you ever heard." The self-deprecation notwithstanding, Kander was more secure writing in the vocal medium.

At Oberlin, Kander, Nikos Psacharopoulos, the future founder of the Williamstown Theatre Festival, and John Goodfriend, who became the CEO of Salomon Brothers, reconstituted the then inactive theater club called Mummers.[37] Kander wrote a number of compositions for Mummers, including a single-movement, antiwar cantata for narrator and chorus called *Requiem for Georgie* (1951), which served as a curtain-raiser for Kurt Weill's *Down in*

Table 4.1. John Kander's extant student compositions

Title	Description	Place and Date	
Da capo	one-act opera	Columbia	master's thesis, text by James Goldman
English folk song arrangements	"Lass from the Low Countree," "O Can Ye Sew Cushions," "The Old Maid," "Early One Morning," "Egg and Marrow Bone"	Oberlin	performed by Ruth Schoeni
Lullaby ("Golden slumbers kiss your eyes")	for soprano and piano		text by Elizabethan playwright Thomas Dekkar (1570–1641)
"Portrait of Geraldine"	soprano and piano	Oberlin, 1950	marked "a song for uninhibited sopranos who sing high B"
Requiem for Georgie	chorus, narrator, and piano	Oberlin	original text by Kander; written for Mummers
Sonata for piano	three movements: moderately fast, slow, fast	1953	"for D. H." (possibly J. H.)
Sonata for violin and piano	3 movements: slow, slow, allegro		
Sonatina for piano	single movement	Oberlin, 1947	
Song	single movement work for violin and piano		
Songs of Ophelia	two songs for soprano and piano	Oberlin	
Theme and variations based on "Happy Birthday"	violin solo		probably a student work
Three songs	"I Hate School," "From My Window," and "Nobody"		original texts by Kander

Table 4.1. (*Continued*)

Title	Description	Place and Date	
Trio for flute, violin, and piano	3 movements: mod-erato, andante, vivace		
untitled	three movements for piano: moderate, andante, allegro		
untitled piece for piano	three movements: slow (very), mod-erato, allegro		
untitled work for oboe, clarinet, 1st and 2nd violin, viola, celli, bass, and harp	3 movements extant: slow, slowly, and leisurely		
untitled work for piano	single movement for piano		highly chromatic and fugal
untitled work for piano	three miniatures		third movement in-corporates a hymn melody
untitled work for piano	single movement		marked lento
untitled work for piano	theme and variations		incomplete
untitled work for piano	single movement		
"White Are the Grasses by My True Love's Tomb"	SSAA chorus	Oberlin	text by Jeanne Tay-lor; "M.M." is given as title
Winterset	opera (act 1, scene 1, and sketches for another scene)	Oberlin	scene 1 is fully orchestrated

the Valley. Kander wrote his own text for the cantata. Georgie is an every-man: he is born, grows into a boy, fishes, gets engaged to Priscilla, is drafted, goes off to war, gets killed in combat to save America for "apple pie," and is mourned by his family and fiancée. The bullet that kills Georgie comes from the gun of a boy like himself. Kander gives this cantata a distinctly theatrical flair. The narrator announces Georgie's death on a descending C arpeggio followed by an E-flat arpeggio in the opposite direction (example 4.2a). Re-

Example 4.2. *Requiem for Georgie* (a) opening phrase (b) closing section

inforcing the bitonal implication of this opening gesture, a dissonant chord sounds six times like a death knell. A waltz portrays the dance where Georgie and Priscilla fall in love. At the end of the cantata, the narrator implores the choir, "sing a requiem for Georgie" (example 4.2b). The choir answers with a Mixolydian melody arranged like a hymn on the words "Requiem aeternam." This phrase ends on a sustained G major chord, which shifts to G minor as the narrator, alternating with repeated choral statements of the Latin text, sings, "His mother misses him, his father misses him and Priscilla Bartlett cries in her sleep sometimes when she dreams." *Requiem for Georgie* is a solid if prosaic student work, and it meant a lot to Kander at the time.

Kander's student art songs are studies in miniature form. He worked with a variety of texts, including some he wrote himself, such as "I Hate School," "Nobody," and "From My Window," which together make up a cycle of songs told from a young boy's perspective. In "I Hate School," the boy avoids telling his father that he is developing an aversion to school because of the girls. A through-composed melody captures the disconnected thoughts of a child as a short recurring figure in the piano, first heard in measure 2, provides a sense of musical cohesiveness (example 4.3). The underlying accompaniment contains a raised 4th above the bass. The climax of the song—a threefold statement of "girls"—occurs on a high F-sharp, after which the voice slowly sinks down to the final note as the boy resigns himself to keeping his thoughts to himself.

Other vocal works composed at Oberlin include "Portrait of Geraldine" (1950), a moralizing satire about a woman who dies a virgin (subtitled "A song for uninhibited soprano who sings high B");[38] "Two Songs of Ophelia," which are based on texts from Shakespeare's *Hamlet*; and arrangements of British folk songs, mostly the same tunes that Benjamin Britten had set. Ruth Schoeni, one of Kander's classmates—and probably the "uninhibited soprano"—who later had a short professional vocal career, performed the folk songs at Oberlin and later in New York with Kander accompanying her at the piano.[39]

At Oberlin, Kander started an opera based on Maxwell Anderson's award-winning play *Winterset*. He completed the opening scene, including the orchestrations. *Winterset* deals with issues of guilt and forgiveness. Mio, the son of an immigrant who was falsely executed for a crime, tries to exonerate his father. He looks for a man named Garth, who was an eyewitness to the crime but was never called on to testify at the trial. Mio finds Garth living with his father and sister Miriame. Trock Estrella, the real killer, recently released from jail, also tracks down Garth to keep him from talking. At a mock trial in Garth's apartment, Trock confesses to the murder. Satisfied with the truth, Mio leaves, but he and Miriame, who have fallen in love, are shot by Trock's henchmen.[40] Anderson wrote *Winterset* in the hope of founding a modern poetic tragedy genre. In an essay that he wrote for the first publication of the play, "A Prelude to Poetry in the Theatre,"[41] Anderson eschews the tendency in American drama to be "journalistic social" commentary and complains

Example 4.3. "I Hate School"

that "our modern dramatists . . . are not poets, and the best prose in the world is inferior on the stage to the best poetry." Prose is the bearer of information, but poetry is the "language of emotion." It is a philosophy to which Kander and his friend and early collaborator James Goldman vigorously subscribed. They believed that words and music should supersede the objective facts of a scene and move the emotions.

Kander set Anderson's text nearly verbatim, deleting only a few short lines.

In the opening scene Trock lurks in a dark street near Garth's tenement along with his henchman named Shadow. Kander employed recitative throughout the scene, save for a small passage for Shadow. The music is through-composed, terse, and permeated with dissonant semitones and tritones. The descending semitone motive occurring in the opening phrase on "you roost" and "gulls" recurs throughout the scene (example 4.4a). Shadow responds to Trock's terse language with an angular line over an ironically playful accompaniment suggestive of a waltz (example 4.4b).

After Oberlin, Kander entered the master's program in composition at Columbia University. He continued to write in the same style and idiom as he did as an undergraduate. For his master's project, he wrote a one-act opera on a libretto by James Goldman, developing it in Otto Luening's thesis seminar. *Da Capo*, as the opera is titled, is a murder-mystery comedy involving nine characters:[42]

Tyrus Belmore	a wealthy man of about fifty
Lucile Belmore	his wife
Larry Belmore	their son, about twenty
Grover Morley	another wealthy man of about fifty
Clarissa Morley	his wife
Laurie Morley	their daughter, betrothed to Larry
Harshly Comma	a private detective
Fanny	a young domestic
Lothrop	a butler

The place is the Belmore mansion, the time late spring, "slightly after six o'clock." Lothrop is in love with Fanny, but she does not reciprocate his feelings. While they prepare dinner for an engagement party for their employer's son, Lothrop receives an envelope containing his obituary and a warning. Shortly thereafter, he is discovered strangled. Summoned by Belmore, Detective Harshly Comma arrives to investigate. (The detective's name was an inside joke between by Goldman and Kander.) Just before Comma solves the case, Lothrop enters nonchalantly and announces that dinner is served.

Da Capo, a comedy in miniature, consists predominantly of recitative. Mixed meter and syllabic text declamation dominate, although occasionally a section in parlando style blooms into an arioso passage. Standing out from the recitative are three major lyrical events, a love duet for Laurie and Larry, an aria for Fanny, and a large-scale ensemble at the climax of the story. Laurie and Larry's duet lampoons the romantic opera duet convention. The

Example 4.4. *Winterset* (act 1, scene 1 opening)

text consists of one word, "love," as though the lovers have lost their command of language (example 4.5). The melody is a continuous thread of short asymmetrical, melismatic gesticulations, modulating nervously every couple of measures as though to laugh at the inane text.

Fanny sings the only solo aria in the opera, a lament about harboring a love that does not speak. It is the emotional high point in the comedy and the most expressive music in the score. Anticipating a device found in many

Example 4.5. *Da Capo*, "Love Duet" (first 6 measures)

of Kander's later musical theater songs, the opening melody incorporates appoggiaturas approached from above, emphasizing important words in the text ("fortress" and "longing") (example 4.6). The accompaniment is sparse but active, consisting of parallel thirds moving by large leaps in both the treble and bass parts. In measure 4, the voice slides from D to C-sharp on "words," triggering a tonally unstable progression of two measures. A series of root-position chords in quick succession (F-sharp [G-flat]–D-flat–A–C–E) produces consecutive cross-relationships between the voice and accompaniment.

After Kander graduated from Columbia, he redirected his creative energy to musical theater. His love of opera never waned, however, and today he still attends the complete season of the Metropolitan Opera as well as several dress rehearsals. In the early 1970s, Kander appeared twice on the Texaco Opera Quiz, holding his own with the other panelists, Walter Sleazac and Terry McHuen. The first of his two Opera Quiz appearances occurred during a performance of *Tosca* and coincided with the return of the Met broadcasts, which had been suspended due to a strike. Edward Downs, the host of the

Example 4.6. *Da Capo,* "In a Fortress"

quiz, asked the panelists to sing a line from an opera that expressed their personal feelings about the end of the strike. Kander came up with Hans Sacks's line from *Die Meistersinger von Nürnberg,* "Wahn! Wahn! überall wahn" (Madness, madness, everywhere madness, or, as Kander translated, "God knows how it happened. Madness all over").

Musicals with James and William Goldman

Kander's lifelong friendship with the Goldman brothers started when he and James Goldman, both ten at the time, attended the same summer camp in Holland Park, Illinois. Kander and James were about four years older than William, but a close bond developed between the three of them. Kander and William were at Oberlin College at the same time. When Kander and James first moved to New York, they shared a two-bedroom apartment. After William finished Oberlin, he too moved to New York, and the three of them shared a nine-room apartment located on 344 West Seventy-second Street, the farthest west building before the Hudson River. The monthly rent was

$275. Kander had the smallest bedroom, which they called "Sneaky Falls," one of many nicknames they made up for things, plus an alcove for his piano. The young trio epitomized a mixture of youthful optimism and Midwest naïveté. They had gone to New York to pursue their respective careers, and it never even occurred to them that they might not succeed: James would become a playwright, William a novelist, and Kander a composer.

Around this time, Kander and James Goldman started writing musicals together, sometimes with William. As noted above, Kander and James felt strongly that poetry, defined in the broadest of terms, was more powerful than the literalism of prose. Putting their theory of art into practice, they started writing metaphorical or symbolic stories, often with an element of fantasy. Ironically, their only musical that saw the light of day, A *Family Affair*, was their one exception to this aesthetic stance. Kander and Goldman's first musical from this period is *Magic Circle* (1956), a bucolic tale set in New Hampshire at the end of the nineteenth century. Kander calls it "a story about prose vs. poetry." An aging vaudeville magician named Christopher Morgan returns to a town once controlled by his family in order to donate a Ferris wheel. He is accompanied by his troupe of performers, his young wife Julia, and an assistant. He and Julia have not yet consummated their four-year marriage. Morgan and his entourage are offered food and lodging by Adam, the present owner of property that once belonged to Morgan. Julie soon falls in love with Adam's son, and Morgan's assistant falls in love with Adam's devoted daughter Sarah. The suspicious townsfolk reluctantly accept the gift, and the magician's wife returns to him. Only the title song seems to have survived from this quixotic musical. It is a duet in which Adam's son and daughter perform a repeated ritual of acting out a princess and prince story.

Jennifer's Travels is based on an idea by James and William, although James alone wrote the script and lyrics.[43] He had a dystopia in mind, noting on the cover of the script that the story uses the past "the same way that 1984 . . . uses the future." The story, which is more like alternative history fiction, is a crime adventure set at the end of the nineteenth century. Victor Morningside, the maniacal brother of the governor of Manhattan, has his brother and niece, Jennifer, kidnapped and attempts to install himself as governor. The hero of the story, Johnathan Smythe, a Byronic figure, rescues them. At first, Smythe and Jennifer take an instant dislike to each other, but soon they fall in love. Goldman's script includes song lyrics, but no music has been found.

Kander and James Goldman's most romantic and lyrical project was a musical adaptation of Jean Giraudoux's *Intermezzo*, which opened on

Broadway in 1950 under the title *The Enchanted*.[44] The heroine, Isabel, communes with the dead, but an inspector charged with protecting the social order demands that she desist. Isabel rejoins the world of the living only after falling in love with a dead person, an experience that reveals to her that the love and beauty that exist in the corporeal world must be embraced. The life-affirming theme and poetry of *The Enchanted* appealed to Kander and Goldman's aesthetic sensibilities, even though critics of the play objected to its overreliance on abstractions.[45] Rather than speaking to the intellect, the play speaks to "a more subtle organ of comprehension which does not ordinarily need to deal with words."[46] Kander felt that *The Enchanted* lent itself to musical treatment, noting that the last scene is "literally conducted" by the doctor, who leads the town in a symphony of daily life (perhaps this scene explains why Francis Poulenc was commissioned to compose music for the original spoken version of the play). Kander and Goldman completed six songs and made a demo recording with the assistance of June Ericson and Bill Lutz:

"I Love You, Isabel" (Supervisor)
"Grammar Song" (sung as counterpoint to "I Love You") (Isabel and students)
"Gossips' Song" (Leonide and Armande [Mangebois sisters])
Diary (middle section of "Gossips' Song") (Isabel)
Duet ("When Twilight Falls") (Isabel and Ghost)
"March for the Supervisor" (Supervisor)

"I Love You, Isabel" epitomizes the lyrical sweep that Kander envisioned for the entire score (example 4.7). The melody bursts forth with a leap of a major ninth over a dominant harmony followed by a stepwise descent. This song marks the moment in the play in which the local superintendent falls in love with Isabel, who is busy reviewing a grammar lesson with her students to a contrasting animated melody consisting of consonant skips of a third and a small ascending scale pattern. At the climax of the scene, the two melodies combine, with the children's lilting patter providing humorous counterpoint to the superintendent's nearly operatic confession.

Kander and Goldman auditioned their score for the famous literary agent Audry Wood and an associate of Wood's at MCA, David Hocker, with the hope of obtaining the musical rights to Giraudoux's play.[47] Their efforts failed, a fact that Kander regrets to this day. (Kander later tried to interest

Example 4.7. *The Enchanted* (a) "Grammar Song"; (b) "I Love You, Isabel";
(c) both melodies together

Ebb in writing *The Enchanted*, but he was turned off by its magical element.)
But the meeting with Wood was propitious, as Hocker's assistant, Dick Seff
(the same man who helped get Ebb's career off the ground), was present, and
he offered to help Kander and Goldman in the future. He came through with
his promise when he convinced his cousin Andrew Siff (they spelled their last
name differently) to produce *A Family Affair*.

The romantic themes, poetic lexicon, and lyrical music of *The Magic
Circle*, *Jennifer's Travels*, and *The Enchanted* do not prepare one for *A Family
Affair*, a broad musical comedy about the trials and tribulations of organiz-

John Kander, William Goldman, and John Goldman. From the personal collection of John Kander

ing, paying for, and surviving a big Jewish wedding. It was billed as a group effort, with Kander, James, and William sharing credit for the script, lyrics, and music, but in reality Kander wrote the music, Kander and James the lyrics, and William the book.[48] A *Family Affair*, which sprang from the Goldmans' memories of their Midwest Jewish upbringing, has some screamingly funny scenes and a solid if conventional musical comedy score, but today it seems a bit too much like a glorified Catskill comedy skit.

The musical springs into action without wasting any time: the curtain rises, Jerry proposes to Sally, Sally agrees, and the trouble begins. The dramatic conflict involves a fight of near biblical proportions between Jerry's parents, Tillie and Morris Siegal, who are proud of their "son the lawyer," and Sally's uncle, Alfie Nathan, a confirmed bachelor. Because Alfie offers to pay for his niece's wedding, he feels entitled to make all of the wedding plans, but only over Tillie's dead body. All pretense of civility is dropped and relationships begin to unravel until these petulant future in-laws come to their senses. As the curtain comes down, the wedding begins.

The cast featured some of the brightest comic talent in the business:

Shelly Berman as Alfie Nathan, Eileen Heckart as Tillie Siegal, Morris Carnovsky as Morris Siegal, and Larry Kert and Rita Gardner as Gerry Siegal and Sally Nathan, the bride and groom. Andrew Siff felt that Word Baker, who had just scored a major triumph with *The Fantasticks*, had the right gentle touch to direct the musical, but after the first previews in Philadelphia it became abundantly clear that he had made an error in judgment. Hoping to reverse the damage, Siff approached Jerome Robbins, George Abbott, and Gower Champion about taking over for Baker. With no one willing or able to step in so late in the process, he nearly closed the show out of town, but he managed to convince Hal Prince to travel to Philadelphia and to take a look at the show. Prince had read the script and listened to the score of *A Family Affair* at Stephen Sondheim's urging, and he basically liked the material, but what he saw in Philadelphia was not working:[49] "The material that I liked so much on paper was impossible to see for the production that was imposed on it, a unit set that looked like a tiered wedding cake, with doughnut turntables that moved at a snail's pace, and a cyclorama of wedding lace in front of which they played the entire show."[50]

Prince was eager to get into directing, so he agreed to take over for Baker. Hoping to recover the charm of the original material, he threw out the gimmickry scenery and got Tony Walton to help him streamline the set. Meanwhile, the writers worked feverishly to fix the weak portions of the show. Despite their heroic efforts, *A Family Affair* opened on Broadway on January 27, 1962 to mostly negative notices and closed after only sixty-five performances. Most of the critics attacked the flimsy book and underdeveloped characters. That Shelly Berman was allowed to perform his famous telephone routine, albeit in the context of ordering a wedding cake, is symptomatic of the lack of confidence in the book that the production team must have felt. The critics also complained about the limitations of the modern suburban setting and reliance on "clichés of Jewish domestic attitudes."[51]

Notwithstanding the drubbing from the press, *A Family Affair* established Kander's reputation as a talented and hardworking musical theater composer, and it also solidified his relationship with Prince. The score (rereleased on CD in 2006) is unabashed musical comedy, from the potpourri overture to the final ensemble number.[52] Reviewing the recording for *The American Record Guide*, Robert Jones noted, "This work has probably the brightest, cleverest, and most original score to reach Broadway in years. The arching melodic contours of *Anything for You* and *There's a Room in My*

House, the driving enthusiasm of *My Son, the Lawyer*, the rah-rah spirit of the Siegals' and the Nathans' marching songs, the rocking Dixieland humor of *Harmony . . .* and the unforgettable oddness of *I'm Worse Than Anybody* suggest a major talent on the horizon."[53] Jerry and Sally's romantic ballads contain momentary flights of lyricism; the parents' songs humorously magnify their character flaws; and upbeat ensemble numbers give the extras moments to shine. Some of the numbers break out of the realistic mode of traditional book songs. For instance, "Siegal's Marching Song" is a football game sequence, complete with a sports announcer, that physicalizes the fight between the families. A few songs are amplified by an offstage chorus, such as Alfie's "Revenge," which is built on the ostinato pattern and rising modulatory trajectory of Ravel's *Bolero*. One of the ensemble numbers, "Harmony," anticipates Kander and Ebb's penchant for old popular musical forms and styles. It is performed by the wedding caterer, who, armed with years of experience at avoiding the minefield of a Jewish wedding, manipulates both sides so that each one thinks it is winning the war. "Harmony" is a rousing Dixieland number, full of syncopated rhythms and close barbershop harmonies sung by the caterer's crew; and Robert Ginzler's orchestration features wailing high reeds and trumpets, thereby reinforcing the New Orleans reference.[54]

Making Ends Meet in the Late Fifties

In the late fifties, Kander earned a living working as a vocal coach, musical director, and rehearsal pianist. He also worked as musical director at the Warwick "musical tent," as it was fondly called, from 1955 to 1957, conducting Broadway classics like *Oklahoma!* and *Finian's Rainbow*. Through these various jobs he made a network of friends who also helped advance his career. In 1955, he was the rehearsal pianist for *The Amazing Adele*, a musical by Albert W. Selden and Anita Loos and which starred Tammy Grimes. The show closed out of town, but two years later, Peter Manz, the dance arranger for *Adele*, who was doing the orchestrations for a Broadway revival of Noël Coward's *Conversation Piece*, hired Kander to be the musical director. Tony Walton, the set and lighting designer for *Conversation Piece*, later designed the sets for *Chicago, The Act, Woman of the Year*, and *Steel Pier*; he also co-produced the first London productions of *Cabaret* with Hal Prince and Richard Pilbrow. In 1956, Kander and Don Pippin played dual pianos for a production of *An Evening with Beatrice Lillie* at the Coconut Grove and Palm Beach in Florida.[55] Pippin later worked on some of Kander and Ebb's musicals, including *Woman of the Year*.

Kander's first experience as a composer for Broadway was as the dance arranger for *Gypsy* and *Irma la Douce*. At the suggestion of Ruth Mitchell, Jerome Robbins hired him for *Gypsy*, apparently impressed with his piano playing for *West Side Story* rehearsals in Philadelphia. Tulsa's "All I Need Is the Girl," arguably one of the most riveting song-and-dance sequences in musical theater, took Kander a couple of tries to get right. Robbins was not satisfied with his first attempt, so one day he improvised a dance while Styne made up something at the piano. Later Kander along with Betty Walberg adapted the tune of the song to fit Robbins's choreography.[56] For *Irma la Douce* Kander got to compose entirely new music. The Paris and London productions of *Irma la Douce* had been hits, but the director, Peter Brook, and choreographer, Onna White, wanted additional dance music for the New York production.[57] One of the highlights of the show was Kander's "Arctic Ballet" (informally known as the "Penguin Ballet"). Kander enjoyed writing this dance, for which he adapted the melody of "Our Language of Love" as a cancan and framed it with music similar to the zany underscoring of Warner Brothers' Looney Tunes. He even sneaked in a quote from Richard Wagner's "The Ride of the Walküre."

Kander tried out a number of potential writing partners during this period. Between *A Family Affair* and his working with Ebb, he wrote specialty material with David Rogers, who is best known as the librettist of the ill-fated *Charlie and Algernon*, which has music by Charles Strouse. Their sketches are lightly satirical and topical in nature, such as "The Launching," which is an astrophysicist's solution to his marital woes.

> I'm launching Louise in a sputnik.
> I'm sending her up into space.
> I'm sure she won't mind,
> She's good and she's kind,
> And I can't stand the sight of her face.

Their collaboration showed promise, but it ended quickly because Rogers was not interested in working as regularly as Kander wanted.[58] In 1957 Kander also worked with the composer Hank Beebe on a musical based on H. G. Wells's short story "The Man Who Could Work Miracles." It too was a brief collabo-

Table 4.2. John Kander's film and television music

Title	Year	Director	Music
Something for Everyone (released in England as *Black Flowers for the Bride*; also known as *The Rook*)	1970	Hal Prince	various
Norman Rockwell's World . . . An American Dream	1972	Robert Deubel	"Faces" (lyrics by Ebb) and variations
Kramer vs. Kramer	1979	Robert Benton	adapted Baroque music
Still of the Night	1982	Robert Benton	waltz
Blue Skies Again	1983	Richard Michaels	ragtime
Places in the Heart	1984	Robert Benton	pentatonic theme and variations
An Early Frost	1985	John Erman	waltz
I Want to Go Home	1989	Alain Resnais	various, including several waltzes
Billy Bathgate	1991	Robert Benton	period score with lush, romantic theme
Breathing Lessons	1994	John Erman	conventional light film theme
Boys Next Door	1996	John Erman	ragtime

ration because, although they enjoyed working together, their strengths and weakness were the same. In 1961, Beebe contributed material to a politically oriented satirical revue called *O, Oysters!*, which opened at the Village Gate and featured Jon Voight and Elly Stone. With Kander's permission, he used a song they had written together called "I'm Afraid."[59]

Music for Film and Television

Kander wrote music for eleven Hollywood and television films spanning more than three decades (table 4.2). His first film, *Something for Everyone*, starring Michael York and Angela Lansbury, was Hal Prince's film directorial debut. The screenplay, by Hugh Wheeler, is based on a novel by Harry Kressing. York's character, Konrad, is a murderous opportunist who charms Countess Von Ornstein, a widow whose fortune has practically dwindled to nothing after her husband's death. Kander wrote German beer garden polkas and marches to capture the post–World War II Bavarian setting of this black comedy. The project was a welcome break for Kander after the nonstop work of 1968, and since Prince did not fully understand the logistics of film scoring, which normally takes place during the postproduction period, he brought Kander with him to Europe.

A couple of years later, Kander wrote music for the 1972 television documentary *Norman Rockwell's World . . . An American Dream,* directed by Robert Deubel, which won an Academy Award for Live Action Short Film. The script calls for a theme and variations, each of which was "to dramatize the changing moods and periods immortalized by Rockwell's paintings." Kander and Ebb wrote a song called "Faces"—a purely diatonic and bucolic thirty-two-measure waltz—on which Kander based the variations.[60] Ebb's lyric was not used in the documentary. In the years that followed, Kander and Ebb were too busy to be able to pursue outside projects. Kander did not return to film composition until after *The Act,* which opened in 1977.

Kander believes that film music "should tell you something that the dialogue is not telling you." This philosophy, which was influenced by Debussy's *Pelléas et Mélisande,* is born out in most of his film scores from this period. His next film, *Kramer vs. Kramer,* was the first of several films that he did with the director Robert Benton. Starring Meryl Streep and Dustin Hoffman, *Kramer vs. Kramer* is about a custody battle between a self-absorbed art illustrator and his wife, whose lack of validation from her husband drives her away. Kander and Benton decided to use Baroque music rather than an original score, hoping to avoid sentimentalizing the subject matter. Kander selected and arranged pieces by Vivaldi and Purcell. Benton shared Kander's views about the function of film music, and he incorporated these pieces sparingly and with great precision. The same can be said for his next two films, *Still of the Night* and *Places in the Heart.* For both films Kander composed a theme and variations. *Still of the Night* is a psychological thriller starring Streep, Roy Scheider, Jessica Tandy, and Joseph Sommers. Streep, a museum employee, encounters the psychiatrist of her murdered lover, who was also her boss. The psychiatrist falls in love with her, solves the murder, and saves her from being murdered. Kander composed a nocturnal waltz theme that captures Streep's vulnerability, frail beauty, and intelligence (example 4.8). The gentle, mostly diatonic theme incorporates a series of suspensions that create an uneasy balance between romance and terror.

Places in the Heart stars Sally Fields, who plays a Depression-era widow and owner of a failing farm, and Danny Glover, a black stranger who saves

Example 4.8. *Still of the Night* (main theme)

her property from foreclosure. Kander devised a folksy pentatonic theme in duple meter. (A waltz version of the theme exists among his papers.) He also wove the classic bluegrass tune "Cotton-Eyed Joe" into the musical fabric of the film.

Following the three Benton films, Kander wrote music for four television movies, one directed by Richard Michaels, *Blue Skies Again*, and three by John Erman, *Early Frost*, *Breathing Lessons*, and *The Boys Next Door*. Erman's interest in serious stories of human interaction attracted Kander, and he, too, shared Kander's minimalist approach to film music. Kander composed two kinds of themes for these movies. For the lighter stories, such as *The Boys Next Door*, he wrote a ragtime or ragtime-inflected theme; for the serious stories a lyrical and primarily diatonic theme, most often a waltz, as is the case in *Still of the Night*. Kander composed a waltz theme for *An Early Frost* (1985), the first television drama to deal directly with AIDS. Although somewhat dated today, *An Early Frost* helped to counter early misconceptions about AIDS and the "gay lifestyle." The story, written by Ron Cowen and Daniel Lipman, the executive producers of the television series *Sisters* and *Queer as Folk*, is about a successful Chicago lawyer who contracts AIDS from his lover. The lawyer seeks solace from his family, who reside in the Boston area. Only when he collapses and ends up in the hospital does he admit to his family that he is gay and has AIDS. In an ending that today seems too sanguine given our current knowledge about the virus, the lawyer returns to his lover, prepared to face his last days. Kander's waltz theme is an apt counterpoint to the Chopin nocturne that the lawyer's mother, a once-promising concert pianist who now teaches students at her home, plays throughout the film.

Kander wrote a rousing cakewalk theme for *Blue Skies Again*, a television movie about a woman baseball player who wants to cross the gender divide and join an all-male team. Ebb wrote a lyric to go with the music, but it was never used. A jaunty rag is featured in *The Boys Next Door*, starring Nathan Lane, a Hallmark Hall of Fame movie about a group home for mentally handicapped men. *Breathing Lessons*, also a Hallmark movie, is based on Anne Tyler's 1988 novel about a woman on a mission to reunite her family. Joanne Woodward played the leading role, and James Garner her husband. A light theme over a plodding quarter-note accompaniment is an effective backdrop to what is essentially a road movie. Although there are hints of ragtime, the theme is similar to the whimsical music heard at the beginning of countless Hollywood family-oriented films.

Kander's last two film scores are more expansive than his earlier ones. Alain Resnais's 1989 film *I Want to Go Home* required Kander to write several distinct themes. The story, by Jules Feiffer, is about an American cartoonist who attends a comic-strip exhibition in Paris given in his honor. He takes the opportunity to look up his estranged daughter, an art student at the Sorbonne. Throughout the film, the cartoonist, played by Adolph Green, argues with a cartoon cat, animated by Feiffer (a device right out of *Woman of the Year*).[61] Kander wrote a series of waltzes: "Major-Minor Waltz," "One More Dance," "Accordion Waltz," "Angry Waltz," "Mysterious Waltz," "Bath Waltz," and "Ragtime Waltz." Shifting between major and minor keys and imbued with appoggiaturas, these pieces have something in common with the music that Kander wrote for his musicals set in Europe, *Cabaret*, *Zorbá*, and *The Visit*.

Kander's most emotionally lush film score was cut before anyone had a chance to hear it. He composed it for *Billy Bathgate*, which starred Dustin Hoffman, Bruce Willis, and Nicole Kidman. The main theme features suspensions, sevenths, and ninths, evoking the romantic scores of a bygone era in Hollywood (example 4.9). The music was orchestrated and recorded by Michael Gibson, but Kander, to use his own words, "was fired" when the studio reedited the film to make Hoffman's part more prominent. Kander's score was replaced with music by Mark Isham.

Example 4.9. *Billy Bathgate* (main theme)

Miscellaneous Compositions

Although Kander never undertook a full-length opera (even turning down
an offer by Lyric Opera of Kansas City), late in his career he had the opportunity to compose music for two critically acclaimed opera singers. Carol
Vaness commissioned *Three Poems*, a song cycle about death, "You," "Plaisir," and "The Last Day." One of Kander's cousins, Lucile Adler, wrote these
poems as a response to her husband's struggle with an illness at the end of his
life. Vaness performed the cycle on her 1987 concert tour and later recorded
them for a CD called *Classical Broadway*.[62] The order of the three songs for
the published music is different from the order on the recording.

Published Music	Recording
"You"	"Plaisir"
"Plaisir"	"You"
"The Last Day"	"The Last Day"

The published score progresses from the shortest poem, "You," to the longest
poem, "The Last Day," an extended text about accepting loss. "You" has a

Example 4.10. *Three Poems*, "You" (opening)

through-composed melody over a peaceful repeated pattern in the accompaniment reminiscent of Satie's *Gymnopédies* (example 4.10). The opening phrase serves as a refrain, recurring in the piano and at the end of the movement.

"Plaisir" opens with a burst of ascending and descending deca-tuplet runs traversing the first six pitches of the Lydian scale. The flutter of rhythmic activity runs throughout the piece, depicting the "crazy bird" metaphor for the wife's eagerness to wake her husband. "The Last Day" starts out with an expressive pentatonic theme in F major sung a cappella (example 4.11). The first three notes of the theme make up a motive that is heard every time the music modulates, which is often. These modulations help underscore the idea of moving toward something elusive. The vocal part is essentially a recitative, but it grows in intensity as the music modulates from F to F-sharp to G. The arrival of the word "come" coincides with a mediant modulation to E-flat, the final key of the song and a symbol of closure.[63] Here, the voice sustains an E-flat for twelve beats as the piano majestically restates the opening pentatonic theme.

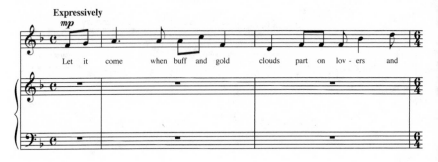

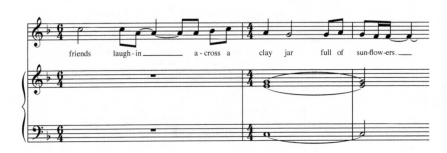

Example 4.11. *Three Poems*, "The Last Day" (opening)

In 1993 Kander won the second Richard Tucker Composer's Commission.[64] Kander chose to write an aria—for Renée Fleming, his favorite living soprano—that is based on a letter written by Sullivan Ballou, a soldier in the Confederate Army, to his wife, Sarah.[65] Ballou wrote the letter, which Kander first heard during Ken Burns's PBS Civil War documentary, the night before going into battle. Among the challenges that Kander had to overcome were how to deal with the extraordinary length of the letter and how to translate the prose text into lyrical musical lines. Kander solved the former problem by having the performer read the greeting and salutation over a piano accompaniment, and the latter by incorporating a simple, flexible theme that can expand and contract.

The aria begins and ends in F, but the interior sections shift between D major and D-flat major. The first sung section is a twenty-four-measure recitative passage in F Lydian over a four-note ostinato in the right hand of the accompaniment, and an F pedal in the left hand (example 4.12a). The first shift away from the key of F occurs on "civilization now leans on the triumph of the government," as pitches from the D-flat scale insinuate them-

Example 4.12. *Letter from Sullivan Ballou:* (a) opening vocal passage; (b) main theme; (c) "Oh, Sarah!"

selves, alluding to the approaching key change. The principal theme is first introduced in D major on "Sarah, my love for you . . ." (example 4.12b). Built on the pentatonic scale, it evokes the nineteenth-century American milieu of the letter. This theme appears several times during the course of the piece, slightly altered to fit the prose text. The music returns to the key of F in measure 78 as the singer cries out "Oh Sarah!" on a high E, an allusion to the accented passing tone on "deathless" in the main theme (example 4.12c). In measure 78, the primary pitch E functions as a suspension within the sub-dominant harmony. The most discordant moment in the aria occurs on the word "always," which is repeated on whole notes over an F chord and A chord in the accompaniment. Despite the sectionalization and expansiveness of this work, it is remarkably economical. Unity is achieved through a few re-curring elements: Lydian mode, E as melodic focal point, subdominant har-mony with 4–3 suspensions, and variations of the main theme.

Music for Plays

When Kander and Tony Walton met in 1957 during *Conversation Piece*, they talked about writing a musical together. Although this musical never materialized, a project that Walton wrote in the early nineties involved col-laborating on a song with Kander. The MS. Foundation for Women invited Walton to direct a live theatrical version of the television special *Free to Be You and Me*. He wrote a skit called *Adelie Penguin* to be incorporated into the production as additional material and asked Kander to write the music. When Walton withdrew from the project, *Adelie Penguin* went into a trunk until Kate Burton, who was staying with the Waltons, secretly sent the script to the Public Theater, which was planning an evening of mini-musicals. The director and choreographer Graciela Daniele was interested in doing it, but when Joseph Papp died, so too did the production of mini-musicals. In 1995 Bridget LeRoy, Walton's daughter, turned her father's original skit into a full-length musical called *Adelie Penguin and the Wibbly Wobbly Walk*, and in-cluded the one song that Kander had written when the show was still part of the *Free to Be You and Me* project.[66] The Bay Street Theater in Sag Harbor, Long Island, which was founded by Walton's other daughter, Emma Walton, and her husband, Stephen Hamilton, produced the musical. *Adelie Penguin* works on a very simple premise: a group of schoolchildren arrives at the pen-guin pool at the zoo only to discover that it is temporarily closed. The kids put on flippers and start to wobble like penguins. After an introduction in which the kids turn into penguins, they act out a thematically structured set of vignettes about diversity and gender.

    Kander also served as musical director for a couple of productions pro-duced by Tony Randall's National Actors Theatre, *The Crucible* in 1991 and *Three Men on a Horse* in 1993. The director of the former, Yossi Yzraely, mixed songs from the early American *The Bay Psalm Book*, which gave the production a feeling of authenticity, with contrasting music by Kander for solo double bass. Kander experimented with nontraditional techniques for the bass, such as double-stops and pizzicato playing.

The pieces examined in this chapter help us to better understand how Kander and Ebb evolved into successful Broadway writers and where their individual artistic interests occasionally led them outside of their collaboration. The musicals they wrote in the fifties and early sixties are particularly instructive in this regard. Ebb and Paul Klein never produced any lasting work, but their musicals were important to Ebb's maturation as a theater writer. Klein's scores have not been located, and much of Kander's compositions from these years exists either in his head or in the form of indecipherable sketchbooks. Perhaps some of Klein's music will surface someday, allowing for further study and even possible productions. Kander still regrets not being able to complete *The Enchanted*, but maybe he will be moved to commit to paper some of the music he remembers.

CHAPTER 5

Kiss of the Spider Woman

Sex, Politics, and the Diva Musical

Kiss of the Spider Woman shows what gay writers and straight producers think Broadway
audiences will accept ten years after *La Cage aux Folles.*
—JOHN CLUM

IN THE MID EIGHTIES, KANDER AND EBB BEGAN WORKING WITH
Manuel Puig on a musical adaptation of his stirring 1976 novel *Kiss of the
Spider Woman.* Set entirely in a Buenos Aires prison, *Kiss of the Spider
Woman* is about the relationship between a leftist political prisoner, Valentin,
and his apolitical homosexual cellmate, Molina, who has been arrested for
"corrupting a minor." In order to escape the harsh conditions of prison life,
Molina, a window designer by profession, describes romantic film plots to
Valentin, who at first sees Molina as an annoyance and objects to the fact that
his plots are from Nazi propaganda films. Molina delights only in the films'
glamour and idealized love stories, preferring to remain blissfully ignorant
of their political content. Valentin's initially derisive attitude about Molina's
fascination with film reflects what Brett Farmer has described as the hetero-
sexually constructed myth that codes "gay cinematic reception," and, by extension, gayness itself, "as deviant and extreme . . . as the obscene other of an
implied, stable, heterosexual norm."[1] Norman Lavers suggests that the clash
of Molina's aestheticism and Valentin's masculine sense of righteousness (and
unconscious aversion to homosexuality) provides Puig a unique opportunity

to examine how society turns men into "oppressors of the weak" and to break down the gender binarism that lumps homosexuals and women into a single category, "the submissive masochistic side of the machismo equation."[2] The reader is thereby forced to examine patriarchal constructions of gender, sex, machismo, and marianism.

Puig's novel treats gender as performance and deconstructs the binary definition of gender as constructed by machismo culture: the submissive woman and the repressive male. Molina acts like a submissive woman because it is the only role that society has made available to gay men. He adopts the ostentatious physical and vocal gestures of the film heroines with whom he identifies, and he nurses Valentin back to health several times during the course of the story and in the end makes the ultimate self-sacrifice. Valentin eventually comes to appreciate Molina and his films. But Valentin performs his prescribed role, too, and with no less conviction than Molina does. Puig limits Molina to the language of Hollywood films and Valentin to the popular jargon of Freudian psychology and Marxism. Molina's campy effeminate persona is inseparable from his projection of himself into his favorite films, and Valentin's lectures are laden with clichés.

It was Ebb who proposed the idea of adapting the novel as a musical: "I just saw it . . . You can get into his [Molina's] head and do all her [Spider Woman's] numbers on screen. It just seemed right to me. I didn't have to go further than that." Ebb might have identified personally with Molina, for words he once used to describe himself could have been intended for Molina: "[I] always lived in a fantasy world as a boy, and my fantasy life started to center itself in the theater when I was old enough to appreciate it in my early teens."[3] The line between the cold reality of life and the comforting illusion of theater is more pronounced in *Kiss of the Spider Woman* than in any of Kander and Ebb's previous musicals. Molina's film fantasies distract him and Valentin from their oppressive surroundings, but these diversions are only a temporary respite. Each prisoner dies a horrible death in the end. Puig's strategy of exploring serious themes through the lexicon of popular culture plays right into Kander and Ebb's strengths. It also appealed to Hal Prince, who agreed without a moment's hesitation to direct the project.

Puig, Kander, Ebb, and Prince first met early in 1986 to discuss the project. At the time of this meeting, Prince was busy with several other projects, including *Phantom of the Opera*, and Puig was living in Brazil, so progress was slow at first, and communication between Puig and his collaborators in New

York was mostly of an epistolary nature. Puig's letters allow us to reconstruct the early evolution of the project, and they reveal that Ebb and Puig clashed over the fundamental concept of the musical.[4]

By May of 1986, Puig had completed a detailed outline for the musical. Puig substituted a single 1940s Hollywood musical for the multiple Nazi propaganda films of his novel. (He had done the same thing when he adapted his novel as a stage play in 1981.)[5] Puig's newly invented Hollywood musical begins with the birth of a girl and an ominous prediction about her demise. She grows into a beautiful but insecure woman and falls in love with a playboy film director. The young woman poses as a maid at the director's house, and, when the Mafia threatens him, she helps him seek safe haven in a fishing village. They fall in love but must return to the city to take care of his financial matters. Gangsters sent by the jealous producer attempt to shoot the director, but the young woman blocks the bullet with her own body. Although she has learned the true meaning of love, she cannot escape her fate.

Nearly half a year passed before Puig's next correspondence with Prince. During that time, Ebb wrote to Puig about concerns that he had with Puig's outline for the film sequences. Ebb pushed for "an obviously different 'concept'" from that of the novel and cited *Follies* and *Cabaret* as examples, but Puig felt that "those [musicals] were atmosphere pieces, . . . not dominated by two strong characters like *Spider Woman*." Ebb was afraid that Puig's vision lacked a sense of style and theatricality. Puig believed otherwise and, according to his own statements, tried to allay Ebb's concerns, claiming that his film musical provided plenty of opportunity to use "exuberant kitsch" and draw on naïf paintings or Henri Rousseau's work for the tropical settings. The cell scenes, he suggested, could incorporate elements from the Bauhaus school, "with its obsession for cages and oppression." Puig's main concern was that the film sequences deepen the audience's understanding of the characters, and he worried that Ebb's insistence on style over content would dilute the main story. Despite these differences, Puig remained enthusiastic about the project, and Ebb evidently had some influence on him, for when he sent Prince a complete script, it included a new movie fantasy, *It Was Written in the Stars*, which he infused with "sex/superstition/terror in the style of the film director Val Lewton."[6] In reality this plot was not that different from the original. It too featured a young woman (here named Perla) who is raised by prostitutes. She falls in love with a wanted man and in the end dies tragically. The new movie plot reflects elements of the Molina-Valentin story.[7]

Puig's new version clearly did not satisfy Ebb's desire for a new concept, for in the late eighties Terrence McNally, a playwright with a reputation for confronting gay themes, replaced Puig. Prince claims that Puig, apart from living in a different hemisphere, "had no sense of the technique necessary in structuring a work for the stage."[8] McNally, who never saw Puig's script (a situation parallel to that surrounding *The Rink*, for which McNally also replaced the original book writer), wrote an entirely new version, including new Hollywood musical sequences in the style of a Rita Hayworth film. No doubt at Ebb's urging, *Man Over Board*, as the new inner-film musical was titled, features MGM-style musical production numbers. It is a story in "glorious Technicolor" about a South American actress named Aurora, who works under the stage name of "La Sueña." Aurora is the mistress of a crime boss known as the "Monster." While on his yacht, Aurora falls in love with a young sailor named Armando. In order to nip this affair in the bud, the Monster roughs up Armando. Aurora heals Armando's wounds with kisses. Later, we learn that Armando is the leader of the resistance movement, "dedicated to overthrowing everything the Monster stands for." At a guerrilla camp high in the mountains, Armando and his forces are training. The Monster pressures Aurora into revealing Armando's whereabouts. "But first," exclaims Molina, "there's a big production number ["A Good Clean Fight"]. We better get out of the way, or we'll get caught right in the middle of it."[9] The burly men of the resistance sing

> If there's one thing in the world
> That could set a man right,
> It's a good clean fight.

Aurora, who believes in Armando's cause, arrives at the camp and warns him of the Monster's plan to destroy him and his men. They devise a counter plan to assassinate the Monster. At a café called Las Calumbas, Armando, disguised as a waiter and concealing a gun, approaches the Monster while Aurora performs "Kiss of the Spider Woman" and "The Day After That." When she is done, the Monster is discovered dead. Armando sweeps Aurora up in his arms. "Goodness and love have triumphed over evil and hate," Molina exclaims.[10] This plot, with its political edge, is a more effective parallel to the Molina-Valentin story than was either of Puig's scenarios.

McNally's treatment of Molina and Valentin's relationship avoids many of the complex gender and political issues raised in Puig's novel and as a result lacks its gritty essence. What remains is a sympathetic story of a developing friendship between a straight man and gay man set against the brutal forces of machismo society, which was probably the only aspect of the original story that seemed tenable for the mostly North American Broadway market. In Puig's *Kiss of the Spider Woman*, the ethnic-sexual other is a central part of the story, but McNally, Ebb, and Kander were not culturally predisposed to treating the ethnic aspects of either Molina's or Valentin's sexual orientation. How else could one explain the fact that neither Molina nor Valentin was played by an actor who could not even pass as Latino? The remaining ethnic elements of the musical are more like exotic trappings for a story than a vehicle for examining homophobia in machismo culture.[11]

McNally makes up for some of the lost thematic complexity by including graphic depictions of homophobia. For instance, guards regularly taunt Molina with anti-gay epithets. Worse, they force him to act out a sex-slave scenario in which he promises to do anything they command. At the dramatic high point of the story the warden, who threatens Molina with death if he does not name names, barks, "Talk you fucking faggot or I'll blow your fucking head off." Instead of betraying Valentin, Molina turns to his former cellmate and says, "I love you." The warden shoots Molina in the head. It is a gruesome scene, and more violent than anything that had ever occurred in a Broadway musical.[12]

The musical's most significant departure from the novel regards the role of the Spider Woman, which the writers completely reconceived. Late in Puig's novel, Valentin, in response to Molina's self-identification with a panther woman, a character in one of Molina's film narratives, insists that Molina is a spider woman:[13]

> "I'm curious . . . Would you feel much revulsion about giving me a kiss?"
> "Mmm . . . It must be a fear that you'll turn into a panther, like with the first movie you told me."
> "I'm not the panther woman."
> "It's true, you're not the panther woman."
> "It's very sad being a panther woman; no one can kiss you. Or anything."
> "You, you're the spider woman, that traps men in her web."
> "How lovely! Oh, I like that."

This exchange, which occurs just 20 pages from the end of the 281-page novel (English translation), marks the first mention of a spider woman. During the last few pages of the novel, Valentin, who lies wounded in the infirmary experiencing the effects of morphine, has a dream in which he narrates a film to his girlfriend, Marta. In order to maintain a level of ambiguity in the text, Puig avoids identifying the speaker. The lines inside quotation marks indicate Marta as the speaker:

> In my cell I can't sleep anymore because he got me used to listening to him tell films every night . . . you don't know how beautiful it is here with this mixture of palm trees, and lianas, at night it's all silvery, because the film is in black and white, "And the music in the background?" very soft maracas, and drums, "Isn't that a sign of danger?" no, it's the music that announces, when they switch on a strong spotlight, the appearance of such a strange woman, with a long dress on, that's shining, "Silver lamé, that fits her like a glove?" yes, "And her face?" she's wearing a mask, it's also silver, but . . . poor crea-ture . . . she can't move, there in the deepest part of the jungle she's trapped in a spider's web, or no, the spiderweb is growing out of her own body, the threads are coming out of her waist and her hips, they're part of her body, so many threads that look hairy like ropes and disgust me, even though if I were to touch them they might feel smooth as who knows what, but it makes me queasy to touch them. . . . and I ask her why she's crying and in a close-up that covers the whole screen at the end of the film she answers me that that's just what can never be known.

Puig incorporated this ending into his script for the musical. Throughout his script, Molina associates himself with Perla, whose situation resembles his own, and Valentin calls him a spider woman. At the end of the novel, Valentin imagines Molina's voice: "A strange creature is ready to save your life, although she can be dangerous, she catches men in her web!" Molina as-sures Valentin that the Spider Woman has discovered what love is all about.

Mira Wiegmann has noted that, in incorporating a spider woman into his story, Puig was drawing from an array of high and low cross-cultural ref-erences, ancient mythological archetypes, and the psychological models of Freud and Jung.[14] In Hindu, for instance, the spider woman, like Molina, is a "weaver of the illusory world of the senses."[15] Puig also evokes the mythologi-cal figure of Ariadne, who disobeys her father (a parallel to Puig's warden) in order to protect Theseus from death.[16] Molina behaves like many a film hero-ine, challenging patriarchal society in order to protect the man he loves.

McNally, Ebb, and Kander preferred the Spider Woman character of Hector Babenco's 1985 film adaptation of Puig's novel, which starred William Hurt as Molina, Raul Julia as Valentin, and Sonia Braga as Leni Lamaison, Marta, and the Spider Woman. Hurt won an Oscar for his performance. The film transformed Valentin's comments about a spider woman to an actual character in one of Molina's movies; the Spider Woman is thus a symbol of Molina's "fantasy image of himself," no longer Valentin's projection onto Molina. She is not the benevolent archetypal spider woman of Puig's novel. She is a more "popular and patriarchal romantic vision" but also a more ambiguous figure. McNally, Ebb, and Kander went even further in this direction, completely separating out the spider woman's beneficent attributes and reassigning them to Aurora, a role they created. Whereas Aurora, Molina's favorite film diva, is warm and nurturing, the Spider Woman, a character in a movie that Molina saw as a boy and has been afraid of ever since, is menacing and duplicitous. These two characters, though, are played by a single actress. The Spider Woman, now a prosaic symbol of death, confronts Molina directly, detached from the film in which he first saw her.

The musical's radical reconfiguration of the Spider Woman is inseparable from the elevation of her role to a musical theater diva. She is an omnipresent symbol of fear and death (as exemplified by the musical's black and red logo and other advertising images), "a negative anima, the shadow of Molina's film diva Aurora. . . . Her eyes probe those on stage and in the audience, reminding viewers that everyone will one day face this darkly beautiful, but terrifying anima."[17] Throughout the musical, she tries to lure Molina into her web with snippets from her opening theme music (see example 5.2) and phrases from the title song. Her theme music incorporates descending glassy chromatic chords, portending Molina's tragic end. Of course, she literally announces Molina's death when she sings the title song toward the end of the musical. Her performance of this song has nothing to do with Molina's film—at least there is no explicit indication that it does. She ostensibly sings directly to Molina.[18]

The road to Broadway was arduous and bumpy for *Kiss of the Spider Woman*. A 1990 workshop at SUNY Purchase produced by "New Musicals," an organization founded to nurture new musicals, was a highly publicized disaster. Hal Prince and Ebb's good friend Marty Bell founded "New Musicals" that very year with the intention of providing writers a working environment away from the pressures of Broadway. They chose Purchase College as their venue because of its state-of-the-art facilities and proximity to Manhattan, and decided on *Kiss of the Spider Woman* to launch the organization. When performances began, several dramaturgical problems remained unresolved, such as an imbalance between the film segments and the realistic prison scenes. *Man Over Board*, Molina's fantasy film from 1947, impinged too much on the main story. "We made every mistake in the book," Ebb admitted; "we really had no idea how to do it up there . . . We had a sailor in it. We had a tap dance number. . . . It was ridiculous." As Kander put it, "We had been tying to tell two different stories at once, and the audience didn't follow it."[19] To make matters worse, Hal Prince had to miss a number of critical rehearsals due to the illness of a relative. A major blow to the production came when Sheridan Morley and Frank Rich decided to review the musical, ignoring pleas from the producer not to do so on the grounds that it was still a work-in-progress. Morley was favorable, but Rich, although admiring of the musical's courage, disparaged the fantasy segments, the casting, the choreography, and the direction; and he questioned the very operation of "New Musicals," insinuating that Prince had spent developmental money on what was essentially a pre-Broadway tryout. Once the *New York Times* decided to publish the review, the other New York papers felt at liberty to review the show as well. Most critics agreed with Rich, complaining that *Man Over Board* overwhelmed the principal story and drew attention away from the important themes of the story (the very thing that Puig had feared about Ebb's approach to the movie sequences). McNally's treatment of the main plot drew much less fire, even though it was a mere reflection of Puig's original story. *Spider Woman* closed in Purchase on a sour note and put an end to "New Musicals."

After the Purchase debacle, *Kiss of the Spider Woman* remained in limbo for a couple of years while McNally, Kander, and Ebb rewrote major portions of the musical. A new producer, Garth Drabinsky, president of the now bankrupt Livent, Inc., produced the revised version first in Toronto in 1992 and then in London in the same year, before bringing it to New York, where it opened at the Broadhurst Theatre in May 1993. Before committing money to the project, though, he insisted on a New York reading.[20] The Broadway production was a solid success, running for 906 performances and earning Kander and Ebb their third Tony Award for best score.

In revising *Spider Woman*, McNally, Kander, and Ebb altered only a few minor details in the main story, but they radically rethought the content and structure of the Hollywood movie within the musical. In so doing, they created a commercial hit and received the approbation of the Tony committee. They went back to the novel's use of multiple film narratives, and they recast the Aurora/Spider Woman, originally played by the North American soprano Lauren Mitchell, with Chita Rivera, for decades one of Broadway's leading divas (Rivera had appeared as the Spider Woman in the reading mentioned above). With unrelated movie-musical vignettes, the new version alleviated the burden of following a complicated secondary plot line. Aurora, a Latin-American star and Molina's favorite film diva, appears in all of the movie se-quences, which lack the psychological depth of Molina's films in Puig's novel and only loosely comment on the main action. They feature exotic musical numbers built on south-of-the-boarder dance rhythms. The Latin-American patina provided enough entertainment and colorful stage settings to appeal to a mainstream audience while creating enough distance from the story to allow them to confront but not feel threatened by the serious themes of Puig's novel.

The first vignette introduces Aurora as she soaks in a bathtub surrounded by servants. It celebrates the diva as diva ("Her Name is Aurora"). It is a single, self-contained scene from Molina's vast mental repository of Holly-wood musicals. The same is true for the subsequent vignettes. Later in act 1, when Valentin's patience with Molina has run out, Aurora appears and sings "Where You Are," counseling Valentin to "learn how not to be where you are." The song helps to distinguish between the real and fictional world. Toward the end of act 1, Molina narrates a nightclub scene from a film called *Bird of Paradise*. Aurora, playing the role of a prisoner, performs "Gimme Love," a love-is-the-only-thing-that-matters song and dance.[21] This number distracts Valentin and thus saves him from having to go to the infirmary. Early in act 2, Molina enthralls Valentin with a scene from *Flame of St. Petersburg*, a film set against the backdrop of the Russian Revolution. Suggested by Valentin, it is the only film fantasy with a strong thematic connection to the main story. Aurora plays Tatyana Alexandrovna, a cabaret singer who chooses to marry her revolutionary lover over a man from the Russian aristocracy. At her farewell performance she sings "Good Times" in a cabaret before all of St. Petersburg, including the tsar.[22] This scene is the last Hollywood sequence in *Spider Woman*. The remainder of act 2 builds toward the dramatic climax of the main story.

Many of the critics who had complained about the Purchase production of *Spider Woman* declared the revised version to be a triumph, but they re-served their most enthusiastic praise for Chita Rivera. Her appearances in the film sequences alone were enough to change Frank Rich's overall opinion about the musical. Rich raved about the "love affair" between Rivera and the audience, a sentiment voiced by nearly every critic.[23] Her diva turn provided enough entertainment to offset some of the issues that the critics had with the main story and the lyrics. The reviews had some guarded praise for the music but, in general, only disparagement about McNally's handling of the main story. John Simon, comparing the musical to Babenco's film, thought that they both dragged the high camp of Puig's novel to a low level but that the musical went even lower than the film.[24] Most critics agreed that McNally reduced Valentin to a two-dimensional macho figure with more bravado and volume than substance and subtlety. The increased importance of the Spider Woman role might have reinforced Molina's identification with her, but it weakened the character of Valentin. As Rich noted, the musical "turns the serious business of police-state torture into show-biz kitch every bit as vacuous as the B-movie clichés parodied in its celluloid fantasies." Critics praised Anthony Crivello, the actor playing the part of Valentin, but his performance did not make up for what they thought was a deleterious downgrading of the role.[25] What upset critics most, however, was a change in Valentin's motives for sleeping with Molina. As made explicit in the song "Anything for Him," Valentin has sex with Molina in order to secure a favor: "If we touch before he goes / He'll make that call." One critic charged the writers with changing the "shattering exchange of contrasting manhoods to a despicable manipulation. . . . a deceit that turns heroism into just another victimizer of a gay man's heart."[26] One can only wonder if the writers' lack of fidelity to Puig's story is an indication that they did not trust the mostly heterosexual audience to accept the fact that a heterosexual man would freely have sex with a gay man.

McNally considered including a scene for Valentin and Molina's mother, who visits him in his cell one month after Molina's death in order to thank him for giving her son dignity: "A life without that—which is what he had—is no life at all. . . . He kissed me goodbye and I'll never see him again. [She is crying.] I wanted to see the man who'd give my son his dignity." This scene, which was cut well before *Spider Woman* opened at Purchase, was too sentimental and maudlin for the harsh facts of the story. That McNally wrote it at all is indicative that he (as well as Kander and Ebb) were promoting themes of acceptance over the more radical and political themes of Puig's novel. McNally's final script does make it clear that Valentin appreciates Molina's love and heroism, but only after he is shot, and by then it is too late to redeem himself for having manipulating his friend.

John Clum's quote at the head of this chapter is more accurate than one might assume from its glib tone. From a commercial standpoint, reducing the story to a diva vehicle paid off, for the unanimous enthusiasm from the critics for Chita Rivera offset their largely negative criticism about Valentin and the weak book. It also placed more importance on Molina and thereby tilted the thematic emphasis away from sexuality and toward survival. One can assume, given Ebb's long-held interest in this theme, that he preferred it this way. Could *Spider Woman* have succeeded on its own terms in the commercial venue of Broadway? Could it have provided the escapism expected by Broadway audiences while dealing uncompromisingly with the themes that were important to Puig? Apparently, McNally, Ebb, Kander, and Prince did not think so.

In order to better understand how much the musical compromises the novel's intentions, we must turn back to Puig's outlines and script for the musical. Puig tried to incorporate as much of the novel's political content as possible. Molina and Valentin's discussions address, among other topics, the treatment of women, the charitable nature of the poor, alienation, and the nature of freedom. Puig even included an allusion to the scientific theories about sexuality and love that give his novel an interesting intellectual dimension. For instance, in the musical Valentin reduces falling in love to a physical function of the body, "the same way your stomach secretes juices for digestion." Molina coyly criticizes reductionist explanations for homosexuality and the belief that gayness in a man can be cured by a woman. Molina also lectures Valentin on the hand gestures of women celebrated in Hollywood films, including the Floradora girl, "all intent on pleasing her man"; the Deco girl, "a woman who starts to think"; and the outdoor girl of the forties, like Paulette Goddard in tennis clothes. The only political detail remaining in McNally's script is an invented passage about the "movement" led by Alberto Golizar, the man who changed Valentin's life with his speeches. Puig's script, even though it is full of political dialogue, never seems preachy or didactic. Rather, political details surface naturally in Valentin and Molina's conversations, in which they discover new things about themselves. In the name of his cause, Valentin refuses sexual gratification, and he struggles with sentiment, which he sees as an obstacle to achieving his goal of stamping out military oppression. Were he committed to a single woman, his death would cause her too much pain. Puig's script artfully illustrates how Valentin's rigid justification for his type of masculinity softens through his contact with Molina. After Valentin has sex with Molina, he experiences an awakening. He learns that, like eating and sleeping, sex is "devoid of moral meaning. . . . [It is] morally banal." Affection, on the other hand, is transcendental. Valentin concludes that neither masculinity nor identity determines sexual behavior. Homosexuals and heterosexuals do not exist. Only people exist. These scenes

John Kander and Fred Ebb performing at the benefit concert for the hospital where Chita Rivera was being treated following an automobile accident (November 1986). Photo by Cliff Lipson; Cliff Lipson/cliff lipson photography (copyright 1986) (Tiff C12)

would have been racy stuff for a musical, even in the nineties, but they would have given the musical more intellectual and political depth.

The evolution of Kander and Ebb's score provides additional insight into why the second version of the musical succeeded. In effect, they wrote a tripartite score consisting of traditional book songs, Hollywood musical songs for Aurora, and haunting surreal music that Molina hears in his imagination (the Spider Woman's music and "The Morphine Tango"). The mixture of diegetic songs and book songs had proved to be a winning formula in *Cabaret* and *Chicago*, but the two types are less in balance here than in those musicals. For the film sequences, Kander and Ebb wrote some of their most exciting production numbers ever. Michael Gibson's brilliant orchestrations gave these numbers a slick Hollywood veneer using synthesizers and a battery of Latin percussion instruments. The Spider Woman music is evocative, well unified, and dramatically effective. The book songs, however, are less uniform and uneven.

Table 5.1. Purchase and Broadway scores for *Kiss of the Spider Woman**

Purchase (1990)†	Broadway (1993)
Act 1	**Act 1**
"A Visit"	
	Prologue (Spider Woman theme)
	"Aurora"
"Over the Wall 1"	"Over the Wall 1" (different from Purchase)
	"Kiss of the Spider Woman" Fragment 1
	"Bluebloods"
	"Dressing Them Up"
	"I Draw the Line"
"Dear One"	"Dear One"
"Aurora"	
"Sailor Boy"	
	"Over the Wall 2" (Purchase "Over the Wall 1")
	"Where You Are"
"Come Out"	
"Marta" (short segment)	"Marta" (with "Over the Wall 3")
	Spider Woman theme
"I Do Miracles"	**"I Do Miracles"**
"My First Woman"	"Gabriel's Letter" and "My First Woman"
"Gabriel's Letter"	
"Everyday"	
"Morphine Tango"	"Morphine Tango"
"You Can Never Shame Me"	"You Can Never Shame Me"
	"The Visit" and "Morphine Tango" reprise
"The Day After That"	
"She's a Woman"	"She's a Woman"
"Gimme Love"	**"Gimme Love"**
Act 2	**Act 2**
"A Good Clean Fight"	
"Cookies"	
	"Russian Movie" / **"Good Times"**
	"The Day After That"
"Never You"	
"Mama, It's Me"	"Mama, It's Me"
	"Anything for Him"
"The Kiss of the Spider Woman"	"The Kiss of the Spider Woman"
"The Day After That"	

Table 5.1. (*Continued*)

Purchase (1990)†	Broadway (1993)
"Over the Wall 2"	
"Over the Wall 3"	"Over the Wall 4" (same as Purchase "Over the Wall 3")
"Only in the Movies"	"Only in the Movies"

*Some of the same songs from both productions have different titles. This table uses the Broadway titles. Songs in the Hollywood musical are in boldface type.
†The Purchase production began with an overture in the form of a medley of tunes from the score.

Because the writers did not alter the main story after Purchase, Kander and Ebb did not need to do much work on the book songs (table 5.1). They cut two of them, "Come Out" and "Cookies," and wrote two new ones, Molina's defining song, "Dressing Them Up," and a trio for Molina, Valentin, and the Spider Woman, "Anything for Him."[27] The rest of the changes amounted to relocating the book songs within the plot. On the other hand, they retained only half of the movie songs, which is no surprise given that these movie sequences were completely rewritten, and they limited the number of songs for the movie sequences to five, three fewer than in the Purchase production.

The multilayered score, although well conceived for the concept of the show, lacks the singularity of purpose in Kander and Ebb's scores for *Cabaret* and *Chicago*. Aurora's film appearances have some metaphorical value, but they relate only tenuously to the main story. By contrast, the cabaret scenes in *Cabaret* did double duty as entertainment and thematic commentary, and the vaudeville format of *Chicago* is inseparable from the content of the musical. The flashy songs and dances of the film sequences in *Spider Woman* cushion the shock of the tragic conclusion of the story. The Hollywood musical is more of a theatrical device than an ideal conveyance of the musical's themes. It provides an escape for Molina and Valentin from the grim realities of their incarceration, but it lacks the social commentary and pathos of Puig's film fantasies.

The Hollywood songs, which the critics generally admired, range from velvety seductive ballads to hot salsa-infused dance numbers. The book songs did not fare as well. The writers attempted to distinguish Molina and Valentin from each other musically, but the result is an uneven mixture of the Broadway idiom and Broadway opera. Molina's music tends to rely on pastiche, such as in "Dressing Them Up," for which Kander wrote a vamp that provides melodic material for the choppy syncopated vocal theme (example 5.1a). In

Example 5.1. Molina's and Valentin's first song (a) "Dressing Them Up,"
(b) "Marta"

contrast, Valentin sings long arching lines as in "Marta" (example 5.1b). In
addition, making Valentin's character less complex caused a musical imbalance between the two protagonists.

Notwithstanding these shortcomings, the score for *Spider Woman* aims
for emotional depth, incorporating a greater dramatic sweep, more extended
musical scenes, and more ensemble writing than do Kander and Ebb's earlier
scores. Kander once said, "The beauty of the Broadway musical form is that it
is so broad and inclusive, you are free to do whatever you want. You are free
to be as operatic as you want."[28] These words are borne out in *Kiss of the Spider Woman*, which is Kander's most operatic score up to that point. Kander's
favorite operas, *Manon*, *Der Rosenkavalier*, and *Pelléas et Mélisande*, engage
him in the emotional world of the characters. For Kander, Richard Strauss
composes the "most beautiful lines about love." He admires Puccini's ability
to bring the listener into the world of the characters and has noted that "Bohème is genius because in no time at all, [Puccini] establishes those people
so brilliantly that you really feel so close to them that it is almost as if you
could do a biography of each one of them." Likewise, he was drawn to the
intense emotional drama between Molina and Valentin, which pushed him
in an operatic direction: "There are sections of . . . *Kiss of the Spider Woman*
which let me extend myself that way, without having to come to terms with

the fact that I would then have to take myself seriously as a composer." There are several direct opera references in his score. For instance, "Dear One" recalls the additive multivoice structure of "Mir ist so wunderbar" from Beethoven's *Fidelio*, in which the texture thickens as each new singer enters with the main theme. The prisoners' guttural utterances are evocative of the revolting hanging scene of Benjamin Britten's *Billy Budd*. Puig himself might have suggested an operatic style, as he mentioned using leitmotifs in one of letters: "Since both characters are so emblematic they could easily carry recognizable musical themes that later mingle and enrich or modify each other."

Kander treats the Spider Woman like an operatic diva, assigning her a theme that, like a Wagnerian leitmotif, recurs throughout the musical. The string of descending chords of the Spider Woman theme (example 5.2) is reminiscent of "The Presentation of the Rose" theme from *Der Rosenkavalier*. Kander claims that he was not conscious of this connection when he wrote it, but Gibson's glassy orchestration makes the reference practically explicit. In retrospect, Kander feels that the Spider Woman's music produces a similar effect to what Strauss was after for the Marschallin: "that you hear a very warm woman's voice singing something great that sounds very sweet in back of it. . . . What I wanted was a warm sound with something behind that said, 'don't take this at face value.'" The last recurrence of this theme is in the trio "I'd Do Anything for Him," which signals the turning point of the musical and is its most operatic moment. In this trio, Molina and Valentin alternate singing a fraught melody against the Spider Woman's sensuous theme. It is the only number in the musical that bridges the prison world and fantasy world, and it leads directly into the portentous "Kiss of the Spider."

Kander almost had a chance to incorporate an operatic idiom into the Hollywood sequences, as McNally, an opera aficionado himself, flirted with the idea of making them about a South American opera diva named Stella Cassadobles. The plot for this scenario is identical to that of *Man Overboard*. Ironically, Molina professes not to be particularly fond of authentic opera music. While describing Stella to Valentin, he exclaims, "What I like best about these sequences is that they use made up music. It's much prettier than the stuff they really sing in opera. Have you ever heard a real opera? Cats in heat are more attractive. But in the movie, Stella gets to sing the most wonderful music. I mean, if we're going to have to listen to opera, it might as well be tuneful!" Molina's superficial attraction to the operatic diva reflects his aestheticist tendency to privilege style over substance. Whereas Kander

Example 5.2. Spider Woman Theme

probably had no objections to the opera diva version, Ebb most likely pushed for Aurora.

The Spider Woman theme forms the basis for "A Visit," a haunting dia-logue between the Spider Woman and Molina mainly in recitative style. "A Visit" is part of Molina's morphine-induced hallucination, in which the two most important women in his life appear, his nurturing mother (the good mother) and the dangerous seductress, the Spider Woman (the phallic mother). The ominous "A Visit" and the mother's tender "You Could Never

Shame Me" form a pair, which is framed by "Morphine Tango" and thereby set off from the real world of the prison. Molina and the Spider Woman's musical dialogue incorporates speechlike rhythms over an ostinato in the accompaniment (example 5.3). The portentous, chromatic Spider Woman theme interrupts the dialogue four times. The opening recitative section is limited to three pitches, F, A-flat, and C, which float over two oscillating chords, D-flat major (I) and F minor in first inversion (iii⁶). D–flat major is the key of this section, but these pitches suggest the key of F minor. The recitative centers on C (5th scale degree of F minor), which occurs eight times within the first eleven measures. These details allude to "Kiss of the Spider Woman," which is not heard until late in act 2. "Kiss of the Spider Woman" is in the minor mode, and the melody is limited to an octave, C-c. "A Visit" modulates abruptly and frequently (D-flat–E-flat–D-flat–G-flat–A–A-flat–A) and lacks tonal closure, thus pointing to a later point in the story and the title song. Kander, Ebb, and Prince experimented with the placement of "A Visit," just as they had for "Cabaret" nearly twenty-five years earlier. At Purchase, the song occurred during the opening scene: the Spider Woman visits Molina in his cell immediately after the arrival of Valentin. Molina chases her away in order to save Valentin from her deadly kiss.

Despite its many strengths and operatic sections, the score is not Kander and Ebb's most seamless effort. Several of the reviews mentioned the operatic potential of Puig's novel but disparaged Kander and Ebb's score. John Simon, with his signature lack of tact, felt that the story could be the basis of an opera but only "in the hands of a major composer." Clive Barnes suggested that only someone like Alban Berg should touch this project and felt that Kander and Ebb trivialized the themes with a conventional score.[29] Linda Winer, who was generally favorable about the music, compared the "Over the Wall" sequences to Beethoven's freedom chorus from *Fidelio*, judging the former to be inferior to the latter. Other writers, such as Jeremy Gerard, questioned the entire enterprise of musicalizing Puig's novel.[30] The score also had its fans—for instance, Ken Mandelbaum, who used the term "Broadway opera" to describe the score, praised the music for its "incredible richness and interconnection of themes and ideas."[31]

Recent critical assessments of *Kiss of the Spider Woman* are also mixed. John Bush Jones relegates the musical to "a same-sex love story" and emphasizes the story's human rights violations over issues of gender politics.[32] Ethan Mordden, who is a writer of gay fiction in addition to musical theater history, more accurately connects the story's focus on sexual and gender identity to

Example 5.3. "A Visit" (first 14 measures)

the fascist political backdrop of the story, preferring the musical's "cream-ing faggot as anti-fascist" over the portrayal of homosexuals in *La Cage aux Folles* and *March of the Falsettos*, a sentiment shared by Ebb.[33]

Personal interpretations of the theme vary widely among the people as-sociated with the musical. Hal Prince sees *Spider Woman* as a story about escape, but Ebb considered it to be about "passion and loyalty and courage."[34] Brent Carver, who created the role of Molina on Broadway, feels that the musical is about "liberation through music, liberation through the imagination."[35] One reading of the musical views it as an AIDS allegory.[36] For John Clum, Spider Woman is mostly about "gay diva worship." In his words, Rivera was "a true diva in a gay-created musical about the role of divas in the life of an unliberated queen."[37] This element—and Ebb might have realized this from the beginning—was a winning commercial strategy. Molina plays the diva in his own musical. He is concerned not with the politics of his movies but with their knowing sense of style (Puig planned to avoid this aspect of the novel in the musical). Like Molina, Ebb claimed to have no interest in politics. Ebb's attraction to projects such as Kiss of the Spider Woman lay in their inherent theatrical value. However, he also valued the provocative nature of his and Kander's musicals. After all, a mixture of serious message and lively entertainment is Kander and Ebb's hallmark. In the case of both Cabaret and Chicago, the form the writers adopted is an effective analogue for the central theme. By comparison, the movie musical in Kiss of the Spider Woman is more diversionary than substantive. Perhaps the writers felt that there was no other viable option for a musical version of Puig's novel, which might explain Puig's departure from the project early on.

In the end, Kander, Ebb, McNally, and Prince were proud of having turned their project around after Purchase and of finding a successful way to present the complex and challenging story. Indeed, Kiss of the Spider Woman is a brave musical. It treats the gay subject with more dignity than do other musicals with gay representations, and it does not back away from depictions of homophobic violence or sex. The writers simplified the complexity of Puig's novel, especially regarding the Hollywood movie sequences and the political aspects, but this adjustment provided relief from some of the darkest book scenes in the musical theater repertory. The film segments featuring Aurora can be read as an analogue for Molina's aestheticism, which he embraces as a strategy for survival in a world in which he feels marginalized and threatened. It is a strategy on which Kander and Ebb had themselves long relied.

CHAPTER 6

Flops and Second Chances

Flora, the Red Menace; The Happy Time; Zorbá;
70, Girls, 70; The Rink; *and* Steel Pier

I am swept along all the time. I have a lot of opinions once I'm part of it. But to get me to be part of it is a cinch. I'm like a puppy. You pat me on the head and I'll go wherever you take me.

—FRED EBB

R EFLECTING THE MIXTURE OF IDEALISM AND PRAGMATISM OF someone who has both produced and directed musicals on Broadway, Hal Prince likes to draw a distinction between a "hit" versus a "success" and a "flop" versus a "failure." Hit and flop refer to financial return, and success and failure to artistic merit. For Prince, a hit musical does well at the box office and may or may not receive accolades from the press. On the other hand, a success is admired on an artistic level but fails to attract an audience. *She Loves Me*, a succès d'estime, was a financial flop. *The Boy from Oz*, starring Hugh Jackman, which most critics considered an unequivocal artistic failure, recouped its initial investment.[1] Rarer is the musical that succeeds both artistically and financially. Kander and Ebb have had their share of these, like *Cabaret* and *Chicago*, but half of their musicals initially lost money: *Flora, the Red Menace* (1965), *The Happy Time* (1968), *Zorbá* (1968), *70, Girls, 70* (1971), *The Rink* (1984), and *Steel Pier* (1997).

These musicals flopped at the box office primarily because of weak books. Each one boasts a solid score but is flawed dramatically. Kander and Ebb made substantial improvements to all but one of these musicals either for a

Broadway revival or a production elsewhere, and these versions are the ones rented for performance today by Samuel French, the leasing agency for all of their musicals except *Cabaret* and *The Happy Time*, which are controlled by Tams-Witmark Music Library and Dramatic Publishing, respectively. Fred Ebb died before getting the opportunity to rework *Steel Pier*, although it is still possible that Kander might someday revisit the project.

The old adage that the whole is greater than the sum of its parts could have been invented for the musical theater genre. In the case of a truly great musical, all of the constituent parts are of high quality and work symbioti-cally to create a seamless whole. Often a recording of a flop musical creates the impression of greatness, causing one to wonder whether the critics even saw the show before writing their reviews. In reassessing such works, one must address the myriad of things that could have gone wrong. Kander and Ebb's "flops" suffered from problematic books, but the book writers, the least understood member of the creative team, were not solely at fault. The entire creative staff of a musical, including the director, producer, lyricist, and com-poser, steer a project in one direction or the other or, even worse, in different directions at once.

Flora, the Red Menace

The names "John Kander" and "Fred Ebb" first appeared together on a Broadway marquee when *Flora, the Red Menace* opened in 1965. They had written one musical, *Golden Gate*, but they were unable to find a producer willing to bet on two unproven writers (see Chapter 8). Their efforts, how-ever, were not for naught, as they used their tuneful score for *Golden Gate* as audition material when Hal Prince was looking for a composer and lyricist to write *Flora*. Although *Flora* closed after only eighty-seven performances, it solidified Kander and Ebb's collaboration and established their career-long association with Prince and Liza Minnelli.

Flora, the Red Menace is based on Lester Atwell's 1963 novel *Love Is Just Around the Corner*, an optimistic tale of survival set in New York during the Depression. Flora Meszaros, the protagonist of the novel, a wannabe fashion illustrator with talent and moxie to spare, inadvertently joins the American Communist Party.[2] No musical had as yet dealt directly with Communism,[3] and in 1964, with the McCarthy era fading into the past, Prince thought that the time was right. With its rich array of characters and engaging story, Atwell's novel seemed a promising project.

Love Is Just Around the Corner is an episodic novel chronicling a year in Flora's life. It is an important year for Flora, for she is hired by Garret and Mellick's Department Store as a fashion illustrator and has a romantic relationship with Harry Toukarian, a fellow artist, a stutterer, and a member of the American Communist Party.[4] Flora has leased a large studio and rents out small portions of it to a handful of struggling artists, including a dancing team with ambitions to get on the Major Bowes' Amateur Hour, a model who suffers through a bloody episode of rhinoplasty, a disillusioned ex-Communist and watch repairman named Weiss, and Harry, the most talented of the lot. Harry pressures Flora into joining the party. Confusing politics and love, she agrees but finds it difficult to conform to the party's draconian rules, and as a result the party officials expel her in perpetuity. Harry, who has no sympathy for Flora's problems with the party, pressures her to have sex with him. By the time Flora is ready to acquiesce, it is too late, for Charlotte, another party member, has caught Harry's interest. Flora's problems with Harry are paralleled by her risky escapades at the office. Several times she barely avoids getting fired, and her hubris eventually gets the better of her. She provokes Mr. Stanley, a production manager who takes an instant dislike to her. Stanley eventually falls for Flora, and they even go out on a date, which ends abruptly when she slaps him after he tries to kiss her. When an advertising manager commissions Flora to design eight murals, Flora accepts, hoping to enlist Harry's help and thereby get closer to him. But Harry goes away to a Communist camp in upstate New York, and when he returns to the city it is too late to salvage Flora's murals. Worse, he announces that he and Charlotte, the ideal Communist, have married. Without Harry's expertise Flora botches the murals, which leads to her dismissal. As the novel draws to a close, Flora is single, unemployed, and forced to give up the lease on her studio. As she packs up her belongings and looks back on her eventful year, Stanley arrives at the studio. He offers to arrange an interview for her with another company and to take her out to dinner.

Flora, the Red Menace opened on Broadway at the Alvin Theater on May 11, 1965, following out-of-town previews in New Haven and Boston. The triangular love story, conventional score, big-band orchestrations, and humorous treatment of the political theme boded well for *Flora*. Moreover, the musical exemplified the highest level of professionalism and craftsmanship that Broadway had to offer. George Abbott's reputation was on a mythological scale; Hal Prince was the wunderkind of Broadway; and the orchestrator, Don Walker, was in high demand. Out-of-town reviews were favorable. So

Marquee for *Flora, the Red Menace*, Shubert Theater, New Haven (1965).
Van William, from the personal collection of John Kander

what went wrong? Was the thirties' setting too bleak a reminder of the Depression? Did the script fail to integrate the political and romantic aspects of the plot? Or was Flora and Harry's relationship too much of an anti–love story for a musical comedy? The show's demise might have simply been the result of an embarrassment of riches on Broadway. After all, *Flora* opened only a couple of months after *Fiddler on the Roof*, whose themes about family and sympathetic portrayal of the Jews of Anatevka struck a chord with audiences, and *Hello, Dolly!*, another runaway hit. Against formidable musicals like these, *Flora* did not stand much of a chance at the box office.

Flora did win one important Tony Award: best actress. Although not a diva role in the traditional sense, Flora Meszaros is one in a long line of strong-willed female leading roles; she is iconoclastic, freethinking, ambitious, confident, and cautiously romantic. Like Hope Charity, Fanny Brice, and Dolly Levi, Flora is not the blue-blooded, objectively pretty ingenue of musical theater's past, but a psychologically complex and ethnically marked

(Hungarian) romantic lead. Minnelli's Italian-American background and idiosyncratic looks served Flora's iconoclastic nature and Eastern European roots. Initially, Abbott wanted Eydie Gorme for the role of Flora, but Minnelli practically pleaded with Kander and Ebb, whom she had met through a mutual friend, Carmen Zapata (née Marge Cameron), to consider her for the part. Abbott was dead set against Minnelli, but when Gorme lost interest, Prince got behind Minnelli and Abbott acquiesced. He eventually warmed up to Minnelli, and she received a Tony Award for her performance.

Hal Prince made two decisions early on that sealed the fate of *Flora*. The first was to hire Abbott to direct the musical. The second was to ask Abbott to write the script. Abbott was not Prince's first choice for book writer. He wanted Garson Kanin, who turned him down and suggested Robert Russell for the job.[5] Russell, whose only previous Broadway experience was as co-writer (with Joseph Stein) of the book for the 1959 musical *Take Me Along*, came up with the appealing title and wrote a draft, but Prince felt unsure about the playwright's vision of the story and detected "an obduracy, an unwillingness to bend, an impracticality, difficult to analyze."[6] It was at this point that Prince asked Abbott to co-write the book, which meant rewriting Russell's script. By 1965, Broadway had experienced an increase in productions of serious musicals, but musical comedy was still the default mode. So it seemed natural for Abbott—and Russell—to turn Atwell's story into a musical comedy. Prince came to regret both of these decisions, acknowledging that Abbott, a wealthy septuagenarian, lacked the "affinity for the material" needed to write a sensitive book and to direct the show. Despite having a good track record for fixing ailing shows on the road, Abbott simply had no sympathy for the characters or the topic.[7] In retrospect, Prince felt that he himself was better suited to direct *Flora*: "My wife's family had been victims of the blacklist, and I knew full well how idealistic and naive and innocent so many of the people who were pilloried really were, and I wanted the show to be about that and so did the original author of the novel."[8] *Flora* was to be the last musical that he produced without also directing, with the exception of the 1977 musical revue *Side by Side by Sondheim*. It was also the last time Russell worked on a Broadway musical.

Kander and Ebb's score for *Flora, the Red Menace*, although imminently clever, polished, and tuneful, has the unmistakable sound of a fifties book musical. The writers made little attempt to evoke a thirties' period style, preferring to stick to the lingua franca of musical comedy at the time. This aesthetic perfectly served Abbott's script, but the score was unable to elevate the musical above its inherent conventionality. The score's limitations were hardly Kander and Ebb's fault, as Abbott cut out many of their most interesting songs, creating an unintentional imbalance between "out-of-the-blue" book songs and novelty songs.[9] What remained was the type of numbers one had come to expect from a musical comedy: waltzes, marches, specialty dance numbers, ballads, and novelty songs, all of them solid, some brilliant, and some expendable.

The overture, a medley of three tunes, announces a fifties-style musical comedy, beginning with a hot swing-band rendition of "Not Every Day of the Week," followed by a mellifluous trombone solo of "A Quiet Thing," and ending with the waltz "Dear Love." Shortly after the show began, "All I Need Is One Good Break," one of Kander and Ebb's earliest songs of survival and self-determination, introduced Broadway audiences to Liza Minnelli and her fearless singing. Harry's "Sign Here" and Ada's "The Flame" are brilliant musical comedy numbers.[10] Also excellent are Flora's belting numbers, "All I Need" and "Sing Happy." "A Quiet Thing," one of Kander's favorite ballads, is an unexpected moment of lyrical introspection for Flora. The pulsating verse, surprising harmonic changes, and tonally distant bridge section became regular features in Kander and Ebb's ballads. The secondary characters have novelty songs, "Palomino Pal" and "Knock Knock." Flora and Harry's duets, "Not Every Day of the Week" and "Hello, Waves," are standard musical comedy fare. Charlotte's "Express Yourself" is an excuse for some slapstick comedy.

The bittersweet story, political backdrop, and Depression-era setting of *Flora* unleashed Ebb's acerbic wit and irony, and Kander's lyricism and versatility. Kander began to make extensive dramatic use of minor keys and mediant key relationships. Ebb started to think more effectively about form and tone. They also sharpened their ability to conceive both serious and comic songs within the framework of the drama. For the first time, they delved into subtleties of character and plot and used Flora's songs to convey her resourcefulness, her vulnerability, and her optimism.

Ebb's vernacular constructions reflect the time, place, and details of the story, and Kander, for his part, used the minor mode to give the score a sense of unity and to reflect Flora's (and the other Communist Party members') Hungarian roots. There are no outstanding musical markers for Flora's ethnicity other than the minor keys and dance rhythms. A likely musical influence on the score is Marc Blitzstein, who had Communist leanings.[11] An excellent example of Kander's use of the minor mode is "Sign Here." The

Example 6.1. "Sign Here"

music starts out in A minor, turns around the 5th scale degree touching on
the upper and lower neighbor tones, and climbs a sixth to the 3rd scale degree
(example 6.1a). A slippery chromatic descending line underscores "Here,
sign, sign here!" The oppressively repetitive two-note motive first heard on
"The rights of man?" lands squarely on B-flat, the lowered 2nd scale degree,
suggesting the Phrygian (or an Eastern European) scale (example 6.1b). The
release ("The winds of change . . .") is in the major mode, a symbol for the
new, modern, and progressive—everything American. Ebb felt that "Sign
Here" "may be the best musical comedy song I ever wrote, because it's smart
and it's deep, and it's important, and it meant a lot to me, and I think he
[Abbott] just played it for laughs . . . it is important what that song was talking
about." "The Flame," a Soviet-inflected character song for Ada, is saturated
with lower neighbor tones and other chromatic inflections (example 6.2a).
For the refrain, Kander reworks melodic material from the verse, which is in
the minor key (example 6.2b).

　　Flora previewed in New Haven and Boston before coming to New York.
The critics were excited about Liza Minnelli and the music but perceived
too many weaknesses in the book. Robert Leeney, writing for the *New Haven
Register*, reviewed the musical favorably but felt that that the humor kept
"the lovers of the piece steadily weighed down by doctrinal comradeship
every time that larger affections try to break through." Kevin Kelly of the *Bos-*

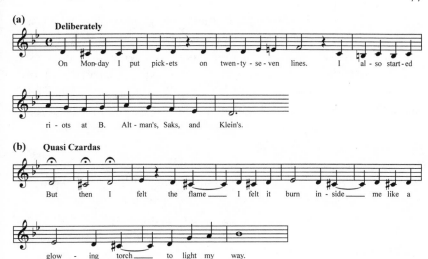

Example 6.2. "The Flame"

ton Globe predicted success for the musical, but he considered Abbott's treatment of the Depression to be superficial.[12] The New York critics, however,
were much less forgiving. Howard Taubman saw Abbott's comrades as having
"little resemblance to human beings. Not even amusing cartoons, they are
only paper cutouts."[13]

Russell and Abbott share credit for the final script, although probably
little of Russell's original material was used. Russell tamed Atwell's episodic
novel and condensed it into a musical comedy format. Abbott further pushed
the musical comedy format. He contrived a formulaic secondary romantic
couple by pairing, as far-fetched as it may now seem, Ada, a Communist
known to her comrades as "The Flame," and one of Flora's renters, a xylo-
phone player called the Cowboy.[14] The two writers had different approaches
to Harry. Russell based him on the unsympathetic character of Atwell's novel,
and Abbott turned him into a more likable character.

The plot of the musical charts the waxing and waning of Flora and
Harry's romance, retaining the novel's one-year time frame. While looking
for employment Flora meets Harry, who, unbeknownst to her, is a member
of the Communist Party. Harry coerces Flora into joining the party. They
fall in love, but their relationship is threatened by Charlotte, who is a more
committed comrade and more sexually available than Flora. A more serious
crisis for Flora arises when her politics and professional life collide. Charlotte

places copies of the *Daily Worker* in Flora's locker at work, which leads to her dismissal. (In an earlier version of the script, Charlotte forms a picket line around Flora's place of employment in order to get her fired.) Flora is eventually rehired after an anonymous phone call (made by Harry to her former employer—his only selfless act in the musical) clears her of any culpability. Although Abbott used Flora's affiliation with the Communist Party as the cause of her dismissal, he treats the threat of Communism no more seriously than does the musical *Silk Stockings*.

Fred Ebb's papers contain unattributable sketches (let us call them "*Flora* early sketches") and an early draft ("*Flora* early draft") that probably represent Russell's work on the script. Assuming that Russell indeed wrote these, they indicate his intention to remain relatively faithful to the spirit and content of *Love Is Just Around the Corner*. Compared to the final script, Russell's dialogue is more politically charged, the characters are more complex, and the emotional stakes are higher. In "*Flora* early draft," Weiss, the watch repairman who rents space from Flora, personifies the musical's anti-Communist sentiment. He is also Harry's sworn enemy. In an attempt to imbed the political nature of the story into the characters, Russell expands the role of Stanley, the model of conventionality and conservatism. Whereas Weiss is Harry's political foe, Stanley is Harry's romantic opposite. Stanley's life is changed when he becomes attracted to Flora. He breaks off his picture-perfect engagement with Claire (a character not in the final version) and pursues Flora. Abbott retained this part of the plot but made it peripheral to the main story. Kander and Ebb composed several songs for Stanley, most of which had to be cut when Abbott decreased the size of his role.

"*Flora* early sketches" include descriptions for several songs with political themes, such as "The Forgotten Man," which Harry sings to Flora during their first meeting:

> This song identifies "The Forgotten Man" as an invention of FDR's. Harry leads, and Flora is impressed with his idealism, with his goodness, and she is excited by his radical appeal for all Forgotten Men to stand together, march together, etc. The pattern of the song can come from the questions on the employment application, all of which Harry manages to convert into propaganda: *job applied for* is a place a man can take to build a better world; *salary desired* is a living wage, with security, etc; recommendations come from Tom Paine, John Henry, Joe Hill, and other Forgotten Men heroes of the folk-singing left wing; *Previous employment* details such anonymous proletarian achievements as the Bonus March, the building of ten thousand Depression

Shantytowns, the selling of a hundred million red Depression apples, and other triumphs of the Depression Unemployed. During the song, Flora is so inspired that she falls for Harry.

If Abbott had any political statement to make, it was to extol American individualism over Soviet collectivism. Kander and Ebb never wrote "The Forgotten Man." In its place they put Flora's wanting song, "All I Need Is One Good Break," which imparts her American-as-apple-pie optimism.

The version of the scene that introduces the characters renting space at Flora's studio includes a description for a song called "Strive and Succeed," which Russell intended as a "sharp contract to the self-pity of 'Forgotten Man.' This is the other side of the social picture of the Depression—the 'Self-Help' bunch with old-fashioned virtues of independence and struggle. They are not taking the Depression lying down, no, sir! They are fighting to get ahead; they are full of Horatio Alger zeal. . . . Each foolish optimist has his bit. It is all proud and sad, because we all know that, two years hence, they will all be on the W.P.A." As the song ends, Flora and Harry enter the studio. Weiss is so angry with Flora for wanting to rent space to a "Bolshevik" that he threatens to leave. Harry, calling Weiss a "A typical Napoleon! . . . a follower of Trotsky," sings about the uprising of the wretched in "The Internationale." As the script states, "Flora has fallen in love with Harry and with Collective Man . . . the song ends in a warm red glow and a kiss."

The American musical has long dealt with themes of self-determination. Broadway's principal female protagonists from Magnolia Hawks to Laurie Williams to Annie Oakley to Gypsy Rose Lee determine their own destiny by overcoming daunting obstacles. According to Ethan Mordden, the focus on individualism is the very thing that makes American musical theater American and distinguishes it from other music theater forms: "That ebullient idealism is why the musical started the twentieth century by gradually conquering the European forms. . . . It's resourceful, protean. There is no equivalent in Singspiel, opérette, or zarzuela to nineteen-year-old Minnelli's jump onto Broadway by playing, more or less, herself. Those arts don't stretch. The American musical, like Walt Whitman, contains multitudes."[15] Abbott's version of Flora celebrates this idea, even though, as Prince admits, his "Communists were cartoon characters, some of them farcical, others evil."[16] Had Abbott aimed for more character development and a more serious exploration of the political aspects of the story, the show might have made a stronger impression.

Kander and Ebb received ample praise for their score, but some critics thought that the music shifted too often between traditional musical comedy and political satire. This perception may be the result of Abbott's script, which made little or no allowance for Kander and Ebb's most dramatic and passionate numbers, which are among the best of the cutout songs from the show.

> "You Feel Too Much" (Stanley)
> "Harry's Lie" (no lyric)
> "Among the People" (Flora)
> "Goodbye" (Flora and Stanley)
> "The Tree of Life" (ballet)
> "I Gotta Right to Know"[17] (Flora)
> "I Believe You" (Flora)
> "Blood on 23rd Street" (Harry, Ada, and Chorus)
> "What Am I Doing Here"[18] (Flora, Charlotte, Harry, and Weiss)[19]

Stanley originally had three songs (including "You Are You," which was later reassigned to Weiss and Flora's other friends). His slowly evolving attraction to Flora in Russell's version provided the basis for some excellent ballads. In "You Feel Too Much," Stanley reveals his sympathy for Flora:

> You feel too much.
> Too many things reach you.
> It's wrong, I think, to feel so much.
> But how can I teach you?
> You're open wide to ev'rything.
> It's always heart not brain.

"Goodbye," a song suggested by Atwell's novel, is a sentimental duet in which Stanley warns Flora not to let the party infringe on her personal life or work. Her response is to accuse him of philistinism. Their conversation progresses from cordial to confrontational, but their attraction for each other is undeniable.

"The Tree of Life" ballet and the extended "Blood on 23rd Street" were entertainments for the Communist Party meetings. "Blood on 23rd Street is a parody of agitprop theater, performed by Harry, Ada, and other party members. Modeled on dramatic ballad sagas such as "The Saga of Jenny" from *Lady in the Dark*, it recounts the riches-to-rags story of Pierpont Packard, who just wants to have fun, until he saves a young woman's honor and falls in love with her. When Pierpont's wealthy father refuses to accept his son's new love interest, Pierpont leaves home, exclaiming, "Money be damned

Example 6.3. "I Got a Right to Know"

if that money means love is denied." Now destitute and starving, Pierpont unites the poor. His father, the consummate capitalist, considers his son to be the enemy and orders him shot. Although critics in New Haven and Boston applauded this number, Abbott cut it from the show, probably because of its considerable length and political nature.

Flora had several excellent songs that were cut. "Among the People," which audiences in New Haven and Boston heard, introduces Flora and her sarcastic humor. It was succeeded by "All I Need Is One Good Break." In "I Got a Right to Know," the most impassioned song that Kander and Ebb wrote for the musical, Flora confronts Harry about his true feelings. The opening phrase rises arduously and slowly from D to F-sharp, lingering along the way on the accented passing tone F-natural, which helps to accentuate the supplicating tone of the lyric (example 6.3). The ultimate melodic goal of the phrase, the note B, is approached by a large ascending leap as Flora pleads with him, "come on." To emphasize Flora's frustration, the accompaniment at measure 7 superimposes accented lower neighbor tones over the opening rhythm of the phrase, a device that Kander uses on other occasions. Abbott may have rejected this song on the grounds that it was too emotional for his script.

Example 6.4. "I Believe You"

The same may also be the case for "I Believe You." The principal motive of this song centers on an accented lower neighbor tone, the 7th scale degree, which resolves to the tonic on the second beat of the opening measure (example 6.4). The harmony for the opening phrase alternates between a tonic triad, A, and a major triad on B (I–II) over a tonic pedal. The D-sharp contained in the B chord, a raised 4th scale degree, is an allusion to a restatement of the opening motive in measure 7 transposed down a fourth. Both before and after *Flora, the Red Menace*, Kander like to incorporate the raised 4th, harmonically, melodically, or both, as he did here.

In 1987, the director Scott Ellis, writer David Thompson, and choreographer Susan Stroman approached Kander and Ebb with the idea of revising Flora for a production at the Vineyard Theater.[20] They felt that the story and existing score contained the seeds of a successful musical. They reconceived the show as a WPA project, as Thompson's script explains: "To create the illusion of this being a WPA project, enormous murals—done in the style of Thomas Hart Benton—should hang on the walls of the theater. They should show scenes of life in New York in the Thirties and reflect the drama, struggles and realities of the common man."[21] Thompson believed that Abbott's script "betrayed" Kander and Ebb's score, which, as we have observed, aimed for complexity of emotions and dramatic conflict. Thompson retrofitted a new story to Kander and Ebb's score, playing down the musical comedy aspects and approaching the leftist politics with greater seriousness than Abbott had done. He invented a narrator, a musician named Willy; replaced the musical couple who audition for the Major Bowes' Amateur Hour with ballroom dancers from the novel; and cut Ada and reassigned "The Flame" to Charlotte. The actors playing the nine principals also play the supernumeraries, mostly the young artists at Flora's studio and the Communists. In a bit of mischievous cross-casting, Thompson assigned the role of Galka, head of the Communist Party, to the same actor playing Weiss, a former Communist.

As the prologue begins, Willy welcomes the audience and explains that the play is made possible by the "Federal Theater Project," an offshoot of the WPA dedicated to theater. The new opening number that follows, sets the tone for the dire economic situation of the period. Strains of this new opening run through the entire show, a unifying technique often employed in concept musicals (such as *Company*). When Flora finally appears, it is to deliver her high school graduation valedictorian speech, which replaces the FDR radio address of the original production.

Kander and Ebb utilized some of the cutout songs from the 1965 version and wrote some new ones. In the application scene, Flora now sings "The Kid Herself," leaving "All I Need Is One Big Break" to be sung by all of the young hopeful artists associated with Flora, as Kander and Ebb originally conceived it. "The Kid Herself" was cut in 1965 because the choreographer, Lee Theodore, thought that Minnelli could not dance, a decision that Ebb always regretted: "It was a very effective—I thought—opening number for that character . . . and then you go to her studio, where everybody sings 'All I Need Is One Good Break,' which introduced all the other characters. . . . and that was our arch, and that was correct, I believe. . . . That was the first of many crushing disappointments I had." Ebb was thus very pleased to see it reinstated for the revival.

Kander and Ebb wrote a new song for Harry called "The Joke," which is a political speech he delivers at a Communist rally. "The Joke" is reminiscent of the menacing mood and terse harmonies of Marc Blitzstein's *The Cradle Will Rock*. Ebb saw "The Joke" as Harry's "metamorphosis." While delivering this speech, Harry overcomes his stuttering. Kander and Ebb also wrote "Keepin' It Hot" to show off the ballroom dancers and "Where Did Everybody Go?," a trio for Harry, Flora, and Charlotte.[22]

The dialogue of Thompson's script is more realistic than Abbott's musical comedy banter, and the dramatic arch is more effective. Thompson completely rethought the events leading up to Flora's dismissal from Garret and Mellicks, and he raised the stakes for Flora and Harry. Late in act 2, when Flora is having trouble meeting her deadline, and with the party forming a picket line in front of the store, she asks Willy to deliver to Stanley an envelope containing her designs. Envelopes accidentally get switched, and the one that ends up in Stanley's hands contains the employee signatures that she has collected for the party. Now forced to cross the picket line in order to save the jobs of her fellow workers, Flora is confronted by Harry, who is charged up from the success of his rally speech. During this encounter, the dramatic climax of the musical, Flora and Harry's political differences destroy their relationship. The 1965 version had, to use Ebb's words, "the dopiest ending," and he and Kander were much more satisfied with Thompson's solution. In *Love Is Just Around the Corner*, Harry's rejection of Flora is connected to his sexual frustration. In Thompson's script, Harry gives Flora an ultimatum: "You make your own decision. Either you are against us . . . or you are with us. But if you're against us—you're against me." Disillusioned by his and the party's intolerance, she takes an action that is the final blow to her relationship with Harry.[23] At the end of Thompson's version, Flora stands alone, literally. Thompson forgoes the possibility of a relationship between Flora and Stanley. The change renders Flora's paean for survival, "Sing Happy," more moving.

Casting for the Vineyard production was a drawn-out process. For Flora, according to Thompson, "We were looking for somebody that was funny, and quirky, and eccentric, and had a larger-than-life personality." Whomever they hired would have to contend with Minnelli's association with the part, so they cast against type, choosing Veanne Cox, a skilled comedienne known for her red hair, pale complexion, and goofy appeal (she played Jerry Seinfeld's heckler and also lost a toe in a well-known *Seinfeld* episode, and she was a stepsister in the 1997 television version of *Cinderella*). Cox evinced none of the character's ethnicity, but she rendered Flora sympathetic and was the perfect foil to her male lead, Peter Frechette. Like Bob Dishy's portrayal of Harry in the original Broadway production, Frechette's Harry was warm and zealous. A later production at the Pasadena Playhouse starred Jodi Benson (the voice of Ariel in the film *The Little Mermaid*), who sang beautifully but was dramatically weak.

In its new incarnation, *Flora* is a cross between a musical comedy and a musical play.[24] In his review of the revival, Walter Goodman of the New York Times approved of the serious tone of Thompson's script, which allowed the "appealing central characters more of a chance to break out of musical comedy convention."[25] Flora remains a part of its time. As the years of the Soviet Union slip further into the past, the musical's politics will seem less relevant, even though its main theme will remain universal. "If the show has a guiding philosophy," Fred Ebb observed, "it is to be true to yourself."[26]

The Happy Time

Immediately after Cabaret, Kander and Ebb were in high demand. In 1967 they wrote industrials musicals for General Electric and Ford Motor Company (see Appendix), and in 1968 they provided the scores for two Broadway musicals, The Happy Time and Zorbá. Neither show, one a comedy of self-discovery, the other a dark story of personal awakening, was a definitive hit. The Happy Time had everything going for it, a charming and beloved source, Robert L. Fontaine's novel of the same name; Broadway's hottest super-director, Gower Champion; the shrewdest and most powerful producer in the business, David Merrick; and a star-studded cast including Robert Goulet and David Wayne. Merrick nearly closed The Happy Time out of town and lost interest in it entirely once it became clear that he would never recoup his investment. Zorbá, too, showed a lot of promise, but Hal Prince, who produced and directed it, cut short the initial Broadway run before it had broken even.[27]

Kander and Ebb's score for The Happy Time is a colorful mixture of pastiche, musical comedy, musical play, and opera. However, the critics, who still had Cabaret ringing in their ears, were caught off guard by its conventionality and offered little more than passing judgment. Walter Kerr's comments are typical: "John Kander and Fred Ebb, lacking that first twist of mind that led them into composing the brittle, sneaky score for 'Cabaret,' are working at half-staff."[28] By most accounts, Gower Champion's concept for the show robbed the score of its charm, stripped key parts of the script, and ruined the musical's chances of success.

Fontaine's novel The Happy Time is a coming-of-age story set in the 1920s told from the point of view of a boy named Bibi, the youngest member of an idiosyncratic French Canadian family.[29] The novel consists of several loosely connected episodes in Bibi's life, all taking place during the year leading up to his first discovery of love. Filling out the novel are the antics of

Bibi's eccentric family, including his debonair and permissive grandfather; his father, a vaudeville musician and armchair philosopher who can turn a request to pass the sugar into an ethics lesson; his mother of Scottish descent (Maman), beneath whose occasional stern demeanor lies a profound maternal love; his alcoholic ne'er-do-well but irresistible uncle; and his budding female cousin. We also get to know an array of other local characters, most notably, a fanatical moralist of a schoolmaster who inflicts corporal punishment on Bibi for allegedly lying until the boy's father and uncles give the educator a taste of his own medicine. Although not monumental, the ordinary events detailed in the novel shape the boy's view of the world as he emerges from childhood and discovers his first true love, a redheaded American who lives next door.

The positive reception of Fontaine's book led to a stage play of the novel by Samuel Taylor, which in turn generated discussion of a possible musical adaptation. Rodgers and Hammerstein, who turned to producing in the mid forties, produced Taylor's play.[30] It was a hit, running for 614 performances, and was turned into a film starring Charles Boyer and Louis Jourdan. Rodgers and Hammerstein had no interest themselves in writing the musical adaptation, and David Merrick eventually acquired the musical rights. By the time Merrick got around to producing it, a new generation of musical theater writers had arrived. He hired Kander and Ebb only after his first choice, Cy Coleman and Dorothy Fields, turned him down. Merrick apparently never considered hiring Taylor to write the book, perhaps because his play was not a workable model for the musical.[31] In any case, the playwright was occupied at the time with his comedy Avanti!, which opened on Broadway just days before The Happy Time. Merrick approached N. Richard Nash, who felt that Fontaine's novel was "too sentimental" and ordinary. According to William Goldman, Nash was more interested in developing an idea of his own "about a small-town Mid-western photographer who comes home every four or five years and wrecks the family. And finally his father makes him tell the truth about the 'glamorous' life he's been leading—that he's a liar and a failure and has never found himself and is always living on the edge of dishonesty."[32] Merrick, eager to exercise his option, allowed Nash to map his prodigal son and homecoming story onto Fontaine's breezy coming-of-age novel.

In effect, Nash transformed Fontaine's story into an adult-oriented story of self-exploration.[33] By centering the story on a new protagonist, a photographer named Jacques, the playwright relegated Bibi to a secondary role, the agent through which Jacques learns to see the truth about himself. Jacques is a traveling photographer and the black sheep of the family, "an artist who could go either way, towards art or commercialism."[34] At sixteen years of age, Jacques left St. Pierre for a life of adventure. For years he has been passing himself off as an international success and bon vivant. Jacques seldom visits home, but chaos usually ensues when he does. Bibi worships him. The musical portrays the visit that changes Jacques's life. He attempts to rekindle a relationship with Laurie, his childhood sweetheart and Bibi's schoolteacher. She still loves him, even though they see the world differently, he with his head in the clouds, she with her feet on the ground (as Kander might say, poetry versus prose). During Jacques's first night in town, Bibi follows his uncle to see "The Six Angels" at the theater where his father works. They stay out all night, and Bibi, drunk with the love he feels for his uncle—and from his first taste of brandy—asks Jacques if he can accompany him on his world travels. Bibi's request gives rise to the dramatic conflict of the story. Jacques asks his brother, Philippe, to let Bibi leave school temporarily, and Philippe refuses, more in defiance of his brother than for reasons regarding Bibi's education. Philippe's decision, however, drives Bibi further into Jacques's arms. Jacques decides to take matters into his own hands and declares that he will take Bibi with him. Grandpère, with the insight that only a parent can have, intervenes and forces Jacques to confess the truth about his life. In one of the most powerful, soul-searching scenes in musical theater, Jacques, no longer able to hide, admits to Bibi that he is a fake, as his father looks on.

Still without a director, Merrick approached Gower Champion, with whom he had worked on several occasions. Champion agreed to direct the musical because it fit in with another projected he wanted to do: Elliot Martin, director of Center Theatre Group in Los Angeles, had approached Champion to direct a dance musical for the opening of the new Ahmanson Theatre.[35] Champion thought that *The Happy Time* was a good project for the purpose.

Nash's script and Kander and Ebb's score suggested an intimate musical with a small orchestra and no chorus,[36] but Champion wanted to give the piece a sophisticated look and fluid rhythm. He decided to present the story as a memory play, which he would convey with the IMAX system, invented by Chris Chapman and Barry Gordon. The result was a show that, in Kander's words, "smothered the intimate subject matter with too enormous a production." Champion pressured Nash to alter his script in order to facilitate his grand vision for the musical. At Champion's request, Nash wrote a prologue and epilogue. In the former, Jacques addresses the audience directly, entreating them to return with him to St. Pierre. Champion spent considerable time and money on creating slides of Jacques's photographs to project against a cyclorama. Champion photographed a series of rose images at Griffith Park Botanical Gardens in Los Angeles, planning to use them as examples of Jacques's work. Since the IMAX system required a large fixed-rear-projection screen, the rest of the set had to be minimal. A revolving platform was devised, and the orchestra sat onstage (although they were back in the pit by the time the musical reached New York). Merrick was forced to book one of the largest Broadway theaters in order to accommodate the projections. The effect was stunning, but Nash's intimate story suffered from the excesses of the production. To use John Kander's words, "The heart of the piece just vanished."

Champion's "step outline" for the opening two scenes gives an idea of the physical flow and visual beauty that he envisioned.

> 1. Jacques . . . enters, speaks to audience, takes their picture. Sings. "The Happy Time," a song of remembrance. Lights fade, leaving cyc[lorama] in color. Add R[ear] P[rojection] pictures illustrating places and things of the song's lyrics. Small town in French Canada. Final photo: The Bonnard family at dinner some years ago—around 1930 (?).
> 2. The Bonnard Dining Room
> Actors enter (carry own chairs?), take position to approximate final photo. Concluding song, Jacques corrects their positions to match photo as he remembers them. Song concludes. Jacques takes close-ups of family. Matching close-ups appear R[ear] P[rojection]. The action is boisterous as Jacques enters scene and becomes one of the family.
>
> Action now changes, becomes subdued, almost slow motion as Jacques, in his memory, now turns to Laurie and Gillie, who are revealed in another part of the stage. Music. Lights shift emphasis. This is a basic technique which we will use through the play.[37]

In these opening moments, Champion set the nostalgic tone for the musical and provided insight into the interior life of the protagonist. In the first pantomimed section, Jacques prepared a photo shoot of a rose: "*Click!* A signal transmitted from Jacques's camera causes a small area of the screen to come alive with a brilliant color photograph of the rose: *Click, Click, click, click!* A series of varying views of the rose appeared on different areas of the screen."[38] The IMAX system was a hit, but, to Nash's resentment, the spectacle did not match the earthiness and charm of his script.

Champion hoped to end the musical with a seven-minute film montage following the death of Granpère while Jacques sings a song called "Being Alive" to Bibi. The film montage would reveal the next three years of Bibi's life and end with a frozen image of Bibi in midair, which dissolves to the glorious strains of "St. Pierre." The live actors would then appear at Bibi's high school graduation. The film turned out to be too technically difficult to pull off and, although stunning to look at, "dwarfed the stage action, rendering it dull and colorless by comparison."[39] The Los Angeles critics responded with unflattering reviews.

In the wake of the negative press, Champion made several drastic changes, mostly to the consternation of Nash, who by this time was rather unhappy. The sets had to be completely revamped. Champion was convinced that audiences did not want to see Robert Goulet in the part of a cad, so he sweetened his role. As Ebb noted, Champion's Hollywood crowd "thought we should change him into a fellow who was simply a misunderstood desperate person who kept up this pretense, not because he was a liar and a sham, but because he wanted his nephew to love him."[40] Nash and Champion clashed over this change, and the director secretly solicited help from the writer Michael Stewart. The version of The Happy Time that opened in New York ended with an anticlimactic epilogue in which Jacques informs the audience that he became a success and is happily married. This ending cuts against the grain of Nash's original concept of "a man who has lost his chances and to whom the nephew means everything."[41] For Nash the theme was "reality versus romance," but for Champion it was about facing the truth before it is too late. According to William Goldman, "what Champion tried with Happy Time was to re[-]create the Dolly! experience. The projections— the razzmatazz part of the show—stayed, because that was the part of the show that was working. The part that wasn't working—the part involving characters—Champion tried to brighten up," and, as result, the show got "soft, gooey, marshmallow-cored."[42]

Champion also took a lot of liberties with Kander and Ebb's score, cutting songs because, in his estimation, they either slowed the momentum or were nonessential to the story (table 6.1). "Jeanne Marie" is a spirited, humorous folk song that Jacques sings first with Bibi and then with the entire family when he returns home. It helped to establish the bond between Bibi and his uncle, but Champion felt that it sapped energy from the first scene. "Allez-oop" is a cancan for the "Six Angels," but at Champion's request Kander and Ebb came up with the more risqué "Catch My Garter." "In His Own Good Time" depicts an argument between Philippe and Suzanne over Bibi's

Table 6.1. Genesis of the score of *The Happy Time**

Demo Recording	Los Angeles Preview†	Broadway (1968)	Goodspeed Opera (1980) and Lyric Opera of Kansas City (1983)
"The Happy Time"	"The Happy Time"	"The Happy Time"	"The Happy Time"
—	"Jeanne Marie"	—	"Jeanne Marie"
"He's Back"	"He's Back"	"He's Back"	"He's Back"
"Allez-oop"	"Allez-oop"	"Catch My Garter"	"Catch My Garter"
"Tomorrow Morning"	"Tomorrow Morning"	"Tomorrow Morning"	"Tomorrow Morning"
"Please Stay"	"Please Stay"	"Please Stay"	"Please Stay"
"I Don't Remember You"	"I Don't Remember You"	"I Don't Remember You"	"I Don't Remember You"
"St. Pierre"	"St. Pierre"	"St. Pierre"	"St. Pierre"
—	"I Don't Remember You" (reprise)	"I Don't Remember You" (reprise)	"I Don't Remember You" (reprise)
"Without Me"	"Without Me"	"Without Me"	"Without Me"
"In His Own Good Time"	"In His Own Good Time"	—	"In His Own Good Time"
"The Happy Time" (reprise)	"The Happy Time" (reprise)	"The Happy Time" (reprise)	"The Happy Time" (reprise)
"(Walking) Among My Yesterdays"	"(Walking) Among My Yesterdays"	"(Walking) Among My Yesterdays"	"(Walking) Among My Yesterdays"
—	"I Won't Go"	—	—
"I'm Getting Younger Ev'ry Year"	"I'm Getting Younger Ev'ry Year"	"The Life of the Party"	"The Life of the Party"
—	—	—	"I'm Sorry" (this number followed "Seeing Things" in the Kansas City production)
—	"Seeing Things"	"Seeing Things"	"Seeing Things"
"If You Leave Me Now"	—	—	—
"A Certain Girl"	"A Certain Girl"	"A Certain Girl"	"A Certain Girl"
"Being Alive"	"Being Alive"	—	"Running"

Table 6.1. (*Continued*)

Demo Recording	Los Angeles Preview[†]	Broadway (1968)	Goodspeed Opera (1980) and Lyric Opera of Kansas City (1983)
"St. Pierre" (reprise)	"St. Pierre" (reprise)	"St. Pierre" (reprise)	"St. Pierre" (reprise)
"The Happy Time" (reprise)	"The Happy Time" (reprise)	"The Happy Time" (reprise)	"The Happy Time" (reprise)

*Musical sketches without lyrics have been found for five songs—"With a Woman by Your Side," "Far from New," "Home Away," "I'm Home," and "Choose Your Friends"—as well as a completed song called "Up My Sleeve," which was never used. "Far from New" might have originally been for *Cabaret*.
†This inventory is based on a recording of a live performance. It is likely that the score changed as Champion continued to work on the show. According to Gilvey, Champion cut "I'm Sorry" before the premiere (John Anthony Gilvey, *Before the Parade Passes By: Gower Champion and the Glorious American Musical* [New York: St. Martin's, 2005], 193).

upbringing. "I Won't Go," the most contrapuntal piece in the score, is an ensemble number in which each member of the Bonnard family threatens to boycott Grandpère's birthday party. At the party Grandpère sings "I'm Getting Younger Ev'ry Year," which was later substituted with "The Life of the Party." "Being Alive" (which predates Sondheim's song of the same name by two years) represents Jacques's emotional breakthrough. Kander and Ebb wrote the ballad "If You Leave Me Now" for Laurie, but it was never incorporated into the show.

The New York critics had many of the same concerns as the Los Angeles critics. They complained about the weak script and placed the blame at Champion's feet. In response to the oversized production, Kerr wrote, "the [IMAX] technique creates a vast cavern, accenting the hole at the heart of things: it [the cyclorama] makes the stage inside it seem dark and gloomy."[43] For Kerr, bloated shows like *The Happy Time* were the source of Broadway's ills at the time.

Ironically, *The Happy Time* was one of the most commercially successful musicals to open on Broadway during the 1967–68 season, and Champion won Tony Awards for best director and best choreographer, which helped to keep the show afloat. Most of the other shows nominated for a Tony Award in the best musical category—*How Now, Dow Jones* and *Illya, Darling*—did poorly by comparison. *The Happy Time* ran for 286 performances, only 7 less than *Hallelujah, Baby!*, that year's Tony Award winner for best musical.

The Happy Time is rarely performed today, and it is hardly ever mentioned in the literature, even though Nash, Kander, and Ebb made considerable improvements to the musical for a revival at Goodspeed Opera House in 1980.[44] Nash restored some aspects of his original script that Champion had eliminated, intensified the drama, and fleshed out the characters. The revised script contains more intense interactions between Jacques and his brother Philippe, his father, and Laurie Mannon. From the beginning Grandpère senses that Jacques is concealing his unhappiness. Laurie is more mature, has two sons, and is more of a match for Jacques. She and Jacques sing "I Don't Remember You" not as a nostalgic ballad, as in the Broadway version, but as a willful song of denial about their true feelings for each other. Nash also brought Laurie's opinion to bear on the fraternal battle between Jacques and Philippe over Bibi's upbringing. She takes Philippe's side when Jacques objects to his insistence that Bibi make a public apology for hanging up naked pictures at his school. Jacques exclaims, "a child has a right to be a fool," but Laurie turns the tables on him, responding, "nobody has a right to be a child—not forever." One must eventually live up to the responsibility of being an adult, she insists. This exchange leads to "Seeing Things," in which they express their different philosophies of life. (In the Broadway version, "Seeing Things" occurred after Bibi's public apology.)

Nash's new script gave Kander and Ebb an opportunity to reconsider some of the songs that Champion expunged. They reinstated "Jeanne Marie," "In His Own Good Time," and "I'm Sorry," and they wrote one new song, "Running," which fills the musical void at the dramatic climax of the story, created when Champion cut "Being Alive."[45] In "Running," Jacques forces Bibi to see him for what he really is. He acknowledges the mistake he made by leaving home and urges Bibi not to commit the same error. Jacques thereby saves his nephew from what would have been a lot of anguish. It is his moment of redemption.

"Being Alive"	"Running"
I'm not wise, Bibi	So you think you've found the answer
Everyone tells me so	Running,
But I have eyes and ears	Some wonderful solution
And I know	Running,
	You're prepared to travel light
Being alive	And to vanish in the night
While you're alive	And the life will be all right?

That's what matters.	Wrong!
. . .	. . .
Open your eyes, Bibi	Look at me,
Open your mind, Bibi	I've been running all my life,
Keep it alive as long as you live.	Looking for a chance to stop,
	All runners do.

Look at me,
Bibi, now I'm running scared,
Maybe time is running out?
That's true,
But just for me,
Not for you.

In his review of the Goodspeed production Frank Rich praised the revised score but attacked the book for being clunky and underdeveloped.[46] He admonished the lack of "esthetic unity" and felt that the best musical moments did little to illuminate character or story, a sentiment first articulated by Martin Gottfried in 1968.[47] In the final analysis, the problems with *The Happy Time* might be a case of too many cooks spoiling the soup. By the time Fontaine's novel was filtered through Taylor's play, Nash's conflation, and Champion's intervention, it had lost its charm and identity. The opposite can be said for Kander and Ebb's next musical, *Zorbá*, which adhered perhaps too closely to a story that had little charm in the first place.[48]

Zorbá

Zorbá reunited Kander and Ebb with Hal Prince, who was intrigued by the prospect of a musical version of Nikos Kazantzakis's 1946 novel *Zorba the Greek*. At first the writers were not receptive to the idea, but when Prince described his theatrical vision for the opening scene, a circle of musicians in a "bouzouki parlor arguing over the meaning of life," they were sold. Moreover, as writers with one flop and one hit they were not yet secure enough to turn down such an offer. As Ebb stated, "This is Hal Prince, this is a major Broadway show, with Herschel Bernardi. And this is the king of Broadway asking you to do it . . . and how can you not do it. Needless to say, fifteen minutes into that conversation, we are panting to do this show, panting, I would have paid *him*. And I hated the novel." Joseph Stein adapted Kazantzakis's novel, which centers on the relationship between Zorbá, a gregarious free agent and the personification of Mediterranean earthiness, and Niko, a reticent Englishman of Greek decent who has inherited a mine on the island of Crete.[49] During his journey to Greece, Niko meets Zorbá, who instantly befriends him. In Crete, Niko falls in love with a young widow, which inflames the jealousy of Pavli, a young man who has long suffered an unrequited love for her. Pavli commits suicide when he learns that the widow has slept with Niko. Thereafter, the islanders shun the widow, and Pavli's father avenges his son's death by killing her. Niko's relationship with the widow is paralleled by Zorbá's romance with Madame Hortense, an old, ailing French courtesan who has lived on Crete since the war. She accepts Zorbá's lovemaking, hoping that he will marry her, and eventually dies in his arms. Niko, sickened by the brutal murder of his lover and disillusioned by the discovery that his mines are barren, decides to return to England. As he is about to board the boat for the return voyage, he enjoys one last dance with Zorbá. He has lost everything, but he has experienced life for the first time.

Today *Zorba the Greek* seems little more than an unenlightened misogynist novel in the guise of an earthy, life-affirming story.[50] The public sacrifice of the widow was already dated by 1964, the year in which Michael Cacoyannis's film version of the novel was released, and the unnamed narrator's "boasted detachment becomes irresponsible and even ugly."[51] When Kazantzakis's novel first appeared, however, some critics admired its timeless quality and equated it with masterpieces like *Candide* and *The Odyssey*.[52] What must have appealed to Prince and his team were the theatricality of the story, the colorful setting, and an attractive leading male role on the scale of Dolly and Mame. The libertine Zorbá is bigger than life and inherently a good man, but he has seen the worst of humanity and has become a moral relativist. Prince understood that the story of *Zorbá* was exceptionally dark for a Broadway musical, so he made the audience observers rather than participants by distancing them from the action, the opposite of what he did in *Cabaret*. He achieved this effect by providing constant reminders that they were watching a theatrical reenactment.[53]

Kander and Ebb were in their element with *Zorbá*, and they produced an excellent score. The exotic locale and ethnic backdrop allowed them to experiment with asymmetrical meters and Greek folk music idioms while also incorporating story songs and vaudeville motifs. The oft-cited opening scene establishes the use of a female narrator called the "Leader," who comments on the story in the manner of a Greek chorus, sometimes with the assistance of the ensemble. When the musicians' opening philosophical debate reaches a fever pitch, the Leader abruptly interrupts and settles the argument in the song "Life Is," which features one of Kander's most memorable vamps (see Chapter 1). Kander and Ebb felt that they did their best work for Hortense's scenes, which are the most presentational segments in *Zorbá*. Musically speaking, they conceived of Hortense as a French stage performer, an effective analogue for her actual former profession of courtesan. Striking the right balance between pastiche and character song, her music includes cancan, popular French ballads, and upbeat cabaret numbers. The dance segments involving Hortense are right out of the Folies Bergère. "No Boom, Boom" is a vaudeville routine performed to music pouring out of Hortense's old horned phonograph and backed by a chorus line of admirals, who suddenly appear out of nowhere. "Happy Birthday" takes place in Hortense's imagination just moments before she dies.

Critics admired Kander and Ebb's score for *Zorbá*, but they attacked the story and the nature of the production. Martin Gottfried blamed Joseph Stein's book and expressed his concern about the long-term consequences of the concept musical.[54] Walter Kerr felt that the concept was altogether ineffective for the story: "much of the evening suggests that Bertolt Brecht has been tamed and made useful on the musical stage; the technique talks to the audience at will, and the players are all members of a café audience."[55] Kerr also felt that the inhabitants of Crete were unlikable: "The community . . . has not seduced us into sharing its special, prickly, earthy, savage and exuberant attack on the desperation of living. We make a note, as an ethnologist might. But it's hard to enjoy the post-mortem revels."

Prince later acknowledged that *Zorbá* had so much in common with *Fiddler on the Roof* that it was bound to pale by comparison. Joseph Stein wrote the book for both musicals; Herschel Bernardi, the first Zorbá, had taken over the role of Tevya from Zero Mostel, and Maria Karnilova, who played Hortense, was the original Goldie. Critics immediately connected the ethnic backdrops of the two works. Ironically, *Zorbá* is actually closer to *Cabaret* than to *Fiddler*. Its plot hinges on parallel romantic couples, one old and one young, with both relationships ending tragically. Moreover, both musicals incorporate performative songs to tell a serious story. Like the emcee in *Cabaret*, the Leader in *Zorbá* glides in and out of the story, now taunting Zorbá, now expressing the thoughts of the young lovers, now observing Hortense's death.

Zorbá's bleakness was a strong contrast to *Fiddler*'s guarded sense of hope. Ebb called *Zorbá* "joyless, from beginning to end, it is joyless." Although

Prince later conceded that *Zorbá* was too dark for Broadway, he never turned against it the way Ebb did. He still considers it a "masterpiece" and is particularly proud of the opening number. However, with ticket sales down, he closed the New York production before recouping the initial investment, noting in an announcement to his loyal investors,

> ZORBA's been rolling with the punches since the summer began. Both our stars have medical problems, and at the end of last week Herschel Bernardi went to hospital for a couple of weeks.
> We have repaid 60% of your investment [. . .] and we have a tour scheduled for January[,] which should easily recoup the rest of the investment and return a profit. . . .
> It's a tough decision. I love the show, and I certainly thought after the reviews that we'd have at least a few seasons, but we then had a consistent run of bad luck.[56]

Zorbá eventually made a handsome profit for its investors when, in 1970, Prince sent out a national touring company starring John Raitt in the title role and Chita Rivera as the Leader. This production was lighter in tone than the Broadway version, and it offset the financial loss of the Broadway run. Kander noted that because he and Ebb "weren't dealing with a diva" this time out, they felt free to make several changes, and they took advantage of Raitt's supple voice by adding a song called "Boubolina." They also turned "The Butterfly," a duet for the Leader and the Widow, into a trio by adding a part for Niko. The revised song is more expansive, incorporating three melodies corresponding to three different emotions. Foster Hirsch wishes that Kander and Ebb had gone in an even more operatic direction: "Nico's struggle between the world of intellect in which he feels safe and the life of desire that Zorbá embodies, and to sustain a larger-than-life dimension the characters (as well as the show itself) require a continuous musical texture that is darker, more 'fateful,' more propulsive, than Kander and Ebb's rhythmic and tuneful song catalogue." Hirsh calls for "a weightier musical idiom" in order to capture "the play's essential material, the elemental battle Kazantzakis dramatizes between sex and repression, with Zorbá as a life-affirming primitive in combat with a community one step above savagery in the evolutionary scale."[57]

A Broadway revival of *Zorbá* opened in 1983, with Anthony Quinn and Lila Kedrova repeating the roles they had famously created for the 1964 movie *Zorba the Greek*. The director of the revival, Michael Cacoyannis, who had also directed the movie, purposely avoided repeating anything that Hal Prince had done, and he rarely consulted with Kander and Ebb. He adopted a cheerier view of the material than Prince had. Kander and Ebb reworked some of the original songs and wrote a new ballad for Quinn, "Woman." These changes did nothing, however, to change the critics' minds about the musical's abject misogyny and dreary theme. Frank Rich noted, "Zorba's gabby philosophy of life, which he passes on to his bookish and repressed young employer Niko, is essentially a platitudinous recipe for reckless womanizing and guiltless irresponsibility; while it once seemed liberating and romantic, it now sounds juvenile."[58] The revival played over twelve hundred performances nationwide and earned over $48 million.[59]

Zorbá's harshest critic, Ethan Mordden, although admiring of the music, lambastes the musical's forced upbeat ending, and in a bit of unadulterated Broadway diva bitchiness offers this summation: "Embrace Zorbá! Herschel Bernardi [Zorbá] cries, to John Cunningham [Niko]. What, and forget all the sadness and failed projects that have brought us to this embrace? . . . Maria Karnilova dies hopeless and abandoned? Embrace Zorbá! The Widow is murdered because she wouldn't accept some jerk's advances? Embrace Zorbá! I think Zorbá is one of the ugliest, most life-denying pieces of evil shit ever perpetrated as a Broadway musical."[60]

Zorbá and The Happy Time are Kander and Ebb's first musicals with strong male protagonists and themes about male bonding. In Zorbá, Niko and Zorba's homosocial relationship is mediated by the female characters, and in The Happy Time Jacques and Bibi's uncle-nephew friendship threatens the peace of the entire family. It is probably a coincidence that these shows occupied Kander and Ebb at the same time. Nevertheless, that neither one was a definite successful might have steered Kander and Ebb back to stories centered around women protagonists. They did not return to male-oriented themes until Kiss of the Spider Woman in the early 1990s.

70, Girls, 70

After Zorbá, Kander and Ebb initiated a musical of their own choosing for the first time. As Kander and Ebb tell it, this project started out with the simple notion of doing "a musical about geriatrics and do[ing] it like a big vaudeville."[61] They knew that they had found a suitable plot when they saw the film Make Mine Mink, starring the famously gap-toothed actor Terry-Thomas. However, legal complications forced them to use the play on which the film is based, Peter Coke's 1958 British farce Breath of Spring.[62]

It took six years, two entirely different plot lines, three book writers, three directors, and a number of cast substitutions for Ebb and Kander's idea to reach fruition. At some point, Ebb and Norman Martin, whom Ebb knew from Camp Tamiment, worked on a scenario about a group of women in a retirement home who successfully execute a robbery. The heroine, Thelma, the newest resident at a "State Home for aged ladies in the state where they grow the best oranges," has old ties to the mob. With Thelma's encouragement and guidance, the other women at the home pull off a bank robbery. A parallel plot features a young male district attorney, Tom, who suspects that the home is involved in some sort of political graft. Tom infiltrates the home with the help of a friend, a female doctor who donates three afternoons a week to the home. There is no hint of any intention to incorporate a vaudeville concept. Ebb and Martin came up with three different versions, each with a different title, *One of the Girls*, *The Golden Age*, and *The Senior Citizens*. They wrote a synopsis for each, but unfortunately these are undated, making it impossible to know if they came before or after Kander and Ebb's decision to use the plot of *Breath of Spring* for the musical.

There are two possibilities regarding the chronology. Either Ebb asked Martin to work on an original idea and later abandoned it for *Breath of Spring*, or Ebb started with *Breath of Spring*, interrupted work on it in order to develop a related but original idea with Martin, and then returned to Coke's play. Making matters more complicated, the Broadway *Playbill* for *70, Girls, 70* credits Joseph Masteroff with the adaptation for *Breath of Spring*. There is no telling from this vague credit whether he incorporated the vaudeville framework or whether Ebb and Martin did so after Masteroff left the project. All that can be stated with certitude is that, after Masteroff left the project, Ebb and Martin coauthored the published script for *70, Girls, 70*.

The plot of Coke's play involves five pensioners, mostly British farce stock characters: Dame Beatrice Appleby, an ex-suffragette who tends to a variety of pet charities; a punctilious and efficient retired brigadier named Albert Rayne; a butch vocal coach named Nanette Parry; Lady Alice Miller; and Elizabeth Hatfield, a straight-laced, high-strung spinster. Except for Miller, they are all lodgers at Dame Appleby's flat. The plot is set in motion when Appleby's devoted housekeeper, Lilly, a former thief whom only Appleby would hire after she got out of jail, gives her employer a mink as a token of her gratitude. The mink, however, belongs to the couple living next door, and Appleby insists that it be returned immediately. Rayne devises a plan to reverse the maid's crime, but it requires the assistance of his fellow pensioners.

The plan succeeds without a hitch, and they enjoy the thrill of the experience so much that they start stealing furs in earnest, using their ill-gotten gains to fund their favorite charities.

Masteroff transferred the action to New York City and substituted the eccentric British characters with senior citizen (ex-vaudevillians in the final script) living together in a retirement home on the Upper West Side called the Sussex Arms Hotel. As the story begins, the residents gather in a drab restaurant, where they have been invited by their friend Ida, whom they have not seen in months. Ida announces that she has taken up robbery following an inadvertent act of shoplifting. She suggests that her friends join her in her new enterprise, if only to be able to afford to fix up their surroundings. They turn her down, but when Eunice inadvertently takes a fur from Sadie's Fur Salon, they, like their British counterparts, devise a plan to put it back without getting caught and in the process get hooked on crime. During their final heist, Ida, in an act of self-sacrifice, allows herself to get caught so that the others can escape.[63] In the last scene, she reappears to tell the audience that she died while in jail, as she had planned all along. She has returned briefly from the world beyond, appearing on a crescent moon (a reference to *Mame*, that survivalist of survivalist diva musicals) in order to spread the message of carpe diem.

It was eventually decided to tell this story as a vaudeville, alternating the action between book scenes, most of them taking place in the retirement home on the Upper West Side, and the Broadhurst Theatre, the actual theater where *70, Girls, 70* was playing. The musical opens as the actors have gathered on the stage of the Broadhurst Theatre to perform a show about old folks. As the story unfolds, the locale shifts back and forth between the theater and the various plot locations.[64] Throughout the proceedings, the characters break the fourth wall to perform specialty numbers. Because the conceptual framework was superimposed onto the story rather than grown from it organically, the concept never fully worked. The show was clever, but audiences had trouble following the transitions between the book scenes and vaudeville scenes.

Kander and Ebb wrote a crackerjack score that bursts with energy and invention, but by design most of the songs are not integrated into the plot. For the most part they function as isolated numbers on a vaudeville bill and cover a wide range of unrelated topics, from sex during old age ("Do We") to the mystery regarding where elephants go when they die ("The Elephant Song"), to the dizzying pace of modern city life ("Coffee in a Cardboard

Cup").[65] Most of the songs are performed as traditional crossovers, which historically were novelty songs performed "in one" (in front of a curtain) while the stage was reset for the next scene. Although entertaining, these self-contained songs distracted from the story. As table 6.2 illustrates, the pre-scribed physical locations for the performance of the musical numbers seem arbitrary, for some of the book songs take place in the theater space rather than at the Sussex Arms, and vice versa.

Not helping matters any, the show was produced on a far grander scale than Kander and Ebb had envisioned. Ebb "wanted it to be like one of those old Alec Guinness British comedies, when you would go to a seaside resort, there'd always be four ladies or six ladies who comprised a teatime orchestra. . . . I wanted six old ladies accompanying the whole show. Many ideas like that went down the drain the minute it went to Broadway."[66] Ebb blamed Ron Field, the first director, for turning the musical into a gaudy extrava-ganza. When Field, the choreographer of *Cabaret* as well as of Ebb's later television projects, committed to directing *70, Girls, 70*, he pushed it toward Broadway with his "big production ideas."[67] When Field left the project, the neophyte director Paul Aaron was hired, but after the Philadelphia opening the more experienced Stanley Prager took over as director. It was too late, though, to reverse course, and the project ended up without a unified direc-torial vision. Ebb later complained, "I had too many collaborators."[68]

70, Girls, 70 opened on April 15, 1971, and closed after a mere thirty-five performances, losing $600,000.[69] It was Kander and Ebb's shortest run. In an odd coincidence, *70, Girls, 70* and *Follies*, both of which featured a troupe of seasoned performers from the vaudeville era pulled from retirement, opened within weeks of each other. The irony was not lost on Ebb, who self-consciously equated *70, Girls, 70* with Woolworth's and *Follies* with Tiffany's. Sondheim was particularly fond of *70, Girls, 70* and included "Home," Ida's first song, on his often-cited list of "Songs I Wish I'd Written (At Least in Part)."[70] Although both musicals use vaudeville, they have entirely opposite points of views. *Follies* deals bitterly with regret, a theme antithetical to Kan-der and Ebb. *70, Girls, 70* is about survival, a recurring theme in their mu-sicals. In any case, neither *70, Girls, 70* nor *Follies* could compete against *No, No, Nanette*, the third musical at the time to feature famous performers from the past. *No, No, Nanette* was a stroll down memory lane without the psychological pain of *Follies* or the bittersweet acceptance of old age in *70, Girls, 70*.

70, Girls, 70 was entertaining, but it lacked clarity and real dramatic con-

Table 6.2. Synopsis, music, and structural plan of *70, Girls, 70* (not including reprises)[*]

	Action	Physical Location	Song Title	Structural Frame
Act 1				
Prologue	Actors introduce themselves and state their ages.	Broadhurst Theatre	"Old Folks"	vaudeville
Scene 1	Ida recounts to her friends how she was led into a life of crime.	Sussex Arms	"Home"	book scene
Scene 2	—	Broadhurst Theatre	"Broadway, My Street"	vaudeville
Scene 3	Eunice accidentally steals a fur from Sadie's. Ida and the "gang" plan how to return it undetected.	Sussex Arms	—	book scene
Scene 4	Harry reviews the master plan in militarily precise detail.	Broadhurst Theatre	"The Caper"	book scene
Scene 5	Led by Ida, the gang succeeds in returning the fur.	limbo, then Saidie's Fur Salon	—	book scene
Scene 6	—	Broadhurst Theatre	"Coffee in a Cardboard Cup"	vaudeville
Scene 7	—	Sussex Arms	"You and I"	vaudeville
	Ida, Harry, Gert, and Eunice celebrate their smashing success.		—	book scene
	—		"Do We?"	vaudeville
	Ida, Harry, Gert, and Eunice decide to rob more furs in order to refurbish Sussex Arms.		—	book scene
	—		"Hit It, Lorraine"	vaudeville

Table 6.2. (*Continued*)

	Action	Physical Location	Song Title	Structural Frame
Scene 8	—	Broadhurst Theatre	"The Caper" (reprise)	book scene
Scene 9	Harry and Ida steal furs as Gert distracts the security men.	Bloomingdale's Fur Salon	"See the Light"	vaudeville
Scene 10	The "gang" count their earnings. Melba and Fritzi join the gang. Walter confesses to being an ex-safecracker. He joins the gang, too.	Sussex Arms	—	book scene
Act 2				
Scene 1	Gert, Harry, Eunice, Walter, Fritzi, and Melba sneak into the Arctic Cold Storage.	Broadhurst Theatre	"Boom Ditty Boom"†	vaudeville
Scene 2	They break into the vault, and then Harry locks them in. They escape using a stick of dynamite.	Arctic Cold Storage Vault	"Believe"	vaudeville
Scene 3a		Broadhurst Theatre	"Go Visit"	vaudeville
Scene 3b	The cops show up to interrogate the residents, who drive them away by acting senile. They decide to pull off one final heist.	Sussex Arms	—	book scene
	—		"70, Girls, 70"	vaudeville

Table 6.2. (*Continued*)

	Action	Physical Location	Song Title	Structural Frame
	—		"70, Girls, 70"	vaudeville
Scene 4	—	Broadhurst Theatre (limbo)	"The Elephant Song"	vaudeville
Scene 5	—	Broadhurst Theatre	"The Caper" (second reprise)	book scene
Scene 6	The final heist. Ida sacrifices herself.	New York's Coliseum	—	book scene
Scene 7	Ida brings the audience up to date.	[Broadhust] Theatre	—	book scene
Scene 8	Harry and Eunice get married.	Chapel	"Yes"	book scene

*Based on the published script.
†"Boom Ditty Doom" replaced "Folk Song," a rock song parody in which one of the female senior citizens belted out "You old bastard" on a repetitive, jerky three-note motive over a monotonous ostinato. "Folk Song" was used in Philadelpohia, but Violet Carson, the actress who performed it, left the cast, and so too went her song.

flict. Audiences had trouble following the inexplicable shifts between the Broadhurst Theatre, where the geriatric performers sang and danced, and the Sussex Arms Hotel, where the named characters acted out a story about a group of poor old folks living on the Upper West Side. Moreover, the casual incorporation of songs further obscured the two structural levels: vaudeville and the book scenes (see table 6.2). For instance, many of the book songs themselves take the form of a vaudeville number. How are we to read these numbers when they bleed into the vaudeville world? A few songs, "You and I," "Believe," and "Yes," fit neither category comfortably. "You and I" is novelty material, but it relates to the geriatric theme and is performed by two Sussex Arms tenants. Melba, a Sussex Arms waitress who has traditionally been cast as an African American, sings "Believe" in order to give Walter confidence to crack the Arctic Cold Storage Vault, but the number is a spiritual, not a book song. "Yes" is more thematic than plot driven, and the deceased Ida sings it at Eunice and Walter's wedding. On the other hand, Harry's "The Caper," which he reprises before each heist, grows out of the story but is performed on the stage of the Broadhurst Theatre as a vaudeville routine. The contradictions and crossovers between the action and the songs reflect the flawed structural concept of 70, *Girls*, 70. To kick off many of the vaudeville songs, the actors shout out a cue to Lorraine, the onstage piano player and herself a senior citizen. She has a number of featured piano solos, all of which underscore the performative nature of the songs. During "Hit It, Lorraine," Lorraine and her upright piano join the cast center stage. It is great fun and a sight to behold, but, again, confusing.

Ebb and Martin did all they could to guide the audience through the transitions. For instance, after the prologue, during which the cast sings "Old Folks," Melba gives the following advice: "I guess you wonder why I'm talking to you. Well, you better get used to it, honey. We'll be doing it all night long. We talk when we want to, sing when we want to, use Lorraine when we want to. And all the while we'll be telling you a story. So, if you don't want to get confused. [sic] Pay attention."[71] That this speech was necessary at all reflects the writers' fear that the format of the show would cause confusion. Ebb later recognized that the structure needed to be made clear to the audience within the first twenty minutes, and he bemoaned the fact that he was never able to fix the problem.

70, *Girls*, 70 previewed in Philadelphia with a cast made up of veteran stage performers, including Lillian Roth, Goldye Shaw, Marjorie Leach, and David Burns. Lillian Roth embodied the heart and soul of Ida, the leading character and brains of the operation. Burns had his last hurrah with 70, *Girls*, 70: he dropped dead of a heart attack onstage after delivering a joke. The audience as well as the other actors onstage thought that his collapse was a pratfall, actually part of the act. It was a fitting end for one of the great Broadway comic actors. Burns played a hotel clerk who spontaneously broke out into song and dance, all to the consternation of the "stage manager," who tried to keep him focused on the story. Burns sang "The Caper," an arduous patter song that has not been performed adequately since (Ebb's indefatigable rendition on the demo recording is unsurpassed).[72] Burns's material was unapologetic shtick. After Burns's onstage death, his part was excised, and his songs were either reassigned or cut.

The Philadelphia critics were quick to point out the confusing dramaturgical structure and loosely constructed plot of 70, *Girls*, 70. William Collins responded with a mixture of annoyance and admiration, seeing the imperfect framework and reliance on nonintegrated songs as a metaphor for the old characters themselves, whose capriciousness "can amuse and annoy us at the same time," and he pinpointed the problem of featuring "oldtime headliners . . . sort of pretending to be themselves as well as somebody else and having moments when the audience is not quite sure which they are."[73] The New York critics agreed with their compatriots to the south but were more enthusiastic about the music. Clive Barnes called it "one of Kander and Ebb's better scores," although he questioned the entire premise of the musical and disparaged the double structure.[74] Walter Kerr was completely dismissive and nastily titled his review "Please, No '80, Girls, 80.'"[75] Notwithstanding the legitimate complaints of the press, 70, *Girls*, 70 was a winner with audiences. One woman even wrote to the editor of the *New York Times* in protest of Kerr's review,[76] and *Show Business* reported, "Rarely have I seen audiences enjoying themselves to the extent that they had been doing at the Broadhurst. It's the type of show where bravos and standing ovations are a nightly occurrence."[77] 70, *Girls*, 70 has developed a following over the years and is one of Kander and Ebb's most produced musicals today.

English audiences did not see 70, *Girls*, 70 until the early nineties. For the English production, which opened at the Minerva Studio in Chichester in 1990 and then transferred to London in 1991, Ebb asked David Thompson, who had done wonders with the *Flora* revival, to help him solve the lingering book problems. Thompson came closer to achieving Kander and Ebb's original conception of an intimate musical. He cut down the size of the cast, retaining the original gang of seven, Eddie, Sadie, Lorraine, and a couple of men who play the security guards and police officers. He also updated the story to the present, and eliminated the vaudeville space, thereby avoiding the disorienting shifts between the Sussex Arms and the theater, as a note in his script explains: "The set pieces should be as simple as possible so that the action of the play can flow continuously. There are very few blackouts in the script and, therefore, the pace of the show should not be interrupted by heavy scenic changes. The different set pieces should be used in a variety of different ways. For example two boxes can serve as seats stage right and left that store various props and can be moved in a variety of configurations. All set changes should take place with music . . . and imagination."

Although eliminating the physical vaudeville playing area seems to go against Ebb's original concept, it alleviated some of the confusion that audiences had—and Ebb gave his approval. Thompson merely left the locations for the songs unspecified, but he also integrated them more into the plot. He also gave the old folks more justification for their crimes by establishing the fact that they are about to be evicted from the Sussex Arms Hotel. This change gives new meaning to the song "Home," which Ida sings after suggesting that they buy the hotel and turn it into a retirement home for actors.

"The Caper" was substituted with "Best Laid Plans," a soft-shoe number. Also excised were "You and I" and "The Elephant Song." Harry and Walter got to sing "I Can't Do That Anymore," a song that Kander and Ebb originally wrote for *Wait for Me, World* (see Chapter 8).

Thompson also decided to present the story as a flashback, beginning with a police lineup (table 6.3). After "Old Folks," Ida explains the situation directly to the audience:

> We are going to do a show for you. Because we are all actors. Would you give me a pink spot? Thank you. I live for pink spots . . . and big entrances . . . and even bigger endings. Where to begin, where to begin! This is what we call a flashback. It's six months ago at the Sussex Arms Hotel. . . . The rooms were cheap and my friends were swell. Let me introduce you to them. There's Lorraine. She's going to play the piano for you. [. . .] Great troopers these boys. They'll be on and off all evening. Oh! And finally there's Eddie, the bellboy—he's going to do a number for you—(Eddie starts to tap)—LATER! So here we are. Our little band of players. And this is how it all started.

During the final fur heist late in the second act, Ida gets arrested, which takes us back to the lineup in the opening scene. She informs the audience that the gang got off by pleading temporary insanity and purchased the Sussex Arms Hotel. She took the full rap for the robberies.[78] (When the show transferred from Chichester to London, Thompson, as requested by the producers, changed the stolen loot from furs to jewelry in order to preempt any possible protest from animal rights groups.)

The British critics were more forgiving than the American critics had been twenty years earlier. It is worth noting that they all commented, either approvingly or disapprovingly, on the campy nature of the production. Citing Susan Sontag's *Notes on Camp*, one reviewer cautioned that camp is good but "only up to a point."[79] The critic of the *Independent* called the musical "corny," "unsubtle," and "unrealistic," but added that "some of the comic scenes . . . have a way-beyond-parody quality which suggests that this musical could become a camp cult."[80] Given the overwhelming unanimity regarding this aspect of the production, one might justifiably wonder why in 1971 no one even mentioned the musical's campy aspects, not even Harry's cross-dressing during the Bloomingdale's heist? That *70, Girls, 70* seems more conspicuously campy today than it once did probably has something to do with current attitudes and assumptions about musical theater: that it is a gay genre with a large audience of insiders. Since the original production of *70, Girls, 70* in 1971, musical theater has because increasingly self-referential. If

Table 6.3. 1971 Broadway production and 1991 London production

	Broadway Production			English Production	
	Action	Song		Action	Song
Act 1			**Act 1**		
Prologue	Actors introduce themselves.	"Old Folks"	Scene 1	Police lineup.	"Old Folks"
Scene 1	Ida recounts to her friends how she was led into a life of crime.	"Home"	Scene 2	Ida recounts to her friends how she was led into a life of crime.	"Home"
Scene 2		"Broadway, My Street"			
Scene 3	Eunice has accidentally stolen a fur from Sadie's. Ida and the "gang" plan to return it undetected.		Scene 3	Same as parallel scene in Broadway production, except that jewelry is used in place of furs.	
Scene 4	Harry reviews the master plan in militarily precise detail.	"The Caper"		Harry reviews the master plan.	"Well-Laid Plan"
Scene 5	Led by Ida, the gang succeeds in their plan.		Scene 4	Led by Ida, the gang succeeds in their plan.	
Scene 6		"Coffee in a Cardboard Cup"	Scene 5		"Coffee in a Cardboard Cup"

Table 6.3. (Continued)

	Broadway Production			English Production	
	Action	Song		Action	Song
Scene 7	Ida, Harry, Gert, and Eunice celebrate their smashing success.	"You and I"	Scene 6	Ida, Harry, Gert, and Eunice celebrate their smashing success.	
	Ida, Harry, Gert, and Eunice decide to rob more furs in order to refurbish Sussex Arms.	"Do We?" "Hit It, Lorraine"		Ida, Harry, Gert, and Eunice decide to steal more jewelry in order to buy the hotel.	"Hit It, Lorraine" "Do We"
Scene 8		"The Caper" (reprise)	Scene 7	Same as parallel scene in Broadway production, except jewelry.	"The Caper/ Best-laid Plan" (reprise) "See the Light"
Scene 9	Harry (in drag), Ida, and Eunice steal furs as Gert distracts the security men.	"See the Light"			

Scene		
Scene 10	The "gang" count their earnings. Melba and Fritzi join the gang. Walter confesses to being as ex-safecracker. He joins the gang, too.	
Act 2		
Scene 1	Gert, Harry, Eunice, Walter, Fritzi, and Melba sneak into the Arctic Cold Storage.	"Boom Ditty Boom"
Scene 2	They break into the vault, and then Harry locks them in. They escape using a stick of dynamite.	"Believe"
Scene 3a		"Go Visit"

Scene		
Scene 8	The "gang" count their earnings. Melba and Fritzi join the gang. Walter confesses to being as ex-safecracker. He joins the gang, too.	"Broadway, My Street"
Act 2		
Scene 1	Gert, Harry, Eunice, Walter, Fritzi, and Melba sneak into the Arctic Cold Storage.	"Boom Ditty Boom"
Scene 2	Same as parallel scene in Broadway production.	"Believe"
Scene 3		"Go Visit" (Eddie and Ida)
Scene 4	Harry and Walter discuss women and marriage.	"I Can't Do That Anymore"

Table 6.3. (Continued)

	Broadway Production			English Production	
	Action	Song		Action	Song
Scene 3b	The cops show up to interrogate the residents, who feign senility. They decide to pull off one final heist.			The cops show up to interrogate the residents, who feign senility. They decide to pull off one final heist.	
Scene 4		"70, Girls, 70" "The Elephant Song"			"70, Girls, 70"
Scene 5		"The Caper" (second reprise)			"The Caper/ Best-laid Plan" (reprise)
Scene 6	The final heist. Ida sacrifices herself.		Scene 5	Same as parallel scene in Broadway production, but the location is International Estate Auction.	
Scene 7	Ida brings the audience up to date.				
Scene 8	Harry and Eunice get married.	"Yes"	Scene 6	Same as parallel scene in Broadway production (plus Ida brings the audience up to date).	"Yes"

hits like *Urinetown, Spamalot, The Drowsy Chaperone,* and *[Title of Musical Here],* not to mention *Curtains,* are any indication, this trend has only increased in recent years. The London production of *70, Girls, 70* luxuriated in "incestuous showbiz references," such as humorous allusions to *Miss Saigon* and *Hello, Dolly!*[81] The self-referentiality allows for a new interpretation of the musical's theme: not only must the "old folks" survive but also the Broadway musical itself. This notion recalls Frank Rich's oft-cited *Harvard Crimson* review of *Follies,* which suggested that the musical was about the death of musical theater.[82] Today, *70, Girls, 70* can be reinterpreted as arguing the same point of view, but from a more positive perspective. It should be mentioned that Kander and Ebb's demo recording of *70, Girls, 70* is quintessential camp, if only because it features two gay men performing a bunch of old lady characters, all of them retired vaudevillians. Ironically, the demo is funnier and campier (and more musical) than the original Broadway cast recording. Notwithstanding the dramaturgical flaws of the original script, perhaps the lack of camp performance by the aging Broadway actors had an impact on the overall perception of the show.

If Ida Dodd's entrance in the English version "prompts a parody of [the song] 'Hello Dolly,'" as one of the English critics claims, "it also underscores her will to survive." Ida dies at the end of the musical, but not without reappearing with a life-reaffirming message. *70, Girls, 70*'s theme of survival is central to much of Kander and Ebb's work. As Kander says, "What's life-affirming about our work, when that survival theme is there, stems from the story and the characters' need to affirm life, to go on, to be brave. We don't impose that. It's there in the material and we translate it in some way, as in that song ["Yes"]."[83] *Follies* is a metaphor for lost dreams and the death of the musical, but *70, Girls, 70* uses theater as a metaphor for life and the survival of musical theater.

The Rink

The Rink was "a very emotional, fulfilling experience" for John Kander, even though it ran for only 204 performances. Kander and Ebb both remained attached to the work because they felt that they had achieved exactly what they set out to do artistically.[84] During the production they also made several close friends and met a number of future collaborators. Two of the cast members, Scott Ellis and Rob Marshall, became part of a group of young artists that Kander and Ebb referred to as the "family." The librettist for *The Rink,*

Terrence McNally, went on to write the books for *Kiss of the Spider Woman* and *The Visit*. Kander and Ebb also took great delight in the fact that Chita Rivera won her first Tony Award for her performance in *The Rink*.

The Rink has the emotional breadth of grand opera and the dramatic depth of classical tragedy, although on the surface it is Kander and Ebb's most pedestrian musical. It takes place in a grimy neighborhood in 1984 and features beer-drinking, blue-collar characters. *The Rink* began as an attempt to create a modern-day musical based on Heinrich Ibsen's verse play *Peer Gynt*, a drama of self-discovery. *Peer Gynt* recounts the life journey of a young man who leaves his home and mother in order to see what lies beyond the borders of his provincial town. Peer escapes the small-minded world that shaped him, but in so doing he becomes an outsider to it. The plot of Ibsen's play had long fascinated Kander, maybe because he identified with the protagonist's desire to get away from home and see the world.[85]

The evolution of *The Rink* recalls that of *70, Girls, 70* in that it took two playwrights, two directors, and two scores to get the show open. Many things changed along the way, some more than once. For example, the name of one of the two protagonists changed from Pia to Jessica to Nedda and to Angel. The location was transferred from Queens to northern New Jersey to the Boston area and finally to "somewhere on the eastern seaboard." Throughout the slow evolution of *The Rink*, one thing remained constant: the conflict between a mother and daughter over the sale of the family-owned-and-operated skating rink.

The playwright Albert Innaurato, who gained notoriety with his 1977 comedy *Gemini*, wrote the first version of *The Rink*. He invented a story of reconciliation between Anna, an Italian immigrant, and her daughter Pia after a decade-long estrangement. When Pia was eighteen she left home and went to California.[86] Now Anna has decided to sell the family's dilapidated roller rink to a disco promoter and retire to Abruzzi, Italy, the place of her birth. As the deal is about to be closed, Pia suddenly shows up. For her the rink represents a part of her life that she has missed, so she attempts to block the sale. Pia's actions unleash the pent-up resentment and anger that she and her mother have been harboring for years.

Innaurato wrote two versions of this story. In the first one, Shelly Silver, a disco and punk rock promoter, offers Anna an attractive sum of money for the rink. An old friend of Pia's, Bob Campbell (Brustein in the second version), encourages her to hold on to the rink and to rent it out as a rehearsal space to young performance artists like him.[87] Innaurato overburdened the basic mother-daughter conflict with implausible subplots that were already out-of-date when they were written. For instance, the character of Mischa O'Keefe, a director of a modern dance troupe who shares Pia's disillusionment with the '60s revolution, leases the rink in order to rehearse a *Peer Gynt* ballet. In a slipshod resolution, Anna gives in to Pia's wishes and throws her daughter a surprise party at which she announces her decision to keep the rink.

For his second version, Innaurato gave Anna a love interest, Hans Rolf, a German immigrant and retired school principal from Phoenix. He also created a character named Frankie, Bob's neurotic brother who competes for and wins Pia's affections. A double marriage is planned, but a county official shows up with a warrant of condemnation of the rink. Shelly Silver agrees to pay Anna $10,000 instead of the original offer of $200,000 for the rink. Pia concedes, realizing that by holding on to the rink she is living in the past.

Kander and Ebb wrote a complete score for Innaurato's version of *The Rink* and recorded all but four songs ("Getting in on the Ground Floor," "Ich und Du," "No Guts, No Glory," and "To Hell with Love").[88]

Act 1:[89]
  "Colored Lights" (Pia)
  "Don't Ah Ma Me" (Anna and Pia)
  "Chief Cook and Bottle Washer" (Anna)
  "The Theatre of My Mind" (Bob)
  "As You Were" (Jean Paul and Simone)
  "Wine and Peaches" (Anna, later Pia)
  "Trust" (Anna, Shelly, Pia, Bobby, Mischa)
  "Getting in on the Ground Floor" (Shelly)
  "Ich und Du" (Dietrich)
  "All the Children in a Row" (Pia)
  "No Guts, No Glory" (Bobby, Misha, Bobby, Jean Paul, Simone, Pia, Anna)[90]
Act 2:
  "I'm What's Happening Now" (Bobby)
  "Tough Act to Follow" (Pia and Frankie and, later, Anna and Hans)[91]
  "Just When You Least Expect It" (Pia and Frankie, and Anna and Hans)
  "To Hell with Love" (Anna)
  "When the Antonellis Were Here" (Anna)

Pia's two extended solo numbers, "Colored Lights" and "All the Children in a Row," form the emotional core of the score. They both recall the past and share a musical motive intended to capture 1960s folk music. There is no overture. The first person the audience sees is Pia (now Angel) as she arrives home. She sings "Colored Lights," in which she recalls the past and expresses optimism about the future. This number establishes the reason why she has returned and sets up the principal dramatic conflict of the story. The vamp for this song imitates the guitar picking of a sixteenth-note pattern alternating between a I chord and a vii chord with a 2–1 suspension over a tonic pedal. Kander's accompanimental pattern establishes the folklike guitar riff (Michael Gibson's orchestration features an acoustic guitar). Angel sings a recitative-like passage about her first recollection. On "Santa Cruz" the harmony shifts to a sultry vii°7/ii over a tonic pedal. Despite these unstable harmonies, the opening four-measure phrase remains rooted in the tonic key. The B phrase, which starts in measure 37, has a higher tessitura and is more animated. The next section is a simple binary waltz (AB) reminiscent of merry-go-round or roller-rink music.

The diagram below illustrates the musical structure of "Colored Lights." The A section (guitar vamp and recitative melody) and B section (waltz) evoke different periods from Angel's past, her time in California and her childhood years at the rink, respectively. Losing her innocence and her inability to move forward has brought Angel back home. The quasi–folk music of the A section and nostalgic waltz music of the B section contrast each other as well as denote specific decades, the late sixties and early fifties. The "Colored Lights" waltz, moreover, is reminiscent of prerock roller rink music, which Gibson's orchestration makes explicit. As the song progresses, it becomes clear that Angel is disillusioned with her life. During the third A section, she waxes nostalgically about her innocent childhood, wishing that she could return to that earlier, simpler time. Memories of her childhood (the waltz music) haunt her thoughts. The waltz returns now in F major, played on a celeste without voice. Anna appears but does not let Angel see her.

"Colored Lights"

Section	Key
A	A major
B	G major
A	A major
B	G major
A	A major
B (orchestra, then voice)	F major
B' (orchestra)	E major
B'	F major

Nothing came of Innaurato's version of *The Rink*, and eventually the playwright Terrence McNally was brought in to write a new script. McNally retained the basic mother-daughter conflict of Innaurato's version, but he reconceived the story as a concept musical. He also raised the stakes to a nearly Sophoclean level by mapping the psychological scars of the past onto the mother and daughter conflict in the present. In his version, Anna's decision to cash in on the rink poses nearly insurmountable emotional challenges for her and her daughter. Angel still resents Anna for having told her that her father, Dino Antonelli, died, when in truth he abandoned the family because he was traumatized by serving in the Korean War. Anna harbors resentment about being abandoned by her daughter. While Angel was flitting about in California—she was a college student, forest ranger, and finally a backup singer in a rock band—Anna witnessed the precipitous decline of her neighborhood, and she was raped. McNally also invented a group of male workers called the Wreckers, who dismantle the rink piece by piece during the course of the musical, take on various other male and even female roles when necessary, and serve as a quasi–Greek chorus.

For the new version, Kander and Ebb retained four songs from their original score, including Pia's "Colored Lights" and "All the Children in a Row." The concept of moving back and forth between the present and past is established in "Colored Lights." In McNally's version of *The Rink*, during the orchestral interlude in "Colored Lights" (the waltz melody in F major), a girl—Angel's younger self—enters the rink and skates. As Angel looks on, she sings the remainder of the melody. The music builds to a sudden modulation to E major, as the full orchestra now takes up the waltz theme, and the ghost of Dino dances with the young Angel. A return to F major shatters Angel's happy thoughts of the past and reminds her of the present. In a recitative style she asks herself, "Leaving home years ago what was I looking for?"

Arthur Laurents was going to direct *The Rink*, but he pulled out of the project. A. J. Antoon was hired to replace Laurents at the suggestion of Jules Fisher.[92] Antoon quickly identified the dramaturgical problems with the script and worked with the writers to solve them. He emphasized realism over nostalgia. He recognized that there would be a romantic edge, but he wanted to play against sentiment, so he asked that the dialogue be "sharp—unsentimental . . . unromantic," thus the frequent "fuck you" interjections and the pot-smoking scene in McNally's script. Antoon envisioned *The Rink* as a play of discovery, with a long dramatic arc slowly revealing bits of information to both the characters and the audience.[93] McNally devised flashback sequences that explain the reasons why Anna and Angel remain fixated on the past. In a key scene, Dino's uncle Fasto tells Angel the truth about her father. It is this confrontation that precipitates Angel's decision to leave home. In another flashback, Angel, now twenty-three years old and pregnant, tracks down her father, who lives in Florida, works a lousy job, and has two sons. As mother and daughter learn about each other's life, they begin to move toward reconciliation. The resolution of their conflict follows the revelation that Angel has a child named after her mother.

Kander and Ebb's score for *The Rink* coalesced slowly. Table 6.4 lists the sixteen songs identified in one of McNally's early drafts, including the four holdovers from the original score. For the final score, the writers eliminated seven of these songs and added six new ones.

The score mixes idioms from jazz, folk, musical theater, and even opera. The different styles help to demarcate the two generations represented by Anna and Angel as well as the fact that one is an Italian immigrant and the other a first-generation American. The opening music of *The Rink*, a juxtaposition of an old roller rink organ (Wurlitzer organ sound) and a "modern" amplified guitar, instantly establishes the different musical styles for the two main characters. Like "Colored Lights," two other numbers stand out for their extended forms and dramatic gravitas: "All the Children in a Row," and the ensemble number "Mrs. A." These three extended numbers anchor the show dramatically and musically and signal a new direction in Kander and Ebb's musical dramaturgy.

"All the Children in a Row" occurs at the climax of the story, immediately after a devastating fight between Anna and Angel. It reveals the truth about Angel's experiences in California and expresses not just her personal disappointment about her life but her generation's disappointment about the unfulfilled promise of the sixties. "All the Children in a Row" conveys Angel's emotional journey through no less than twenty-six key changes and a fragmentary melodic construction. The modular structure of the song is a symbol of Angel's fragmented life. The use of the guitar vamp from "Colored Lights" at the beginning and end of the number helps to create an emotional connection between this song and Angel's hope to recapture the happiness of her youth. The formal divisions of the song, shown in table 6.5, correspond to the structure of the text, changes in pace and time frame, and the chronology of the scene. The "a" and "b" phrases are intended to evoke California and the sixties. Ebb incorporated specific references to the sixties and the "Summer

Table 6.4. Score as indicated in the early draft and the final score (songs originally written for Innaurato's version in bold)

McNally's Early Draft		Final Score	
"Colored Lights"	Pia	"Colored Lights"	Angel
"Chief Cook and Bottle Washer"	Anna	**"Chief Cook and Bottle Washer"**	Anna
"Don't Ah Ma Me"	Anna and Pia	**"Don't Ah Ma Me"**	Anna and Angel
		"Blue Crystal"	Dino
"Familiar Things	Pia	"Under the Roller Coaster" (same as "Familiar Things")	Angel
"Not Enough Magic"	Dino	"Not Enough Magic"	Dino, Angel, Anna, Sugar, Hiram, Tom, and Dino's father
		"We Can Make It"	Anna
"After All These Years"	Wreckers	"After All These Years"	Wreckers
		"Angel's Rink and Social Center"	Angel and the wreckers
"What Happened to the Old Days"	Anna, Lino, and wreckers	"What Happened to the Old Days"	Anna, Mrs. Silverman, and Mrs. Jackson
		"Colored Lights" (reprise)	Angel
		"The Apple Doesn't Fall"	Anna and Angel
"All the Children in a Row"	Pia		
"Lecce"	Anna and wreckers		
"Gelati"	Lucky as Lenny		
		"Marry Me"	Lenny
		"We Can Make It" (reprise)	Anna
"Eight Ducks" (also called "Moments")*	Pia, Anna, and Guy (as Dino)		
		"The Rink"	Wreckers
"Wallflower"	Anna (Angel was later added to this number)	"Wallflower"	Anna and Angel

Table 6.4. (*Continued*)

McNally's Early Draft		Final Score	
"Yesterday Is Yesterday" (from *Golden Gate*)[†]	Wreckers		
"Murphy's Law"	Anna		
		"All the Children in a Row"	Angel and Danny
"When the Antonellis Were Here"	Anna, Pia, and wreckers		
"Well, Anyway" (based on music from "Colored Lights")	Anna and Pia		
		Coda (based on the toast from "We Can Make It" and "Colored Lights")	Anna and Angel

*In this song, Pia relives the time her father shot all of the ducks at a carnival booth. Unknown to her at the time, Dino conspired with the owner of a booth to fix the game so that he wins.
†*The Rink* marks the second time that Kander and Ebb tried to reuse "Yesterday Is Yesterday," which initially belonged to the score for *Golden Gate*. The first time was for *Flora* (see above).

of Love," including Janis Joplin, Ken Kesey, and the rock band Steppenwolf. The "c" phrase is a majestic melody hailing the glory days of California during the sixties—a yearning for a past that probably never really existed. The melody, in D-flat major, captures the mood with a flat-seventh "blue" note. The music of "d" imitates a protest march, although the deliberate tempo and strummed off-beat quarter notes have the effect of mocking the youthful optimism and defiance that Angel remembers. Between the B section and the return of the A section, Angel discovers that her father is still alive. It is 1971. She hunts him down and confronts him. When she tells him that she is pregnant, he sends her on her way.

"Mrs. A." also stands out for its operatic dimensions (table 6.6). Involving Anna, Angel, Lenny, and three of Anna's suitors, this cacophonous ensemble has an intentionally fragmented structure and lack of tonal unity. It moves back and forth in time and sometimes portrays the past and present simultaneously, recalling themes heard earlier in the story and combining them to create both Anna's and Angel's nightmarish memories of the past. Anna's melody (B), the most substantial new material, anchors the number.

Table 6.5. Musical structure and key scheme for "All the Children in a Row"

Sections	Phrase	Key	Lyric	Alternative Lyric
A	α*	G		
	a		All the children in a row	
			Leaving home behind.	Confident and brave.
	a		We've a war to win, you know	
			We've a life to find.	
	b	E	Have you been to Monterey	
			Didn't Janis sing?	
	b′		Kesey's bus came by today	
			Steppenwolf is king.	
	a	G	All the children in a row	
			Flowers in their hair.	
	a′		Why do people turn away?	Eldridge Cleaver, Bobby Seale
			Man, it isn't fair.	
	a	G-flat	Leary's in the slammer now	
			Boy, is that a mess.	
	a′		Light a match and burn the card	
			Doctor Spock says "yes."	
	b	E-flat	Marching proudly arm in arm†	All the children in a row
			Singing Dylan songs	Acapulco calm.
	b′		No one is a stranger here	"Easy Rider" knocked me out
			Everyone belongs.	Spread the tiger balm.
	c	D-flat	California's warm as love	California's warm as love
			I'm with friends, I know	I belong I know.
			In the gallant army of‡	
			All the children in a row.	
	d	B-flat	Who can change things? We can!	Who will change things? We can!
			Who will change things? We will!	
B	e	A-flat	And me and Danny running hand-in-hand	
			Frisbees on the sand.	
	e		[Danny: Wanna be my old lady? Whaddaya say?]§	

Table 6.5. (*Continued*)

Sections	Phrase	Key	Lyric	Alternative Lyric
			Me and Danny Burgers on a bun Banners in the sun. [Danny: Might as well be my old lady. Everybody says you are anyway!]	
	f	B-flat	Turning in the night, hungry [Danny] Look it, you're my wife, ain't you? Promise not to laugh, will you? Answer me one thing, honest. Please don't tell a soul I asked you.	
	recit	C	Where's Cambodia?	
	e′	E-flat	[Angel] Me and Danny, walking down the street "How we gonna eat?" [Danny: Dudes who ain't got no old lady—they move on, you know.]	
	e″	g	Me and Danny, why'd you pick that fight? No, it's not all right We were brave together, strong together Where's it gone?	
	g	f-sharp	["Do you need to take that stuff?" "Come on, Danny, that's enough!"] We can make it, we'll survive Danny, you're too stoned to drive!	Danny, you're too stunned to drive.
	—	B-flat	(The music sounds like a car crash, in the distance a siren wails. Danny is gone.)	
	e	F-f	Me and Danny, I don't understand Where's the world we planned?	

Table 6.5. (*Continued*)

Sections	Phrase	Key	Lyric	Alternative Lyric
	g′		["You promised me 'Someday.' Oh, Danny that should have been your middle name— 'Someday.'"]	
	h	A-C	In California, it doesn't ever snow In California, living's kind of slow.	
	e**	F	[Dialogue between Angel and Dino.]††	
	e**			
	e″**	a		
	e**	F-f		
	g′**			
A′	α	F		
	a		All the children in a row Confident and brave	
	a		We've a war to win, you know We've a world to save	
	b	D	No one thinks we matter much No one understands	Three Dog Night's in San José Have you got a ride?
	b′		But we made a difference by The joining of our hands	What about Kent State today? Seven of 'em died!
	c	C	California's warm as love I belong, I know To the gallant army of All the children in a row!	
	d	D	Who keeps marching? We do! Who's the future? We are! We are! We Are!	

*Guitar vamp from "Colored Lights" indicated by α.
†"Proudly marching arm in arm" on the original Broadway cast recording.
‡"In the gentle army of" on the original Broadway cast recording.
§Spoken dialogue in brackets.
**Phrases played as underscoring by orchestra.
††This section is not on the original Broadway cast recording.

Table 6.6. Musical structure of "Mrs. A," *The Rink*

Key	Men	Anna	Angel	Lenny
C	A theme			
F–A-flat		B theme		
A		Dialogue underscored by "We Can Make It"		
C	A (Men)			
C				C theme ("Marry Me")
E			D theme ("Familiar Things")	
C	A			
A-flat–B	A	B		
E-flat	A	B	B	

The A theme is sung by the men as they harass Anna. Lenny reprises the rhapsodic "Marry Me," after which Anna sings a verse of "Familiar Things."

Kander and Ebb originally wrote *The Rink* as a star vehicle for Chita Rivera. Many top-notch actresses were considered for the part of the daughter, including Jessica Harper, Linda Hart, Mary Testa, Laurie Beechman, Terri Klausner, Patti LuPone, Judith Ivey, and Priscilla Lopez. However, when Liza Minnelli practically begged Kander and Ebb to let her play Rivera's daughter, they could not refuse her. Adding Minnelli to the equation, however, turned *The Rink* into a double-diva show. Rivera and Minnelli had already developed a professional rapport when the latter filled in for Gwen Verdon during her leave of absence from *Chicago* in August of 1975. However, whereas *Chicago* had benefited from the high-powered pairing, *The Rink* suffered from it. By most accounts, Minnelli performed brilliantly (although she missed too many performances), but audiences apparently had trouble accepting her as a ragtag, pot-puffing flower child.

The Rink attracted audiences for a time because of its star power. It also drew severe reactions from the critics, which caused business to taper off once Minnelli left the show. Ironically, McNally suffered the brunt of the critics' attacks, even though he was not even responsible for the basic story line. Frank Rich lavished praise on Chita Rivera and remarked positively on the music and orchestrations, but he added that "no glossy Broadway professionalism can mask the work's phony, at times mean-spirited content—or give credence to its empty pretensions."[94] He accused McNally of writing "psychobabble" and mere "ciphers" for characters: "Almost every male character is a crude sexual adventurer, and both women are presented as reformed 'tramps.'" Of the lyrics, Rich singled out "All the Children in a Row," complaining that they "characterize the idealists of an entire decade as ineffectual Frisbee throwers and draft-card burners."[95] Ebb felt that Rich completely missed the point: "I was kind of annoyed that [Frank Rich] didn't understand the real intent of that line 'Where's Cambodia!' Then he went off on Terrence McNally and the whole show."[96] What probably irked Kander the most was Rich's assertion that Proust rather than Ibsen was the musical's source of inspiration. The flashback sequences reminded a few critics of *Follies*,[97] and Richard Cerliss of *Time* likened McNally's script to "a domestic mini-drama swathed in poignancy—*A Tree Grows in Brooklyn* mixed with *Terms of Endearment*."[98] Both Benedict Nightingale and Douglas Watts picked up on the classical elements of the story, with the former glibly calling *The Rink* "an inverted 'Electra' on wheels,"[99] and the latter insinuating that the time frame of a single day adheres to Aristotelian unity of time. In general Kander and Ebb's score faired much better than McNally's script. Watts sensed an indirect connection between the music and Italian romantic opera and called the writers "an outstandingly professional team of songwriters who go for the throat—and I don't mean that disparagingly, for Verdi, among others, was a master at it." Clive Barnes, the sole dissenter and a long-time ardent Minnelli fan, called the musical "ambitious" and McNally's book "lean and hard even in its sentimentality."[100]

The Rink had its British premiere in Manchester in 1987, and it opened in London the following year. The British press was generally more favorable than the American press and even had a few positive comments about the script. Like some of their American counterparts, the London critics saw similarities to *Follies*, but they could not resist making a superficial connection to *Starlight Express*.

In the mid nineties, McNally, Kander, and Ebb revised *The Rink*, moving it up to the present (the nineties) in order to make it more relevant to contemporary audiences. They shifted attention from Angel to Anna. They relocated "Colored Lights" to a later place in the story, after Angel learns that Anna had been molested by muggers. The new version of the musical begins with a dialogue scene for the Wreckers followed by Anna's wanting song, "Chief Cook and Bottle Washer." McNally included several topical references, such as Save the Whales, Tom Cruise, and Oprah. In the first scene, one of the

Wreckers establishes the contemporary time frame: "This place survived the hurricane of thirty-seven, that big fire in '57. It survived two wars, rock 'n' roll, disco, VCRs, Watergate, Vietnam, Jimmy Carter, Reagan, Bush, Madonna, Michael Jackson and Michael Jordan. People went through all that and they still liked to skate together." The nineties' setting robs the story of its historical dimension involving Angel as the archetypal sixties' reject with bittersweet memories of the past. The new time frame also cuts against the folk musical allusions in "Colored Lights" and precludes using the Korean War as the cause of Dino's breakdown. Apparently, the writers did not want to substitute the Vietnam War for the Korean War. Instead, Dino moves away and settles in Texas, McNally's home state, simply because he is unhappy with Anna and his life running the rink.

The most significant musical change for this version involves "All the Children in a Row," the song most lambasted by the critics back in 1984. The further the story got from the 1960s, the less relevant the song became. So Kander and Ebb tried to write an effective substitute, "It's a Great Big World." The new song dramatizes Angel's cross-country search for her father; in each verse she is in a different city and has a different job. She starts out as a restaurant hostess.

> Good evening, sir.
> Dinner for three?
> I have a nice table.
> Follow me.

As she works, she thinks about finding her father.

> And I wonder if I'll ever find my father.
> I need to see . . .
> I need to find my father.
> Here's a phone book . . .
> Antonelli . . .
> God.
> God, it's a great big world.

Although more fitting for the new version of the story, "It's a Great Big World" did not have the emotional power of "All the Children in a Row," so Kander and Ebb tried combining the two songs. The final result ("All the Children in a Row revised," dated 8/6/96) is the weakest of the three versions, too much of a compromise, and the sections borrowed from the first and second versions work at cross-purposes. The opening section of the song begins:

Table 6.7. Phrase structure and key scheme of the revised "All the
Children in a Row"

Section	Key
aa	G
bb′	E
aa′	G
c	G
d (new theme)	E-flat
bb′	E
aa	G
c	G
d	E-flat
bb′	E-flat
e ("California")	D-flat
f	B-flat
gg	A-flat
gg′	E-flat–g
accident	f-sharp
g/b (underscoring)	F-f
hec	A–C–E-flat
d*	A-flat
aa	F
bb′	D
e	C
α**	C

*A version dated 3/95 ends at the end of this section. This table represents the version
dated 8/6/96.
**α = vamp from "Colored Lights" plus the opening phrase

> All the children in a row
> Running for their lives
> Seems to me I wrote the book,
> How a kid survives.

This version lacks the sense of purpose of the original "All the Children."
Modulations occur with the frequency found in the other versions, but here
they lack strong dramatic justification and thus seem random (table 6.7). The
original version's decisive lack of musical continuity was part of its dramatic
effectiveness. In the new version, there are simply too many ideas vying for
attention, and they weaken the underlining drama.

Kander and Ebb also experimented with a new finale. Ebb and McNally
wanted to use "When the Antonellis Were Here," a charming song dating

back to Innaurato's version of *The Rink*. Kander never warmed to the idea, though. They tried it in a workshop reading but ended up opting for something closer to the 1984 ending. Anna and Angel sing a brief recitative based on the "a" theme of "All the Children."

> ANGEL: All that looking back
>   Was it dumb, I mean?
> ANNA: If we hadn't looked
>   We'd have never seen.
> [ANGEL]: Will you help me know·
>   Calmer days and nights?
>   Will you help me find
>   Other colored lights?
> ANNA: I don't know where.
> ANGEL: Well, anyway.

Despite the writers' efforts and the insight of their combined years of experience, *The Rink* might simply be too much prose and not enough poetry. McNally understood the stakes: "It's not conceived of as an entertainment. . . . We're asking a lot from our audiences."[101] *The Rink* is probably too dated and uneven to become a main part of the repertory. As one critic noted, it is "a serious treatment of a mother-daughter relationship in a genre strong on cotton candy."[102]

Steel Pier (1997)

When the revival of *Chicago* opened, Kander and Ebb were just embarking on rehearsals for *Steel Pier*, which reunited them with the creative team and star of the 1991 hit *And the World Goes 'Round* (see Appendix).[103] After *And the World Goes 'Round*, Susan Stroman (choreographer), Scott Ellis (director), and David Thompson (book writer) decided to write a dance musical specifically for Karen Ziemba. They considered a broad range of sources, including *Ball of Fire*, Gypsy Rose Lee's *G-String Murder*, *Tootsie*, and *Purple Rose of Cairo*. Ebb liked the Sydney Pollack film *They Shoot Horses, Don't They?* but everyone else wanted something more romantic. "Our goal," according to Thompson, "was to deliver an American love story." As a child Kander visited the real Steel Pier in Atlantic City, and he remembered it as being a magical place where women wore elegant gloves, and men bow ties. Given the setting, time frame, and romantic criterion, they devised a story about a woman struggling to break out of a dead-end marriage.

The plot is an inversion of sorts of the Orpheus myth. The heroine, Rita Racine, a woman in her thirties, has been forced by her husband, Mick Hamilton, a ruthless and corrupt dance marathon promoter, to travel from city to city to compete in the humiliating competitions, which Mike fixes so that Rita always wins. As the musical opens, Rita and Mike arrive at the Steel Pier for what they have agreed will be their last marathon, for she wants to settle down and lead a normal existence. She pairs up with a daredevil pilot named Bill Kelly. During the telescoped time frame of the marathon, they fall in love, and Rita decides to escape from her abusive marriage. Bill, we later learn, died in an air show accident, and he has come back from the world of the dead in order to help Rita, but he cannot remain with her. Like their mythological models, Bill and Rita can only be together spiritually in the incorporeal world.

What appealed to Thompson was the "myth of a man going into a world where a woman is trapped and asking her to follow him out and to help find a way to free her." As Orpheus enters "the marathon of the underworld to save Eurydice, so too does Bill arrive at the dance marathon to save Rita." Kander sees an even stronger parallel with the Orpheus story: "As long as she [Rita] doesn't look back, they can be together." Whereas Thompson and Kander were enthralled by the romanticism of the story, Ebb was never fully comfortable with it. Tony Walton, the set designer for *Steel Pier*, also thought that the conclusion of the story begged too many questions and pushed the audience's suspension of disbelief to the breaking point. In contrast, Kander was untroubled by this aspect of the story: "It's like if you fall in love and you try to analyze it, you can analyze yourself right out of the feeling. So sometimes you just have to go with your feeling." In the end, Kander and Thompson won out. The production was visually and musically beautiful. Walton designed an enchanting set that captured the nostalgia and romanticism of the story. Gibson's orchestrations shift from swing to lush waves of sound. Stroman's choreography featured an array of popular social dances from the '30s (rumba, fox-trot, quickstep, the Grind Snake) as well as the Charleston from the '20s and dances like the Lindy. But the critics echoed the minority opinion of Walton and Ebb.

Steel Pier is Kander and Ebb's least cynical musical. In this respect, Kander and Ebb were prisoners (or victims) of their own success, and critics were quick to comment on the shift. Ben Brantley called *Steel Pier* the "anti-'Cabaret . . . anti-'Chicago'" musical, and he thought that it was "dishearteningly fizz-free."[104] He glibly suggested that "It is apparently time to leave the party, the razzle-dazzle, the driving grind of show business, and go home to consider gentler, more spiritual matters." Were this conclusion born out in Kander and Ebb's three post–*Steel Pier* works—*All About Us* (*Skin of Our Teeth*), *The Visit*, and *Minstrel Show*—Brantley's words might be justified, but these new musicals all invoke the self-referential elements and stoicism of their earlier works. Brantley forced the comparison, calling Rita Racine Sally Bowles's and Roxie Hart's "more passive, ingenuous cousin." Rita, as Brantley makes clear, wants not to "make it" in but to "escape" from the dance marathon. Brantley felt that this shift in sentiment underscored the musical's weaknesses: "The new point of view lacks drive and energy, and Mr. Kander and Mr. Ebb are simply more engaging when they're in a more cynical mood." The review was by no means a death sentence, but the producer got cold feet and decided to cut off the financial lifeline necessary to keep the show afloat long enough for it to find its audience.

CHAPTER 7

Divas or Anti-Divas?
The Act *and* The Woman of the Year

The diva musical is about a woman's escape from the humdrum. . . . To closeted gay men, the diva heroine was a figure of identification. Where does one find magic if one is different and must try to hide one's difference?
—JOHN CLUM

I N PREVIOUS CHAPTERS WE OBSERVED HOW CAMP AND DIVA WOR-ship—in musical theater they are always closely allied—informed the style, themes, and topics of Kander and Ebb's musicals. These features were not new to musical theater when Kander and Ebb began their career, but they became more pronounced during the early years of their collaboration. Although the composer-lyricist Jerry Herman might be more famously identified with the diva musical, Kander and Ebb stand out for their career-long devotion to specific divas, primarily Liza Minnelli, Chita Rivera, and Karen Ziemba.[1] Kander and Ebb's diva musicals encompass a full spectrum of concerns important to gay men and women: survival, self-determination, sexuality and gender, and the relationship between theater and real life. Moreover, Kander and Ebb are the only writers of their generation to perpetuate the diva musical into the twenty-first century.

The gay male's identification with the celebrated female performers of high art (opera, ballet, drama), low art (popular music, television), and everything in-between (cinema, musical theater) is inseparable from the way that gay men negotiate their identity within a hostile society.[2] Of all the arts, the

Broadway musical, as Stacy Wolf points out, "is the one performance form that features women as neither passive objects of desire nor subjects of vilification."[3] It is largely for this reason that musical theater has been labeled a "gay genre." For gay men in particular, the diva musical represents, to use Daniel Harris's phrase, "the almost universal homosexual experience of ostracism and insecurity."[4] The most celebrated diva roles (on stage and film) "transgress [. . .] conventional notions of femininity [and by extension gender] or expand them almost to the breaking point."[5] Al LaValley notes that divas such as Carol Channing, Ethel Merman, and Hermione Gingold are "loud, somewhat obscene women, who violate the decorum one is taught to expect socially from women."[6] Minnelli's portrayal of Sally Bowles is all sexual bravado and performance. (To quote Clum, "she is more a fag hag than a sexually promiscuous woman.")[7] It is not the diva's femininity that most gay men desire; they want the same things that the characters these women play want. This desire helps to explain why acting out the lines, roles, and personas associated with these women lies at the heart of gay camp performance. Kander and Ebb's own performances of the diva roles they created attest to the power of camp to "allow outmoded emotions to flourish not just for their sentimentality but their seeds of rebellion against a more conformist modernity. . . . [C]amp treasures an excessive theatricality and outrageousness as an avenue to heightened emotions."[8] Terrence McNally, an outspoken gay playwright and librettist for three of Kander and Ebb's diva musicals, is more than a little familiar with gay diva worship. At least four of his plays — The Ritz, Love! Valor! Compassion!, Lisbon Traviata, and Master Class — treat musical theater and opera as signifiers of gayness and, to borrow a phrase by Wolf, "a site for the performance of camp."[9]

Gay men have long privileged musical theater singing, especially the emotive singing of the diva, because, notes Paul Robinson, it "gives expression to the character's deepest emotions, to say precisely and emphatically just what the character feels, to speak, as it were, the character's profoundest identity."[10] Musical theater queens identify most with those diva figures, such as Momma Rose and Sally Bowles, who negate the same "system of assumptions" that stigmatize and silence the homosexual.[11] A gay man (or woman) might thus identify with the self-actualization achieved by the diva through the act of singing — in particular belt singing — and hopes to achieve it him (or herself).[12]

Like Jerry Herman, Kander and Ebb sometimes chose source material that was already woven into the fabric of gay subculture. However, they also transformed a lot of frumpy, unglamorous female characters into diva roles, such as Flora Meszaros, Roxie Hart, Angel and Anna Antonelli, and Rita Racine. Jerry Herman's musicals celebrate the diva as diva, and, once he came up with a successful formula, he stuck with it throughout his career. By way of contrast, Kander and Ebb, who were pioneers in the concept musical, looked for the most effective way to tell a particular story and explore a specific theme, and usually came up with a show business metaphor for the central theme. They wrote stories about women who appealed to them as characters, who try to make something better of and for themselves.

Kander and Ebb tailor-made works to showcase the talents of their favorite divas. They wrote the two musicals examined in this chapter, *The Act* and *Woman of the Year*, for Liza Minnelli and Lauren Bacall, respectively. Produced in close succession, these musicals happen to be Kander and Ebb's least distinguished work, although both were commercially successful and the latter won several Tony Awards, including awards for best musical and best score. Neither Kander nor Ebb considered *The Act* or *Woman of the Year* to be among their best work. Ebb acknowledged that "*Woman of the Year* was a mistake." He signed on to do it because of the cachet of working with Lauren Bacall and the well-known title, but he never felt "any real conviction or passion about it."[13] *The Act* started out with a good premise, but it never fully came together. Ebb recalled, "We've had shows that won strong critical approbation—*The Act* was one, at least with the New York critics—that I thought were actually rather sloppy efforts on our parts."[14] Kander remembers being at a "total loss" during *The Act*.

Comparing Minnelli to Streisand, Clum points out that "Liza didn't go the faux glamorous route. . . . She was the ugly duckling who worked harder than anyone else—sang harder, danced harder, acted harder to earn an audience's love." In Chapter 4 we observed how Ebb helped to manufacture the Liza Minnelli persona, in effect transferring his own diva worship of Judy Garland onto her daughter. Gay men adored Garland because of her "identification for [them] at a time when they had nothing but silence or negative comments from any corner of the culture and often had internalized their society's hatred."[15] Clum calls Minnelli Garland's "heiress apparent" and points out that Garland herself tried to set up her daughter as "as her successor with her fans"—although Ebb and Kander witnessed occasions in which Garland could not refrain from upstaging her daughter.[16] Minnelli did not achieve international diva status until the release of the film *Cabaret* and *Liza with a Z!*, which occurred only a couple of years after Stonewall and her mother's death. Minnelli's ascendancy as a diva set the stage for *New York, New York, The Act,* and *The Rink.*

Lauren Bacall is a different sort of diva. Whereas Minnelli earned her diva credentials through hard work, determination, and her inherent talent, and constantly felt the need to prove herself worthy of the diva label, Bacall was the classic diva. Bacall's reputation as a diva preceded her first appearance in a Broadway musical. She did not need to sing and dance. She just needed to appear. In a bit of campy bitchery, Clum describes Bacall's Broadway appearances:

> another Broadway baritone, can't carry a tune, and her voice sounds lower than that of her leading man. . . . She can't really dance. She is a Presence, which means most of the musical work goes to the supporting cast. . . . But Bacall is a celebrity, a star at a time in which there is a dire shortage of musical stars. And she represents those two essential aspects of the Broadway diva. She is a figure of nostalgia and she is a survivor in a show about survival.[17]

Bacall had proven that she could attract musical theater audiences when she starred as Margo Channing in *Applause*, the musical based on *All About Eve*. (It is worth noting that Ebb's friend Ron Field, who choreographed *Cabaret* and *Zorbá* and who was slated to direct *70, Girls, 70*, was the director and choreographer of *Applause*.) John Clum calls *Applause* "a Grand Musical Debut for a camp figure, forties film siren."[18] Bacall's Margo was sympathetic to gay men, as exemplified by her relationship with her gay hairdresser.[19] In *Woman of the Year* the same sort of relationship exists between Bacall's Tess Harding and her personal assistant, played by Roderick Cook.) Coming on the heels of Stonewall, *Applause* was informed by the more enlightened attitudes about homosexuality that that event engendered. A decade later, Bacall suggested the idea of a musical version of the 1941 film classic *Woman of the Year* to Peter Stone, who in turn got Kander and Ebb interested in the project.

Kander and Ebb enjoyed working with Bacall, who was willing to try anything. She wanted to be treated like "one of the boys," to use one of the song titles from *Woman of the Year*. Kander and Ebb even called her Jimmy, after a phone call during which Ebb mistook Bacall for the actor James Coco. The name stuck because, as Kander recalls, she liked "being Jimmy and we liked that it was something special between us . . . It's funny to talk about her as a pal, but she is pal-like in our relationship with her."[20] During a rehearsal of the song "I Wrote the Book," Ebb stood in for her because, as he later joked, "I walk like Bacall. I'm about as graceful as she is."

Woman of the Year is Kander and Ebb's most conservative and conventional musical. By way of contrast, The Act contains all of the hallmarks of a Kander and Ebb musical. It is a story about the survival of an actress down on her luck and told in the form of a Las Vegas nightclub act. The score, some of it excellent, consists mainly of the songs she performs during her act. We have seen similar structures in Cabaret, Chicago, and 70, Girls, 70. Unfortunately, in the case of The Act the show-within-a-show framework did not transcend itself enough to appear to be more than a venue for Minnelli to sing and dance and emote. Nor does the showbiz venue serve as an effective metaphor for the heroine's life.

The Act

The Act (1977) was conceived by Marvin Hamlisch, who wanted to split the music with Kander and use Ebb as their mutual lyricist. Kander and Ebb were uninterested in such an arrangement, but they liked the idea enough to write the entire musical themselves. Supposedly based on the life of Shirley MacLaine, The Act is about the comeback of a once in-demand movie star named Michelle Craig (originally Mayer). Film offers have dried up, so she has decided to do a Las Vegas nightclub act. The idea seemed ideal for Minnelli, who insisted that Scorsese direct, despite the producers' reservations.

The Act went through a shaky four-month out-of-town period, playing Chicago, San Francisco, and Los Angeles, in each city under a different title, respectively, In Person, Shine It On, and The Act. The title was not the only thing that changed. Stanley Donen was going to write the script, but George Furth took over. The most drastic change, however, was the unpublicized replacement of Scorsese with Gower Champion. Scorsese's experience in film did not prepare him to direct a Broadway musical, and, by all accounts, he was uninterested in learning. According to Cy Feuer, "The biggest problem was that he [Scorsese] didn't understand staging. He couldn't figure out how to bring actors on and off, how to set up a scene."[21] To make matters worse, Scorsese and Minnelli were getting high after rehearsals, which began to affect the company's morale. When Feuer decided to replace Scorsese, he first approached Michael Bennett about taking over, but the director was either unavailable or unwilling to do so. Feuer eventually convinced Gower Champion to intervene but only on the condition that he not get directorial credit. In lieu of marquee billing, the published script for *The Act* is "lovingly and gratefully dedicated to Gower Champion."[22]

George Furth came up with a concept of a nightclub act that opens up into book scenes, an inversion of the backstage musical formula. An explanatory note in the published script reads: "Whereas in most musical comedies the procedure is to break from the book into musical numbers, in this production the procedure will be to break from the night club act into the book." The action also shifts between the past and present. Scenes from the past focus on Michelle's marriage to Dan, which collapses because of Michelle's overdependence on him. During her nightclub act, which takes place in the present, Michelle sings, dances, jokes, and tells autobiographical stories to her fans, sometimes in the form of flashbacks. The confessional tone and nightclub setting seem just right for Ebb's experience as a producer of television specials (see Chapter 4) and Minnelli's ingratiating stage personae. Kander and Ebb originally conceived of the score as a real nightclub act without any direct reference to the plot, but Champion wanted more emotional return from the music. He thus recontextualized the musical numbers within the story of Michelle's life, allowing them to perform double duty as diegetic songs and book songs.

The opening number of *The Act* is also the opening of Michelle's Las Vegas debut, a tightly wound, disco-inflected song called "Shine It On." After the applause, Michelle starts to recount her life, speaking directly to the Las Vegas audience. Her delivery recalls the rehearsed spontaneity and mannered intimacy of Minnelli's concerts. At one point, Michelle unctuously announces that her ex-husband Dan is in the audience. Michelle's next number, "It's the Strangest Thing," which Kander and Ebb salvaged from their Horatio Alger musical (see Chapter 8), is a touching ballad that alludes to events in Michelle's life. A flashback occurs midway through the song, taking us back to an audition during which Michelle sang the same song for Dan. It is an effective use of a cinematic device.

The critics accused George Furth of writing a thin, ineffectual book, which failed to elevate what was essentially a nightclub act to the level of musical theater.[23] Ironically, Furth had originally included intricate backstories, but under Scorsese's direction they were cut in favor of more nightclub scenes. According to Tony Walton, who designed the sets for *The Act*, Scorsese eliminated the most interesting parts of Furth's script, but the playwright chose the path of least resistance, and by the time Champion took over it was too late to salvage the cut scenes.

Despite mixed reviews, audiences were willing to come as long as Minnelli showed up, even paying $25 for a Saturday night orchestra seat, a record-setting figure at the time. By most accounts, Minnelli was wonderful and entirely dedicated to the show. Even though her larger-than-life personality negated the character she was playing, the book was so superficial that the audience did not seem to care. (Minnelli had no understudy, so performances had to be canceled whenever she was unable to perform, which was not infrequent.) Edwin Wilson noted that "The role [of Michelle] is not a vehicle for Miss Minnelli; only a kind of costume to set her off. It takes her nowhere. She is just the same—and this is the mark of cabaret—at the end as at the beginning."[24] This is not the kind of endorsement that the producers needed in order to keep the show running after Minnelli's departure.

In 1994 the actor and director Walter Painter started working with George Furth on a revised version of *The Act*. In order to make the musical more viable, they distanced it as much as possible from the aura of Minnelli. They changed the title to *Comeback*, renamed the protagonist Michelle McNally, and changed the venue from a Las Vegas nightclub to a concert stage. They left the score mostly intact, but Painter hoped to convince Kander and Ebb to write a couple of new songs. Painter contacted Shirley MacLaine about the possibility of starring in this version, but the project has been put on hold indefinitely.

Kander never entirely embraced *The Act* and wondered why anyone would care about two protagonists who do nothing but argue. However, *The Act* marks an important moment in his life. He met Albert Stephenson, one of the dancers in the show, and they have been together ever since.[25]

Woman of the Year (1981)

Woman of the Year is Kander and Ebb's fourth-longest-running musical, not including their revivals. Opening in the early days of the Reagan era, this conservative musical comedy appealed to mainstream audiences more interested in seeing a Hollywood legend than in dealing with gender issues. Bacall was ideal for the role. Her physical beauty and femme fatale mystique made her an irresistible Tess Harding. And she had proved back in 1970 that one need not have musical and dancing talent to carry a diva musical. She spoke-sung her way through her songs, joining the pantheon of nonsinging Broadway musical stars.

Stone's script gently argues for, if not turning back the clock on the feminist movement, at least slowing down its momentum. His answer to the gender equality debate is a defeat for radical feminism thinly disguised as a reciprocal compromise. He updated the original story by turning Tess into a Barbara Walters–type morning show hostess ("television anchor diva") and Sam Craig, the plainspoken sportswriter of the film, into an editorial cartoonist for a New York daily.[26] Sam's new vocation softens the rough edges of the role created by Spencer Tracy. Act 1 is a flashback that takes place in Tess's mind as she is about to accept the award for "Woman of the Year." She recalls how Sam walked into her life after she attacked the funnies on national television. The rest of the act charts the rise and fall of their relationship: they meet, fall in love, marry, argue, and separate. In act 2 Tess, as unfathomable as it might seem, seeks marriage counseling from her ex-husband and his frumpy, suburban second wife in Colorado. Convinced that her marriage is a casualty of her ambition, Tess returns to New York and quits her job so that she can dedicate herself to Sam. Sam insists that she can have it both ways as long as she strikes a balance.

Although garnering Kander and Ebb their second Tony Award, their score for *Woman of the Year* is, by their own assessment, not their best work. The score is pure musical comedy, containing the requisite number of comedy songs, love ballads, charm songs, and upbeat ensemble numbers. Highlights of the score include Sam's ballad "Sometimes a Day Goes By" and "The Grass Is Always Greener," a comedy song for Tess and her ex-husband's new wife, Jan Donovan, played unsurpassably by Marilyn Cooper. "Sometimes a Day Goes By" has become one of Kander and Ebb's most frequently covered ballads. "The Grass Is Always Greener" is one of Broadway's legendary eleven o'clock numbers. As the title suggests, Tess, a self-engrossed urban professional, yearns for the simple existence of a middle-class housewife. Cooper's deadpan performance—which earned her a Tony Award for best featured actress—left little doubt that the Women's Liberation Movement had bypassed Colorado. The reciprocal envy that Tess and Jan express for each other's worlds encapsulated the conflicted attitude of an entire generation of women.

JAN: Is your picture up at Sardi's?
   That's wonderful!
TESS: What's so wonderful?
   You can clean an oven
   That's wonderful!
JAN: What's so wonderful!
   First, you get the E.Z. Off.

Raquel Welch replaced Bacall after about a year, and later Debbie Reynolds took over the role. In a comparison of the three divas, Mel Gussow called Bacall "an imposing, Barbara Walters woman of the world," Welch "a glamorous Wonder Woman," and Reynolds "the most down-to-earth of the three."[27] Welch brought more irony to Tess than Bacall, and Reynolds gave a self-knowing "nudge to the audience." Bacall returned to the role of Tess in 1983 for the national tour, for which Stone, Kander, and Ebb made several changes.[28] A revised opening number for Tess replaced the original one, which brought to mind the ostentatious theme music of television awards shows, with a more supple melody. Ebb's new lyric for the song introduced a more defiant Tess. Retained from the original version of the song are the "chirp, chirp" interjections of the offstage chorus, an avian metaphor for Tess's autograph seekers.[29] Kander and Ebb also added a song called "Here We Are, the Two of Us" (which may have been influenced by a song of the same name from Simon Says [see Chapter 4]), which constitutes an entire comic scene: hoping to enjoy a night out on the town alone, Sam and Tess sing the first verse; with each subsequent verse more people enter until the stage is overcrowded. The song cleverly illustrates the collision of Tess's professional and private lives.

The Act is never performed today. On the other hand, Woman of the Year has become a popular vehicle for actresses overseas. It is not necessarily a coincidence that these two works, which were written one after the other, represent a nadir in Kander and Ebb's collaboration. Between the two productions there was some tension in their relationship. Another cause might have been the changing cultural climate, especially on Broadway. The so-called English invasion was under way, which marginalized traditional musical comedy as well as the concept musical, both distinctly American in origin. Kander and Ebb did not try to alter their style or jump on the bandwagon, preferring to stick to what they knew best. In the case of The Act, the diva overshadowed dramatic considerations, which, as we saw in the previous chapter, are indispensable to the success of a musical. The diva always survives, but the roles keep changing. *Woman of the Year* is simply too conventional and mediocre to be placed in the same group as diva musicals like *Gypsy, Mame*, and *Chicago*. It is also true that Tess Harding is forced (or chooses) to conform, the opposite of how a diva traditionally acts. Although Tess has all the markings of a diva—a masculine sense of ambition, a husky voice, pants, and a gay sensibility—she is not a diva but rather an anti-diva.

For Kander and Ebb the diva musical is a form of empowerment, a means of personal expression. They found other ways to express their identities as gay artists. As we have seen, Ebb lived out his innermost desires through Liza Minnelli, and Kander, when given the opportunity, wrote music for Renée Fleming, one of the most celebrated divas of our time. But they always returned to the diva musical, which John Clum, right after the epigraph at the head of this chapter, offers up as "escape from the provincial, where one is hated. . . . an antidote to grayness and the strong sense of entrapment. In the process the diva gains glamour and power."

CHAPTER 8

Musicals Abandoned and Imagined

N O STUDY ON KANDER AND EBB WOULD BE COMPLETE WITHOUT at least a brief account of the musicals that they either never completed, abandoned for lack of a producer, or considered but could never get off the ground. These projects, almost as many in number as their Broadway musicals, are a treasure trove of Kander and Ebb material and a window into their working method. They replicate many of the aspects of their musicals that we have already observed, such as the dramatic use of presentational songs. Several use framing devices and deal with the sort of themes running throughout their collaboration.

Golden Gate (1962–63)

Kander and Ebb started out their collaboration by writing specialty material for nightclub performers. They rarely, if ever, refused an opportunity to get a song onstage. A lot of this material is similar to the skits and songs that Ebb had written with Paul Klein, and Kander with David Rogers (see Chapter 4). For example, Lynn Carter, a female impersonator, performed songs like "I Didn't Raise My Girl [to Be a Bunny]," in which a mother complains about the fact that her daughter is working as a Playboy Bunny.[1] It was not long, though, before they were writing their first musical, *Golden Gate*.

The playwright Richard Morris, who was an acquaintance of Ebb's, approached them with an idea for a musical set in the aftermath of the 1906 San Francisco earthquake. He had already begun writing the script. *Golden*

Gate is about Murphy, an ex-pugilist who has taken it upon himself to oversee the welfare of the city during its reconstruction and to care for its still unclaimed children, his "Royal Wards."[2] He has a nemesis, Auntie, a profiteer and proprietor of a parlor hall for young women and the personification of political corruption. The battle for the soul of the city plays itself out against the struggle between Murphy and Auntie. They also fight over Angel Casey, a half-Cherokee, half-Irish street urchin who has come to San Francisco to seek her fortune. Her love interest, a wealthy Italian immigrant named Bruno Del Grande, also squares off with Auntie. The story coalesces around a public debate between Murphy and Auntie over whether to rebuild San Francisco out of the ruins of the earthquake or to relocate to nearby Oakland.

Morris's original script has not been found, but a later outline, which Morris might have written for a possible television version, helps us to piece together the plot as the playwright probably first conceived it.[3] A note appearing on the title page of the outline, probably intended as a joke, lists Sammy Davis, Jr. as Murphy, Liza Minnelli as Angel, Angela Lansbury as Auntie, James Caan as Bruno, and Bob Fosse as director. Because of *Golden Gate*'s seminal importance in Kander and Ebb's career, the entire plot synopsis along with the musical plan is given here.

Plot Outline	Songs
Act 1:	
On a ferry shuttling survivors of the earthquake from Oakland back to San Francisco, Murphy, the self-appointed "Emperor" of the city, meets Angel Casey, who has come to California to seek her fortune. She and Bruno Del Grande, a wealthy Italian immigrant also on board, are strongly drawn to each other.	"Golden Gate"
Angel is eager to take on the world.	"I'm One of the Smart Ones"
But Auntie, a corrupt madam, attempts to lure Angel into her employ.	
Murphy tries to protect Angel, even double-crossing her by returning a gold watch that she has pickpocketed to its rightful owner.	

In Golden Gate Park, Angel helps Murphy to care for the children. Robby Morgan treats them to a joy ride on an automobile.   "Emperor"

Angel is not as impressed with Robby as Murphy would like her to be.

At tent city, Murphy feeds the children and puts them to bed.   "Dear Lord"

Murphy sends his aide Tsung Lee to impersonate Auntie's cook Chin Wa, using this ploy to sneak into Auntie's parlor and spy on her.   "Yesterday Is Yesterday"

Auntie instructs her protégés on how to squeeze political secrets out of their male clientele.

Murphy is disappointed to discover Angel working for Auntie, who is teaching her the tricks of the trade.   "Etiquette"

In an attempt to cause a decline in the value of San Francisco real estate, Auntie conspires with Bruno Del Grande to create the appearance of a land grab in Oakland ("the new promised land").

Del Grande and Angel go out on a date. He kisses her. They argue and then make up.   "Start All Over Again"

Murphy meets them on the street, and warns Bruno to beware the company he keeps.

Murphy and Tsung Lee teach a sailor from Missouri not to say "Frisco"   "Everybody's Favorite City"

Auntie spreads propaganda in favor of relocating to Oakland, as Murphy campaigns in favor of rebuilding San Francisco.

Angel is angry with Bruno for wanting to abandon the city.

Act 2:

When his followers comment on the Emperor's cushy life, Murphy complains that with his responsibilities he has no time of his own.	"The Royal Rounds"
Murphy presents designs for the Golden Gate Bridge to Del Grande, who refuses to fund it.	
Tsung Lee teases Del Grande that he will someday marry Angel Casey.	"I Bet You Two Dollar"
Auntie cites Nostradamus's prediction about San Francisco in order to convince Bruno to build a new Barbary Coast, which they will control. She asks him to appear on stage with her at a debate at the North Beach Ladies Garden and Political Club.	"Sin City, My Home"
Angel comes to Murphy bearing gifts. She is about to move into a house paid for by Bruno. She pleads with Murphy not to fight Auntie.	
Murphy feels that he has failed Angel.	"A Simple Thing Like That"
Bruno visits Angel in her glamorous new surroundings. He gives her a diamond necklace, but what she really wants is marriage. When Bruno leaves to go to the symphony, Murphy arrives with the purse she left at the park. He does not approve of her life.	"There's Nothing Wrong with My Life"
One of Auntie's flunkies has discovered that Murphy is a former pugilist from an Oregon logging camp. His nickname was "Donkey." He apparently blinded a man. Auntie taunts Murphy with this information.	
Feeling he has failed everyone, Murphy gives up on his mission, until Angel and	"Anywhere You Are"

Tsung Lee rekindle his resolve to fight
for the city.
At the Ladies Garden and Political Club,   "Emperor" (reprise)
Murphy and Auntie publicly debate the   "Golden Gate"
    relocation issue. Angel and Robby
    sit together. Bruno arrives with Miss
    Puchelli. He is jealous of Robby. To
    Auntie's dismay, Bruno claims that he
    will not abandon San Francisco or his
    love, Angel. Auntie tries to counter
    with claims that their land is good for
    nothing except grazing. Tsung Lee
    enters with Auntie's ledger. Having lost
    the battle, Auntie goes to Los Angeles,
    "where sin is considered an art form."

Golden Gate marks the end of an era rather than the dawn of a new one.
It is a traditional book musical, and Kander and Ebb wrote a conventional
score. Each number fits into one of the conventional song categories of a
typical fifties musical: march ("The Emperor"), ballad ("Anywhere You Are"),
comedy song ("Etiquette" and "I Bet You Two Dollars"), and charm song
("I'm One of the Smart Ones" and "Start All Over").[4] Kander and Ebb made
no attempt to imply the musical patois of turn-of-the-century San Francisco.
One noteworthy feature is the use of some melodies as musical recollections
and emotional signposts. For instance, "The Royal Rounds" takes its opening from the theme of "Emperor." In another example, the common-time
melody of "Golden Gate" is recast in triple meter for the nostalgic "Yesterday
Is Yesterday." Some melodies reappear as countermelodies in the accompaniment of new songs.[5]

Morris, Kander, and Ebb never found a producer for *Golden Gate*, but
they did not stop trying for two decades. They rewrote it twice, first in 1970
and then in 1982, in the hope of getting a production. Morris's revised scripts,
one of which is titled *The Emperor of San Francisco*, eliminate the egregious
racist humor and simplify the conflict between the political factions. With
these changes, however, the musical lost some of its dramatic energy. For example, in place of the climactic debate between Murphy and Auntie, Murphy tricks Auntie into transferring her resources to Oakland, thus turning her
own scheme against her.

As *Golden Gate* lay fallow, Kander and Ebb started to pilfer some of the songs for other projects. Liza Minnelli sang "I'm One of the Smart Ones," with orchestrations by Jonathan Tunick, in her 1974 concert at the Winter Garden Theatre (see Chapter 4). "A Certain Girl," which is included on the *Golden Gate* demo recording but not in Morris's original or subsequent scripts, found its way into *The Happy Time*. The song "Dear Love" from *Flora, the Red Menace* originally belonged to *Golden Gate*. In the end, with so many songs sacrificed to other projects, a production of *Golden Gate* no longer seemed viable.[6]

Tango Mogador (c. 1971)

Tango Mogador came closer to a Broadway production than *Golden Gate* ever did. In 1971, the producing team of Cy Feuer and Ernest Martin suggested to Abe Burrows that he turn an unused screenplay by Rod Amateau (which was based on the 1867 novel *Under Two Flags* [*Coeur Vaillant se Fait Royaume*]) into a musical. They envisioned a "comic operetta" extravaganza with a cast of fifty.[7] *Under Two Flags*, by the nineteenth-century English novelist Ouida (the nom de plume of Marie Louise de la Ramée), had inspired a number of Hollywood films. Amateau's version was a spoof of the desert-movie genre based on a treatment of the novel by Harold Nebenzal, who co-produced the film version of *Cabaret* with Feuer.[8]

The action of the musical takes place in Mogador, Morocco, in 1928. The hero, François, who has dedicated his life to protecting the honor of the French Foreign Legion, arrives in Mogador to investigate the killings of a number of Legion officers. His fiancée, Clothilde, remains in France, where she spends most of her time combing her hair. Upon his arrival in Mogador François falls in love with Germaine, a French ex-patriot and the main attraction at the Café Mogador. But François has a rival, a German Legionnaire named Ulrich Metzger, who takes pleasure in reenacting a rape scene with Germaine. (In the words of John Kander, "He liked to dress her up as a nun and fuck her.") Metzger, who is actually an ex-officer in the Kaiser's army, has conspired to infiltrate the Legion and take over the territory for Germany. When discovered, he is captured and condemned to face the firing squad. In the epilogue, which jumps ahead several years, Peter Watkins, the journalist who covered the story, lies injured in a hospital bed awaiting a visit from the French president, who turns out to be none other than François. The nurse taking care of Watkins is the now reformed Germaine. These characters are humorous caricatures of a typical cast of the desert-movie genre: a sexually ambiguous military officer, an earnest war reporter, a Dudley-Do-Right-like hero, a commanding officer who—like Gilbert and Sullivan's Sir Joseph Porter—has risen in rank far beyond his level of competence, a world-weary and altruistic chanteuse, a vapid femme fatal, and a Germanic sociopath.

Burrow's script called for Kander and Ebb to engage in a high degree of silliness. No written music has been found, but there is a recording of fourteen numbers. The score is a cross between musical comedy and operetta, with a strong Gilbert and Sullivan influence. Sometimes these two styles humorously compete, as in "He Doesn't Love Me," in which Ulrich explains his perfidy, to the strains of a waltz in a minor key, as the result of not being loved as a boy. The rhythmic character of the waltz evokes the motor rhythms of Chopin's piano work nicknamed the "The Minute Waltz" (op. 64, no. 1), but midway through the song Ulrich breaks into a vaudeville two-step. Nowhere is the influence of Gilbert and Sullivan more evident than in "Military Man," a three-part chorus in the form A B A/B C A/B/C. Some of the songs are vintage Kander and Ebb, especially the cabaret numbers that Germaine performs during the interior scenes at the Café Mogador, such as the torch ballad "Sad Am I." In another scene, Germaine leads the Legionnaire patrons in "La Legion" (using the French pronunciation), a spirited march and chorus capturing the liberty-fraternity-equality sentiment of French World War I songs. Germaine also performs "Tango Mogador," a song and dance in the minor mode that builds to a bacchanalian frenzy as the music modulates continually upward, like Ravel's *Bolero*. "Morocco Marie" and "Sand" are chorus-girl numbers with the sort of double entendres that Ebb loved to write (such as "My Garter" from *The Happy Time*). "The Mass" is a musical tour de force in which the whores of Mogador, who are gathered at the café for a mass hosted by Germaine, sing gossipy chatter over a chanted Kyrie, occasionally joining in the prayer.

A press release announcing *Tango Mogador* appeared in the *New York Times* in late 1971. Ironically, the article began with a question that seems to suggest an anti–Kander and Ebb as well as anti-Sondheim sentiment: "Do you yearn for the days when musicals were mostly fun and you came out of the theater humming love songs instead of dolefully ruminating upon the inadequacies of human relationships?"[9] By mid 1972, contracts were signed and discussions about casting were held, but, for reasons still not clear, by October the production was put on hold indefinitely, and the musical sat idle for nearly a decade.[10] Then, in the mid 1980s, Peter Stone came to Kander and Ebb with an idea of doing a backstage murder-mystery musical called *Who Killed David Merrick?* Kander and Ebb thought that *Tango Mogador* would be fun to use as the show-within-a-show. *Who Killed David Merrick?* is the progenitor of the Broadway show *Curtains*, which uses an entirely different show-within-a-show (see Chapter 9).

Wait for Me, World (1972)

Shortly after *Tango Mogador* was put on hold, Dale Wasserman, the creator of *Man of La Mancha*, approached Kander and Ebb with an idea for a musical about Horatio Alger. *Wait for Me, World*, as he titled the work, is the type of story that had always appealed to Kander and Ebb; it has a showbiz milieu, presentational songs, and an inner story–outer story framework. Wasserman concocted a panoramic rags-to-riches narrative similar to the novels on which the real Alger made his fame and fortune. He framed this story within another story about a personal crisis in Horatio Alger's life. The Algeresque inner plot is about a young orphan and Irish tenor from Ohio named Phil Fallon, who has come to New York to pursue his dream. Phil has read Alger's novels and subscribes to their optimistic philosophy. When Alger first meets Phil, he is singing on street corners. Phil has business savvy, and he soon forms a theatrical troupe, recruiting a dancer named Louisa, whom he eventually marries, and a few other young performers. In the process, he makes an enemy, Rattery, the local organized-crime boss, who sends his thugs to extort "protection money" from Phil. Alger helps Phil out of this mess and urges Phineas Barnum to hire him. In pure Horatio Alger excess, there is more to this happy ending. Mrs. Mulligan, a tough-talking but sentimental proprietor of Alger's favorite watering hole, turns out to be Phil's mother; and Jiffy Kinch, an alcoholic and ex-vaudevillian whom Phil hires to teach him the tricks of the trade, is his father. The story ends with a double wedding of Phil and his father to Louisa and Mulligan, respectively.

Wasserman wove Alger's daydream sequences throughout Phil's story. In the opening scene, Alger fantasizes about a ceremony at which the greatest literary figures of his time have gathered to lionize his talents. Lavinia, Alger's muse, who represents his desire for literary greatness, appears to him here and throughout the musical, in a mirror, on the street, and as his opponent during a chess match. In the final scene, Lavinia forces Alger to choose between being a popular fiction writer and being an author of great literature. The confrontation grows heated as he challenges her, "You began in my imagination. You must end there, too." She vanishes as Alger accepts his destiny to be an inventor of the American dream rather than the author of the great American novel. His dreams are not about heroes, but about farm boys and city vagrants.

Kander and Ebb's score is a veritable catalogue of late nineteenth-century American popular songs, featuring a march, a ragtime, a sentimental ballad about a mother, a music hall dance number, and an Irish ballad in three-quarter time about orphanhood (table 8.1). Although Wasserman kept the project alive for many years, Kander and Ebb started to recycle the songs into other projects and eventually lost interest. "It's the Strangest Thing" found its way into *The Act.* "I Can't Do That Anymore" was used in *'Ol Blue Eyes Is Back* and then was interpolated into the English production of *70, Girls, 70* (see Chapter 6).

St. Teresa (1970s)

What a missed opportunity *St. Teresa* must have felt like to Kander and Ebb. A fictional story based on the life of Eva Peron, *St. Teresa* stands out not only for its prescient subject matter, but also for being the only work Kander and Ebb conceived as an opera. Ebb, who came up with the idea, put considerable effort into the dramaturgical design, writing pages of backstory, and completed a libretto. The plot centers on a love triangle involving a peasant named Teresa; Miguel, her eventual husband and their country's president; and Fernando, his second-in-command. As in the Guinevere-Arthur-Lancelot triangle, despite their mutual love for each other, these three characters end up destroying each other against the politically charged backdrop of a Latin-American revolution. Ebb was particularly interested in the theme of political and personal corruption through power. To use his own words, "our love of each other is the most important element in life; and that to put anything above that love is to destroy ourselves."

The story, set in the present in "a country to the south," calls for seven main characters and a number of supernumeraries.

Fernando	Leader of the revolution and, afterward, president
Miguel	His dearest friend and second-in-command
Teresa	His mistress; later, his wife
Ramon	His lieutenant; later, chief of security
Diego	A labor leader of national importance
Teodoro	An editor and leader of the intellectual community

Table 8.1. Songs from *Wait for Me, World*

Song	Character	Song Type
"We, the Greatest Writers in America Today"	Greatest living American writers at the time, and later Lavinia	
"Far Away from Home"	Phil	sentimental Irish ballad about being an orphan
"I Love Music"	Gottenhimmel (a pawnbroker), Phil, and Alger	march
"Wait for Me, World"	Alger and later Lavinia	
"The American Way"	Rattery, The Committee, and Alger	described but never written
"Machine"	The Mechanical Chess Marvel (a wax figure of Barnum's that comes to life)	
"It's the Strangest Thing"	Mrs. Mulligan	ballad (later used in *The Act*)
"I Can't Do That Anymore"	Jiffy Kinch	Music Hall (or vaudeville) soft shoe
"The Bowery Rag"	Phil and his troupe	ragtime
"Mother"	Louisa, joined by Plug-Uglies	sentimental ballad about a mother
"Easy Living"	The Troupe	two step about the high life ("The mode will be 'take your turn,' featuring each of The Troupe in his speciality"—a Minstrel Show song type)

Felice   Mistress to the president
Soldiers, officers, peasants, ambassadors and members of the diplomatic corps, cabinet ministers

The prologue is uncannily similar to the opening of Tim Rice and Andrew Lloyd Webber's *Evita*. A tolling bell announces the death of St. Teresa and a group of peasants enters while chanting the Litany of Saints. This funeral scene dissolves, and there is a flashback to Teresa as a peasant girl. She is dancing suggestively for some soldiers as Fernando and his men enter with a group of captured prisoners. He orders that the prisoners be executed, and Teresa along with them. She convinces him to spare her life by making seductive overtures. As a romantic relationship develops between Fernando and Teresa, Miguel worries that it will compromise their revolutionary mission. Matters are further complicated when Miguel himself falls in love with Teresa. Fernando, Teresa, and Miguel set aside their personal feelings long enough to see the revolution through to its successful conclusion. Fernando is sworn in as president. In act 2, Fernando succumbs to the corruption of power and Teresa to the corruption of wealth, and Miguel looks on in horror as the revolution falters. Teresa eventually wins over the masses, though, and they begin to call her saint. By act 3, Teresa has developed a stigmata and believes that God has chosen her to rule. Fernando, suspicious of Miguel and influenced by Teresa, orders Miguel's execution. However, he leaves Teresa when she pressures him to agitate for her canonization. From the throne Teresa hears the litany of saints and, finally, "Santa Teresa."

Ebb meticulously planned out each musical segment in advance of writing the libretto. A small sample from Ebb's notes (see below) is indication enough of his understanding of the characters' motivations and of the dramatic impact of the music. Particularly interesting is the reference to Mozart's adagio-allegro aria pair (cavatina-cabaletta) and how the double arias will function dramatically. These, the only such documents found among Ebb's papers, demonstrate how well-honed Ebb's skills as a dramatist had become. It is interesting to note that Teresa mediates the homosocial relationship between Fernando and Miguel, which occasionally tips toward the homoerotic, a situation similar to that found in *Zorbá*, which predates this project by just a couple of years.

Act 1:

Scene 1   Teresa's temptation of Fernando. While this is vigorous and
           sensual, its subtext is one of feverishness and blank desperation.
           This is an enormous display of will, effort and temperament. The
           number may well close with her physical collapse.

Scene 2   The music lies in their regret at parting when they've only just
           found each other; and in the passion of their decision not to part.
           (There is something both romantic and ironically appealing in a
           love duet that comes out of:

           . . .

At any rate, the scene ends musically with the two of them locked together on the bed.

Scene 3   The moment belongs to Fernando and Miguel; it's their revolution and Teresa is the outsider. The sense of raw joy and ass slapping that the present script has is probably right. There are two soldiers who have fought for seven years and suddenly they've brought it off. The emotional possibilities in the moment are considerable. Wonder, shock, refusal or inability to take it in, tears, whatever the decision, the number is critically important. The love that Fernando and Miguel have for each other is difficult to dramatize within the confines of the show. They can talk about each other—as they do in the preceding scene—and there is a quick chance of seeing them working together in the opening. But this is the one real chance we have to dramatize—to show in Action—what these two men mean to each other. The emotional values of the decay to their relationship, in which so much depends, will never come to life and play for us without this scene.

Scene 4   It is possible that the entire scene is composed. The oath of office and the benediction are singable enough. So, of course, is the contribution of the crowd. As before, the crowd functions to punctuate the music of the scene. However, taped noises of mobs are never effective and it seems to me imperative that crowds in this show always sing. Not only is it a convention that we set up right at the beginning, it is both an expressive opportunity and a tradition. It also seems to me that Fernando's speech to the people (in the following scene) must be sung. In that event, it seems likely that the two scenes are musically constructed like the large Mozart adagio: allegro arias. That is to say, I want to suggest that scene five is possible as a trio with Teresa having the dominant part and the chorus punctuating it into sections. Teresa needs to dominant the trip both because it is a statement of her love for Fernando and because her feelings, while not more important than the men's, are more varied. There is no close to the scene or the music. Rather, on a sustained c[h]oral sound, Fernando and Miguel walk to the balcony. Also important here is the fact that Teresa is no longer an outsider. They are three now: the duet of the scene before has become a trio.

By all indications *St. Teresa* would have been Kander and Ebb's most operatic work, with the orchestra integrated to a degree not found in their other musicals. In fact, Kander fleshed out the accompaniments more than was his usual practice at this stage of a project. Kander and Ebb completed the prologue, the first two scenes, and some sketches. The recitatives are direct and effective, a contrast to the aimless sung-through scenes in the "poperettas," as they have been called, that appeared during the eighties and nineties. The closed numbers weave motives into the orchestral parts. Kander employed modal scales and other novel musical techniques, such as metrically unmeasured sections, to create varied musical textures.

In the prologue, a chorus of peasants sings an unmetered monophonic chant in transposed Mixolydian in praise of three saints (example 8.1). Evoking the haunting open sonority of early medieval polyphony, half of the chorus harmonizes the chant melody at the fifth. The texture thickens with vocal doublings at the octave and the addition of orchestra. When the dynamic level of the chanting reaches fortissimo guitars enter, announcing the first scene with a Latin-tinged ostinato pattern in mixed meter. In an attempt to reverse Fernando's decision to have her shot, Teresa sings "I am one of you," which features an unaccompanied sensuous Lydian melody (example 8.2). A single-line countermelody in the orchestra provides a supple accompaniment. The dramatic intensity builds as the texture thickens and the music modulates to the mediant. This theme reoccurs in a later scene when Teresa addresses her public.

In scene 2 Fernando, studying Teresa as she sleeps, sings a gentle arioso unified by a recurring "Mariachi trumpet" motive in the accompaniment: parallel thirds moving by step over a syncopated figure in the bass (example 8.3).[11] After a fight between Fernando and Miguel, Teresa awakens and sings a lyrical aria about a dream in which she saw God. It features a sweeping melody with sparse accompaniment (example 8.4). Like Fernando's aria, it is through-composed and built on a recurring motive.

After hearing these initial sketches, the opera director Frank Cosaro discouraged Kander and Ebb from pursing the project any further, apparently making no allowances for the Broadway venue for which the musical was intended. Cosaro's perfunctory opinion derailed what might have been Kander and Ebb's only opera. Any interest that they might have had in completing the work came to an end when they started *70, Girls, 70*, which pushed them further toward the concept musical and vaudeville styles. From this point Kander and Ebb's musicals swung between two extremes, one oriented in

Example 8.1. *St. Teresa*, Prologue and opening of scene 1

vaudeville and Broadway musical comedy, the other in a more lyrical and operatic style. This bifurcation of their output—sometimes present in a single score—characterizes their overall output and reflects their opposing personalities and tastes.

Promising Proposals

In 1967 Hal Prince, Kander, and Ebb considered working with William Goodhart on a musical version of Keith Waterhouse's 1959 novel *Billy Liar*.[12] The main character is a Walter Mitty type who escapes into his imagination in order to avoid lectures from his family about responsibility. In his day-dreams he appears as a musician in a military band, a servant, a political

Example 8.2. *St. Teresa,* "I Am One of You"

aide, and a member of a scientific committee. Goodhart intended the musical, which he titled *Head of America*, as a serious critique of the vapidity of American culture following the exuberance of the fifties: "I would like to extend by implication, Billy's mental state to represent a general cultural phenomenon. One way of doing this is to give the entire show a certain bizarre, irrational, dissident quality, so that suspense is created because the *Head of America*, that is America itself, teeters on the edge of madness." The project fell through when it became clear to Prince, Kander, and Ebb that a collaboration with Goodhart was unlikely to succeed.

In the early seventies, Kander and Ebb were briefly involved in two unrelated television projects with animal themes. The first of these was a musical version of the fairytale *Puss in Boots*. Richard Morris, the librettist for *Golden Gate*, completed a script, which is dated 1971, but the project never got off the ground, and Kander and Ebb did not write any music. The second animal musical, *The Zoo*, had an original story by Ron Cowen and Seth Glassman. They wrote the musical as a protest of the then inhumane conditions at the Central Park Zoo. The story is about a group of animals at the zoo who liberate themselves from the urban blight, kids, noise, and pollution of New

Example 8.3. *St. Teresa*, "So Gently She Sleeps"

York City. Led by a radical pigeon named Isadora, they take Noah's Ark to
a utopia that she has read about called "Paradise Lost." The writers hoped
to cast Fred Gwynne as Vincent the Giraffe and James Coco as Buster the
Gorilla, Isadora's romantic interest. The songs include "Isadora," "The Duck"
(about ducking projectiles thrown at the animals by kids), "Paradise Island,"
"The Difference Between Us" (a duet for Isadora and Buster), and "Better
Than Massachusetts" (a vaudeville ensemble number for all of the animals).
Just as this project was getting started, Fosse obtained the rights for *Chicago*
and enlisted Kander and Ebb's services. *The Zoo* was shelved permanently.

In the early nineties, Ron Cowan and Daniel Lipman proposed a musical
based on William Maxwell's novel *So Long, See You Tomorrow*. The novel
is told from the point of view of a seventy-five-year-old man who struggles
to come to terms with a life-shaping event that occurred when he was a boy
living in Lincoln, Illinois. He had a friend named Cletus, whose father, a tenant farmer, killed his wife and her lover, and then took his own life. Decades
later, the old man seeks Cletus's forgiveness for showing little empathy during the tragedy. Cowan and Lipman invented a narrator named Willy, after

Example 8.4. *St. Teresa,* "I Dreamed of God"

William Maxwell, "to create the structure and mood of a memory piece."
A single young actor would have played the seventy-five-year-old narrator,
the narrator as a young boy, and the part of Cletus, so as to walk literally
in the shoes of his friend. Cowen and Lipman's proposal notes, "As plain,
simple Midwestern people, giving voice to their feelings is often difficult and
unfamiliar to them. It is, therefore, through song that they can release their
love, their longings and disappointments—everything that they're unable to
say." This sentiment is one that Kander shares, and the dark human story and

notion of redemption would have appealed to Ebb. Unfortunately, Maxwell did not want to see his introspective novel turned into a musical.

Around 2003 Kander and Ebb almost got to play themselves in a film called *Bye Bye Blues*, written by Charles Badaracco and Stanley Donen (the co-director of *Singing in the Rain* and director of *Lucky Lady* [see Appendix]). *Bye Bye Blues* is a movie-musical-within-a-movie-musical about the movie musical business. In the story Kander and Ebb are hired to write the music for the musical. As the film begins, Max Coleman, an aging film director, imagines the opening of the film he wants to make. It is a story about a failed architect who becomes romantically involved with a hooker and addict, "a metaphor for what happens if we give up." Max hopes to get Paul Newman to star in the film, but when his plan does not pan out, he realizes that the only way to get his film financed is literally to kill himself on screen. Kander and Ebb had a few songs ready to go, including "This Life," which they pulled from the first version of *All About Us* (see Chapter 9), but the movie was never made.

When asked if there were any musicals that he wanted to write but never got around to doing, Ebb mentioned *Smile*, the 1975 television movie satire about beauty pageants. Taking place behind the scenes of a televised pageant and exploring the effect of this sort of entertainment on the individual participants, *Smile* seemed a natural for Kander and Ebb. James Goldman agreed to write the book, but negotiations broke down and the rights went to Marvin Hamlisch and Howard Ashman, whose version of *Smile* ran briefly on Broadway in 1986. Ebb also wanted to do a musical based on *La Strada*, and he even wrote to Federico Fellini to inquire about the rights. Ebb could recite Fellini's response verbatim: "Dear Mr. Ebb, I thank you for your letter. . . . But after all, sir, having refused the rights of *La Strada* to Giancarlo Menotti, Leonard Bernstein (and he lists all these people who've asked for the rights, [including] Samuel Barber), I see no reason to grant them to you, a person whose background I know nothing about."

Like fans of Verdi's who still mourn the fact that he never finished his *King Lear*, Kander and Ebb fans have reason to regret the fact that so many of their musicals never reached fruition. That so many good ideas never saw the light of day says a lot about the diminishing opportunities for musical theater writers during the four decades of Kander and Ebb's career. Around the time they met, writers were experiencing increasing difficulty in getting a musical produced. As a result, several musicals by Kander and Ebb and other writers of their generation took years, in some case even decades, to find a

producer, and many projects were simply abandoned out of frustration. However, Kander and Ebb never allowed their frustration to sap their creative
energy. While in their seventies they wrote four new musicals, the subject of
the next chapter. So far, only one of these has appeared on Broadway, but, at
eighty-one years old, Kander continues to court potential producers. And in
all likelihood he will soon begin a new project. He always regretted not being
able to complete *The Enchanted;* who knows?

CHAPTER 9

"A Tough Act to Follow"
Curtains *and Three New Shows*

We're going to entertain you, and you're going to have fun, but at the same time, we're going to lead you to a place that's very dangerous and very controversial. What you take out of this, where you get, you're going to have to sort out yourself. But in the meantime, we're going to entertain you.
—DAVID THOMPSON

D URING THE 2005 TONY AWARDS CEREMONY, CHITA RIVERA AP-peared at the podium to pay tribute to Fred Ebb and the composer Cy Coleman, both of whom had recently passed away. "My two close friends," she announced, "Fred Ebb and John Kander." Rivera recovered elegantly from her slip of the tongue by acknowledging how unnatural it was to follow the name Fred Ebb with any name other than John Kander, who happened to be home, alive, and well and watching the awards ceremony. Ironically, Ebb had loved to joke that someday he would ask Cy Coleman to replace John Kander.

A Broadway tribute to Fred Ebb was held on November 14, 2004, at the Ambassador Theater on the set of the revival of *Chicago*. Joel Grey kicked off the event by performing "Willkommen," accompanied by Kander. Karen Ziemba, Debra Monk, Brent Barrett, Brian Stokes Mitchell, Chita Rivera, Wayne Brady, and Liza Minnelli also performed. Terrence McNally spoke openly about his deceased friend, humorously pointing out his complex, sometimes contradictory character with regard to sexuality, religion, and friendship. McNally's tribute, something of a cross between an outing, a backhanded compliment, and a genuine homage, opens a window onto the real Fred Ebb, who was, by most accounts, complicated, occasionally misanthropic, often overwhelmingly generous, and eternally devoted to his friends. He loved Liza Minnelli, Chita Rivera, Dorothy Loudon, Carol Channing, and Lauren Bacall. And he loved John Kander. And yet, as he aged, Ebb's cynicism, which had served him for many years as a lyricist, started to mute the colors of his rainbow, to paraphrase John Kander. Ebb was happiest when he was performing, but that pleasure had been diminished by a bout with throat cancer in the late nineties and because of other physical ailments. In his final days Ebb acknowledged that he was a sad man. Those close to him felt that he had begun to give up on life. But Ebb never stopped writing, and he was excited about his latest project, *Minstrel Show*.

Ebb's death stunned the theater community, but it did not deter John Kander from completing the four musicals that he and Ebb were working on at the time: *Curtains*, *All About Us*, *The Visit*, and *Minstrel Show*. Although saddened by the loss of his collaborator, Kander rebounded with the verve and resilience of a young composer eager to get his first musical on Broadway. Kander has joked that he will never get to retire, but at this point he seems to have no interest in slowing down. Since 2004 he has guided *Curtains* to Broadway, completed the score for *Minstrel Show*, and overseen workshops and stage productions of *All About Us* (*The Skin of Our Teeth*) and *The Visit*. Except for *Curtains*, these musicals deal with weighty topics and serious themes. *All About Us*, based on Thornton Wilder's *The Skin of Our Teeth*, posed some of the greatest challenges the writers ever had to face. *The Visit* is their bleakest and most operatic musical. *Minstrel Show* promises to be their most provocative work, surpassing even *Cabaret* for its inflammatory subject matter. *Curtains*, a musical comedy, celebrates the world of musical theater. Scott Ellis, the director of *Curtains*, has called it Kander and Ebb's valentine to Broadway. It had its world premiere in the summer of 2006 at the Ahmanson Theatre in Los Angeles; opened on Broadway on March 22, 2007, a few days after John Kander's eightieth birthday, and closed on June 29, 2008, after having played 511 performances and 26 previews. A national tour is scheduled to begin in the fall of 2009. *All About Us* and *The Visit* have both been produced twice at regional theaters. So far *Minstrel Show* has had two readings in New York with professional actors.

Curtains

Kander and Ebb started writing *Curtains* in the mid eighties when Peter Stone approached them with an amusing idea for a musical he called *Who Killed David Merrick?*, a combination backstage musical and murder-mystery spoof. Stone's concept played right into Kander and Ebb's expertise in the play-within-a-play framework. The plot, set in the late 1980s, satirizes the theater world, its main targets being the critic John Simon, *A Chorus Line*, Andrew Lloyd Webber, and playwrights like Edward Albee and Lanford Wilson. Stone, who was president of the Dramatist Guild from 1981 to 1999, seriously worried about the state of American theater and might have intended the musical as a lighthearted protest about the situation. *Who Killed David Merrick?* takes place in Boston during the pre-Broadway tryout of a failing musical. Kander and Ebb suggested that they use the plot and songs of the defunct *Tango Mogador* for the musical within the musical. Stone liked the idea, as *Tango Mogador* was itself a spoof of the Hollywood desert film and therefore offered some self-contained humorous scenes. He retitled the musical *Sand* and incorporated eight songs from the score.

The cast of *Who Killed David Merrick?* includes the types of stock characters seen in Hollywood backstage musicals: the flamboyant and ornery English director, the paranoid Russian musical director, the self-absorbed has-been B-movie star, the sexy actress with hopes of taking the place of the leading lady, the once idealistic playwright who has sold out, his dutiful and perceptive wife, the husband-and-wife songwriting team, the philistine business manager, the wealthy female backer, the jaded theater critic, and an array of lesser players including a gaggle of homosexual chorus boys. Stone, who had attended Bard College and the Yale School of Drama, was known for his dramaturgical acumen. It is also worth nothing that he had won an Edgar Award for his screenplay for the film *Charade*. So is not surprising that he devised backstories and motives for each character. Most of these details do not actually surface in the play, but they provided a compass for Stone as he unraveled the various strands of the plot.

Back story for the Characters in *Who Killed David Merrick?*
    Author's (to be wife) [Laura], at Yale music (plays the flute) fell for author, having gone out with both [author and critic].
    During one period (author works nights, critic goes to movies), wife-to-be had brief dalliance with critic—more like one-night stand—which she immediately regretted and which he never forgot.

After school, author's career progresses: after a verse-play, two neo-Brechtian serio-comic dramas done in Regional (one won a prize) and one Broadway play—a strong denunciation of materialism told as a game-show which was quite well-received—that didn't run; two films (one original, one adaptation of "The Mayor of Casterbridge"), a TV docu-drama on American Indians; he augments his income by teaching Amer. Lit. at a girl's college in Upstate N.Y.

Finally, author writes a new play—an anti-militarist, anti-imperialist, anti-interventionist black comedy in the form of a pastiche on desert foreign legion plays and films, and based loosely on Ouida's 1878 novel, "Under Two Flags." He calls it "Sand."

. . .

Pre-production goes swimmingly. Casting is easy, everyone agrees with the choices. Rehearsals are smooth and optimistic. In fact, everything is marvelous. Until the opening in Boston.

When *Who Killed David Merrick?* begins, the final curtain is coming down on the first Boston preview of *Sand.* In the next scene, the writers, business manager, and principal backer of the show lament the murderous reviews from the Boston critics. Not willing to abandon ship—and lose all that money—they commit to reworking the show while David Merrick raises additional money in New York in order to keep the production afloat. Soon thereafter, however, Charlene, an actress and Merrick's mistress, announces that the producer has been murdered. Lieutenant Salvatore Cioffi of the Boston police, who happens to be a devotee of the theater and an amateur actor, arrives on the set of *Sand* to investigate the homicide. Because he saw a performance of *Sand* and loved it, Cioffi insists that the show must go on as he proceeds with his investigation of the killing. He quickly becomes smitten with one of the actresses, Nikki. Their relationship develops during the course of the investigation, even though at one point he has to consider her a suspect like everyone else. Georgia and Aaron, the songwriting team, seemingly modeled on Comden and Green, compose a new song, "Where Were You?," and as they sing it Cioffi questions each suspect—meaning everyone associated with the production. Cioffi's chief suspect is Charlene, that is, until she is herself discovered dead at the end of the first act. Now with two murders on his hands, Cioffi widens his investigation. He eventually gathers the entire cast onstage and accuses Oscar, the business manager, of committing both murders, suggesting that he killed Merrick because he was going to turn him in for embezzlement and Charlene because she witnessed the first murder and was trying to blackmail him. Oscar is ceremoniously led away in handcuffs, but the arrest was actually staged by Cioffi so that the real murderer would expose him or herself. It is Darin, the Boston theater critic and ex-roommate of the playwright. There is one more surprise to come: as the final curtain is about to descend, David Merrick is heard approaching from offstage. It turns out that the entire musical was a rehearsal of a play-within-a-play-within-a-play.

Lieutenant Salvatore Cioffi gives the musical its charm and emerges as its hero, solving not only the murders but also the problems with *Sand*. Throughout his investigation, he offers the advice of a seasoned dramaturge:

> Excuse me, I know I'm not a member of the company—but I'm a member of the audience and I know what I like. And I think you've got a wonderful show here. I really do. Maybe it isn't as good yet as it can be—it's too long, I'm sure you know that—and sometimes the book and the score seem to be fighting each other—and some of the performances aren't quite there yet—but that's why you're in Boston. Sure, I know it's discouraging to get bad reviews—but did you know that a play opened in this very same theatre fifty years ago that the critics hated? It was called "Our Town." And don't forget "Oklahoma" and "Hello Dolly" and "Fiddler on the Roof"—they all got bad reviews out of town but *they* didn't give up. I bet anything that "Sand" will be a big hit, too. All you have to do is work hard and believe in it as much as I do.

Cioffi sometimes has trouble differentiating between his investigation and musical theater. When he reviews his notes after questioning all of the suspects, he mentally conjures up "The Line-Up" to the vamp for "One" from the musical *A Chorus Line*, zeroing in on twelve suspects, each of whom he presses for answers while adopting the tone and manner of Zack from *A Chorus Line*. Each suspect sings his or her alibi, often with direct references to *A Chorus Line* (see below). Cioffi follows with a soliloquy that paraphrases Bock and Harnick's "Tradition," substituting the word "suspicion." His recitative grows into a full-fledged dramatic aria, "Blood on Her/His Hands" ("Somewhere in the Midst of this Mystery"). The very end of the song paraphrases the final line of Billy Bigalow's "Soliloquy" from *Carousel* (in a reprise of "The Line-Up," Cioffi quotes "Puzzlement" from *The King and I*). "The Line-Up" exemplifies the farcical nature of the score and underscores Kander and Ebb's deliberate intention to parody operetta and musical theater, especially for the fantasies occurring in the lieutenant's imagination.

Alibis in "The Line-Up":

Belling (director)	"He fired me"
Carmen	"I gave him two million"
Charlene	"He loved me"
Oscar	"Motive ten, alibi three"
Harry	"I got a part on 'All My Children'"
Jessica and Liselotte	"We share a love that dares not speak its . . . name" (a tango)

By October 1986, Stone had completed a draft of the script. He had also renamed the musical *Curtains*, preferring the pun to the insider's joke of the original title, and changed the name of the never-seen producer to David Mishkin (in 2002 he changed the name again, to Sidney Bernstein). He included a lot of topical humor, even targeting abortion. At this stage in the process, Stone, a dramatist first and librettist second, was thinking more dramaturgically than musically. It is thus not surprising to find several long stretches of dialogue without music, some of it overly burdened with expository detail. (Stone's script for the 1969 musical *1776* has the distinction of containing the longest scene in a musical without music.) He indicated seven book songs, and six songs for *Sand*.[1]

Score According to Peter Stone's First Complete Draft of *Who Killed David Merrick?* (*Curtains*) (book song titles in bold)

Act 1:

Scene 1	"We Are Responsible" (from Tango Mogador)
Scene 2	**"What Kind of Man"**
	"Collaboration" (for songwriters)
Scene 3	"La Legion" (from *Tango Mogador*)
	"The Man Is Dead"
	"The Show Must Go On"
	"Where Were You" (first of two versions written)
Scene 4	**"A Line-Up"**
Scene 5	"Thinking of Her" (from *Tango Mogador*) (sung by Grosvenor)
	"Thinking of Him" (sung by Laura)
	"Thinking of Her" and **"Thinking of Him"** together
Scene 6	"Sand"

Act 2:

"Thinking of Her," one of the songs taken from *Tango Mogador*, deserves special attention, as Kander and Ebb transformed it into a duet by
adding a countermelody and additional lyrics. In *Tango Mogador*, François sings "Thinking of Her" (let us call it "Thinking 1") while his thoughts
roam between his respectable fiancée in France and the forbidden woman
with whom he has just had a tryst in Mogador. The new version of the song
("Thinking 2") bridges the outer and inner stories of *Curtains*. While the
François character in *Sand* (renamed Grosvenor) sings the original melody
and lyrics ("Thinking 1"), Laura, the unappreciated wife of the playwright
of *Sand*, sings the newly composed portion of the song ("Thinking 2"). The
two parts of the song have starkly contrasting styles, corresponding to, respectively, the operetta-like hero of *Sand* and the vulnerable playwright's wife (example 9.1). "Thinking 1," a ballad in the musical *Sand*, has a lilting, diatonic
melody, not unusual for a fifties musical theater ballad; the counter piece,
"Thinking 2," which is a book song, develops a terse one-measure motive and
features the type of dissonant, brittle lyricism of some of Kander and Ebb's
best ballads. Pauses in the melodic line and a flood of triplets perfectly match
the introspective lyrics.

Mike Nichols was slated to direct *Curtains* in 1987, but for reasons unknown the production fell through, and the musical sat idle for nearly fifteen
years. The *New York Times* announced productions in 1991 and 1998, the
latter to be directed by Tommy Tune, but neither one panned out.[2] Then,
in 2002, Scott Ellis took an interest in the project and directed a semistaged
reading. Stone decided to replace *Sand* with a newly invented Pirandellian
musical called *Harlequinade*, which is previewing in Detroit. As *Curtains* begins, a scene from *Harlequinade*, which is itself a play-within-a-play, is under
way: Arlecchino introduces a company of commedia dell'arte players. Suddenly, a Nazi lieutenant interrupts the performance and accuses the actors
of being spies and members of the Free French Resistance (Ernst Lubitsch's

(a)

As we speak I'm think-ing of her. Look-ing at you, but

think-ing of her.

(b)

Think-ing of him.⎯⎯⎯ Think-ing of him.⎯⎯⎯ Some-times it seems I

spend ev' - ry mo - ment of Think - ing of him. Think - ing of him.

Example 9.1. *Curtains* (*Who Killed David Merrick?*), (a) "Thinking of Her" ("Thinking 1"), (b) "Thinking of Him" ("Thinking 2")

1942 film *To Be or Not to Be,* with a screenplay by Edwin Justus Mayer, begins with a similar comical twist). The actor playing Pierrot seizes the lieutenant's gun and shoots Columbina.

Stone also tinkered with the main story. For instance, he gave more weight to Cioffi's dramaturgical interventions. At the beginning of his investigation, Cioffi takes time out to proffer an unsolicited critique of *Harlequinade*: "Excuse me—I know I'm not a member of your production, but I'm a member of the audience and I have to tell you you've got a wonderful show here. . . . I found the theme, which demonstrates the thin line between reality and the illusion of reality to be both profound and original. Which is why I particularly admired your brilliant ending, Mr. Cates, when both the actors and the audience don't know if it's supposed to be part of the play or not." And he has an opinion about the music, too: "And the show has a beautiful musical score. What a fantastic idea to put most of the songs in that same, two-four tempo which accentuates what Broadway does best. Especially that lovely song in the second act, 'Thinking of Him.' You people don't know how lucky you are! Because putting on a Broadway musical has to be one of the most fabulous things a person can ever do!" The advice works, and the detective becomes a true musical theater hero, saving the show, solving the murders, and getting the girl.

At one point, Stone playfully extended the Pirandellian theme of *Harlequinade* to the main story by revealing in the final scene that *Curtains*, the musical we are watching, is itself a play-within-a-play-within-a-play. The musical *Harlequinade*, which is previewing in Detroit, is about a musical previewing in Philadelphia about a musical previewing in Boston. The last note in Stone's script suggests that this surreal illusion could continue ad infinitum like a hall of mirrors: "During curtain call: the 'bare brick back wall' suddenly rises (it's yet another curtain) and, behind it, a new bare brick back wall is revealed. This one is real. Or is it?" Aware that he was taking the joke too far, for the actual reading Stone eliminated the Detroit frame.

With *Sand* out and *Harlequinade* in, Kander and Ebb had to write several new songs to replace the *Tango Mogador* numbers. They also reworked some of the book songs and wrote a few new ones. The revised score contains sixteen numbers, three new songs for *Harlequinade* and ten book songs (not including reprises):

Musical Numbers for the 2002 Version of *Curtains* (book song titles in bold; songs written for *Harlequinade* in roman type)[3]
Act 1:

       "Come One, Come All" (new) (Arlecchino)
       "Curtains" (new) (Columbina)
       "All Because of You" (new) (Pierrot)
       "What Kind of Man" (Stan, Georgia, Aaron, Carmen, and Oscar)
       "Where Were You?" (Georgia and Aaron)[4]
       "Out of Town" (new) (Actors)
       "The Man Is Dead" (Company)
       "Special People" (Carmen, Oscar, and Cioffi)
       "A Line-Up" (Cioffi, Charlene, Oscar, Harry, Jessica, and
          Liselotte)
       "Where Were You?" (reprise) (Nikki)
       "Say Hello" (new) (Jessica)
       "Where Were You?" (reprise) (Nikki)
       "Thinking of Him [Her]" ("**Thinking 1**" and "**Thinking 2**")
          (Laura and Jessica)[5]
       "Come One, Come All" (reprise) (Arlecchino)

Act 2:

"A Line-Up: Part Two" (Cioffi)
"He Did It" (Company)
"It's a Business" (new) (Carmen and Company)
"Thinking of Him" (reprise) ("Thinking 2") (Laura and Stan)
"He Did It" (reprise) (Company)
"Tough Act to Follow" (new) (Cioffi, Nikki, and Chorus)
"Come One, Come All" (reprise) (Cioffi and Company)
"Curtains" (reprise) (Cioffi)
"All Because of Me" (reprise) (Darin)
"Out of Town" (reprise) (Company)
"Curtains" (reprise) (Company)

The only remaining song from *Tango Mogador* that remains is "Thinking of Her" (retitled "Thinking of Him") ("Thinking 1"), which Nikki (the ingenue) sings as the playwright's wife sings the new countermelody ("Thinking 2") written for *Who Killed David Merrick?* But the director of *Harlequinade* detests "Thinking of Him" and demands a new song from Aaron and Georgia, something more like Andrew Lloyd Webber. The joke here is based on the fact that Lloyd Webber is himself often accused of being derivative, especially of Puccini. Sarcastically, Aaron plays a strain from "Che gelida manina" from *La Bohème*. The boorish director thinks that he has struck gold, and the opportunistic producer, Carmen, exclaims, "Ten people will know. Ten *million* will get goose bumps." Stone takes the joke one step further: after Aaron and Georgia sing their "new" song (a Puccini melody by any other name) for the cast, Harry blurts out, "It sounds just like something from 'Phantom.'" Later, Aaron exclaims, "I'm sorry, Christopher, but I can't go through with it. I refuse to steal from Puccini!" Georgia gets in her two cents: "From Sigmund Romberg maybe, but not Puccini!"[6]

The 2002 reading of *Curtains* spurred further interest in the show, but Stone died in 2003 just as rewrites got under way. Scott Ellis suggested Rupert Holmes, a specialist in mystery and detective fiction, as a good candidate to take over as book writer.[7] Ebb remained cautiously optimistic about Holmes's ability as a dramatist until one day in his kitchen, where the writer improvised a scene with such aplomb that Ebb gave him a big hug and welcomed him to the "family." Holmes adhered to the basic premise of the musical but wrote a completely new script. He relocated the story to 1959, the symbolic end of the

Rodgers and Hammerstein era, and aimed for a more "good-hearted" tone, to quote Holmes. He streamlined the plot, eliminated some of the charac- ters and consolidated others, reconceived the motives of the murder suspects, and reconfigured the murders. By conflating the book writer and composer, and the book writer's wife and lyricist, he reduced four key characters to two: a composer, Aaron, and his ex-wife and lyricist, Georgia. Aaron and Georgia have both agreed to work together on the musical in the hope of rekindling their love, not unlike the leading characters in *Kiss Me, Kate.*

The producer Sidney Bernstein is no longer the first to be killed. Holmes gave that honor to Jessica Cranshaw, a hell-on-wheels diva whom nobody likes or respects. She is poisoned by hydrocyanic acid shot into her throat as she accepts roses during the curtain call. Sidney Bernstein is killed off at the end of the first act. In a hilarious sight gag, his body is discovered hanging from the drops as the curtain descends during a rehearsal. Holmes also kills off the stage manager. In addition to a third murder, he added a second mur- derer. Holmes also further developed Cioffi's romance with Niki (along with changing the spelling of her name).[8] Niki is a local Boston actress, hired by the producers as a public-relations stunt, and the only one in the cast to re- ceive favorable notices from the *Boston Globe.*[9] Holmes also changed Cioffi's first name to Frank because, in his mind, the lieutenant "was simply not a Sal- vatore or a Sal. He was barely a Cioffi. There was nothing in any way Italian or ethnic about him. I had no problem retaining the Cioffi name, as it sounded more like a friendly cup of coffee at a Chock full o'Nuts lunch counter than something Sicilian. But I drew the line at Salvatore. Our Lieutenant might have been a Doug, a Ray, a Dave, a Brian, but simply not a Salvatore."

For the inner musical, Holmes initially went back to *Tango Mogador* (*Sand*), renaming it *Song of the Legion.* In short time, however, he decided that, given the current political climate, the colonialist backdrop ran the risk of being unintentionally offensive, as he stated in a memo to Scott Ellis and John Kander: "I've tried a different inner musical, keying out of our last meeting, and I personally find it to be sunnier and cleaner . . . an American Western retelling of the basic premise of 'Robin Hood.' I like the clear con- trast between the stage-bound show biz people and the Wild West charac- ters. I also enjoy the idea that Jessica Cranshaw's role is somewhat parallel to the Marlene Dietrich role in 'Destry Rides Again.'"

The country and western musical comedy, which he cleverly titled *Robbin' Hood*, is appropriate for the 1959 setting for *Curtains.* As the curtain rises, the final scene of *Robbin' Hood* is under way, and the cast is belting out the finale, a rousing paean to the Kansas way of life. The number ends with a tongue-in-cheek allusion to "Oklahoma!": K-A-N-S-A-S U-S-A.

Score for the World Premiere of Curtains (book song titles in boldface; * = song was originally written for *Who Killed David Merrick?*; ** = song was written for the 2002 reading; *** = new song; **** = song has *terminus ante quem* of 1968[10]

Act 1:

> "Wide Open Spaces"*** (Jessica, Niki, Bobby, Bambi, and Ensemble)
> **"What Kind of Man?"*** (Carmen, Oscar, Aaron, and Georgia)
> "Thinking of Him"* ("Thinking 2") (Georgia, Aaron, and Bobby)
> **"The Woman's Dead"*** (Entire Company)
> **"Show People"**** (earlier titled "Special People") (Carmen, Cioffi, and Company)
> **"Coffee Shop Nights"*** (Cioffi)
> "In the Same Boat 1"**** (Georgia, Niki, and Bambi)
> **"I Miss the Music"*** (Aaron)
> "Thataway!"*** (Georgia and Ensemble)

Act 2:

> **"The Man Is Dead"** (reprise of "The Woman's Dead") (Sasha)
> **"He Did It"**** (listed in Stone's 1986 outline) (Company)
> **"Kansasland"*** (Niki, Randy, Harv, Bambi, and Ensemble)
> **"It's a Business"*** (Carmen and Stagehands)
> "In the Same Boat 2"**** (Bobby, Randy, and Harv)
> **"Thinking of Him"**—Reprise* ("Thinking 2") (Aaron and Georgia)
> **"A Tough Act to Follow"*** (Cioffi, Niki, and Ensemble)
> "In the Same Boat 3"**** (Company)
> "In the Same Boat 1, 2, and 3"**** (Company)
> "A Tough Act to Follow"—Reprise* (Company)

Between 1986, when Stone first suggested the idea for the musical, and the Broadway premiere in 2006, the score had several different lives, and the final score retains at least something from every incarnation: a few new numbers (some with lyrics by Kander and some by Kander and Holmes), songs from the 2002 version, songs from *Who Killed David Merrick?*, and one of Kander and Ebb's trunk songs, "In the Same Boat," which dates back to the sixties. Ironically, not a single song from *Tango Mogador* is used, although "Thinking of Him" ("Thinking 2") remains, detached from "Thinking of Her" ("Thinking 1"). It functions simultaneously as a ballad from *Robbin' Hood* and a book song: As Georgia sings the song during a rehearsal after taking over for the deceased Jessica, Aaron (Georgia's ex-husband) and Bobby (who pretends to be her new lover in order to make Aaron jealous) express their feelings about her while singing a counter melody. In act 2, Georgia and Aaron reprise the song during their reconciliation.

Evolution of "Thinking of Her"/"Thinking of Him"

Tango Mogador	*Who Killed David Merrick?* (c. '86)	*Curtains* (2002)	*Curtains* (2005–07)
"Thinking of Her"	"Thinking of Her/Him"	"Thinking of Her/Him"	"Thinking of Him"
("Thinking 1")	("Thinking 1" and "Thinking 2")	("Thinking 1" and "Thinking 2")	("Thinking 2")

"In the Same Boat" is a three-part song that Kander and Ebb originally wrote in the sixties for a Ford Motor Company trade show (see Appendix) and interpolated into Carroll O'Connor's television special in 1973 (see Chapter 4). After reading Holmes's script, Kander observed that "In the Same Boat" could perform double duty as an eleven o'clock number for both *Curtains* and *Robbin' Hood*. Holmes ingeniously wove it into the story, introducing one part at a time and not allowing the three parts to be heard together until late in act 2. It is a number that Aaron struggles to make work throughout the show, and he composes three versions based on the same harmonic progression, not one of which delivers the punch that the director demands. When all hope is lost, Cioffi cries out, "I've solved it"—not the murder, but the song. He suggests that the cast divide up and sing all three parts together (à la "When the Foeman Bares His Steel" from *The Pirates of Penzance* and "The Tea Party" from Jerry Herman's *Dear World*). As they do so, Cioffi rushes frantically between the three groups, singing and dancing all of the parts. Everyone loves the results, and Cioffi receives the credit.

Curtains premiered in 2006 in Los Angeles. It starred David Hyde Pierce as Lieutenant Cioffi, Debra Monk as Carmen, Karen Ziemba as Georgia, Jason Danieley as Aaron, and Edward Hibbert as the English director. The entire six-week run was sold out, and audiences were consistently enthusiastic. William David Brohn supplied the orchestrations. His fifteen-piece orchestra, which sacrificed strings in order to have full brass and woodwind sections, evoked the sound of fifties musical comedy. Anna Louizos's sets effectively differentiated between *Robbin' Hood* scenes and backstage book scenes. The "In the Same Boat" trio incorporated a steamboat, which appeared in a puff of steam, perhaps as a reference to *Show Boat*. William Ivy Long's costumes captured the explosion of color of golden age musical comedy. Reviews were generally favorable, although everyone seemed to have some bone to pick. Some critics complained about the thinness of the show-within, wanting something of greater substance, but Holmes felt that *Robbin' Hood* need not relate to the outer story (as does *Taming of the Shrew* in *Kiss Me, Kate*), which, as a murder mystery, is already one of the most complicated plots in the musical theater repertory.

All of the leading actors from the Los Angeles premiere repeated their roles for the Broadway run. The production remained pretty much as it had been, with one notable exception. Kander expanded Aaron's ballad "I Miss the Music," adding a middle section that is a thinly veiled message to Fred Ebb. The new section includes the self-referential lyric, "She says something / You say something / She writes a line / You play a vamp," to which the pit piano responds with a vamp that only Kander could have written. Aaron and Georgia sing a reprise of the song in act 2 during their reconciliation. Ben Brantley of the *New York Times* appreciated the "hushed poignancy" of "I Miss the Music," but he felt lukewarm about the rest of the show, calling it "thrill-starved."[11] Brantley complained that the musical lacked a sharp satirical edge, which he assumed was caused by the change in book writers. John Lahr of the *New Yorker* countered Brantley's dismissive review: "'Curtains' is ingeniously put together and smart about show business."[12] Karen Ziemba, Debra Monk, and David Hyde Pierce received Tony nominations, as did Kander and Ebb for best score and Rupert Holmes and Peter Stone for best book. Pierce won the Tony for best actor in a musical, but the Tony for best musical went to *Spring Awakening*, as did the majority of other awards for which it was nominated. During the live telecast of the Tony Award ceremonies, Kander appeared onstage to a hearty standing ovation and introduced a number from *Curtains*, "Show People," which the entire cast performed. *Curtains*, it should be noted, did win the Drama Desk Awards for outstanding book of a musical, beating out *Spring Awakening*.

All About Us

In 1997, still smarting from the poor reception of *Steel Pier*, Kander and Ebb took on the challenge of turning Thornton Wilder's quixotic play *The Skin of Our Teeth* into a musical, a feat that others had tried and failed to accomplish, including Leonard Bernstein and Comden and Green. This project sprang from Kander and Ebb's desire to work again with Joseph Stein, the librettist for *Zorbá*. The metaphysical playfulness of Wilder's play, its blend of cynicism and optimism, and its self-referential theatricality make it a perfect vehicle for Kander and Ebb, whose earlier musicals incorporate some of the same devices found in the play, such as the play-within-a-play framework and Brechtian stagecraft. It is thus surprising that at first Ebb was uncomfortable with the device of moving in and out of reality, but Kander and Stein were enthusiastic and convinced Ebb to join them. (Ebb felt equally reticent about *The Enchanted* and *Steel Pier*.)

Thornton Wilder wrote *The Skin of Our Teeth* during World War II to illustrate the cyclical nature of the human condition. The story centers on the Antrobuses, an archetypal American family. George Antrobus, the family patriarch, is an inventor of things such as the alphabet and the wheel; his wife, Maggie, is supportive of her husband and intervenes when their children get into trouble; their daughter, Gladys, is a sweet but manipulative girl; and their son, Henry, turns out to be an enemy of the state. Sabina, their housekeeper, breaks through the fourth wall to editorialize the play. She also threatens the Antrobuses' marriage when she tries to seduce George at Atlantic City after she wins a beauty contest. The play is in three acts, which take place in, respectively, Excelsior, New Jersey, during the coming of a new Ice Age; Atlantic City after the ice has retreated but as a devastating rain is portended; and back in Excelsior immediately after a calamitous war in which Henry and George fought on opposing sides.

Wilder's plays do not translate easily into a musical idiom, with the exception of *The Matchmaker*, the playwright's most traditional comedy. The playwright himself had a strong sense of which plays might and might not work as a musical, and he instructed the executors of his will on the matter. He even refused Aaron Copland and Leonard Bernstein the rights to *Our Town*,[13] although his estate recently permitted both a musical and an opera based on *Our Town*.[14] In 2003, Wilder's nephew, Tappan Wilder, wrote, "like a mountain that refuses to be conquered, the play [*The Skin of Our Teeth*] has so far resisted all attempts to be adapted as a major film, opera, or musical."[15] He let Kander, Ebb, and Stein's musical go forward, but not without personally intervening, such as forbidding the appearance of Jesus at the end of act 1.

How can music be integrated into such a topsy-turvy story? Whereas *The*

Matchmaker has a tightly bound narrative and *Our Town* well-defined characters, *The Skin of Our Teeth* has a cyclical structure and archetypal characters. The wrong music could easily undercut the play's edgy tone and singular point of view. Wilder, after seeing a performance of his play, warned against a uniformity of pacing, which "prevents both the serious aspect of the play [from] emerging . . . and prevents a real sense of excitement in the possibility of danger before the oncoming ice."[16] Kander, Ebb, and Stein remained mindful of the pacing issue and understood that they ran the risk of ending up creating a musical revue rather than a cohesive musical theater work.

Kander and Ebb wrote an eclectic score, which includes a spiritual, hymn, tango, march, lullaby, opera, and a number of songs in the musical theater idiom. They resuscitated several songs cut from earlier shows and wrote some concerted scenes in which the chorus responds in the style of Gilbert and Sullivan's chain finales. Although such a mélange might suggest a lack of unity or intentionality, the music's eclecticism is in fact the score's strength, serving as a unifying agent, controlling the pace, and determining the tone. Compared to the grandiloquence that a score by Leonard Bernstein would no doubt have had, Kander and Ebb's is frothy and unforced, but it aims to elevate the subject matter.

Current Score (2007)[17]

Part 1:

"Eat the Ice Cream" (Sabina)
"Sabina" (Mrs. Antrobus and Sabina)
"A Telegram" (originally titled "A Hologram") (Telegram boy)
"We're Home" (Gladys and Henry)
"The Wheel" (George)
"Warm" (Mammoths)
"Whole Lot of Lovin'!" (Socrates, Plato, Moses, and Homer)
"When Poppa Comes Home" (Gladys)
"Save the Human Race" (similar to the act 1 finale in the Signature Theatre version) (Company)
"A Discussion" (Wisemen)

Part 2:

"Rain" (Esmeralda)
"Beauty Pageant" (Company)
"World Peace" (Sabina)

"He Always Comes Home to Me" (Mrs. Antrobus)
"You Owe It to Yourself" (Sabina)
"Nice People" (Henry)
"The Promise" (Mrs. Antrobus)
"The Promise" reprise (Mr. Antrobus)
"Rain" reprise (Esmeralda)
"Military Man" (Company)

Part 3:

"Lullaby" (Gladys, Maggie, and Sabina)
"Another Telegram" (Telegram boy)
"Nice People" reprise (Henry)
"The Skin of Our Teeth" (George)
"At the Rialto" (Sabina)

One of the recycled songs, "Military Man," started out in *Tango Mogador*, appeared in the first Kander and Ebb revue—*2 by 5* (see Appendix)—was interpolated into the first version of *Kiss of the Spider Woman*, and was planned for *Curtains* before ending up in *All About Us*. "Military Man" exemplifies the strongest elements of the score: surprise, humor, and cagey political commentary. Connecting the second and third parts of the musical, which are performed without an intermission, "Military Man" is a tour de force trio satirizing the irrational repetitiveness of war and military service. It works so well as an introduction to the segment of the play that depicts the aftermath of a devastating war that it is hard to imagine it in the context of any other musical. The first part of the song is a march celebrating meaningless military ceremony and spectacle, the second part a comic patter in the style of "I Am the Very Model of a Modern Major-General" from *The Pirates of Penzance*, and the third a jubilant cheer for war. The number becomes increasingly absurd as the melodies are combined and the singing soldiers drop dead one by one.

Part 1	Part 2	Part 3
Don't you just love a parade	Plus which you never have to worry some-	Three cheers for conflict my boys.
The epaulette and the braid	one else is thinking for you	Three cheers for war. War! War! War!
The reverential salute	And it's very nice to	Hats off for waging a
The sound of clicking	give your brain a rest	battle

your boot. | In case you ever have a | And giving the enemy
problem you can | what for.
hurry to the chaplain
And immediately get it
off your chest.

"Skin of Our Teeth" is an optimistic anthem in the tradition of grand finales like "Walk On" from *Carousel* and "Make Our Garden Grow" from *Candide*. The only such song in Kander and Ebb's entire output, it is the single galvanizing event among the musical's madcap action and campy pastiche score. It represents George's personal apotheosis, but it also symbolizes the universal message of Wilder's play. Stylistically speaking, "Skin of Our Teeth" is not bound to the rest of the score. A short recitative introduction gives way to the main theme, which grows out of a three-note motive (G–A–B-flat) first heard over a subdominant harmony (example 9.2). The long opening phrase postpones the arrival on the tonic until measure 7. The melody flows with an uncharacteristic rhythmic freedom, following the natural stresses and accents of the words. The first half of this melody (measures 1–4) emphasizes the upper portion of the tonic scale and avoids a cadence, thereby sustaining tension throughout the phrase. In the next measure, the melody begins a long, arduous descent toward the tonic. The cadence on the tonic in measure 7 is answered by an orchestral fanfare. This fanfare, a retrograde version of the motive transposed up a fifth and occurring over a tonic pedal in the bass, contains a raised 4th scale degree heard as part of a II chord. There is ample evidence in Kander's music, spanning back to his student compositions, to conclude that for the composer the raised 4th had emotive power. *A Letter from Sullivan Ballou* is just one of many examples in which he uses a raised 4th in conjunction with an emotional sentiment (see Chapter 4). In "Skin of Our Teeth," along with the expansive lyrical theme, speechlike rhythms, and majestic fanfare, the raised 4th conveys hope, a rare sentiment for Kander and Ebb.

In 1998, Eric Schaeffer directed the first production of the musical at the Signature Theatre in Arlington, Virginia. Since Wilder's estate disallowed the use of the original title, the musical was called *Over and Over*. Later, the estate briefly permitted the use of the original title but then rescinded its permission, resulting in the current title, *All About Us*. The Washington, D.C., critic Lloyd Rose accused the writers of approaching "the problem of telling

Example 9.2. *All About Us*, "The Skin of Our Teeth" (chorus, first 8 measures)

this odd, awkward story by figuring out how many songs could be gotten out of it," and he complained that "the numbers aren't set up by the book." It probably did not help matters that Dorothy Loudon, who was featured in several small roles, detracted from the narrative, either hamming it up or forgetting her lines.[18] What the Signature Theatre production illustrated was the unforgiving nature of *The Skin of Our Teeth*, let alone a musical version.

The writers rectified many of the problems when they presented workshop readings in New York in 2004 and at the McCarter Theatre in Princeton, New Jersey, in 2005. The director of these workshops, Gabriel Barre, used an interracial cast for the Antrobus family in order to reflect the play's universality focus on humankind: an African American for George, a white actress for Maggie, an Asian American for Gladys, and a Latino for Henry. He used the same concept for a 2007 production at the Westport Country Playhouse, but a white actor played George and an African American played Maggie.[19]

Sylviane Gold, who reviewed this production for the *New York Times*, had more to say about Eartha Kitt, who played the Fortune Teller, than about anything else. However, she did underscore the intrinsic danger of musicalizing Wilder's play, noting that "parables create a distance that undercuts the emotional intimacy that grounds a musical."[20] In her final analysis, Gold claimed that the musical "never achieves the critical mass that transforms a collection of discrete numbers into an all-embracing universe," but her judgment may have been skewed by her bias against the play, which she calls "a bubbly mash of anachronism, absurdity and high purpose." In fact, the writers did come close to achieving the necessary unity of purpose among the constituent parts, as the critic herself ultimately acknowledges. Ebb, perhaps because of his negative frame of mind toward the end of his life, lost confidence in the musical. He quipped, "We're beating a dead horse. I don't think it's going to get up and walk." Time will ultimately tell whether the lack of stylistic unity and musical continuity are the musical's key strengths or its intractable weaknesses. The future of *All About Us* is uncertain because Wilder's estate remains reluctant about the viability of a musical version of *The Skin of Our Teeth*.

The Visit

The genesis of Kander and Ebb's next work starts with Barry Brown, who had wanted to produce a musical version of Friedrich Dürrenmatt's 1956 dark play *The Visit* (*Der Besuch der alten Dame*) ever since he first saw it. When he obtained the musical rights to the play, he went directly to Kander and Ebb.[21] Kander liked the idea immediately, for he felt that the play's heightened style lent itself to musical treatment.[22] He had seen the American premiere of *The Visit*, directed by Peter Brooks and starring Alfred Lunt and Lynn Fontanne, as well as Harold Prince's 1973 production at the New Phoenix Repertory Company, starring Rachel Roberts and John McMartin. McMartin was subsequently cast in the leading male role for the world premiere of Kander and Ebb's musical.[23]

The Visit is about Claire Zachanassian's brief return to Güllen, the town of her youth, where, at the age of sixteen, she fell in love with Anton Schill and became pregnant. Anton lied under oath that the child was not his and bribed other citizens of the town to discredit her reputation. Claire fled the town, lost the baby, and became a prostitute. She married a string of wealthy husbands and eventually became the richest woman in the world. She has methodically and secretly purchased Güllen's sources of income, forcing the town to the brink of financial ruin. As the play begins, the citizens of Güllen anxiously await Claire's visit, hoping that she will save the town. Their prayers will be answered, announces Claire upon her arrival, but only on the condition that the citizens give her justice by executing Anton. They react with indignation, but their collective outrage soon turns to justification and eventually to action. Claire takes Anton's dead body with her to Venice for a burial.

Dürrenmatt's "tragic comedy," as he himself called his play, premiered in Zurich in 1956, when Europe had barely begun to come to terms with the horrors of fascism, Nazism, and World War II. It addresses issues of guilt, retribution, justice, greed, love, redemption, mob rule, the corruptibility of wealth, and the illusion of morality as a socializing force. The play is at once satirical, romantic, tragic, and nihilistic. The inevitability of its conclusion has led some critics to see the play as a modern Greek tragedy, with the economic necessity facing the town being an analogue for fate. The moral dimensions of the play are inherent in the motivations and actions of the characters, who rationalize their immoral behavior in ways typical of humankind throughout history: they displace their own guilt onto Anton, they blame the victim, they distort the consequences, they inflate their sense of self-righteousness, and they suggest that the ends justify the means.[24] Ironically, because they never exhibit essential human goodness, the vengeful Claire comes off as the most sympathetic character in the play.

Terrence McNally, the librettist for *The Visit*, altered only a few minor details of Dürrenmatt's play. He changed the name of the male lead from Alfred Ill to Anton Shell and the name of the town from Güllen ("excrement," or "shit," in Swiss dialect) to Brachen (which refers to fallow land). The 1964 black-and-white film version of *The Visit*, directed by Bernhard Wicki, deviates far more radically from the play; in particular, Claire, renamed Karla and brilliantly and frighteningly rendered by Ingrid Bergman, decides on a crueler fate than death for Anton, who is played by Anthony Quinn. Once the citizens of the town decide to kill Anton, she commutes his sentence to life in the town, thereby forcing him to live among the neighbors who would have willingly executed him for material comfort. In contrast to Karla's (Claire's) absolutism in the film, McNally complicates Claire's conflicted emotions of revenge and love by dramatizing the feelings that Claire and Anton once felt for each other and suggesting that some of their love has survived the years. This decision opens up the story to musical possibilities and increases the fantasy elements of Dürrenmatt's text.

Kander sees a thematic parallel between Dürrenmatt's bleak post—World War II horror story and Franz Lehár's fin de siècle operetta *The Merry Widow* (*Die Lustige Witwe*), and he believes that Dürrenmatt had the famous operetta in mind when he wrote the play. *The Merry Widow* is about a fictitious Eastern European country, Pontevedro, which is on the verge of economic collapse. The Pontevedrian ambassador to France fears that one of its wealthiest citizens, Hanna Glawari, will marry a Parisian and keep her money in France. He charges his fellow countryman Count Danilo Danilowitch with keeping Hanna from marrying a foreigner. Danilo and Hanna had a romantic affair when she was a poor peasant girl, but his uncle refused to let him marry beneath his station. Like Dürrenmatt's anti-heroine, Hanna became rich when her husband died.

With this parallel in mind, Kander imagined the most "decadent European operetta style," something "Lehárish." He invoked the arch manner of Viennese operetta as a symbol of the hypocrisies hidden beneath the social airs of European society both before and after the war. He and Ebb also incorporated musical comedy tropes (table 9.1). The starkly contrasting styles effectively articulate the play's inherent tragic-comic dichotomy. The relative banality of the musical comedy numbers negates the romantic sweep of the serious numbers. The contrast is unusual and surprisingly effective.

Claire and Anton dominate the score. "You, You, You" floats through the story (example 9.3) as a musical emblem of their youthful romance. It is a nostalgic piece in the style of a Viennese waltz, first heard instrumentally in the prelude (in the first production). The song proper is sung by Anton's younger self in a later scene as the older Anton and Claire walk in the woods and recall their romance. The principal motive consists of three dotted half notes on the same pitch occurring over changing harmonies. An E-flat appoggiatura in the fourth measure triggers a move toward the minor key. The music teeters delicately between the major and minor modes.

In the prelude, the theme of "You, You, You" appears in the top voice of a series of dissonant chords suggestive of a death knell (example 9.4). The first

Table 9.1. Score for *The Visit**

	Musical Style	Character
Act 1		
Prelude	operetta	Instrumental
Prologue	operetta	Chorus
"Out of the Darkness"	operetta	Townspeople
"At Last"	musical comedy	Claire
"A Happy Ending"		Townspeople
"You! You! You!"	operetta	Younger and older Claire and Anton
"I Know Claire"		Anton
"You Know Me"	musical comedy	Mathilda and Annie
"Look at Me" (You! You! You!)	musical comedy	Anton, Claire, Young Anton, Young Claire, bodyguards, Rudi, and Eunuchs
"Look at Her"		Ensemble
"All You Need to Know"		Claire
"A Masque"	operetta	Mayor and townspeople
"Eunucks' Testimony"		Louis and Jacob
"Winter"		Claire
"Yellow Shoes"	musical comedy	Townspeople
"I Own It"	musical comedy	Claire
"I Would Never Leave You"	musical comedy	Rudi, Lenny, Benny, Louise, and Eunuchs
Act 2		
J. S. Bach Choral†		Townspeople
"A Confession"		Claire
"I Would Never Leave You"	musical comedy	Rudi, Lenny, Benny, and Claire
"Back and Forth"		Otillie and Matilde
"The Only One"		Schoolmaster
"A Car Ride"		Family
"Love and Love Alone"	musical comedy	Claire
"In the Forest Again"	operetta	Anton and Claire
Finale ("A Happy Ending")‡		Townspeople

*This score represents the version prepared for the panned production at the Public Theater. It is also the last version before Ebb's death. Songs without a musical style designation escape easy characterization. "The Visit" and "I'll Wait" were cut from the score used in *Chicago*. An additional song, "The Goodbye Story," was never used, but Kander has not entirely given up on it. He is currently writing new music for the production of *The Visit* at the Signature Theatre in Arlington, Virgina.

†"O haupt voll blut und wundern"

‡The act 1 finale is a mini-opera, a *tableaux vivant* performed by the entire town at the banquet in Claire's honor. It is not Kander and Ebb's best operatic scene, but it imbues the story with a bit of absurdist theater.

Example 9.3. *The Visit*, "You, You, You"

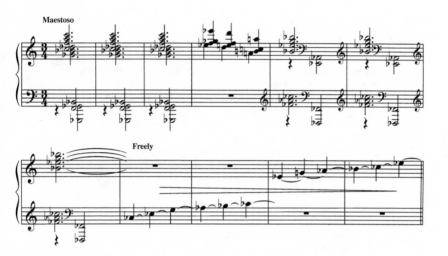

Example 9.4. *The Visit*, Prelude

sonority heard consists of two major triads a half step apart, F and G-flat. The texture, made up of dissonant vertical sonorities, dissolves into a horizontal unfolding of the hexachord first sounding in measure 5, the opening bitonal sonority transposed down a step. The eerie melody and bitonal harmonies of "You, You, You" announce the dichotomy of the score and the comic-tragic underpinnings of the story.[25]

The short prelude segues into a section marked "prologue" in the score, during which several things happen: dancers perform a pantomime depicting Young Anton and Young Claire. He carves a heart in a tree trunk, summer turns to winter, and the older Anton appears from behind the tree (this opening was cut for the production at the Signature Theatre [see below]). The Prologue also introduces the townsfolk as they eagerly await the arrival of Claire's train. Measure 7 introduces the first half of a motive associated with Anton, each note harmonized by an augmented chord (example 9.5a), a har-

(a)

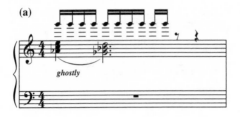

(b)

(c)

Example 9.5. *The Visit:* Prologue, (a) measure 7; (b) measures 18–19;
(c) measure 27

mony derived from the hexachord first heard in the prelude. A disembodied
G-natural pedal tone in sixteenth notes is heard two octaves above. In measures 18–19, the complete four-note "Anton" motive is heard, and then the
ensemble portentously repeats the name on these four notes (example 9.5b).
Recalling the ascending line at the end of the prelude, the next section ends
with a horizontal unfolding of the three augmented chords of the preceding
eight measures (9.5c) followed by a lush restatement of "You, You, You." The
remainder of the prologue alternates between portions of "You, You, You,"
"Winter," and a dissonant section based on the augmented harmony associated with "Anton."

Claire's first solo, "At Last," and last solo, "Love and Love Alone," share the same melodic design and harmonic structure, although they project opposite moods. "At Last" establishes a number of musical markers for Claire: the 6th scale degree as primary tone, sinewy chromaticism, and harmony alternating between tension and stasis (or vice versa). By tracing the structural pitches of "At Last" (the reduced staff of example 9.6b), one can easily see that A, the 6th scale degree, is prolonged for the first eight measures, with G and B functioning as lower- and upper-neighbor tones. A sequence of this phrase at the fourth follows, except at measure 11 the melody moves up a semitone, not a whole tone, as one would expect. From E-flat the line then descends a tritone, returning to A, which does not resolve, even at the cadence on C major, thereby creating an unsettled feeling. This semitone alteration in the sequence and unresolved primary pitch at the cadence belie Claire's friendly words and anticipate the ironic twist of her visit.

"Love and Love Alone" is a melancholy song evocative of Weill's Berlin theater music (example 9.6d). The sentimental lyric, which is among Ebb's best, and the music perfectly match Claire's bittersweet resignation.

When you're young,
Feeling oh so strong,
What can prove you wrong?
Love and love alone.

When the sun
Seems forever bright,
What can dim its light?
Love and love alone.

So beware young love,
Lost in a kiss.
There's a truth, young love,
Simple as this.
Ev'ry fond hello
Ends in goodbye.
What seems certain
To live will die.

So enjoy
All the time there is.
If you're his be his.
Make each day your own.
When tomorrows come

And your heart is stone,
What has made it numb?
Love and love alone.
Ya da da . . .

The melodic contour of this song is based on that of "At Last." The bridge, which is the emotional high point of the song, forces the voice into a higher tessitura (example 9.6e). The two pick-up beats, rhythmically echoing the opening two notes of the song, lead forcefully to F, which is harmonized by a half-diminished $ii^{4/2}$ chord over a tonic pedal. This chord resolves irregularly, moving directly to the tonic. The effect is one of sustained tension moving to a point of stasis. The bridge of "At Last" has essentially the same harmony and melody, although somewhat more rhythmically animated (example 9.6c). The vamp of "At Last" (example 9.6a) alludes to the fluctuating harmonies of the bridge, only in reverse, moving from I^{+6} to $[Ger^{+6}]/I$ (Kander's spelling).

The emotional climax of The Visit occurs in a lengthy operatic scene called "In the Forest Again," which starts out as a dialogue between Claire and Anton. Anton attempts to invoke memories of their past love in the hope that Claire will rescind her decision. With several distinct themes, including the emblematic "You, You, You," this number has an expansive range. The sectional structure and shifts between the past and present effectively portray both Anton's disquieting mixture of fear and residual passion and Claire's conflicted emotions of anger and love. The first theme (example 9.7a) is a simple music-box waltz in D major, during which Anton asks Claire about the child he never saw. The next major section features an undulating melody in F major (example 9.7b), as Claire recalls the time when she and Anton made love "on the straw." In the next section (example 9.7c), Claire tells Anton what she plans to do with his coffin. She sings a short, terse theme that quickly spans the interval of a minor seventh, mostly through large downward leaps over an F pedal point. Several repetitions of this theme finally give way to yet another new idea, this one in A major (example 9.7d). It is associated with Anton and Claire's surviving spiritual love after he is gone. Claire's ideal love is like that obtained in Wagner's "Liebestod." (Ebb even invokes Wagner in the lyric.) This section builds to a restatement of "You, You, You" in A-flat. A final passage of dialogue underscored by several key changes segues into "The Convocation," during which the people of Brachen vote to kill Anton and carry out the deed. A strain of "Love and Love Alone" is heard, followed by a phrase of "Out of the Darkness" sung by the ensemble, and then another

(a) "At Last"

(b)

At last! At last! The old la-dy pays a vi-sit. Let's

stop and think, Just how ma-ny life-times is it? Oh

Example 9.6. *The Visit,* "At Last": (a) vamp; (b) chorus (measures 1–15); (c) bridge (first 4 measures), and "Love and Love Alone"; (d) chorus (first 7 measures); (e) bridge (first 8 measures)

Example 9.6. (*Continued*)

(d)

When you're young, feel - ing oh so strong, what can prove you wrong?

Love and love a - lone.

(e)

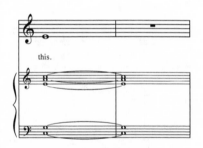

So be - ware, young love, lost in a kiss. There's a truth, young love, sim-ple as

this.

Example 9.6. (*Continued*)

phrase from "Love and Love Alone." The final pitch, the 6th scale degree, is sustained as the curtain descends.

The Visit, although a stylistic departure from Kander and Ebb's other musicals, inclines toward the stylized theatricality that we have observed throughout their career. How appropriate, then, that Derek McLane, the set designer for the Goodman production, framed *The Visit* as a story within a story: "This is Claire's piece of theatre, a show she is, in a sense, putting on for the town of Brachen and for Anton." McLane captured the emotional

Example 9.7. *The Visit*, "In the Forest Again"

(c)

Quietly, with Building Passion

CLAIRE

I'll take your cof - fin to Ca - pri.

I have it planned.

mp

You'll spend e - ter - ni - ty with me.

(d)

ten. *ten.* *ten.* **Fervently**

We'll be to - ge - - - ther high u - pon the

ten. *ten.* *ten.*

Example 9.7. (*Continued*)

Example 9.7. (*Continued*)

aspect and psychological mood of the piece by evoking the landscapes of the artist Caspar David Friedrich, rather than using a traditional musical theater set.[26] He also hung a giant eye from the middle of the proscenium to add to the surreal tone of the story. When Claire's train pulled into the station in the first scene, she appeared on a lift in the middle of the stage in a puff of smoke, like "an ascension from Hell."

So far, the Fates have conspired to keep *The Visit* from reaching Broadway. Angela Lansbury agreed to play the leading female role, but she had to withdraw from the project for personal reasons. In 1999, she participated in a private reading directed by Frank Galati and recorded a few songs from the score. The inimitable Philip Bosco read the part of Anton, and two Kander and Ebb alumni, John Cunningham (*Zorbá*) and Mary Louise Wilson (*Flora and Cabaret*), also participated. This reading led to the production at the Goodman Theater in Chicago in 2001, which Galati also directed and which starred Chita Rivera and John McMartin. The critical reception in Chicago was mixed. The *Chicago Sun-Times* critic complained about the score's eclecticism.[27] On the other hand, the *Chicago Tribune* called the musical "more wonderful in more ways than one ever would have suspected."[28] A move to Broadway seemed imminent, but events of September 11, 2001, precluded opening such a dark musical at that time. In 2003 the Public Theater showed interest and planned a production starring Rivera and Frank Langella, but this production fell through when Barry Brown, who was the primary financier of the project, withdrew funding.

Galati directed a second production of *The Visit* as part of the 2007–08 Kander and Ebb Celebration at the Signature Theatre. Rivera repeated her role as Claire, and George Hearn appeared as Anton. Again McLain provided the sets, this time using a wooden platform and doorways in a brick wall. Kander cut several songs and wrote a few new ones, including "I Must Have Been Something," in which Anton revels in the thought that he was irresistibly attractive to Claire.[29] He also cut the prelude and prologue because the decision was made not to begin with reminiscences of the past.

By most accounts, this production was an improvement over the Goodman production. Some critics, however, struggled with the attenuated nature of Claire's anger. Charles Isherwood called the musical "honorable but conflicted" and complained that Claire's musical reminiscences of her relationship with Anton undercut the intensity of her quest for revenge. Recalling both John Simon's and Clive Barnes's comments regarding the score of *Kiss of the Spider Woman*, Isherwood states that it would require a composer like Berg or Weill to find "an authentic musical language" for *The Visit*.[30] Writing for the *Washington Post*, Nelson Pressley also addresses Claire's tempered anger, claiming that "that Shakespearean spirit of romance—wistful, gradually wise—seems to have enveloped the hardy old pros who are putting together this musical again."[31] Peter Marks's review calls the production "admirable if not consistently embraceable" and emphasizes the effectiveness of Ann Reinking's choreography, comparing it to Agnes de Mille's dream ballets.[32] He, too, sees the flashbacks as detrimental to the tone of Durrenmatt's play. Kander feels that the new production "is close to our [his, Rivera's, and Hearn's] very best work" and hopes to see *The Visit* on Broadway in the near future.[33]

Minstrel Show

Kander and Ebb's last collaboration is their most direct assault on racial prejudice in America and their most unsettling work. In Kander's words, it has "something in it to offend absolutely everybody."[34] Kander and Ebb's only work based a real historical event, *Minstrel Show* is about the Scottsboro Boys trials. David Thompson and Susan Stroman came up with the idea around 2000. At the time, Ebb was at an emotional nadir. *Steel Pier* had a disappointing run, the planned production of *The Visit* at the Public Theater had fallen through, and he was still recovering from cancer surgery. What Ebb needed most was a new project, and he was unequivocally enthusiastic about this one. Thompson recalls that

> When we did mention it to Fred, he jumped. He lit up so quickly. I've never seen anything light up faster with Fred. If he was a little lethargic in the way he signed onto *Steel Pier*, he couldn't work fast enough on this one. He was way ahead of me when we were writing, which was not typical of Fred. . . . He knew immediately. This was the embodiment of that notion [Kander and Ebb's approach to the genre], which is, we are going to entertain you, and you are going to have fun, but at the same time we're going to lead you to a place that is very dangerous and very controversial, and what you take out of this, where you get, you're going to have to sort out yourself, but in the meantime we're going to entertain you as you go.

The Scottsboro Boys case is among the most infamous racial injustices in twentieth-century America. In March 1931, nine black youths were traveling aboard the Southern Railroad from Chattanooga to Memphis, where they hoped to find work. They allegedly scuffled with a group of white boys and forced all but one of them from the train. News of this melee reached Paint Rock, Alabama, and when the train pulled into the station there a "posse" of armed white men was waiting and hauled them off to a jail in Scottsboro. Two female stowaways who were also on the train, twenty-one-year old Victoria Price and seventeen-year old Ruby Bates, accused the black boys of raping them, hoping to deflect attention away from their own illicit activities.[35] The legal proceedings that ensued dragged on for decades, involved the governor of Alabama, the U.S. Supreme Court twice, the Communist Party, and a Jewish lawyer from New York, and ultimately ruined the lives of all nine of the falsely accused defendants.

The first series of trials resulted in convictions and death sentences for eight of the Scottsboro Boys (a mistrial was declared for the youngest boy, who was only twelve). With the NAACP reluctant to take on a case involving rape, the Communist Party (through its legal channel, the International Labor Defense), saw an opportunity to promote itself to southern blacks and sent Samuel Leibowitz, a Jewish trial lawyer from New York, to represent the black youths during the appeals process, which resulted in a U.S. Supreme Court ruling that overturned the convictions and ordered new trials.

At the second trial, Haywood Paterson emerged as the most militant of the accused men and eventually became the sacrificial lamb of the case—"the man whose defiant pride had marked him from beginning as the most visible, the most hated of the Scottsboro defendants."[36] In a famous rejoinder to the prosecutor's incriminating questions regarding the defendant's guilt, Paterson indignantly claimed, "I was framed in Scottsboro." Leibowitz discredited Victoria Price's testimony, and Ruby Bates, who had gone into hiding, suddenly emerged in the courtroom and recanted everything she said at the first trial. In his closing remarks, state attorney general Thomas Knight Jr. declared, "Show them . . . that Alabama justice cannot be bought and sold with Jew money from New York."[37] Despite the reversals and Leibowitz's formidable defense, the jury returned guilty verdicts and death sentences for most of the men.

When the same verdict and sentence were handed down at Haywood Patterson's third trial, Leibowitz again appeared in front of the Supreme Court, arguing that not a single black person appeared among the county's jury pool. Again, the Supreme Court overturned the verdict. Alabama continued to press for the death penalty, but the protracted trials started to be a financial drain on the state, and soon all of the defendants except Patterson were released. Four of the freed inmates were celebrated as heroes. They went on a speaking tour, performed, and even participated in a reenactment of the trial, but they all died ignominious deaths. In his next trial, Patterson was sentenced to a seventy-five-year prison term, but he escaped in 1948 and fled to Michigan.[38] Two years later, he killed a man in a barroom fight, in self-defense, or so he claimed, and two years after that he died of cancer while festering in prison. He was thirty-nine years old. In 1976, Clarence Norris, by then the last living Scottsboro Boy, received a pardon from Governor George Wallace.

Thompson, Stroman, Kander, and Ebb decided to tell this story in the form of a minstrel show. By adopting this form, the writers are able to unpack various conflicts embodied in the Scottsboro Boys case, such as those between the North and South, the poor and middle class, and African Americans and Jews. The segmented structure of a minstrel show—the alternation of jokes and singing, the use of a narrator, and direct addresses to the audience—also helps to tame the sweeping narrative of the Scottsboro Boys story. Twelve male actors in blackface appear in the traditional semicircle of a minstrel show. The Interlocutor, the two endmen, and nine middlemen, who play the defendants, act out key incidents in the case and sing a variety of songs—including "coon" songs, plantation songs, and Victorian parlor songs—which progress or comment on the action. The score, which is on the surface a pastiche of popular songs, is, in effect, a self-reflexive critique of art and racism. The musical is thus no mere musical documentary about the Scottsboro Boys. It is ultimately a denunciation of popular culture's (and musical theater's) complicity in propagating and perpetuating racist attitudes in America. Like Spike Lee's 2000 film *Bamboozled*, it acknowledges the still ubiquitous presence of minstrelsy in contemporary culture and the continued exploitation of African Americans. Earlier musicals and at least one opera evoked the minstrel show, such as Lerner and Weill's *Love Life* (1948), a bleak assessment of modern marriage, and *Gentlemen, Be Seated* (1956), an opera about the Civil War; but in these works, the minstrel show is a theatrical conceit and serves only to perpetuate racist attitudes. In *Minstrel Show*, it is both form and content.

Minstrel shows, to quote Thompson, "made fun of all sorts of social forms, whether it was the upper class, [political] parties, things that were fashionable, elegant, the white man, the understanding of certain things."[39] They used gender, class, politics, and race to entertain and to convey a sense of superiority. However, the minstrel show fostered a culture of "Uncle Tom," for the comic, dramatic, and musical elements were all designed around the pejorative depiction of African Americans. For this reason, the minstrel show milieu has as much metaphorical potential as does the cabaret in *Cabaret* and the vaudeville in *Chicago*.

A minstrel show typically contained three segments: "The Opening," "The Olio," and "The Walk Around." It usually began with a parade of the entertainers into the theater, some carrying chairs, all dressed in black coats and white vests. They assembled on stage positioning themselves in a semicircle. Upon the cue "Gentlemen, be seated," they sat down in their prescribed places and the show began. At the ends of the semicircle sat the endmen, Mr. Tambo and Mr. Bones, between whom sat the middlemen. Tambo and Bones often joked with each other, with one serving as straight man. An Interlocutor narrated the proceedings, but his authority was often undermined by the banter of the endmen.

Thompson adopted a three-act structure to correspond to the minstrel show's tripartite division. Mr. Tambo, Mr. Bones, and the Interlocutor act as the conscience of the piece. Bones and Tambo present most of the expository information, and they frequently break through the fourth wall. The stilted acting style of a minstrel show, along with other metadramatic devices, creates a sense of dislocation between the story and the audience. The Interlocutor serves as an emcee and stands somewhat removed from the action, thereby providing a lens for the audience. The nine middlemen play the Scottsboro Boys.

As suggested by real events of the case, Haywood Patterson, the most outspoken of the nine accused men, is the point-of-view character. As Thompson sees him, "he's not noble, he's not grand, he's not somebody who delivers through his actions great sacrifice, but he is somebody who at the end because of his defiance causes change." In the prologue, Patterson is alone on stage and lectures the audience on the subject of truth.

> The truth? Nobody's much interested in the truth. Inside the courthouse, truth was no defense anyhow. Not for the nine boys standing trial. They just wanted a show. The same goddamn show they'd been lining up to see for the past hundred years. What choice did we have? But to sing and strut . . . sing and strut. [*Patterson is hit with a hard-edged spot. The minstrel show begins.*] Hang 'em from up high! Spin 'em 'round and 'round! Stretch 'em by the neck! Dey make you gasp. Make you sigh! Make you cry sweet tears of joy! Dey's de dancin,' prancin,' entrancing' Scottsboro Boys.

This speech establishes the main theme of the musical and takes the audience back to the beginning of the case as Haywood regresses from an educated, self-respecting man into an Uncle Tom. As he speaks, he literally "blackens up," assuming the role constructed and propagated by whites. His transformation illustrates that race, like gender, is performed.

Thompson's script is remarkably compact, and it allows the music to do much of the work. Initially, Thompson designed the show to have several scenes, each one constructed around a single song.

Act 1:

Overture	"Minstrel Parade" (Instrumental)
1.	"Commencing in Chattanooga" (Haywood and the Scottsboro Boys)
2.	"Two Innocent Southern Girls" (Ruby Bates and Victoria Price)
3.	"Come Right In, Sit Right Down, Make Yourself at Home" (Mr. Bones and Mr. Tambo)
	"It Ain't Right" (Haywood)

4.	"No Sir!" (Scottsboro Boys)
5.	"Beyond the Little Green Gate" (Prison guards)[40]
6.	"Hey Little Boy"[41] (Tambo and Bones)
7.	"Silver Shinin' Moon" (Haywood)
8.	"Christ Is a Nigger" (Scottsboro Boys)
9.	"The Finale/The Reprieve"

Act 2:

1.	"Scenes from a Sanctum" (Interlocutor and Tambo)
2.	"I Sees the Truth" (Tambo)
3.	"Zip Coon, the Carpetbagger" (Bones)
4.	"I Couldn't Say" (Wench Song) (Victoria)
5.	"I Know'd It Was Wrong" (parody of grand opera) (Ruby)
6.	(The Bully Song) "Nobody Tells Me" (form of shivaree) (Haywood)
7.	"The Verdict" (Tambo)
8.	"Zip Coon Get His Comeuppance" (Bones)
9.	"Justitia fiat coelum ruat" (Interlocutor)

Act 3:

1.	"Walk Around Boys" (Scottsboro Boys, Tambo, and Bones)
2.	"Stand Up" (Mama Patterson [Ruby Bates in blackface])
3.	"White Sugar" (Scottsboro Boys)
4.	"Shootin' Coon" (Tambo and Bones)
5.	"Nobody's Nigger" (Haywood)
6.	"No Sir!" (Haywood and Interlocutor)
7.	"They Can't Do Us Like They Done Us Like They Did Before" (Scottsboro Boys)

Thompson's script is not as fragmented as this musical plan suggests. Each act has its own rhythm and dramatic sweep, rather than being broken into small scenes anchored by a single song. Thompson simplified the complex legal case and limited the courtroom action to a bare minimum, thus avoiding the appearance of a documentary.

Act 1 starts with "Commencing in Chattanooga," which depicts the infamous train ride. At Scottsboro, the boys are accused first of fighting with some white youths and then of raping Victoria Price and Ruby Bates. A trial

John Kander and Fred Ebb. From the personal collection of John Kander

is held, although it is a foregone conclusion that death sentences will be handed out—a fact personified by the inept and drunken court-appointed lawyer (in real life the only member of the bar who was willing to represent the Scottsboro boys). Up to this point, the story unfolds linearly and with historical accuracy, but, as each man is led off to the electric chair, Haywood turns to the audience and declares, "It didn't happen that way," and he shouts at Mr. Bones and Mr. Tambo, "Tell them the truth!" With a jeering laugh, Mr. Bones retorts, "That wasn't the truth, but that sho was fun!" Then follows the announcement of a Supreme Court declaration of a mistrial.

Act 2 opens in 1933 as a round of second trials is about to begin. Samuel Leibowitz arrives from New York to argue the case on behalf of the nine men. Ruby Bates reads a statement during the trial that exonerates all nine of them. The boys serve as her back-up singers as she performs "Never Too Late to Atone." The attorney general, played with a Southern Baptist bravado by Mr. Tambo, claims that the Jewish lawyer's money bought Ruby's revisionist history of events. Haywood, who has learned to read and write during his imprisonment, imagines himself lecturing the court—but the Interlocutor reminds him that he never actually did.

As act 3 begins, five years have passed, and the boys are waiting on death row. Bones and Tambo provide an update.

> BONES: Oh to be sure, there were mo' trials.
> TAMBO: And mo' verdicts.
> BONES: Trial Number Three!
> TAMBO: Guilty!
> BONES: And Trial Number Four!
> TAMBO: Guilty!
> BONES: And Trial Number Five!
> TAMBO: Guilty!
> BONES: And Trial Number Six!
> TAMBO: Guilty!
> BONES: Did you say guilt-less?
> TAMBO: Noooo-sir!
> BONES: Did you say guilt-free?
> TAMBO: Noooo-sir!
> BONES: Did you say guil-TEE?
> TAMBO: Yessssss-sir!

The remainder of the act is a telescoping of the real events that transpired. A deal is struck between Leibowitz and the judge, who agrees to acquit the four youngest men provided that the lawyer bring no more appeals. Haywood poses a simple question of logic to the lawyer: "If they're innocent how can *we* be guilty." Leibowitz gets Haywood a parole hearing in front of the governor, but he warns him that he must plead guilty: "the truth will not set you free. But a lie will. After all, it's easier to believe a lie than to believe a colored boy telling the truth." But Haywood, facing a certain death, refuses to admit guilt for a crime that he did not commit. Given an opportunity to address the audience, Haywood dances a soft shoe ("I Ain't Gonna Take It Anymore"). After a production number involving all of the Scottsboro Boys, each one recounts what happened to him after prison. Roy Wright killed himself; Andy Wight lived destitute and was buried in an unmarked grave; Olen Montgomery died a homeless drunk; Charlie Weems worked in a laundry; Ozzie Powell remained unemployed; Willie Roberson died of asthma; and Clarence Norris died of Alzheimer's disease (and "forgot the whole thing"). The Interlocutor calls for "a happy, happy ending" and a cakewalk. The opening parade music rings out, but this time the boys do not participate. Instead, they stare out at the audience. When the Interlocutor insists, "Gentlemen, be seated," each one knocks over his chair and wanders out of the theater. The "boys" have become men. By refusing to follow the Interlocutor's orders, they destroy the minstrel show and shatter the falsehoods of the past, the mold of injustice.

With *Minstrel Show*, Kander and Ebb were working in familiar territory. More like *Chicago* than *Cabaret*, their score—still a work-in-progress—consists entirely of presentational songs, although these are also part of the dramatic narrative. The score includes several classic minstrel show tropes, including parodic set pieces such as a grand opera parody, a Bully Song, a shivaree, and a "coon song." The score surveys idioms associated with African-American music, from minstrel tunes to boogie-woogie. Pentatonic themes evoke early minstrel melodies such as Dan Emmit's "Dixie." "Commencing in Chattanooga" begins with a propulsive boogie-woogie piano figure and incorporates blue notes in the melody. "Welcome to the County Jail" also uses boogie-woogie as the underlying accompaniment. In "Alabama Ladies," Victoria and Ruby "perform in the style of the Dolly Sisters, with complete innocence and sweetness." The song features a genteel two-step melody devoid of syncopation and thus musically distances the two ladies from the black defendants. It is a stylistic contrast to the previous songs, but a few features belie Virginia and Ruby's low-class pedigree, such as an intrusive blue note on "Wouldn't melt in our mouth" and a shift to the relative minor in the bridge. Mr. Tambo and Mr. Bones sing most of the songs while playing characters in the story.

Musical Numbers in the Current Version of *Minstrel Show* (2005)[42]
    "Minstrel Parade" (Overture) (Instrumental)
    "Commencing in Chattanooga" (All)
    "Alabama Ladies" (Ruby and Victoria)
    "Walk Right In" (same as "Come Right In . . .") (Mr. Bones and Mr. Tambo)
    "Nothin'"[43] (Haywood)
    "Electric Chair" (same as "Hey Little Boy") (Mr. Bones and Mr. Tambo)
    "Go Back Home" (Haywood and Boys)
    "Shout" (All)
    "Make Friends with the Truth" (Haywood)
    "That's Not the Way We Do Things in New York" (Leibowitz [Mr. Bones])
    "Never Too Late to Atone" (Ruby and Boys)
    "Jew Money" (Attorney General [Mr. Tambo])

Example 9.8. *Minstrel Show,* "Parade Music"

aria (not yet composed) (Mama Patterson)
"Southern Days" (Boys)
"It's Gonna Take Time" (Interlocutor)
musical scene (only final portion is on the demo recording) (Haywood,
   Tambo, and Leibowitz)
"The Scottsboro Boys" and "You Can't Do Me" (Haywood, Interlocutor, and
   the other boys)[44]

At the beginning of *Minstrel Show,* a bass drum and cymbal announce
the opening "parade music." A clarinet plays a syncopated four-measure
pentatonic tune (example 9.8). These features evoke the Dixieland milieu
of the South and, by extension, minstrelsy. An accompaniment is added as
the tune builds and repeats, progressing through a series of modulations and
eventually winding its way back to the original key. The orchestra holds the
penultimate dominant chord of the final cadence as the Interlocutor com-
mands, "Gentlemen, be seated!" This straightforward cakewalk accompanies
the entrance of the players and establishes the minstrel show milieu and an
"upbeat" tone as ironic commentary on what is about to take place.

The creation of this number is the stuff of musical theater legend. Thompson remembers the day it happened:

   One day we're having a meeting and he [Ebb] announced, "I dreamed the
   opening number. Let me explain it to you." He went on and defined the opening number. . . . That was not something that Fred was making up. He knew
   that he dreamed that number . . . the whole minstrel march and the way that

it comes together. And Kander went and sat down at the piano—I mean, this sounds so corny, but that's the way it was. Kander went to the piano; he wrote that march; and Fred was now just beside himself. He was screaming that it was the best thing Kander's ever written. He told us exactly where we were, what was happening, why it was right, what was evocative about it, and how—back to the point I was making originally—how it should be staged.

Haywood's first solo, "I Haven't Done Nothin,'" is a "coon song." One of several racist song types popular from 1880 to World War I, coon songs derogatorily depicted African Americans. The term "coon song" was used by performers and audiences alike, but Larry Hamberlin prefers the more descriptive term "Negro dialect" song.[45] In reviving this discredited song genre (Hamberlin notes that "few musical genres are today held in lower esteem"), Kander and Ebb once again feature a derogatory form of entertainment in order to arouse anger, as they did with "If You Could See Her Through My Eyes" in *Cabaret*. Haywood, by imitating the white South's depiction of an ignorant black man, produces the same sense of self-loathing and alienation that Amos Hart does in "Mister Cellophane," which is itself modeled on Bert Williams's performance of "Nobody" (see Chapter 3). Haywood also sings "Make Friends with the Truth," the most didactic number in the show. The finale juxtaposes a coon song ("I Ain't Gonna Take It Anymore") and Haywood's final speech about rising up and throwing off the shackles of slavery. During tap dance breaks, the freed Scottsboro Boys recount the miserable lives they led after their release.

Interlocutor (singing)	Haywood (speaking)
So give us some time, Haywood	
	This is *my* time!
And try to behave	
	I will rise up!
Remember it hasn't been so	
Many years since your	
Granddad was only a slave.	
	I am not a slave! I am not a boy!
	I am a man! I know my purpose!
	And I am alive!
	(*singing*)
	We won't stand still
	Our hands in our pockets

What was a whisper
Is now a roar.
You can't do us
If you do us
Like you did us before.

(*speaking*) And now the grand finale
of our show! One day! One day came
indeed! One day! The truth was told.
One day! The wrong was righted!
One day! The boys were free! Their
lives were not for naught. instead, the
human spirit soared! And the world
will always owe a debt of gratitude
to the Scottsboro Boys! Hallelujah,
human beings at last!

Boys
Every member of society
Celebrates our notoriety
Step right up and meet
The Scottsboro Boys.

etc.

Before Ebb died, he and Kander had identified the need for a few additional songs. Kander ended up writing the lyrics for these himself. "That's Not the Way We Do Things in New York," Leibowitz's defining song, illustrates the hypocrisy of Northern tolerance and the mere semblance of social justice in Northern cities:

Back in Manhattan ask anyone.
There's no bigger voice for equal rights than me.
I fight for it! I live for it.
Just ask my cook, Jemima.
Just ask my chauffer, Rufus.
Just ask our colored laundress.
I'm sure they'll agree.

Like "When You're Good to Mama" from *Chicago*, this song, too, reflects the complicated history of Jewish-Black relations. That Leibowitz, a liberal Jew, will probably be played by a black actor in blackface will further underscore the troubling nature of this history. So too will district attorney Knight's song, "Jew Money." The performance of "Jew Money" by an actor in blackface playing a Southern bigot and anti-Semite encapsulates what scholars such as Jeffrey Melnick have discussed regarding early Jewish performers, such as Eddie Cantor, who used blackface to hide their own ethnicity.[46]

Questions still remain regarding the casting of *Minstrel Show*. Doing the show without blackface would soften the impact of the story, but should the cast be white or black, or both? Kander envisions an interracial cast all starting out in blackface, and as the story advances the blackface is wiped off the white actors. The roles of Victoria, Ruby, and Haywood's mother also present interesting possibilities, as minstrel shows usually featured an all-male cast and thus required cross-dressing for the female roles.

Minstrel Show revisits many of the elements of Kander and Ebb's musicals from the very beginning: the press, the ethnically marked lawyer, prostitution, race politics, and gender are all an intrinsic part of the story. Just as Roxie Hart does after her acquittal, Ruby Bates went on to a minor career in vaudeville, and some of the freed Scottsboro Boys made a few stage appearances. *Minstrel Show* also explores issues haunting America today as American culture becomes more heterogeneous but not without tremendous resistance. Only time will tell, but in its current state *Minstrel Show* avoids the racist assumptions of several well-intentioned shows such as *Show Boat* and *South Pacific*. It treats racial discrimination of the past with irony and an awareness of the present. It does not avoid uncomfortable topics, such as the hypocrisy of allegedly nonracist Northern whites. Shortly after *Curtains* opened on Broadway in 2007, David Thompson dreamed that Ebb was yelling at him and Kander "to get busy and open the show." Perhaps he will not have too long to wait.

Legacy

While working on *Minstrel Show*, Ebb disclosed to Kander that he was unhappy with how his life had ended up. Ebb's mood had undergone a noticeable change for the worse. The fact that working on a show was the only thing that made Ebb happy was not easy for Kander to bear. Ebb put a lot of pressure on Kander to work, but he was becoming more difficult to be around. They started spending less time together, even communicating by fax and phone. One of Ebb's last communiqués to Kander, a typed fax, exhibits the mixture of self-deprecating humor, admiration, and neediness that characterized their complex relationship in its final phrase:

I've written this [lyric] in the hope you'll find it something that can work for us as a song for Ruby in the Second Act. The form and the rhyme scheme though hardly set or finished at least allows me room to give her an important and possibly sensational number. I tried working with the last format I gave you and I know you tried setting it. It just didn't give me enough room to expand and help the character be funny and vulgar and true. So forgive me for ignoring the first try. Here's the one I really like. I hope you'll agree. Naturally it's a very, very preliminary draft, but it will give you some idea of how I'd like to go. Feel free to hate it and permanently lose my friendship. Also, feel free to like it and permanently gain my love and support.

Yours in Christ,
Fred Ebb

One senses a razor sharp mind and passion for the material, as well as the give-and-take that Kander and Ebb had enjoyed throughout their collaboration. But there is also something forced about the humor. Ebb asks for Kander's professional approbation, tying it to their friendship. Ebb had always been a demanding and insecure collaborator, but now he needed Kander more than ever.

On June 15, 2004, the New York Public Library for the Performing Arts held a press conference to announce the bequest of Ebb's and Kander's papers, as well as those of Jerry Bock and Sheldon Harnick. On hand to host the event was Hal Prince, who had produced and directed musicals by both teams of writers. He brought them out on stage for a casual discussion about musical theater. Reporting for the New York Times, Jesse McKinley wrote, "Mr. Ebb, 68, and Mr. Kander, 77, shamelessly worked the crowd, playfully bickering about everything from Bob Fosse's perfectionism . . . to their method of creating a musical." Ebb made himself the center of attention, the seasoned comedian, and Kander played the straight man. In typical fashion, Ebb complained that he felt "deeply hurt" by the insinuation that he purposely hammed it up, even though he clearly did. The ceremony was one of Ebb's last public appearances, and he was in his element. Ebb's papers are now accessible to scholars and students. Unfortunately, these materials do not include the tapes and recordings in Ebb's possession at the time of his death. Kander's papers will eventually join Ebb's, but not for many years, one hopes. These materials will spur further critical studies of their musicals.

With three new musicals ready for Broadway, Kander and Ebb are still a force in American musical theater. Their legacy will endure, and their musicals will continue to reach new audiences. Cabaret is performed all over the world. *Chicago* has been seen in nearly five hundred different productions in the United States since 2000 alone and has appeared in most major cities around the world. The Kander and Ebb revue *And the World Goes 'Round* (see Appendix) is a perennial favorite. *Flora, the Red Menace, Zorbá, 70, Girls, 70, The Rink,* and *Steel Pier* are produced with relative frequency. *Woman of the Year* is rarely produced in the United States but is enormously popular overseas. The recent success of the film version of *Chicago* and the success of the long-running stage revival has brought continued fame and fortune to Kander and Ebb.

As the first study of Kander and Ebb's collaboration, this book has laid out the facts of their career and has attempted to view their musicals in the context of American popular culture at a time of tumultuous changes. These two men from the thirties managed to write their music and write it their way while speaking to ever-widening audiences about monumental issues. Materials yet to be examined will no doubt reveal more about their lives and art, such as James Goldman's papers at Cornell University, Nikos Psachorapolis's papers at the New York Public Library, and George Abbott's theater memorabilia, which have been bequeathed to Temple University. And there is more still to come from Kander and Ebb themselves. One still hopes for Broadway productions of *The Visit* and *All About Us.* Susan Stroman, David Thompson, and Kander plan to forge ahead with *Minstrel Show* in the coming months. Kander still thinks often about his partner and gets a little bit of help from him now and then: "And as far as the new material is concerned, I've sort of tried to channel Fred in my head and write the way I think he writes. . . . Every once in a while I look up or down or wherever the hell he is, and need him or curse him for cutting out like this. But mostly he's, he's around."[47]

Appendix

Trade Shows

It is hard to imagine today that in 1966 Kander and Ebb were still facing an uncertain future, but at that point neither one had a bona fide hit to his name. In addition to the poor showing of *Flora, the Red Menace*, Kander's *A Family Affair* (1962) and Ebb's *Morning Sun* (1963) were both box office failures; and *Golden Gate* sat collecting dust. Moreover, *Cabaret* was anything but a sure bet, and its daring subject matter must have caused Kander and Ebb considerable anxiety. It is no wonder, then, that they were still available for hire during the months leading up to the world premiere of *Cabaret*, and that when asked to write a musical for General Electric Utility's executives' conference in Williamsburg, Virginia, they accepted. Such work was common in the sixties, as many corporations commissioned musicals for their conferences and annual meetings. These musicals, referred to in the trade as "industrials," had a promotional, instructional, or self-aggrandizing purpose. For young writers like Kander and Ebb, industrials provided a training ground, an opportunity to work with top-notch theater professionals, and a source of income. The show for GE, *Go Fly a Kite*, featured several talented actors: Valerie Harper, Ted Thurston, and Mary Louise Wilson (who played Charlotte in the original cast of *Flora, the Red Menace*, Fräulein Schneider in the 1998 revival of *Cabaret*, and Edith Bouvier Beale in *Grey Gardens*, for which she won a Tony Award in 2007).

Conceived by a GE employee named Lou Marsh, *Go Fly a Kite* consisted of three segments, one for each day of the three-day conference. Kander and Ebb wrote the script, working from song ideas provided by March and a co-worker named Ted Cooke.[1] The opening song welcomes the conferees to historic Williamsburg:

> Welcome, welcome stranger
> to Williamsburg.
> Glad to see you, stranger
> in Williamsburg.
> Where the breezes are light and airy
> You'll meet a charming couple known as William and Mary.

In the first book scene, Richard the Leprechaun, named after Benjamin Franklin's Poor Richard's Almanac, guides a couple of tourists on a time-traveling journey to the past and future. A series of vignettes follows, each one dealing with a theme relevant to the future of General Electric, such as "Improving the Quality of Power" and "Our Emerging Markets." At the start of each day's session, a GE executive delivered a speech on the planned topic for the day. Kander and Ebb's demo recording, which contains only days 1 and 3, and the souvenir recording given to the conferees do not entirely correspond, but the existence of a conductor-piano score make it possible to determine the final version of the score.[2]

> 1st Day
>   "Williamsburg Opening"
>   "I Got a Proper Perspective" (countermelody to opening number)
>   "Thru the Magic Door"
>   "Philadelphia" (based on opening)
>   "Let Me Put It to You That Way Ben"
>   "Go Fly a Kite"
>   "Atom Is Evil"
>   "Mr. Young" (short melody)
>   "Perfect Control"
>   "A Big Fat Wife"
>   "We're Makin' Our Own"
> 2nd Day
>   "Welcome 2nd Day"
>   "No! No! Not That"
>   "P.D.M. Can Do"
>   "34 Years from Today"
>   "You've Got to Understand the Problem"
>   "Be Direct with Me"
>   "Technological Witchcraft"
>   "Something in Common"
>   "Super Mink"
> 3rd Day
>   "Manpower"
>   "I Protest"
>   "We're Twenty One" (short melody)
>   "That Great Big A Go Go in the Sky"
>   "You Can't Trust No More"
>   "Absolutely Available"
>   "Heaven Out of Hell"
>   "Make a Woman Out of Your Wife"
>   "Times Have Changed"
>   Ultimo Finale

One of the highlights of the score is "Be Direct with Me," for which Ebb provided a Cole Porteresque lyric and Kander a sultry samba, as Porter himself would have most likely done.

Don't be transitive
Don't be tentative
Don't be alternately positive and negative
For like Washington
I'll always be D. C.
So please be direct
Flow to me direct
Oh please be direct with me!

Kander and Ebb also wrote an industrial show for Ford Motor Company. Titled *Action '68*, it was intended to promote Ford's new model lines.[3] The songs were completed in early 1967, well in advance of the actual performances. Neither Kander nor Ebb could remember if it was ever performed, probably because they were in rehearsals for *Cabaret* at the time. *Action '68* did not have a story line. It consisted of an overture, six songs, and a number of promotional films.

Continuity[4]
Overture
"Action '68" (song)
"One from Column A" (song)
"Op Art"
"Under Your Sombrero" (song)
"Better Ideas" (song)
"LTD Reveal"
"LTD Narration"
"LTD Film"
"One from Column A" (song)
"XL Reveal"
"XL Narration"
"Action '68" (song)
"In a Balloon" (song)
"Torino 2 Door Reveal"
"Torino 2 Door Narration"
"Op Art"
"Fast Back Reveal"
"Finale" (reprise of "Better Ideas")

Featured prominently in the overture is "In the Same Boat," which eventually ended up in *Curtains* (see Chapter 9). Kander has quipped, "we spent our entire career trying to use it."

In 1967, Kander and Ebb wrote "Hey Litterbug" for the "Citizens Committee to Keep NYC Clean" campaign. The pop group Jay and the Americans recorded the song. Kander and Ebb also provided music for the annual Inner Circle dinner, sponsored by political reporters. The evening featured Mayor John Lindsey of New York. Kander accompanied, Ron Fields choreographed the event, and Chita Rivera and Josephine Premise appeared alongside the mayor in a piece entitled "Fun City, U.S.A."

Funny Lady and Other Films During the Seventies

The notoriety that Kander and Ebb enjoyed in the early seventies brought them a string of offers from Hollywood. They wrote a couple of songs for the 1975 Stanley Donen film *Lucky Lady*, which starred by Liza Minnelli, Gene Hackman, and Burt Reynolds, who played three rum-running bootleggers at the end of Prohibition.[5] An offer the same year to write the music for *Funny Lady* was too tempting to turn down. The project inspired them to write some excellent songs, but the studio treated them with such indifference that the experience forever soured them on Hollywood. Thereafter, they limited themselves mainly to films involving Minnelli, including *A Matter of Time* in 1976, directed by Vincent Minnelli, and *New York, New York*, directed by Martin Scorsese.

Funny Lady, the sequel to Julie Styne and Bob Merrill's *Funny Girl*, deserves special mention because it is Kander and Ebb's only traditional Hollywood book musical. It also posed several challenges, such as writing for a demanding superstar, maneuvering through the thicket of Hollywood bureaucracy, and coming up with a score that captured the period setting and theatrical milieu of the story and that would simultaneously seem to be a natural extension—but not an imitation—of Jule Styne's *Funny Girl* score. They also had to contend with the studio's decision to include authentic period music, including Billy Rose's "Paper Moon." Kander and Ebb wrote ten original numbers, only six of which ended up in the film: "How Lucky Can You Get," "Honey Lamb," "Blind Date," "Isn't This Better?," "I Like Him/I Like Her" (counter melody to "Paper Moon"), and "Let's Hear It for Me."[6]

Kander and Ebb's sophisticated writing for *Funny Lady* went entirely unnoticed by the critics. It is a tribute to their sense of period style that their songs blended with the oldies used in the film, like "More Than You Know" and "If I Love Again." Vincent Canby accused Kander and Ebb of writing "with a gun at their heads, being told to come up with song-by-song equivalents to the great 'Funny Girl' numbers by Jule Styne and Bob Merrill."[7] In this respect, the studio tipped its hand by insisting that Fanny's (Streisand's) self-affirming number "Let's Hear It for Me" be arranged and filmed in the same manner as "Don't Rain on My Parade" from *Funny Girl*. The studio failed to consult Kander about this decision, and when he found out about it he was so angry that he went back to his hotel and charged up his expense account.

New York, New York

New York, New York (1977), like *Funny Lady*, featured new songs by Kander and Ebb plus authentic period jazz standards such as "Honeysuckle Rose." The movie did not call for any book songs. Kander and Ebb's contributions, "Theme from New York, New York," "There Goes the Ball Game," and "But the World Goes 'Round," are all sung by Minnelli's character. They also wrote a mini Hollywood musical called "Happy Endings" for the film-within-the-film sequence and an earlier version of "Theme from New York, New York," which Robert DeNiro rejected out of hand (example A.1).[8] In the context of *New York, New York*, "Happy Endings" is a movie-within-a-movie about an actress playing an actress who stars in a movie musical about herself. As the inner Hollywood musical documents the rise and fall of the fictional actress played by Minnelli's character, the outer Hollywood musical documents the rise and fall of the character played by Minnelli. Put in simpler terms, inside the film we are watching is a film about the film we are watching. "Happy Endings" is a spoof of the extended musical scenes interpolated into MGM

Example A.1. First version of "Theme from New York, New York"

musicals, for example, the Mickey Spillane parody starring Fred Astaire and Cyd Cha-
risse in *Band Wagon* (1953). Ebb felt that "Happy Endings" "was a pretty good piece, but
the way he [Scorsese] staged it and shot it, it was stupid. It doesn't make any sense. . . . I
mean it's incomprehensible. And it's a very nice, witty piece with some good songs in it."
Ultimately, Scorsese knew that it was not working and cut it. The whole sequence can be
heard on the soundtrack and seen on the director's cut video release of the film.

Mid-Career Revues and Specialty Material

In 1973, Kander and Ebb appeared in concert as part of Maurice Levine's "Lyrics and
Lyricists Series" at the 92nd Street Y. *An Evening with John Kander & Fred Ebb*, as the
event was called, featured songs up to and including *Chicago*, which was still in development at the time. A recording of the event, now out on CD, is one of only two commercially available examples of Kander and Ebb performing their music.[9] One reviewer of
the recording calls Ebb "an irrepressible performer" and quips, "one gets the feeling that
it would be necessary to attack him with bludgeons to get him *not* to perform a song." It
is telling of Ebb's performance that the same reviewer compares him to Al Jolson.[10] This
recording exemplifies the onstage relationship between Kander and Ebb. Ebb, who dominated their public performances, does all of the talking, introducing each song and entertaining the audience with personal reminiscences, as Kander sits quietly at the piano.

In 1976, Seth Glassman conceived and directed the first revue dedicated to Kander
and Ebb, *2 by 5*, which opened at the Village Gate Downstairs. The title alludes to the
two writers plus the two men and three women who constitute the cast. *2 by 5* is a cabaret entertainment featuring mainly Kander and Ebb's hit songs, with the singers sitting
around a piano located center stage and standing only to perform their songs. Glassman
also incorporated a couple of songs from Kander and Ebb's trunk, "Ten Percent" from
Chicago and "Military Man" from *Tango Mogador*. He made no effort to connect the
songs thematically or to provide any sort of narrative, preferring to let the music speak for
itself.

In the late seventies, Phyllis Newman, the wife of Adolph Green, asked several writers,
including Kander and Ebb, to contribute material for a one-woman musical that she and
Arthur Laurents were developing. *Mad Woman of Central Park West*, as the show was
eventually titled, belongs to the first wave of musicals dealing with feminist themes.[11] Newman created the show as a means to address the "many changes going on in society con-
cerning men, women and children."[12] It started out in 1979 at the Hudson Guild Theatre
under the title *My Mother Was a Fortune-Teller*. Kander and Ebb's contribution, "Cheer-

leader," was added the following year when Newman took the retitled version of the show to the Studio Arena Theater in Buffalo. "Cheerleader" is an edgy song about a woman who is so exhausted from seeking the approbation of everyone in her life that she stands on the brink of a nervous breakdown and is self-medicating herself into oblivion.[13]

Sam Found Out (1988)

In 1988, Liza Minnelli, still commanding a large following, starred in a television special called Sam Found Out, which consisted of three segments, each beginning with the line "Sam found out." Alexander Cohen, who co-produced the special with Ebb, came up with the gimmick of asking three different writers to create a play starting with the same line, originally suggesting "Somebody told Roy" but ultimately using "Sam found out." Minnelli played the main female role in all three segments, in each opposite a different male star. In the first segment, a drama by Lanford Wilson, Minnelli played an addict and prostitute who entraps her pimp, played by Ryan O'Neal. In the second, a comedy co-written by Terrence McNally and Wendy Wasserstein, she played a dance instructor who dates one of her dance-challenged students, played by Lou Gossett Jr. In the third segment, a mini musical comedy by Kander and Ebb, she played John Rubenstein's fiancée. Their marriage plans are threatened by her devotion to her dog, Sam, who does not approve of her choice of husband. When faced with deciding between Rubenstein and the canine, she chooses the latter. Kander and Ebb also wrote the opening number, in which Minnelli explains to the television audience what the special is all about. Cohen hoped to produce a second version of the special using the line "You've committed adultery," with August Wilson writing the drama, Neil Simon the comedy, and Cy Coleman, Betty Comden, and Adolf Green the musical. This second edition never materialized.

And the World Goes 'Round (1991)

Shortly after the revival of Flora, the Red Menace, Scott Ellis, Susan Stroman, and David Thompson brainstormed ideas for another Kander and Ebb project. They settled on a revue called And the World Goes 'Round, which premiered at the Whole Theater Company in Montclair, New Jersey, in 1989 and began an open-ended run in New York at the Westside Theatre in 1991. It was a solid hit and is still performed regularly around the country, having replaced 2 by 5 as the favorite Kander and Ebb revue. Unlike 2 by 5, whose nightclub formula was outdated by the nineties, And the World Goes 'Round is more than a string of Kander and Ebb hit songs. Ellis, Stroman, and Thompson devised smooth transitions between songs and paid close attention to the overall pacing. One of the musical highlights of the revue is a duet, arranged by the musical director David Loud, that combines "I Don't Remember You" from The Happy Time and "Sometimes a Day Goes By" from Woman of the Year. The New York production featured Karen Ziemba, whose rave reviews jump-started her career and who soon became the newest member of the Kander and Ebb "family." Ziemba later starred in Steel Pier, appeared in the Broadway revival of Chicago and several Kander and Ebb workshops, and starred in Curtains.

Miscellaneous Songs in the Eighties and Nineties

Throughout their career, Kander and Ebb continued to write specialty material for various occasions, such as the song "Oscar" for Minnelli to sing at the Forty-Fourth Annual Academy Awards ceremony in 1972 and "The Music Makers" for Minnelli and Dudley

Moore to sings at the sixtieth ceremony in 1988. In several instances, critics went out of their way to applaud these songs. For example, in 1984, Kander and Ebb wrote three songs for Hal Prince's unmemorable baseball revue called *Diamonds*:[14] the opening number, "Winter in New York," which celebrates the perennial arrival of the baseball season; the closing number, "Diamonds Are Forever"; and a third song, "Charge!," a story about a musical protégé who turns down several scholarships from conservatories in order to pursue his baseball interests and ends up playing organ at the ballpark. Theirs were the only songs that Frank Rich praised in an otherwise dismal review of the show. Rich also commended "No, My Heart," the song that Kander and Ebb wrote for the 1985 Broadway revival of Noël Coward's *Hay Fever*.[15]

Liza Minnelli's last major film appearance was in the 1991 movie *Stepping Out*, which is based on a stage comedy by the British playwright Richard Harris. Minnelli's role, Mavis, is an ex-performer, a dedicated dance instructor, and a survivor—in short, a quintessential Kander and Ebb character. Harris, who adapted his own play for the screen, transferred the action from London to Buffalo, which suited Minnelli's hard-boiled Mavis. Kander and Ebb wrote the song "Stepping Out," which Minnelli-Mavis and her amateur dance students perform at the end of the film (for the 1987 Broadway production, the director Tommy Tune used "Shaking the Blues Away"). Minnelli had featured "Stepping Out" a year earlier in one of her concerts.[16]

Notes

INTRODUCTION

1. A ceremony was held at the White House. A picture of Kander with Bill and Hillary Clinton is proudly displayed on the ground floor of his townhouse. Kander's medallion is hidden away on a tall shelf on the second floor next to his three Tony Awards. Ebb, who recounted the event glibly, exhibited the medallion and photograph in a prominent spot in his living room.

2. John Kander and Fred Ebb as told to Greg Lawrence, *Colored Lights: Forty Years of Words and Music, Show Biz, Collaboration, and All That Jazz* (New York: Faber and Faber, 2003).

3. Throughout this book, all of the quotations of Kander or Ebb without a citation are taken from the author's personal interviews with the writers.

4. Kander and Ebb can be seen performing live in concert on *Broadway & Hollywood Legends: The Songwriters: Alan Jay Lerner and Kander & Ebb*, Sonny Fox Productions LAN8036, DVD.

5. Ebb never turned down an occasion to perform these numbers. Once he even sang for a Republican-sponsored event, despite his Democratic affiliation, because it was being held at the Palace Theater. For this occasion Ebb had to hire a substitute pianist because Kander refused to accompany him.

6. Gerald Mast coined the term "metaphorical musical" (*Can't Help Singin': The American Musical on Stage and Screen* [Woodstock: The Overlook Press, 1987], 320). John Bush Jones prefers "fragmented musical" because it describes the fragmentation of the narrative and the modular structure (*Our Musicals, Ourselves: A Social History of the American Musical Theatre* [Hanover: Brandeis University Press, 2003], 269).

7. Scott McMillin, *The Musical as Drama: A Study of the Principles and Conventions Behind Musical Shows from Kern to Sondheim* (Princeton: Princeton University Press, 2006), 22.

8. Ibid., 25–30. McMillin invokes Brecht, who objected to the political and economic basis of musical theater, in explaining the dramatic potential of alternating between "book time" (spoken scenes) and "lyric time" (songs and dances).

9. Mast, *Can't Help Singin'*, 320.

10. Jesse Green, "What Good Is Sitting Alone in Your Room?," *New York Times*, 27 August 2006.

11. Steve Swayne, *How Sondheim Found His Sound* (Ann Arbor: University of Michigan Press, 2005), xv.

12. Other artists who worked with both Sondheim and Kander (and Ebb) include the designer Tony Walton, directors Alain Resnais and Susan Stroman, and playwrights Jules Feiffer, George Furth, and Hugh Wheeler. This list leaves out the countless performers who appeared in their musicals.

13. Terrence McNally, "An Operatic Mission: Freshen the Familiar," *New York Times*, 1 September 2002.

CHAPTER 1. Forty-Two Years of Musicals

1. Kander's paternal genealogy has been traced to as far back as 1774, the birth year of his great-great-grandfather, Herz Hirsh Kander. Herz lived in Karlsruhe, Baden. The composer's great-grandfather, Myer, the first Kander to come to America, settled in Baltimore.

2. For several decades, Ebb shared his apartment with his friend Ed Aldridge, but by all accounts they were never romantically involved. Aldridge was the stage manager for several of Kander and Ebb musicals, including *Cabaret*.

3. In an effort to interest Ebb in opera, Kander took him to *The Passion of Jonathan Wade* at New York City Opera. He knew that he had failed when he looked over and saw Ebb asleep. See Brian Kellow, "On the Beat," *Opera News*, 8 April 2006: 8.

4. John Kander and Fred Ebb as told to Greg Lawrence, *Colored Lights: Forty Years of Words and Music, Show Biz, Collaboration, and All That Jazz* (New York: Faber and Faber, 2003), 5 (hereinafter *Colored Lights*).

5. Records indicate that Kander scored "exceptionally high" on the pre-entry aptitude tests. He received a Visual Signaling Certificate with a ranking of proficient and achieved a speed of eight words per minute at semaphore, flashing light, and international code.

6. Margaret Ross Griffel, "Opera at Columbia: A Shining Legacy, *Current Musicology* 79 & 80 (2005): 111–12.

7. In an unpublished article that Ebb wrote in 1967 ("By Jupiter by Now") about the Off-Broadway revival of Rodgers and Hart's *By Jupiter*, for which he supplied additional lyrics, he claims to be thirty-five, which would confirm 1932 as the year of his birth. Corroborating this date is a 1963 newspaper article about Ebb's musical *Morning Sun*, which gives his age at the time as thirty-one (William Bender, "A Play with a Built-in Role," *New York Herald Tribune*, 19 June 1963). Ebb was never forthright with Kander about his age.

8. *Colored Lights*, 6.

9. Jim Caruso, "Well Said, Fred," *Theater Mania for Theater Everything*, 27 November 2001, http://www.theatermania.com/content/news.cfm/story/1793 (accessed 6 November 2006).

10. A movie version starring Sandra Dee and Jimmy Stewart was released in 1963.

11. *Colored Lights*, 21.

12. Ebb met Ballard in the fifties when she was working at the Bon Soir, a nightclub in Greenwich Village. She occasionally paid the struggling writer for special material. Ballard was with Ebb when he saw Liza Minnelli in her first musical, the 1963 Off-Broadway revival of *Best Foot Forward*. See Kaye Ballard with Jim Hesselman, *How I Lost 10 Pounds in 53 Years: A Memoir* (Boulder: Argent Books, 2004), 62–63.

13. The song lost to Leslie Bricusse and Anthony Newley's "What Kind of Fool Am I." "My Coloring Book" was covered by several other vocalists, including Barbra Streisand.

14. Marilyn Stasio, "The Difference Between Kander and Ebb," *American Theatre* 14 (1997): 13.

15. Frank Rich, "All the Best of Kander and Ebb," *New York Times*, 19 March 1991.

16. David Richards, "3 for the Show: Sounds of Music, Sounds of Battle," *New York Times*, 24 March 1991.

17. Unpublished interview with Jeffrey Scott Neuman, 25 June 1997. Neuman wrote his master's thesis on Kander and Ebb's use of vaudeville in *70, Girls, 70* and *Chicago*. I am grateful to him for sharing his research materials.

18. Ibid.

19. Ibid.

20. Jack Babuscio, "Camp and the Gay Sensibility," in *Camp Grounds: Style and Homosexuality*, ed. Davie Bergman (Amherst: University of Massachusetts Press, 1993), 24.

21. Mark Slobin, *Tenement Songs: The Popular Music of the Jewish Immigrants* (Urbana: University of Illinois Press, 1982), 182.

22. Al Kasha and Joel Hirschhorn, *Notes on Broadway: Conversations with the Great Songwriters* (Chicago: Contemporary Books, 1985), 97.

23. Ibid., 205.

24. Showtime Entertainment released a remastered version of *Liza with a Z!* on DVD in 2006. This "Collector's Edition" includes bonus features and the original soundtrack (Sony BMG Music Entertainment A681271).

25. The Yiddish word "Meeskite," which, according to the song lyric, means "ugly, funny-looking," is one of the few non-English words in *Cabaret*. Ebb used the word in an alternative punch line for "If You Could See Her Through My Eyes": "She isn't a Meeskite at all." Ebb's original line—"She wouldn't look Jewish at all"—incited protests and threats from Jewish leaders in Boston to boycott the show.

26. After Jack Gilford, the original Schultz, left the cast of *Cabaret*, "Meeskite" became less effective, and many contemporary productions of *Cabaret* forgo the song. Ebb, who, according to Kander, was the only other person able to effectively perform "Meeskite," approved of cutting the song because he felt that it slowed down the action.

27. While working on "Bobo's," Kander and Ebb received news that a good friend had committed suicide. Ebb insisted that they concentrate on the song in order to keep their minds off the tragedy.

28. John Kander, "Kander on Kern," *Stereo Review* 29 (1972): 50.

29. To commemorate the opening of *Woman of the Year*, Ron Melrose, the dance arranger for the musical, presented Kander with "Kander Vamp Medley," a compilation of the composer's vamps with the tempo indication of "just right."

30. Harold Bloom, *The Anxiety of Influence: A Theory of Poetry*, 2nd ed. (New York: Oxford University Press, 1997).

31. Although Thompson normally goes by the first name of Tommy, this book uses David, his professional name and the name appearing on his published scripts.

32. For a discussion of Kander and Ebb's incomplete and unproduced musicals see Chapter 8.

33. Andrea Most, *Making Americans: Jews and the Broadway Musical* (Cambridge: Harvard University Press, 2004), 10.

34. Robbins took pains to ensure that *Fiddler* not appear too ethnic. Hal Prince, who came to Jewish themes late in his career, has noted, "The show was a success because for non-Jews it wasn't Jewish: It was about family." See Abigail Pogrebin, *Stars of David: Prominent Jews Talk About Being Jewish* (New York: Broadway Books, 2005), 297.

35. "Irving Berlin, Eddie Cantor, Dorothy and Herbert Fields, George and Ira Gershwin, Oscar Hammerstein, Lorenz Hart and Richard Rodgers, Jerome Kern, Kurt Weill, George S. Kaufman, Moss Hart, Frank Loesser, Frederick Loewe, Alan Jay Lerner, Yip Harburg, Leonard Bernstein, Betty Comden, Adolph Green, Jerry Ross, Richard Adler, Jerry Bock, Sheldon Harnick, and Stephen Sondheim" (Most, *Making Americans*, 2). Loewe and Hammerstein were not raised Jewish, but they both had Jewish fathers. Hammerstein's first wife was Jewish, and there is no question of his support of Jewish causes.

36. *Colored Lights*, 5.

37. Pogrebin, *Stars of David*, 299; and private conversation.

38. Pogrebin, *Stars of David*, 299.

39. Stacy Wolf, *A Problem Like Maria: Gender and Sexuality in the American Musical, Triangulations* (Ann Arbor: The University of Michigan Press, 2002), 21.

40. John M. Clum, *Something for the Boys: Musical Theater and Gay Culture* (New York: St. Martin's, 1999), 2.

41. For an excellent study on this topic see Joseph Morella and George Mazzei, *Genius and Lust: The Creativity and Sexuality of Cole Porter and Noel Coward* (New York: Carroll and Graf, 1995).

42. Bruce Kirle, *Unfinished Show Business: Broadway Musicals as Works-in-Progress* (Carbondale: Southern Illinois University Press, 2005), 166.

43. Raymond Knapp, *The American Musical and the Formation of National Identity* (Princeton: Princeton University Press, 2005), 5.

44. Clum calls the mid 1960s "the last gasp of the diva musical" (*Something for the Boys*, 167).

45. Ibid., 197.

46. Knapp, *The American Musical*, 3.

CHAPTER 2. The Divinely Decadent Lives of *Cabaret*

1. Interview, *The News Hour*, PBS, 26 January 2005.

2. "Sally Bowles" was first published alone in 1937. Other stories were published in separate issues of John Lehmann's journal *New Writing*.

3. Antony Shuttleworth, "In a Populous City: Isherwood in the Thirties," in *The Isherwood Century: Essays on the Life and Work of Christopher Isherwood*, ed. James J. Berg and Chris Freeman (Madison: University of Wisconsin Press, 2000), 150.

4. John Van Druten, *I Am a Camera* (n.p., Dramatists Service Inc., 1951).

5. The *New York Times* review of the film called it "meretricious, insensitive, superficial and just plain cheap." The screenwriter for the film, John Collier, turned the stage play into "a Bohemian bedroom farce, barely recognizing that "Nazi hoodlums were then abroad." See Bosley Crowther, "I Am a Camera," *New York Times*, 9 August 1955.

6. Hal Prince, *Contradictions: Notes of Twenty-Six Years in the Theatre* (New York: Dodd, Mead, 1974), 134–35.

7. Linda K. Brengle, "Divine Decadence, Darling!: The Sixty-Year History of the Kit Kat Klub," *Journal of Popular Culture* 34 (2000): 152.

8. Scott McMillin, *The Musical as Drama: A Study of the Principles and Conventions Behind Musical Shows from Kern to Sondheim* (Princeton: Princeton University Press, 2006), 23.

9. One of Ebb's sketches lists a possible running order for the Berlin Songs: "Angel of Love," Two Ladies," "I Don't Care Much," "Tomorrow Belongs to Me," "Herman, My German," "A Mark in Your Pocket," "Yodelin," "Liebchen," Policeman," and "Bucher." Sketches exist for all of these titles except "Yodelin," "Policeman," and "Bucher." No music has been found for "A Mark in Your Pocket." Sketches also exist for a number of other Berlin Songs: "Berlin, Berlin, Berlin" (lyrics only), "A Little Geld" (alternatively titled "Good Neighbor Cohen")—which later supplied the melody for the new "Money Song" used in the film version of *Cabaret*—"Haven't They Ever," "Welcome to Berlin," and "This Life." Kander and Ebb interpolated "This Life" into *All About Us* (see Chapter 9), and they planned to use it for the film *Bye Bye Blues* (see Chapter 8).

10. A description on the music reads: "On the forestage, in a spotlight, a VERY FAT, BALD LITTLE MAN and TWO SEXY LADIES." In John Kander's studio hangs a painting of this very scene. The odd color choices and distorted figures evoke German Expressionistic painting.

11. Ibid., 134.

12. Prince, *Contradictions*, 126.

13. Harold Prince Papers, Billy Rose Theatre Collection, The New York Public Library for the Performing Arts. Masteroff used the name Ernst instead of Fritz.

14. Memo from Hal Prince to writers, 15 July 1966, John Kander Papers (*Cabaret* materials), Billy Rose Theatre Collection, The New York Public Library for the Performing Arts.

15. Prince, *Contradictions*, 125. Raymond Knapp, *The American Musical and the Formation of National Identity* (Princeton: Princeton University Press, 2005), 240.

16. Jack Babuscio, "Camp and the Gay Sensibility," in *Camp Grounds: Style and Homosexuality*, ed. Davie Bergman (Amherst: University of Massachusetts Press, 1993), 19.

17. Jonathan Dollimore, *Sexual Dissidence: Augustine to Wilde, Freud to Foucault* (Oxford: Clarendon, 1991), 311; as quoted in Dennis Denisoff, *Aestheticism and Sexual Parody 1840–1940*, Cambridge Studies in Nineteenth-Century Literature and Culture, no. 31 (Cambridge: Cambridge University Press, 2001), 123.

18. Al LaValley, "The Great Escape," *American Film* 10.6 (April 1985): 31.

19. Brett Farmer, *Spectacular Passions: Cinema, Fantasy, Gay Male Spectatorships* (Durham: Duke University Press, 2000), 111.

20. Although there have been other excellent portrayals of Sally—for example, by

Judi Dench and Natasha Richardson—Minnelli remains closely associated with the part, if only because of the international reach of film.

21. Andrew Britton, *Katharine Hepburn: Star as Feminist* (London: Studio Vista, 1995), 87; as quoted in Farmer, *Spectacular Passions*, 112.

22. Christopher Isherwood, *The World in the Evening*, 125; as quoted in Denisoff, *Aestheticism and Sexual Parody 1840–1940*, 135.

23. An earlier version of the ending reads: "We have a couple of problems / Which I am cognizant of / She's tall, you can tell / And she's Jewish as well / But if you could see her through my eyes / You'd know why I'm madly in Love!"

24. Bruce Kirle, *Unfinished Show Business: Broadway Musicals as Works-in-Progress* (Carbondale: Southern Illinois University Press, 2005), 117.

25. Denisoff, *Aestheticism and Sexual Parody 1840–1940*, 135.

26. Joseph Bristow, "'I Am with You, Little Minority Sister': Isherwood's Queer Sixties," in *The Queer Sixties*, ed. Patricia Juliana Smith (New York: Routledge, 1999), 147.

27. Shuttleworth, "In a Populous City: Isherwood in the Thirties," 159.

28. Some Germans who saw *Cabaret* on Broadway swore that they recalled hearing the song in Germany when the Nazis were in power (John Kander and Fred Ebb as told to Greg Lawrence, *Colored Lights: Forty Years of Words and Music, Show Biz, Collaboration, and All That Jazz* [New York: Faber and Faber, 2003], 64 [hereinafter *Colored Lights*]). Many people said the same thing about "Edelweiss" from *The Sound of Music*.

29. Friedrich Hollaender, *Schall und Rauch: Lieder und Chansons des gleichnamigen Berliner Kabaretts aus der Zeit nach dem 1. Weltkrieg* (Mainz: Schott, 1983), 6–9.

30. *Colored Lights*, 69.

31. The 6th scale degree is also the primary pitch of "The Ballad of Mack the Knife."

32. Raymond Knapp points out that "Tomorrow Belongs to Me" is stylistically a Siciliano, a folk dance connected with the pastorale: "The natural images are from the beginning as specifically German as possible (stag, forest, linden tree, Rhine) while generically pastoral in their clichéd evocations of meadow and storm" (*The American Musical and the Formation of National Identity* [Princeton: Princeton University Press, 2005], 246). The dance is transformed into the type of waltz one would hear at a German Beirgarten, the setting for the song in the film.

33. By 1930 Tauber, a popular Austrian tenor, was beyond his prime.

34. Kander considers this song a cheap attempt at humor and was not sorry to see it cut permanently. Ethan Mordden suggests that this number was meant to evoke Claire Waldoff's song "Hermann Hesst Er," a send-up of Hermann Göring, but Kander denies that this was the case (Mordden, *Open a New Window: The Broadway Musical in the 1960s* [New York: Palgrave, 2001], 153).

35. A different version found among Ebb's papers reads: "I once had a liebchen in Berlin / Throw me the key down 920 / Threw down the key and she asked me in (cho[rus]) / Climbed up the stair to my liebchen's place / Opened the door to her husband's face."

36. Only the lyric has been identified.

37. This song was contemplated for the male patrons at a bar.

38. One sketch of this song is titled "That Pair in the Mirror."

39. McMillin, *The Musical as Drama*, 184.

40. Judith Butler, *Gender Trouble*, 10th ed. (London: Routledge, 1999), 171–80.

41. Suzanne G. Cusick, "On Musical Performances of Gender and Sex," in *Audible Traces: Gender, Identity, and Music*, ed. Elaine Barkin (Zurich: Carciofoli Verlagshaus, 1999), 25–49.

42. This attitude helps to explain why in America today most men reject singing while renegotiating their voices during adolescence. The term "ideology of separate spheres" refers to the nineteenth-century belief in intrinsic differences separating men and women.

43. With the exception of the Baroque castrato, male singing as it relates to gender and sexuality has received little critical attention, as opposed to female singing, which has generated a great deal of literature.

44. A related but different example of characterization through singing is found in *My Fair Lady*. The lack of sustained vocalization of Henry Higgins, another exception to the typical musical theater romantic lead, is not only a contrast to Eliza's exuberant singing, as Raymond Knapp has noted ("Henry Higgins can talk but can't sing, and Eliza can sing but can't talk"), but also expresses a sexual identity that is not yet fully matured or acknowledged, which, given his and Pickering's "shared domestic situation," creates a degree of ambiguity. See Knapp, *The American Musical and the Performance of Personal Identity*, 286–90.

45. Marty Baum acquired the film rights to *Cabaret* after seeing a performance of the last road company in Seattle, and he hired Cy Feuer to produce it. See Cy Feuer with Ken Gross, *I Got the Show Right Here: The Amazing, True Story of How an Obscure Brooklyn Horn Player Became the Last Great Broadway Showman: Producer of Guys & Dolls, How to Succeed in Business Without Really Trying, Can-Can, and Many, Many More Legendary Shows* (New York: Simon and Schuster, 2003), 243.

46. Stephen E. Bowles, "*Cabaret* and Nashville: The Musical as Social Comment," *Journal of Popular Culture* 12 (1978): 552.

47. Hugh Wheeler also worked on the final version of the screenplay. See Randy Clark, "Bending the Genre: The Stage and Screen Versions of *Cabaret*," *Literature Film Quarterly* 19 (1991): 51.

48. Mitchell Morris, "*Cabaret*, America's Weimar, and Mythologies of the Gay Subject," *American Music* 22 (2004): 147. My discussion of the film is based on an early version of the screenplay (John Kander's papers).

49. Feuer, *I Got the Show Right Here*, 24.

50. Max comes with a fascinating backstory: his grandfather acquired land in Argentina in order to grow grapes. There is a moment in the story when Max feels impelled to defend his wealth to Brian: "He [my grandfather] did not foresee the time when it would be a great convenience to have a bit of foreign reserve." Max also flew in the German Luftwaffe during World War I, and he tells Brian, "I was terrified of being killed . . . nor had I the faintest ambition to kill Englishmen . . . the French . . . but always I have had this penchant for Englishmen."

51. Bowles, "*Cabaret* and Nashville," 552.

52. Clark, "Bending the Genre," 58.

53. The choppy cross-cutting reflects the disconnection between Sally's life and her stage persona. The final song, "Cabaret," achieves a similar effect. Sally sings "Cabaret" as Brian's train pulls out of station. Brian can be seen mouthing the opening strains of "Willkommen." This image comes from the ending of the stage version, during which

Cliff, sitting in his train compartment with pen and notebook in hand, sings "Willkommen." (Sally performs "Cabaret" a couple of scenes earlier.) He has begun to write the
novel that will become the source of *Cabaret*. Suddenly, though, the emcee appears and
joins Cliff in singing "Willkommen." By the end of the song, the emcee is alone except
for the theater audience, who, as McMillin notes, "sees itself in the place of Nazi spectators" (*The Musical as Drama*, 207). The discomforting effect is magnified by Boris Aronson's giant mirror, in which the audience can see their reflection. As the reprise of "Willkommen" suggests, in his last appearance, Cliff is like the emcee, "who always seems
to know what is going on inside and outside the cabaret even as he seems to remain
detached from it." This parallel, along with the final seconds in which the audience is left
by themselves in the theater/cabaret, illustrates the musical's message that "one cannot
enter into the cabaret, a metaphor for Nazism on the rise, and then leave it behind as
though one were free of the experience," and makes the audience "recognize that [their]
own attendance at the cabaret has the same political implications Cliff discovered"
(201–2). The end of Fosse's movie is similar.

54. Kander and Ebb had not anticipated the degree to which Fosse transformed the
musical, but they admired his vision for the film.

55. Morris, "*Cabaret*, America's Weimar, and Mythologies of the Gay Subject," 150–
51.

56. As Morris notes in "*Cabaret*, America's Weimar, and Mythologies of the Gay
Subject," "a rhetoric of authenticity" swirled around the promotion of the film (149).

57. Ibid., 148.

58. Letter from Hal Prince to Kander and Ebb, 23 May 1986.

59. Frank Rich, *New York Times*, 23 October 1987.

60. Alan Cumming appeared as the emcee and Jane Horrocks as Sally Bowles.

61. The trombonist and arranger Michael Gibson became Kander's principal orchestrator starting with *Woman of the Year* (1981). Before 1981, Kander had worked primarily
with Don Walker and Ralph Burns (Robert Ginzler did the orchestra arrangements for
A Family Affair), who were the personification of professionalism but less collaborative
than Gibson. Kander and Gibson developed a special working relationship, and, after
Gibson's death from cancer in 2005, Kander put off choosing a replacement as long as
possible, finally hiring William David Brohn, whom Gibson had suggested as his possible
successor, just months before *Curtains* went into rehearsals in 2006.

62. Gibson devised a flexible orchestration that could accommodate the various
musical skills of the actors who came into the production during its run (as well as in the
future).

63. John Bush Jones, *Our Musicals, Ourselves: A Social History of the American
Musical Theatre* (Hanover: Brandeis University Press, 2003), 343.

64. Roger Copeland, "Cabaret at the End of the World," *American Theatre* 16
(1999): 90.

65. Linda Sunshine, "Introduction," in Joe Masteroff, *Cabaret: The Illustrated Book
and Lyrics* (New York: Newmarket, 1999), 13.

66. Copeland, "Cabaret at the End of the World," 26.

67. Sunshine, "Introduction," 13–14.

68. Copeland, "Cabaret at the End of the World," 25–26.

69. Ibid.

70. Ibid.

71. Jones, *Our Musicals, Ourselves*, 345.

72. Renaud Machart, "Un 'Cabaret' vif et impeccable," *Le Monde*, 30 October 2006.

CHAPTER 3. *Chicago*

Epigraph. Ethan Mordden, *Broadway Babies* (New York: Oxford University Press, 1983), 175.

1. Louis Calta, "Gwen Verdon to Star in Musical Revival of 'Chicago,'" *New York Times*, 6 December 1972.

2. Thomas H. Pauly, introduction to Maurine Watkins, *Chicago* (Carbondale: Southern Illinois University Press, 1997), xv.

3. Ibid., xxiv.

4. Maurine Watkins, *Chicago* (Carbondale: Southern Illinois University Press, 1997), 38.

5. The Ginger Rogers film might have also influence Ebb's decision to use a vaudeville concept. In the film Fred Casely, Roxie's murder victim, is half of a two-person theatrical agency, and she shoots him because he refuses to take her on as a client. Before Roxie is hauled off to prison, Casely's partner shows up at her apartment to sign her as a client, and Jake, a photographer, wastes no time in turning her case into a cause célèbre. Roxie is not the killer, but she agrees to take the rap when she realizes that the publicity will boost her chances for a career in show business. Amos is the real killer, and his confession at the end of the film steals the spotlight away from Roxie. Ebb originally wanted to incorporate this idea.

6. Jeffrey Scott Neuman, "'And That's Show Biz, Kid': Self-Referential Theatricality in the Musicals of John Kander and Fred Ebb," (master's thesis, University of Colorado–Boulder, 1998), 51–52.

7. Lionel Abel, *Metatheatre: A New View of Dramatic Form* (New York: Hill and Wang, 1963).

8. Richard Hornby, *Drama, Metadrama, and Perception* (Lewisburg: Bucknell University Press), 31–118.

9. Neuman's use of the term "performative reiteration" in reference to Kander and Ebb's musicals is based on a concept from Judith Butler's discussion of gender. See Neuman, "'And That's Show Biz, Kid,'" 65. Butler uses the term to argue that gender is something constructed through repetitive performance. See Chapter 2, note 41.

10. Neuman, "'And That's Show Biz, Kid,'" 88.

11. Arnold Shaw, *The Jazz Age* (New York: Oxford University Press, 1987), 167.

12. Nicholas E. Tawa, *The Way to Tin Pan Alley* (New York: Schirmer, 1990), 64.

13. One of Ebb's earlier drafts includes a scene involving a knife-throwing act.

14. In fact, some critics misidentified some of the vaudeville references. For instance, one thought that the model for "Mister Cellophane" was the emasculated professor of *The Blue Angel*, and another suggested that it was Ted Lewis, whose rendition of "Me and My Shadow" was well known. See Neuman, "'And That's Show Biz, Kid,'" 87.

15. Neuman, "'And That's Show Biz, Kid,'" 65–78.

16. Kander and Ebb wrote three versions of "We Both Reached for the Gun." The first one includes a group of nuns, who, as manipulated by Billy, create a diversion dur-

ing Roxie's first interview with the reporters. The following is just one of many colorful verses that Ebb wrote for this version: "Gather 'round me chillun / And I'll tell you 'bout the killin' / Of that South Side stud Sylvester Belvedere[.] / He just left me home one evening[,] / Said 'I'm going 'round the corner / Just to get myself a pig foot and a beer'[.] / Well now, 'near a month went by / Fore he come knockin' saying 'Hi' / Oh babe, that dinner was delicious, doncha know / I ran upside his [h]ead / And then, of course, I shot him dead / Cause honey, no one in the world could eat that slow!" The second version of the song is a waltz.

17. James Winston Challender, *The Function of the Choreographer in the Develop-ment of the Conceptual Musical: An Examination of the Work of Jerome Robbins, Bob Fosse, and Michael Bennett on Broadway Between 1944 and 1981*, Ph.D. diss., Florida State University, 1986, 247.

18. Martin Gottfried, *Broadway Musicals* (New York: H. N. Abrams, 1979), 342.

19. John Kander and Fred Ebb as told to Greg Lawrence, *Colored Lights: Forty Years of Words and Music, Show Biz, Collaboration, and All That Jazz* (New York: Faber and Faber, 2003), 120 (hereinafter *Colored Lights*).

20. As quoted in Gottfried, *Broadway Musicals*, 336.

21. Interview with Chita Rivera, 13 June 2005.

22. Ghosts of these supernumeraries later circled around Roxie when she sang "I Am My Own Best Friend."

23. Kander and Ebb's rendition of "Loopin' the Loop" is included on *Chicago: The Musical*, Tenth Anniversary Edition, Sony BMG, 82876–89784–2 (2006). Ben Bagley's *Contemporary Broadway Revisited* (PSCD-131) includes a rendition of "Ten Percent" by Mark Sendroff and of "Loopin' the Loop" by Susan Stroman and Jan Newberger, both recorded with full orchestra; and *Lost in Boston I* (Varese Sarabande, VSD/VSC-5475) contains a performance of "Ten Percent" by Harry Groener, also with full orchestra. Kander and Ebb tried unsuccessfully to place "It" into the film of *Chicago*.

24. Burns's orchestrations for *Chicago* are unmatched. He fashioned an authentic-sounding twenties jazz band featuring muted trombones, saxophones, two pianos, tuba, banjo, and even solo violin. Chita Rivera, a great admirer of Burns's work recalled, "He was so smart, so hot, so bad, so naughty. He was rich."

25. As can be heard on recordings of the musical, *Chicago* begins with the sounds of a muted trombone solo. The unaccompanied melody is the opening phrase of "All that Jazz." The conductor's count-off ("a 5, 6, 7, 8") kicks off the band in an upbeat rendition of "Loopin' the Loop."

26. Stephen Farber, "Stage View," *New York Times*, 3 August, 1975.

27. Cline Barnes, *New York Times*, 4 June 1975.

28. Clive Barnes, "Liza Minnelli Lends Talents to 'Chicago,'" *New York Times*, 15 August 1975.

29. Several songs incorporate the flatted third during the final cadence of the refrain: "All That Jazz," "We Both Reached for the Gun," "Roxie," "I Can't Do it Alone," "I Know a Girl," "Mister Cellophane," and "When Velma Takes the Stand."

30. Edward A. Berlin, *Ragtime: A Musical and Cultural History* (Berkeley: Univer-sity of California Press, 1980), 130.

31. Measure 5 of the A section contains the seeds for the secondary rag motive of the B section.

32. Mark Slobin, *Tenement Songs: The Popular Music of the Jewish Immigrant* (Urbana: University of Illinois Press, 1982), 184.

33. Jack Gottlieb, *Funny, It Doesn't Sound Jewish: How Yiddish Songs and Synagogue Melodies Influenced Tin Pan Alley, Broadway, and Hollywood*, Modern Jewish Literature and Culture, ed. Sarah Blacher Cohen (n.p., SUNY Press, 2004), 107–8. Gottlieb uses the label "Yinglish" to describe such songs and to emphasize the fact that they were written and performed expressly for non-Jewish audiences. Whereas Yinglish songs usually feature a verse in the minor key and a refrain in the major key, Yiddish songs remain in the minor key throughout.

34. Samson Raphelson, preface to *The Jazz Singer*, as quoted in Jeffrey Melnick, *A Right to Sing the Blues: African Americans, Jews, and American Popular Song* (Cambridge: Harvard University Press), 103.

35. *Colored Lights*, 139.

36. The film received thirteen Oscar nominations and won in eight categories: performance by an actress in a supporting role, art direction, cinematography, costume design, directing, film editing, sound, and motion picture of the year.

37. McMillin, *The Musical as Drama: A Study of the Principles and Conventions Behind Musical Shows from Kern to Sondheim* (Princeton: Princeton University Press, 2006), 174.

38. Don Shewey, "The New Season/Movies; It Ought to Be a Movie, They Said, and Said . . . ," *New York Times*, 8 September 2002.

39. At one point, word spread that Hawn and Minnelli were going to co-star as Roxie and Velma, respectively.

40. Richards had already thought of the possibility of presenting musical numbers in Roxie's imagination. In a memo regarding Gelbart's first screenplay, he suggested that "Roxie can be told by Billy early in the script to start thinking of her life as a movie . . . a big musical movie. Her musical fantasies can take her (and us) anywhere" (copy of memo to Harvey Weinstein, 15 September 1995, John Kander's papers).

41. See Gillian B. Anderson, Thomas L. Riis, and Ronald H. Sadoff, introduction to *American Music* 22 (2004): 4.

42. Randy Clark, "Bending the Genre: The Stage and Screen Versions of *Cabaret*," *Literature Film Quarterly* 19 (1991): 54.

43. McMillin, *The Musical as Drama*, 177.

44. Gelbart also subordinated Velma to Roxie and played down their contentious relationship. Instead of teaming up with Velma at the end of the film, Roxie works solo, starring in a movie of her life called *The Roxie Hart Story*. Early in the musical, "All That Jazz," which is no longer Velma's song, underscores a long segment illustrating Roxie's backstory. She married Amos—whom Gelbart thought of more as a "big slob" along the lines of John Goodman than as a "nebbish"—to escape from her oppressive father, only to find that she merely substituted one lousy situation with an even worse one. These episodes explain why Roxie eventually found herself in an extramarital relationship with a vacuum cleaner salesman. As her affair progresses, Roxie sings a reprise of "Nowadays."

45. Billy also serves as Roxie's business manager.

46. They also experimented with a variety of comic vaudeville routines, such as "The Doctor Is In," which Roxie imagines when she undergoes a physical examination to de-

termine if she is really pregnant: Velma plays a nurse, and the leering doctor has a bushy mustache. Roxie, appearing exaggeratedly buxom, rushes onto the stage jiggling, accompanied by "a filthy BOOM-BOOM from the drummer." After being chased around the stage, Roxie stops and says, "Please, Doctor. I need an examination." The doctor replies, "So will I, if you don't stop running away." A suggestive shadow play acted out behind a curtain follows—similar to the one that Rob Marshall used for "Two Ladies" in the 1998 revival of *Cabaret*. Velma pulls back the curtain to reveal that all Roxie has in her mouth is a gigantic thermometer. As the imaginary world slowly dissolves, the real world takes over. To elicit one final guffaw, the stage doctor hits a meter that measures Roxie's pregnancy: "It lights up and a rabbit falls on Velma's head. Honk honk." "Me and My Baby" was to have immediately followed this vignette.

47. Hugh Jackman was also mentioned as a possibility (Rick Lyman, "Movie Musical's Hard-Won Harmony; 'Chicago' Is a Hit, but Its Path to the Oscars Was Paved with Feuds," *New York Times*, 19 March 2003).

48. Raymond Knapp, *The American Musical and the Performance of Personal Identity* (Princeton: Princeton University Press, 2006), 111.

49. *Colored Lights*, 213.

50. The lyric of "I Move On" expresses a familiar Ebbian point of view about surviving in a mean world. The instrumental break between the bridge and the final A section contains ricochet triplet rim shots imitative of a machine gun. Marshall incorporated these rim shots into "The Honey Rag." Kander and Ebb wrote two other numbers, "It's a Criminal Thing" and "In Other Words Chicago," before settling on "I Move On. All three songs feature the 6th scale degree as the primary pitch. The lyric of "It's a Criminal Thing" equates romance with cliché criminal speak—"now I'm confessing," "I'll serve my time." As he did in "All That Jazz," Ebb fills the lyric with historical references, such as "Charlie's wife is back in Burlesque," "Shimmy-ing around the Hancock Tower," and "In the town O'Leary's cow once set off."

51. There is one moment in the film that is intended to solicit audience sympathy for Roxie: as Morton slams the heavy steel door on her cell for the first time, the camera moves in on Renée Zellweger. In total isolation and unobserved by any other human being, she appears genuinely frightened and vulnerable.

52. Lyman, "Movie Musical's Hard-Won Harmony." Marty Richards is currently working on a musical adaptation of Woody Allen's *Bullets over Broadway* with Rob Marshall, Bill Condon, and Marvin Hamlisch.

CHAPTER 4. Fred Without John and John Without Fred

1. Apart from feeling intimidated by the prospect of working directly with Rodgers, Ebb did not care for the premise for *Rex*.

2. One minor exception is a children's musical called *Adelie Penguin* (see below).

3. These belong to a collection that Ebb labeled "Verses from a Point of View."

4. Two songs once listed on Charles Strouse's Web site are apparently incorrect (http://www.charlesstrouse.com/collaborator.html).

5. Trinity Music paid Ebb and Klein a weekly salary to keep them on as staff writers. See Jonathan Klein, "Morning Sun, the Making of a Musical" (5/20/83), Fred Ebb

Papers (Box 98, folder 10), Billy Rose Theatre Collection, New York Public Library for the Performing Arts (hereinafter Fred Ebb Papers).

6. "That Do Make It Nice," The Hudson Bay Music Co., 1955. Best-selling record by Eddy Arnold (RCA Victor).

7. *Isn't America Fun.*

8. On the recording Ebb is heard addressing a certain Carol, for whom the recording was intended. It also contains "The Revolution Is Late."

9. At Tamiment the song was performed by four women, three models, and a seamstress.

10. Howard Taubman, "Topical Revue," *New York Times,* 14 May 1963.

11. Thompson wrote the libretto for *Once Upon a Mattress* (1959) and *Thoroughly Modern Millie* (2002). Around 1963 Ebb and Thompson wrote *How to Be Thoroughly Unpleasant,* a humorous how-to booklet on misanthropy. The book was published in 1965 with cartoon illustrations by Sandy Hoffman: Fred Ebb and Jay Thompson, *How to Be Thoroughly Unpleasant* (New York: Kanrom, 1965).

12. It is unclear whether this skit was ever performed.

13. Ebb and Klein wrote a similar skit called "Four in Hand," which takes place during a rehearsal of a television show. It featured Kaye Ballard, Harold Lang, Larry Storch, and Faye de Witt.

14. The description of the director ("English to the teeth . . . It is highly doubtful that even his mother loved him") anticipates the role of the director in *Curtains.*

15. Mary Deasy, "Morning Sun," *The Virginia Quarterly Review* (Summer, 1952): 402–16; reprinted in *The Best American Short Stories 1953 and The Yearbook of the American Short Story,* ed. Martha Foley (Boston: Ballantine, 1953), 106–18. Deasy is the dedicatee of the volume.

16. William Bender, "A Play with a Built-in Role," *New York Herald Tribune,* 19 June 1963.

17. According to Jonathan Klein, Paul's son, at some point in the fifties his father and Ebb met with Carol Burnett, Rosalind Russell, and Betty Davis to discuss ideas for projects, but nothing came of these meetings.

18. Tahse produced several national tours of Broadway shows and was behind the ABC After School Specials.

19. The script contains several allusions to Lewis Carroll's novel, and some of the titles of scenes in the script match chapter titles of the book, such as "Down the Rabbit Hole" and "A Mad Tea Party." "Tweedle-Dum or Tweedle-Dee" is a reference to *Through the Looking Glass.*

20. Lyric sheets exist for four other songs: "Live a Little," "Such a Business," "Lead Balloon," and "Jabberwocky." Except for "Live a Little," these songs are listed in the 1964 script.

21. Ethan Mordden, *Open a New Window: The Broadway Musical in the 1960s* (New York: Palgrave, 2001), 175 and 177.

22. This list of song titles and the running order are taken directly from the original program (Showcard). The nonvocal musical numbers, which are mostly dances, inside brackets appear in Ebb's script but not in the program.

23. Musical theater scholars have used the term "wanting song" to describe a num-

ber that establishes a character's dramatic motivation. Eliza Doolittle's "Wouldn't It Be Loverly" from *My Fair Lady* is an example.

24. In his review Taubman cites this number for its effectiveness.

25. Howard Taubman, *New York Times*, 7 October 1963.

26. Gene Palatsky, "'Morning Sun' Off the Beam," *New York Evening News*, 7 October 1963.

27. Norman Nadel, *New York World Telegram and Sun*, 7 October 1963.

28. Maxine Kietm, WNYC.

29. Letter from Richard Rodgers to Mrs. Klein, 22 October 1963, Fred Ebb Papers.

30. Dialogue with Liza Minnelli, Fred Ebb, and John Kander (1974), Theatre on Film and Tape Archive, New York Public Library for the Performing Arts.

31. George Gent, "Liza Minnelli Is Given a Special by N.B.C.," *New York Times*, 30 March 1970. This review does not mention Ebb's association with the special.

32. Alessandra Stanley, "Broadway Baby, Resurrected, at 26," *New York Times*, 31 March 2006.

33. Anthony Newley joined Liza in the vaudeville segment, which featured "A Certain Girl" from Kander and Ebb's *The Happy Time*. The next segment imagined Broadway "In the Year 2525" and featured songs by Randy Newman and Jimmy Webb. Minnelli also sang "Maybe This Time," which she claimed (falsely) was written for her.

34. Stanley, "Broadway Baby, Resurrected."

35. Ebb wrote Minnelli's first club act, which premiered in 1965 at the Shoreham Hotel in Washington, D.C. He also wrote and directed *Liza Minnelli Live from Radio City Music Hall* (1993), *Minnelli on Minnelli* (1999), and *Liza's Back* (2002), all of which included new special material by Kander and Ebb.

36. Howard Thompson, "Frank Sinatra Returns in Lively N.B.C. Show," *New York Times*, 19 November 1973.

37. Several years later, Psacharopoulos asked Kander to compose incidental music for a production of *Peer Gynt* that he was directing at Yale University. Kander wrote a lengthy score for oboe and string orchestra. Psacharopoulos ultimately decided not to use the new music, but he failed to inform Kander of his decision until after the composer had traveled from New York to New Haven to see a performance. Their friendship survived, but the slight tested Kander's capacity for forgiveness. He recalled, "I rewrote the score for trumpet and waste basket. . . . I could have killed him."

38. Geraldine never listened to dirty jokes, drank bourbon, nor swam naked, but, as the text boldly exclaims, "Virtue is its own reward." Kander conveys the sentiment of the text with two dry recitative sections supported by piano tremolos.

39. Private interview.

40. The 1936 film version of *Winterset*, starring Burgess Meredith, ends less tragically, with Trock being accidentally killed by his henchman, who mistakes him for Mio.

41. Maxwell Anderson, *Winterset* (Washington: Anderson House, 1935), v–xi.

42. A draft of the libretto is labeled "An Untitled Grotesque in One Act."

43. One of Goldman's scripts has a 1964 copyright, but it probably dates from the late fifties.

44. Jean Giraudoux, *The Enchanted*, adapted by Maurice Valency (New York: Random House, 1950). The new title was used in order to avoid confusion with Noel Cow-

ard's *Intermezzo*. The original French version of the play appeared briefly on Broadway in 1957.

45. Brooks Atkinson, "'The Enchanted' by Giraudoux Put On at the Lyceum in Valency's Adaptation," *New York Times*, 19 January 1950.

46. Maurice Valency, "Bellac, France: Giraudoux Viewed Life and the World from the Town of His Birth," *New York Times*, 15 January 1950.

47. Wood represented Maurice Valency, who did the English translation for the Broadway production and owned the American rights.

48. The California Playhouse produced *A Family Affair* in 1963 and used different billing, crediting Kander with the music, Kander and James Goldman with the lyrics, and James and William Goldman with the book.

49. Hal Prince, *Contradictions: Notes of Twenty-Six Years in the Theatre* (New York: Dodd, Mead, 1974), 87.

50. Ibid., 88.

51. Howard Taubman, *New York Times*, 29 January 1962.

52. The overture on the original Broadway cast recording is different from the one used in the theater, but both are conventional medleys of several tunes from the score.

53. Robert Jones, "'A Family Affair,'" *The American Record Guide* (April 1962): 622.

54. The cutout song "Mamie in the Afternoon" describes Alfie's sexual exploits. Perhaps it was too explicit for 1962. Kander and Ebb refashioned the song as "Arthur in the Afternoon" for Liza Minnelli to sing in *The Act*.

55. Lillie hired Kander "first for his good looks and secondarily because he could play piano." See Bruce Laffey, *Beatrice Lillie: The Funniest Woman in the World* (New York: Wynwood, 1989), 187.

56. Theodore Taylor, *Jule: The Story of Composer Jule Styne* (New York: Random House, 1979), 213.

57. The music for *Irma la Douce* is by Marguerite Monnot, and the lyrics and book are by Alexandre Breffort (English lyrics and book by Julian More, David Heneker, and Monry Norman).

58. In his a one-man autobiographical act called *Naked on Broadway*, Rogers includes two of the songs he wrote with Kander, "Don't Move" and "I'll Never See That One Again."

59. Beebe's reputation as a composer rests on his choral music and church musicals. He also wrote the an Off-Broadway revue called *Tuscaloosa's Calling Me* (1975) and the 1977 revival of *Hellzapoppin!*, which closed prematurely in Boston.

60. According to the script, the documentary was to open in darkness. The first sound heard, a banjo, corresponds to a red splash, which is slowly revealed to be the forge in Rockwell's painting of a blacksmith's shop. This opening was eventually replaced with a shot of Rockwell's easel and brushes underscored by Kander and Ebb's "Faces."

61. Tony Walton created the talking animated feline for *Woman of the Year*.

62. *Classical Broadway*, Bay Cities BCD 1038.

63. Mediant relationships also figure in the overall key structure of the cycle: G–C–E-flat (C–G–E-flat on the recorded version).

64. Ned Rorem received the award the previous year.

65. John Kander, *Three Poems by Lucile Adler* (New York: Fiddleback Music, 1987);

A Letter from Sullivan Ballou (New York: Warner Bros., 1999). Male singers, including Brian D'Arcy James, have also performed "Letter to Sullivan Ballou."

66. This production included a new song by Jerry Bock and Sheldon Harnick called "Isms" and the British Music Hall novelty number "The Wibbly Wobbly Walk."

CHAPTER 5. *Kiss of the Spider Woman*

Epigraph: John M. Clum, *Something for the Boys: Musical Theater and Gay Culture* (New York: St. Martin's Press, 1999), 188.

1. Brett Farmer, *Spectacular Passions: Cinema, Fantasy, Gay Male Spectatorships* (Durham: Duke University Press, 2000), 24.

2. Norman Lavers, *Pop Culture into Art: The Novels of Manuel Puig*, Literary Frontiers Edition, no. 31 (Columbia: University of Missouri Press, 1988), 38.

3. John Kander and Fred Ebb as told to Greg Lawrence, *Colored Lights: Forty Years of Words and Music, Show Biz, Collaboration, and All That Jazz* (New York: Faber and Faber, 2003), 8 (hereinafter *Colored Lights*).

4. Fred Ebb Papers, Billy Rose Theatre Collection, New York Public Library for the Performing Arts.

5. Puig used the *Panther Lady* segment from his novel. The play was first produced in Spain and Brazil, and then in London in an English translation by Allan Baker.

6. Letter from Manuel Puig to Hal Prince, Rio de Janeiro, 21 December 1986, Fred Ebb Papers (Box 65, folder 10), Billy Rose Theatre Collection, New York Public Library for the Performing Arts (hereinafter Fred Ebb Papers).

7. Puig liked his handling of Marta and Molina's mother. They appear only once as themselves, but they remain a presence throughout, for they were to be played by the same actresses who play the major roles in the movie fantasy. Letter from Manuel Puig to Hal Prince, Rio de Janeiro, 24 February 1987.

8. Communication with Prince, November 2007.

9. Kander and Ebb had tried to interpolate "Military Man," a song with a long history, into this spot (see Chapter 9).

10. McNally considered a couple of different endings for the Hollywood film. In one, Armando is shot and killed by one of the Monster's henchman, and in the other Aurora takes the bullet in order to save Armando, not unlike Puig's second scenario for the inner musical.

11. David Román and Alberto Sandoval, "Caught in the Web: Latinidad, AIDS, and Allegory in *Kiss of the Spider Woman, the Musical*," *American Literature: A Journal of Literary History, Criticism, and Bibliography* 67, no. 3 (1995): 557.

12. In Puig's novel, Molina's death occurs when, as authorities are about to arrest him, he is silenced by gunshots fired from a passing car carrying members of the resistance.

13. In order to create a certain degree of ambiguity for the reader, Puig does not identify which character is speaking.

14. Mira Wiegmann, "Re-visioning the Spider Woman Archetype in *Kiss of the Spider Woman*," *Journal of Analytical Psychology* 49 (2004): 397–412.

15. Ibid., 399.

16. Ibid., 401.

17. Ibid., 406.

18. In McNally's first draft, the Spider Woman urges Molina to tell Valentin about her movie, *The Kiss of the Spider Woman*. When he claims to have forgotten it, the Spider Woman taunts him: "I haven't! A little boy and his mother in the balcony of the Cinema Goya, a Thursday matinee. He should have been in school. She let him play hooky . . . A beautiful woman in a strong spotlight. Silver lame that fits her life a glove . . . She's earning a mask, it's also silver but, poor creature, she can't move, because there — in the deepest part of the jungle — she's trapped in a spider's web, or rather the spider web is growing out of her own body, the threads are coming out of her waist and hips."

19. *Colored Lights*, 182.

20. This reading marks Chita Rivera's first association with the project.

21. Before McNally came up with the scenario for *Bird of Paradise*, the same song was going to be used for a film called *Amazon Love*.

22. In the early draft referred to above, Aurora stoically sings "Good Times" as she faces a firing squad.

23. Frank Rich, "For the Musical, a Love Affair Beyond the Liaison in a Latin Jail," *New York Times*, 4 May 1993.

24. John Simon, *New York*, 17 May 1993.

25. Brent Carver, although not Hispanic, delivered a critically acclaimed performance as Molina.

26. Linda Winer, "A 'Kiss' Is Still a 'Kiss' but Less," *Newsday*, 4 May 1993.

27. "Come Out," a song with a double entendre sung by Molina's "queer" friends, provided comic relief, perhaps a bit too much of it, and it took place in the real world outside the prison. In "Cookies," Molina and Valentin each thinks to himself about whether he can trust the other. For both versions, Kander and Ebb wrote several songs that were never incorporated (original score: "I'll Dance Alone" [part of the opening segment], "Man Overboard" [Aurora], "Thank You Very Much" [Gabriel], "There Is No Law Against It"; revised score: "You Owe It to Yourself" [Aurora], "I Like It Here" [Aurora], "Disobey" [Aurora], "Reciprocity"). "There Is No Law Against It" was a song for Valentin and Peter Pelican, a character from a movie that he narrates for Molina while suffering from food poisoning. In the original interrogation scene, the violent beatings are underscored with comic vaudeville music, which is reminiscent of the surreal "Round and Round" from *The Fantasticks*, in which Luisa, in a disturbing sort of cognitive dissonance, experiences pleasure as others suffer. Kander and Ebb substituted the vaudeville music with "I Like It Here," but they ultimately settled for a more dissonant musical portrayal of the interrogation.

28. Marilyn Stasio, "The Difference Between Kander and Ebb," *American Theatre* 14 (1997): 14.

29. Clive Barnes, "Kiss of Death, 'Spider Woman,'" *New York Post*, 4 May 1993.

30. Jeremy Gerard, *Variety*, 10 May 1993.

31. Ken Mandelbaum, *Theater Week*, 24–30 May 1992.

32. John Bush Jones, *Our Musicals, Ourselves: A Social History of the American Musical Theatre* (Hanover: Brandeis University Press, 2003), 341.

33. Ethan Mordden, *The Happiest Corpse I've Ever Seen: The Last 25 Years of the Broadway Musical* (New York: Palgrave, 2004), 251.

34. As quoted in Mervyn Rothstein, "The Spider's Web," 31 July 1993, 10.

35. As quoted in Rothstein (12).

36. Román and Sandoval, "Caught in the Web," 553–85.

37. Clum, *Something for the Boys*, 190.

CHAPTER 6. Flops and Second Chances

1. Robert Simonson, *"The Boy from Oz* Recoups Investment," *Playbill*, 8 September 2004 (http://www.playbill.com/news/article/88272.html).

2. Lester Atwell, *Love Is Just Around the Corner* (New York: Simon and Schuster, 1963).

3. *Candide* was a thinly disguised protest against McCarthyism. See Ethan Mordden, *Coming Up Roses: The Broadway Musical in the 1950s* (New York: Oxford University Press, 1998), 172.

4. An early draft of the script (probably written by Russell) includes a note about Harry's handicap: "Harry is supposed to stammer, and not to stutter, and his blockages cover complete words or complete syllables, and should be accompanied by occasional 'complete stoppage of speech.'" In Atwell's novel, Harry is a stutterer, and no production of *Flora, the Red Menace* has made him otherwise. The script describes Galka, the head of the local party, as a "Red Savanorola."

5. Carol Ilson, *Harold Prince: A Director's Journey* (n.p., Limelight Edition, 2000), 121.

6. Ibid., 122. Russell was better known as a film writer. His screenplays include *The More the Merrier*, which was nominated for an Academy Award in 1943, and *Walk, Don't Run* (1966). He also made numerous documentaries and business and educational films.

7. John Kander and Fred Ebb as told to Greg Lawrence, *Colored Lights: Forty Years of Words and Music, Show Biz, Collaboration, and All That Jazz* (New York: Faber and Faber, 2003), 39 (hereinafter *Colored Lights*).

8. Ibid., 50.

9. Scott McMillin coins this term in order to distinguish such numbers from diegetic songs, which "have a built-in detachability" (*The Musical as Drama: A Study of the Principles and Conventions Behind Musical Shows from Kern to Sondheim* [Princeton: Princeton University Press, 2006], 112–14).

10. Dialogue in an early draft of the script (probably by Russell) provides the ideas for these two songs. In one of Ada's speeches, for instance, she modestly underestimates her accomplishments for the week: "This past week, I have done very little! Beyond giving the Party twenty-four hours out of every day, what have I done? Nothing! A good Communist should do more! I picketed! I protested! I rioted! I heckled! I bit a landlord trying to evict a poor family! But what is this? Routine!"

11. Kander admired Blitzstein, whom he met at a party following the premiere of *No for an Answer*. Kander became inebriated enough to abandon all inhibitions and sing "The Ballad of the Bombardier" as Blitzstein accompanied him on the piano. Looking back he remarked, "Where the fuck did I get the nerve?"

12. Kevin Kelly, *The Boston Globe*, 15 April 1965.

13. Howard Taubman, "The Theater: 'Flora, the Red Menace,'" *New York Times*, 12 May 1965.

14. Even more absurd, in an early draft of the script, Ada inherits a fortune from her

grandmother and gives up on her comrades, who want her to fund their political activities.

15. Ethan Mordden, *Open a New Window: The Broadway Musical in the 1960s* (New York: Palgrave, 2001), 113.

16. Hal Prince, *Contradictions: Notes of Twenty-Six Years in the Theatre* (New York: Dodd, Mead, 1974), 118.

17. One version of this song bears the title "I Gotta Right to Know, Harry," another the sexier title "I Gotta Right to Know, Baby."

18. "What Am I Doing Here?" is an a cappella quartet for Flora, Charlotte, Harry, and Weiss, each of whom is caught in a compromising position. Little else in Kander and Ebb's early musicals is as contrapuntally complex as this number, which one script labels an "Operatic Trio."

19. One of Kander's sketchbooks contains melody lines for the following numbers: "Botch" (or "Butch"), "Comrade," "Express Yourself" (different version), "Fifty," "Flame" (different theme), "George," "Happy Song," "I Can Go On," "I Believe You" (different version), "I Never Knew," "If I Were You," "In the Same Boat" (different from the song of the same title from *Curtain*), "Just Around the Corner," "Look on the Bright Side," "Me of All People," "Never Before" (two versions), "Never Better," "No Bed of Roses," "Rainbow," "Sheridan Square" (two versions), "Sitting Pretty" (two versions, both different from the song of the same name from *Cabaret*), "That'll Do Nicely," "The More I Get To Know You," "The Sun Comes Up," "Union Man," and "You Ain't Seen Nothing Yet" (lyric exists on separate sheet).

20. Ellis and Stroman first met in 1980 while working on the ill-fated *Musical Chairs*.

21. David Thompson, *Flora, the Red Menace* (New York: Samuel French, 1988).

22. According to a note in one of Kander's sketchbooks for *Flora*, this number may have been written for the original version of *Flora*.

23. Stanley threatens to fire everyone on Flora's list, but she counters by threatening to make public a love note from him to his mistress, which would upset his plans to marry the boss's daughter. Her tactic works in that Stanley fires only her. Flora still hopes against hope that things will work out for her and Harry.

24. Rodgers and Hammerstein created this term for *Oklahoma!* The musical play initiated a period of improved musical theater book writing, higher artistic standards, and greater dramatic integrity. In contrast to musical comedy, the musical play emphasizes realistic human behavior, in contrast to the hyperrealism of musical comedy. The music aims for real emotional expression. Humor emerges from characters, as opposed to one-liners. See Mordden, *Open a New Window*, 57–58.

25. Walter Goodman, "The Stage: 'Flora, the Red Menace,'" *New York Times*, 7 December 1987.

26. Stephen Holden, "In 'Flora' Two Music Men Return to an Early Love," *New York Times*, 29 November 1987.

27. According to a notice in the *New York Times* (Louis Calta, "'Zorba' and Musical, 'Company,' to Occupy Harold Prince in '70," 12 November 1969), Prince was going to bring *Zorbá* back to Broadway after the national tour.

28. Walter Kerr, *New York Times*, 28 January 1968.

29. Robert Fontaine, *The Happy Time* (New York: Simon and Schuster, 1945).

30. Richard Rodgers, *Musical Stages: An Autobiography*, 2nd ed. (Cambridge: Da Capo, 2002), 268. Hammerstein was particularly eager to produce the play.

31. Although the action of the play revolves around Bibi, the boy is no longer the point-of-view character, and the scene in which he discovers love is less effective than the parallel scene in the book. Taylor adapted his play for television with the hope that it would lead to a regular series. He had written the script for only one musical, Rodgers's *No Strings*.

32. As quoted in William Goldman, *The Season: A Candid Look at Broadway* (New York: Harcourt, Brace and World, 1969), 291.

33. Other changes made to Fontaine's novel relate either to directorial concerns or to demands of the genre. For example, Sally, Bibi's girlfriend, no longer appears. Laurie, Jacques's love interest, is an amalgam of Fontaine's schoolteacher and Mignonette, a vaudeville performer whom Bibi's father hires to help Maman with the house chores. In the play, Mignonette ends up engaged to Uncle Desmonde.

34. John Anthony Gilvey believes that Nash used aspects from three of Fontaine's novels, *The Happy Time*, *My Uncle Louise*, and *Hello to Springtime* (John Anthony Gilvey, *Before the Parade Passes By: Gower Champion and the Glorious American Musical* [New York: St. Martin's Press, 2005], 184).

35. Ibid., 182.

36. Goldman, *The Season*, 292.

37. Gower Champion Papers, Collection No. 346, Box 2, Charles E. Young Humanities Research Library, UCLA, Los Angeles.

38. Gilvey, *Before the Parade Passes By*, 189.

39. Ibid., 199.

40. Ibid., 197.

41. Ibid.

42. Goldman, *The Season*, 295.

43. Walter Kerr, *New York Times*, 28 January 1968.

44. The Signature Theatre in Arlington, Virginia, included a production of *The Happy Time* for its Kander and Ebb Celebration in 2008.

45. "I'm Sorry" is derived from an episode in Fontaine's novel. At the insistence of his father, Bibi apologizes publicly to his schoolmates for his bad behavior. The song recaptures some of the quality of Fontaine's Bibi that was lost when Nash departed from the original novel.

46. *New York Times*, 7 May 1980.

47. Martin Goldfried, "'The Happy Time,'" *Women's Wear Daily*, 19 January 1968.

48. The version produced at the Goodspeed was repeated with great success at the Lyric Opera of Kansas City in 1983.

49. Early sources (including a published version of Joseph Stein's book [New York: Random House, n.d.] and the original Broadway cast recording of *Zorbá*) use "Nikos," but later sources (the recording of the 1983 Broadway revival and the script currently leased by Samuel French for productions) use the more authentic "Niko."

50. Nikos Kazantzakis, *Zorba the Greek*, trans. Carl Wildman (New York: Simon and Schuster, 1952).

51. Edmund Fuller, "The Wild and Wily Zorba," *New York Times*, 19 April 1953.

52. Ibid.

53. Foster Hirsch, *Harold Prince and the American Musical Theatre*, expanded ed. (Cambridge: Cambridge University Press, 1989), 69.

54. Martin Gottfried, "Zorba," *Women's Wear Daily*, 18 November 1968.

55. Walter Kerr, "'Zorba'—Palette or People?," *New York Times*, 24 November 1968.

56. Harold Prince to Investors, n.d., Harold Prince Papers, Billy Rose Theatre Collection, New York Public Library for the Performing Arts.

57. Hirsch, *Harold Prince and the American Musical Theatre*, 70.

58. Frank Rich, *New York Times*, 17 October 1983.

59. Dena Kleinman, "'Zorba's' Lessons for Anthony Quinn, *New York Times*, 31 July 1986.

60. Mordden, *Open a New Window*, 211. Mordden does not even bother to mention the 1983 revival in his book on the eighties (*Happiest Corpse*).

61. John Wilson, "Kander and Ebb," *BMI: The Many Worlds of Music* 3 (1973): 33.

62. Peter Coke, *Breath of Spring* (London: Samuel French, 1959).

63. The role of Ida was originally intended for Ruth Gordon.

64. Ken Mandelbaum, *Not Since Carrie: 40 Years of Broadway Musical Flops* (New York: St. Martin's Press, 1991), 270.

65. For David Thompson "The Elephant Song" has a "Noël Coward sensibility": "It was cut because it requires a very certain type of person to deliver that; it's sort of a cross between Bea Lillie and Judi Dench. I think Dora Bryan's humor was probably a lot more bawdy than it was erudite. And I think that's probably why it was dropped." Bryan played Ida in the English production.

66. Ibid. Kander saw *70, Girls, 70* as a "very blue-collar, Off-Broadway, backyard piece that should not have been on Broadway, or at least not in a large theater" (*Colored Lights*, 95).

67. Jeffrey Scott Neuman, "'And That's Show Biz, Kid': Self-Referential Theatricality in the Musicals of John Kander and Fred Ebb (master's thesis: University of Colorado–Boulder, 1998).

68. Ibid., 28. According to Neuman, Ebb wrote both a screenplay and a teleplay for *70, Girls, 70*, but neither one has been found (32).

69. Mandelbaum, *Not Since Carrie*, 270.

70. Marc Eden Horowitz, *Sondheim on Music: Minor Details and Major Decisions* (Lanham: Scarecrow, 2003), 172.

71. Fred Ebb and Norman L. Martin, *70, Girls, 70* (New York: Samuel French, 1971).

72. "The Caper" still stymies performers. When Burns died, the song was reassigned to Hans Conried, who delivers a respectable rendition of it on the original cast recording. At the 2006 Encores! production, George Irving struggled with the song even at half-speed. Most of the song was cut altogether from the English production.

73. William Collins, "Second Thoughts on '70, Girls, 70': Are Elders Really Running Things?," *Philadelphia Inquirer*, 12 March 1971.

74. Clive Barnes, "'70, Girls, 70' Arrives," *New York Times*, 16 April 1971.

75. Walter Kerr, "Please, No '80, Girls, 80,'" *New York Times*, 23 April 1971.

76. "To further instruct the authors that they wrote the play in the wrong sequence is to add insult to injury . . . I was charmed by the notion that the first caper was the return-

ing of a coat . . . I found that ironic, amusing and terribly original . . . Bravo Ebb, Kander and Martin!" Barbara Cooney, To the Editor, "Championing '70, Girls,'" *New York Times* (date unknown).

77. Fred Armstrong, "A Sad Closing," *Show Business*, 20 May 1971.

78. Thompson experimented with the ending. In one draft, only Ida is arrested, as occurs in the original Broadway production. In his final script, the entire gang is part of the opening lineup, but Ida takes the rap.

79. Irving Wardle, *Independent on Sunday*, 23 June 1991.

80. Paul Taylor, *Independent*, 21 June 1991.

81. Wardle, *Independent on Sunday*.

82. Frank Rich, *Harvard Crimson*, 26 February 1971.

83. *Colored Lights*, 99.

84. Ibid., 162.

85. As mentioned in Chapter 4, Kander had written incidental music for a production of *Peer Gynt* at Yale University.

86. Character descriptions, John Kander Papers, Billy Rose Theatre Collection, The New York Public Library for the Performing Arts.

87. Innaurato's script refers to Bob as a structuralist theater director.

88. Kander and Ebb's demo recording includes "Everybody's for Sale," which Innaurato did not incorporate into either script, and "Finaletto" (otherwise known as "Well Anyway").

89. This song list is a composite of Innaurato's two treatments. Kander and Ebb retained "Colored Lights," "Don't Ah Ma Me," "Chief Cook and Bottle Washer" (with different opening section), and "All the Children in a Row" for the final score of *The Rink*.

90. This song contains the toast from the final score.

91. This song ended up in *Curtains*.

92. Fisher claims that McNally never saw Innaurato's script (see Don Nelsen, "The Risks in 'The Rink,'" *Leisure*, 5 February 1984).

93. A. J. Antoon papers, Billy Rose Theatre Collection, New York Public Library for the Performing Arts.

94. Frank Rich, "A Daughter's Roots," *New York Times*, 10 February 1984.

95. Howard Kissel, "'The Rink,'" *Women's Wear Daily*, 19 February 1984.

96. *Colored Lights*, 172.

97. Douglas Watt, "'Rink' Glides & Tumbles," *Daily News*, 10 February 1984.

98. Richard Cerliss, "A Coney Island of the Mind," *Time*, 20 February 1984.

99. Benedict Nightingale, "'The Rink' Succumbs to Charmless Predictability," *New York Times*, 19 February 1984.

100. Clive Barnes, "Chita & Liza Set the Wheels in Motion in 'Rink,'" *New York Post*, 10 February 1984.

101. Samuel G. Freeman, "For McNally, a New Show and an Old Struggle," *New York Times*, 5 February 1984.

102. Ibid.

103. Karen Ziemba appeared in the 2005 summer workshop of *Skin of Our Teeth* at the McCarter Theatre Center in Princeton, and as Georgia in the world premiere of *Curtains* in 2006 and in the Broadway production, for which she received a Tony Award

nomination. Debra Monk, who won a Tony Award for her performance in *Steel Pier*, has remained a part of this group. She appeared in the 2004 workshop of the same musical as well as in the 2005 workshop reading of *Curtains*. Monk repeated her *Curtains* role for the premiere in 2006 and the Broadway production, and received a Tony Award nomination.

104. Ben Brantley, "Party's Over, Chum, Just Keep Dancing," *New York Times*, 27 April 1997.

CHAPTER 7. Divas or Anti-Divas?

Epigraph. John M. Clum, *Something for the Boys: Musical Theater and Gay Culture* (New York: St. Martin's Press, 1999), 168.

1. Other grand dames of the theater to have starred in Kander and Ebb musicals include Lotte Lenya, Judi Dench, Barbra Streisand, Gwen Verdon, Raquel Welch, Debbie Reynolds, Shirley MacLaine, Karen Ziemba, Ann Reinking, Queen Latifa, and Eartha Kitt.

2. Alexander Doty, *Making Things Perfectly Queer: Interpreting Mass Culture* (Minneapolis Press: University of Minnesota Press, 1993), 6.

3. Stacy Wolf, *A Problem Like Maria: Gender and Sexuality in the American Musical*, Triangulations Series (Ann Arbor: The University of Michigan Press, 2002), 16–17.

4. Daniel Harris, *The Death of Camp: Gay Men and Hollywood Diva Worship, from Reverence to Ridicule* (New York: Hyperion, 1997), 10.

5. Clum, *Something for the Boys*, 175.

6. Al LaValley, "The Great Escape," *American Film* (April 1985): 32.

7. Clum, *Something for the Boys*, 155.

8. LaValley, "The Great Escape," 31.

9. Wolf, *A Problem Like Maria*, 20–21.

10. Paul Robinson, "The Opera Queen: A Voice from the Closet," *Cambridge Opera Journal* 6 (1994): 288–89.

11. Ibid., 290.

12. For more on the diva musical see Chapter 7.

13. John Kander and Fred Ebb as told to Greg Lawrence, *Colored Lights: Forty Years of Words and Music, Show Biz, Collaboration, and All That Jazz* (New York: Faber and Faber, 2003), 155 (hereinafter *Colored Lights*).

14. *Colored Lights*, 146.

15. Clum, *Something for the Boys*, 151.

16. Ibid., 154.

17. Ibid., 180.

18. Ibid.

19. Bruce Kirle, *Unfinished Show Business: Broadway Musicals as Works-in-Progress* (Carbondale: Southern Illinois University Press, 2005), 194.

20. *Colored Lights*, 156.

21. Cy Feuer with Ken Gross, *I Got the Show Right Here: The Amazing, True Story of How an Obscure Brooklyn Horn Player Became the Last Great Broadway Showman: Producer of Guys & Dolls, How to Succeed in Business Without Really Trying, Can-Can, and Many, Many More Legendary Shows* (New York: Simon and Schuster, 2003), 266.

22. George Furth, *The Act* (New York: Samuel French, n.d.). The infamous out-of-town tryout period of *The Act* is documented in a *New York Times* essay by Cliff Jahr: "'The Act,' the Drama Backstage Is Not an Act," *New York Times*, 23 October 1977; reprinted in Steven Suskin, *Second Act Trouble: Behind the Scenes at Broadway's Big Musical Bombs* (New York: Applause Theatre and Cinema, 2006), 18–27.

23. Richard Eder, *New York Times*, 31 October 1977.

24. Edwin Wilson, "Broadway Lit with Vegas Sparkle," *Wall Street Journal*, 1 November 1977.

25. Stephenson's other Broadway appearances include *Irene* with Debbie Reynolds and *A Day in Hollywood, A Night in the Ukraine*. He is currently on the faculty of the Circle in the Square theater program.

26. Ethan Mordden, *The Happiest Corpse I've Ever Seen: The Last 25 Years of the Broadway Musical* (New York: Palgrave, 2004), 13.

27. Mel Gussow, "Debbie Reynolds in 'Woman of the Year,'" *New York Times*, 28 February 1983.

28. The published script includes the following statement: "Following its successful run on Broadway, WOMAN OF THE YEAR enjoyed a highly acclaimed national tour, with some members of the original cast returning to the roles they created. During this time, several songs and scenes were substantially altered or replaced by new ones, and it is the resultant final version which is printed here. Therefore, any discrepancies between the Original Cast Recording and the music and lyrics herein are intentional changes, made by the authors. No other version is available." Peter Stone, Fred Ebb, and John Kander, *Woman of the Year* (New York: Samuel French, 1981), 7.

29. Ethan Mordden sees this new version of the title song as "a more pointed defiance of gender discrimination" (*The Happiest Corpse I've Ever Seen*, 14).

CHAPTER 8. Musicals Abandoned and Imagined

1. The lyric concludes: "If only I'd have guessed / When I took my rabbit test / The mother of a Bunny I'd be / Though she walks around in fur / I wish that I were proud of her. / The way she must be proud of me! (She falls off the stool.)" Ebb also wrote "The Boy from Fire Island" for Carter to sing to the music of "The Girl from Ipanema."

2. Morris based his protagonist on a real-life character named Emperor Norton, a self-proclaimed hero who lived from 1819 to 1880.

3. It is reasonable to conclude that the outline represents the earlier version, as it includes the Chinese character Tsung Lee and his song "I Bet You Two Dollar" (Morris preferred the ungrammatical "dollar" for Tsung Lee, but Kander and Ebb's demo recording uses "dollars," even though Ebb wrote a Chinese accent into the lyric). Tsung Lee is not a character in either of the revised versions, one of which features Angel and Bruno singing "I Bet You Two Dollars." A note by Morris on one of the scripts suggests that Tsung Lee is from an earlier version: "In the rewrite, Indian Tom Toms could effectively replace the Oriental influence of the original song, to fit Angel."

4. Lehman Engel, *The American Musical Theater*, rev. ed. (New York: Collier, 1975), 77–119.

5. Kander and Ebb recorded two versions of "Nothing Wrong with My Life." This number anticipates the mature, ironic side of Kander and Ebb more than any other song

from the score. In the version of the song corresponding to the plot described in Morris's outline, Angel, when put on the defensive by Murphy, tries to justify her new lifestyle. In the other version, Angel declares to Robby Morgan that she loves him. When she starts to break down, a strain of "I'm One of the Smart Ones" is heard in the accompaniment, which underscores the irony of her choices.

6. There are two demo recordings of *Golden Gate*. Neither one includes "Sin City, My Home" or "I'll Always Love You," the former of which is mentioned in the outline and the latter in the 1982 script. Tsung Lee's "Happy New Year" and "A Certain Girl," which are on the second demo recording, are part of neither the outline nor either of the scripts.

7. John Sutherland, introduction to *Under Two Flags* by Ouida [Marie Louise de la Ramée] (Oxford: Oxford University Press, 1995), [i].

8. Screenplay by Rod Amateau, story by Harold Nebenzal, and adaptation by David Robinson, Abe Burrow Papers, Billy Rose Collection, New York Public Library for the Performing Arts.

9. Lewis Funke, "'Tango,' Anyone?," *New York Times*, 10 October 1971.

10. For the part of Germaine, Burrows considered Georgia Brown, Tammy Grimes, and Margaret Whiting. He suggested Ken Howard, George Chakiris, or Robert Morse for the role of François, and over ten different actors for Peter Watkin, including Jack Cassidy, Dean Jones, Gordon McRae, and Bert Convy. Contenders for the part of Clothilde included Virginia Vestoff, Leslie Warren, Nancy Dussault, and Susan Watson. In his notes for the Broadway cast recording of *Curtains*, Rupert Holmes intimates that the delay was due to Burrows's health problems. See "The Fall and Rise of Curtains," Original Broadway Cast Recording of *Curtains*, Blue Note Label Group, 20070946 9221226 (2007).

11. In Ebb's description of this scene, Teresa sleeps as Fernando studies Hollywood films such as *Viva Zapata* and *Juarez* in order to learn from the mistakes of the revolutionary protagonists in those films. Fernando and Teresa's first love scene follows; she is aware that, for her, victory for the revolution means losing Fernando: "a Catholic country and Presidents do not have whores."

12. A stage version of the novel by Waterhouse and Willis Hall premiered in the West End in 1960.

CHAPTER 9. "A Tough Act to Follow"

1. Stone had outlined several songs that, with one exception, Kander and Ebb never wrote: "One for All, All for One" (which became "Collaboration"), "The Show Must Go On—But Without Me," "What Next?" (for the writers), "Are You Crazy" (for the composer), and "He Did It" (which made it into the final version of *Curtains*).

2. Enid Nemy, "On Stage," *New York Times*, 5 January 1990; and Rick Lyman, "On Stage and Off," *New York Times*, 24 October 1997.

3. Other songs were written for this version of *Curtains* but were never integrated into the script, including a different version of "Collaboration" (for *Harlequinade*) and "Art," the theater critic's song of justification. "Old School Ties," a song for the critic and playwright, was probably intended for this version.

4. The melody of "Where Were You" is based on *"Tu sol comandi, amor!"* from *La*

Bohème. Kander and Ebb wrote an entirely different song called "Where Were You?" for the version of *Curtains* that used *Sand* as the inner musical.

5. Stone's outline includes this duet.

6. Holmes and Kander attempted to incorporate the Puccini joke of the 2002 version. When Aaron informs Belling that the tune is by Puccini, the director quips, "Eight people will know that and we can easily have them destroyed." Later, Aaron insists, "I'm not going to steal from Puccini, Chris. Maybe one of your *British* composers do [*sic*] that—but I'm an American. We steal from Aaron Copland." Oscar, the garish business manager straight out of the garment industry, later quips, "You know, I've been selling imitation Pucci designs for years. I never knew the guy did operas." Kander and Holmes ultimately thought that the joke was too forced, and they gave up on it.

7. Holmes wrote the 1985 hit musical *The Mystery of Edwin Drood*, the television series *Remember Wenn*, and the recent novel *Swing*.

8. Stone based the name of the actress on a real actress named Niki Harris and may have intentionally altered the spelling of the first name to "Nikki" to distinguish the character from the real person (communication with Rupert Holmes, 13 November 2007).

9. In Holmes's first draft (dated 19 February 2005), when Niki (Holmes's spelling) learns that only she has received good notices, she blurts out, "It's like finding out you've been mentioned in Adolph Hitler's will."

10. The score for the Broadway production varies only slightly from the score of the Los Angeles premiere. In additional to some shuffling of the song order, Kander reworked "I Miss the Music" and reprised it along with "Thinking of Him" in act 2. The 2005 reading included "Out of Town," which Kander and Ebb wrote for the 2002 version; "The One About Us," a duet for Aaron and Georgia; "Where Were You?" from the 2002 reading; and "Don't Even Think About It," which was later replaced by "Thataway."

11. Ben Brantley, "Stagestruck Sleuth, Crazy for Clues and Cues," *New York Times*, 23 March 2007.

12. John Lahr, "Sleuths and Truths," *New Yorker*, 2 April 2007.

13. Anne Midgette, "Voices Raised in Song at Grover's Corners," *New York Times*, 27 February 2006.

14. The musical, which is titled *Grover's Corners*, is by Harvey Schmidt and Tom Jones. It had a workshop production in 1984 at the Westbeth Theatre Center in New York and a fully staged production in 1987. The opera, by Ned Rorem and based on a libretto by J. D. McClatchy, premiered as recently as February 2006.

15. Thornton Wilder, afterword to *The Skin of Our Teeth* (New York: Perennial Classics, 2003), 130. Tappen mentions the Stein-Ebb-Kander musical.

16. Wilder, afterword, 137.

17. The first performance of *All About Us*, which took place at the Signature Theatre in Arlington, Virginia, in 1998, included several songs that were subsequently cut: "Oh Me, Oh My," "Someday Pasadena," "As You Are" (written for Innaurato's version of *The Rink*), "This Life" (originally written for *Cabaret*), and "Sweet Home" ("We're Home"). An earlier reading included a couple of songs that were not used for the Signature Theatre production, "Freeport, N.J." and "What For," and made several references to musical theater, quoting "Tomorrow" from *Annie* and "Maybe This Time" from *Cabaret*. Sabina's second-act solo, "World Peace," which Kander wrote just before the 2007

Westport production, is a parody of the canned responses of pageant contestants during the question-and-answer portion of the contest. The song "Warm" is in a script dated 6 November 1998 as well as the score, but it is not on a live recording of the Signature Theatre production. "A Discussion," which was originally titled "I Don't Get It," was written for the 2004 workshop, in which it was the opening number.

18. Personal interview with Michael Gibson.

19. This production used some of Michael Gibson's orchestrations from the Signature Theatre production with additional orchestrations by William David Brohn, the orchestrator for *Curtains*.

20. Sylviane Gold, "Historical Mayhem, Set to Music," *New York Times*, 22 April 2007.

21. Kenneth Jones and David Lefkowitz, "Lansbury & Co. Read, Sing *The Visit* Behind Closed Doors Dec. 6–17," *Playbill On-Line*, 6 December 1999.

22. Richard Christiansen, "Getting 'The Visit' on Stage Was a Drama in Itself," *Chicago Tribune*, 30 September 2001.

23. In 1997, shortly before he began composing music for *The Visit*, Kander saw Gottfried von Einem's opera version, *Besuch der alten Dame* (*The Visit of the Old Lady*) (1971), at the New York City Opera, but he claims that it had no influence on his own score.

24. Richard I. Evans, *Albert Bandura: The Man and His Ideas—A Dialogue* (New York: Praeger, 1989), 39–50.

25. The second act opens with the J. S. Bach chorale "O haupt voll blut und wunden." Overlapping the final cadence on E(tonic), the orchestra begins a restatement of the final phrase in F major. The pick-up beats, however, are coupled with the opening notes of "Winter" in the key of B minor. The bass line continues as a dissonant countermelody of the Bach chorale, ending on an F-sharp major chord, which, when coupled with the F major chord in the upper voices, recalls the bitonal element of the Prelude.

26. Quoted in Davi Napoleon, "A Dish Best Served Cold," *Entertainment Design*, 1 February 2002.

27. Hedy Weiss, "A Strange 'Visit' to a Twisted Place," *Chicago Sun-Times*, 2 October 2001, 46.

28. Richard Christiansen, "Setting a Dark Story to Music, 'The Visit Shines,'" *Chicago Tribune*, 2 October 2001.

29. The running order of songs for this production was as follows: act 1: "Out of the Darkness," "At Last," "I Walk Away," "I Know Claire," "A Happy Ending," "You, You, You," "I Must Have Been Something," "Look at Me," "A Masque," "Testimony," "Winter," and "Yellow Shoes"; act 2: "Chorale," "A Confession," "I Would Never Leave You," "The One-Legged Tango," "Back and Forth," "The Only One," "Fear," "A Car Ride," "Winter" (reprise), "Love and Love Alone," "In the Forest Again," and "Finale."

30. Charles Isherwood, "Vengeance Revisited, with Singing," *New York Times*, 31 May 2008.

31. Nelson Pressley, "A 'Visit' with Very Familiar Faces of Broadway; Signature Plugs into Star Power of Rivera & Co.," *Washington Post*, 1 June 2008.

32. Peter Marks, "Dancing in the Dark: 'The Visit' with Chita Rivera," *Washington Post*, 29 May 2008.

33. Pressley, "A 'Visit.'"

34. Liane Hansen, "A Conversation with Composer John Kander," *National Public Radio Weekend Edition*, 19 March 2006 (13:00–14:00 p.m.).

35. Mark S. Weiner, *Black Trials: Citizenship from the Beginnings of Slavery to the End of Caste* (New York: Alfred A. Knopf, 2004), 246–73.

36. *The American Experience: Scottsboro: An American Tragedy*, written by Barak Goodman, produced by Daniel Anker and Barak Goodman (PBS Home Video, WGBH Educational Foundation, 2001), videocassette.

37. Weiner, *Black Trials*, 267.

38. Patterson published his account of the ordeal, *Scottsboro Boy*, and Clarence Norris published *The Last of the Scottsboro Boys* in 1979.

39. Personal interview with David Thompson.

40. The title of this song refers to the electric chair at Kilby prisons (where the Scottsboro Boys were taken after they were convicted), which was located behind a green gate. Thompson "dummied" this title into a scene in which the guards sing to the boys after they arrive at the prison.

41. Kander and Ebb wrote "Hey Little Boy" instead of "Beyond the Little Green Gate." Guards sing it only to Roy Wright, the youngest boy. Thompson feels that this song is "brilliant, evil, extraordinarily theatrical—and pure Kander and Ebb."

42. The song titles are given as they are listed on the demo recording.

43. Replaced "So Bury Me Like You Do a Cat."

44. On the demo recording, "The Scottsboro Boys" and "You Can't Do Me" (which is the song inspired by the title "They Can't Do Us Like They Done Us Like They Did Before" in Thompson's 2003 outline) are part of a continuous musical scene, which includes a reprise of "It's Gonna Take Time" and "Minstrel March" (same as "Minstrel Parade"). According to the playwright, the sequence will probably proceed as follows: "Zat's So" (which is not yet written), "You Can't Do Me," "The Scottsboro Boys," and "The Minstrel March."

45. Larry Hamberlin, "National Identity in Snyder and Berlin's 'That Opera Rag,'" *American Music* 3 (2004): 380–81.

46. Jeffrey Melnick, *A Right to Sing the Blues: African Americans, Jews, and American Popular Song* (Cambridge: Harvard University Press), 103–14.

47. Hansen, "A Conversation with Composer John Kander."

APPENDIX

1. Walter Marks provided additional music, and Larry Wilcox did the musical arrangements and orchestrations.

2. There are four extant cutout songs from *Go Fly a Kite*: "Aren't You Happy That You're Alive" (three-part song, music lost), "Don't Drink the Water," "Second America," and "Watch Your Language." The song "Don't Drink the Water," which Kander and Ebb might have written for a different occasion, has several other titles: "See America First," "South of the Border," "Down Mexico Way."

3. Other titles were considered: *Where the Action Is, The Action's Here, Get in on the Action, The Action . . . 68, Action: 68, Action Unlimited,* and *On the Move*.

4. Titles followed by "reveal" indicate music that accompanied the unveiling of a car model.

5. *Lucky Lady* marks the first association between Kander and the orchestrator Ralph Burns.

6. The unused songs are "Funny, She Ain't," "Western Union Operator," "If I Leave You Now" (which was probably written for *The Happy Time*), and "Keep Them Happy." "I Like Him/I Like Her," twin soliloquies for Fanny and Billy sung in counterpoint to Billy Rose's "It's Only a Paper Moon," is another number that is at once a real song and a book song. It provides a dialectical basis for the scene that sets up an opposition between the stage and the real world. As Billy auditions "It's Only a Paper Moon" for Fanny, she sings an interior monologue to Kander and Ebb's new music. When Billy sings his chorus, the song stops being diegetic altogether.

7. Vincent Canby, "Streisand as Fanny Brice (Continued)," *New York Times*, 12 March 1975.

8. "Happy Endings" starred Minnelli and Larry Kert, who had appeared in Kander's *A Family Affair*.

9. The recording was originally released in 1978 as part of a three-album set that included the evenings with Sammy Cahn and Jerry Herman.

10. John S. Wilson, "The Lyricist as Performer," *New York Times*, 9 September 1979.

11. Walter Kerr, "Two Women, Both Alone, Two Moods," *New York Times*, 9 July 1978.

12. Carol Lawson, "Miss Newman Ready for Glory," *New York Times*, 16 May 1979.

13. According to the *New York Times*, Kander and Ebb were writing a song called "Show Off."

14. Frank Rich, "'Diamonds,' A Revue About Baseball," *New York Times*, 17 December 1984. The other contributing writers included Cy Coleman, David Zippel, Howard Ashman, and Betty Comden and Adolph Green.

15. Frank Rich, "'Hay Fever,' Noel Coward Comedy," *New York Times*, 13 December 1985.

16. For Minnelli's last live concert, *Liza's Back*, in 2001, Kander and Ebb wrote two new songs, "Liza's Back" and "Don't Smoke in Bed."

Index

Italicized page numbers indicate musical examples (*e*), photographs (*p*), and tables (*t*).

Credits

Music and Lyrics

Music

Lyrics

Text